AF866113

Law in Eastern Europe

A SERIES PUBLISHED IN COOPERATION WITH LEIDEN UNIVERSITY AND THE UNIVERSITIES OF TARTU AND GRAZ

General Editors

Benedikt C. Harzl and Joseph Marko

VOLUME 72

The titles published in this series are listed at *brill.com/laee*

Institute of Law Studies Polish Academy of Sciences

Ministry of Science and Higher Education
Republic of Poland

Doskonała
Nauka II

This project is co-funded from the state budget, allocated by the Polish Minister of Science and Higher Education under the 'Excellent Science II' Programme, Poland.

This work is licensed under a Creative Commons Attribution-NonCommercial-NoDerivs 4.0 International License. https://creativecommons.org/licenses/by-nc-nd/4.0/

This book is available as an open access publication via https://www.degruyterbrill.com.

ISSN 0075-823X
ISBN 978-90-04-75462-1
ISBN 978-90-04-75463-8 (PDF)
DOI https://doi.org/10.1163/9789004754638

Library of Congress Control Number: 2026948467

© 2026 the author(s), published by Koninklijke Brill BV, Plantijnstraat 2, 2321 JC Leiden, The Netherlands

Brill Nijhoff and Koninklijke Brill BV are part of De Gruyter Brill.
www.degruyterbrill.com

Questions about General Product Safety Regulation: productsafety@degruyterbrill.com

Contents

Tables and Graphs

Tables

Graphs

Abbreviations

Official Journals

ECR	European Court Reports
JoL	Journal of Laws (Poland) (Poland – publication of statutes)
JoL OCCP	Journal of Laws of the OCCP
MP	Monitor Polski (Poland – publication of secondary legislation)
OJ	EU's Official Journal

Scientific Journals

AUWrP	Acta Universitatis Wratislaviensis. Prawo
C&R	Revista de Concorrência e Regulação
CLJ	Competition Law Journal
CMLRev	Common Market Law Review
CLPD	Competition Law and Policy Debate
CPI	Competition Policy International
CzPH	Czasopismo Prawno-Historyczne
ECJ	European Competition Journal
ECLR	European Competition Law Review
ELJ	European Law Journal
EPS	Europejski Przegląd Sądowy
GLJ	German Law Journal
GSP	Gdańskie Studia Prawnicze
iKAR	internetowy Kwartalnik Antymonopolowy i Regulacyjny
JAE	Journal of Antitrust Enforcement
JCLE	Journal of Competition Law and Economics
JECLP	Journal of European Competition Law and Practice
KPP	Kwartalnik Prawa Publicznego
MoP	Monitor Prawniczy
OSP	Orzecznictwo Sądów Polskich
OZK	Österreichische Zeitschrift für Kartellrecht
PiP	Państwo i Prawo
PPC	Polski Proces Cywilny
PPH	Przegląd Prawa Handlowego
PPP	Przegląd Prawa Publicznego
PS	Przegląd Sądowy

PUG	Przegląd Ustawodawstwa Gospodarczego
R&G	Regulation and Governance
RPEiS	Ruch Prawniczy, Ekonomiczny i Socjologiczny
ST	Samorząd Terytorialny
YARS	Yearbook of Antitrust and Regulatory Studies
ZaöRV	Zeitschrift für ausländisches öffentliches Recht und Völkerrecht
ZNSA	Zeszyty Naukowe Sądownictwa Administracyjnego
ZNUJ	Zeszyty Naukowe Uniwersytetu Jagiellońskiego

Other Abbreviations

ACM (NL)	Autoriteit Consument & Markt (NL)
AdCom	Advisory Committee
ADO	authorised disclosure officer
AI	Artificial Intelligence
APC	Administrative Procedure Code
CA	(Polish) court of Appeal
CAP	Competition Agency Procedures
CCCP	(Polish) Court for Competition and Consumer Protection
CEE	Central and Eastern Europe
CECI	Central European Competition Initiative
CMA (UK)	Competition & Markets Authority (UK)
CPC	Civil Procedure Code
CT	(Polish) Constitutional Tribunal
EC	European Commission
ECA	European Competition Authorities
ECN	European Competition Network
ECtHR	European Court of Human Rights
EFTA	European Free Trade Association
ERO	(Polish) Energy Regulatory Office
EU	European Union
EUCO	European Court of Human Rights
EUMR	EU Merger Regulation
FDI	Foreign Direct Investments
FSA	(Polish) Financial Supervision Authority
HAC	(Polish) Head Administrative Court
ICN	International Competition Network
LPP	legal professional privilege
MoU	memorandum of understanding

MWG	Merger Working Group
NB	*nota bene*
NCA	national competition authority
NGA	non-government advisor
NGO	non-government organisation
NRA	national regulatory authority
OEC	(Polish) Office for Electronic Communication
OCCP	(Polish) Office for Competition and Consumer Protection
OECD	Organisation for Economic Co-operation and Development
PI	public information
PPC	Penal Procedure Code
PSC	Polish Supreme Court
TFEU	Treaty on the Functioning of the European Union
UN	The United Nations
UNCTAD	UN Conference on Trade and Development
US DOJ	US Department of Justice
WTO	World Trade Organization
VAC	(Polish) Voivodeship (Regional) Administrative Court

CHAPTER 1

Introduction

1 The Subject and Aim of the Book

Poland's economic transformation from a centrally planned economy under a communist regime to a market economy grounded in the rule of law is widely regarded as a relative success within the broader context of post-socialist transitions.[1] The process was comparatively peaceful and orderly – particularly when compared with the experiences of other Central and Eastern European (CEE) states, such as Romania and Bulgaria, where political instability and institutional discontinuities significantly hampered reforms and the Europeanisation of both states.[2] Although the liberal architects of the Polish economic reforms presented them as rational and necessary, many have been – and still are – unwilling to acknowledge their far greater social costs. Yet among the least disputed elements of the transition was the decision to dismantle state monopolies and lay the foundations for free competition in an increasingly open domestic market. This placed competition law at the forefront of Poland's legal transformation and made it an essential pillar of the emerging regulatory state. Despite its great potential and impressive initial achievements, competition law has not become a cornerstone of modern economic governance in Poland, unlike in the EU and many other European countries. This paradox will be explored in the book.

Despite recurring claims that Poland's systemic transformation is complete, I proceed from a different premise. The transformation has not concluded; instead, Poland has entered a new phase in which earlier legislative and institutional choices are being tested, reinterpreted, and, in some respects, reversed. In this context, I examine how Polish competition law and its enforcement architecture have developed since 1989, and whether they are currently moving towards a robust and accountable regulatory system.

The adoption of competition law was integral to establishing a market economy, serving both internal and external functions. Domestically, it was necessary to ensure the efficient functioning of markets previously dominated

1 M. Piątkowski, *Europe's Growth Champion. Insights from the Economic Rise of Poland*, Oxford 2018.

2 A.L. Dimitrova, *Understanding Europeanization in Bulgaria and Romania: following broader European trends or still the Balkan exceptions?*, European Politics and Society 2021, no. 22(2).

© 2026 THE AUTHOR(S) | HTTPS://DOI.ORG/10.1163/9789004754638-002
This is an open access publication distributed under the terms of the CC 4.0 license BY-NC-ND.

by state monopolies; externally, it served as a key instrument in preparing Poland for accession to the European Union. Yet, while the Polish legislator drew heavily on EU models, the system was adapted to local institutional and economic constraints, resulting in a framework with distinctive procedural and institutional features.

Polish competition law and its enforcement system have gradually evolved under the influence of EU law, resulting in a high level of formal harmonisation. EU competition law itself is undergoing a period of conceptual reorientation, experimenting with new regulatory instruments – most notably in digital markets – and postponing overdue systemic reforms, such as revising the EU Merger Regulation (EUMR).[3] These broader European developments heighten the significance of domestic interpretations and institutional choices. In Poland, this has particularly underscored the central role of the President of the Office of Competition and Consumer Protection (OCCP), whose strategic preferences have shaped enforcement practices in ways not mirrored across all EU jurisdictions. Some neighbouring states, for instance, have adopted more technocratic or judicialised models, while others have experienced varying degrees of political entanglement in the governance of national competition authorities (NCAs). This comparative diversity underscores the importance of examining Poland's institutional trajectory.

Competition law does not operate in isolation, and the Polish system must be analysed within a broader international and regional context. Globally, competition law is undergoing significant conceptual shifts, driven by the rise of the digital economy and by growing pressures to incorporate new objectives – ranging from sustainability to broader fairness considerations – into enforcement.[4] These developments represent structural changes that differ markedly from earlier, more evolutionary shifts, such as the rise and demise of the 'more economic approach'.[5] The contemporary landscape demands expedited regulatory responses, institutional adaptability, and renewed theoretical reflection. In this climate, examining the Polish system may appear counterintuitive; however, it is precisely at moments of conceptual uncertainty that historical and institutional analysis becomes most valuable. Understanding how current structures came into being – what motivated their

3 Council Regulation (EC) No. 139/2004 of 20.01.2004 on the control of concentrations between undertakings, OJ L 24, 29.1.2004.

4 For an overview, refer to M.C. Iacovides, K. Stylianou, *The new goals of EU competition law: sustainability, labour rights, and privacy*, European Law Open 2024, no. 3(3).

5 P. Ibáñez Colomo, *The rise and decline of the 'more economics-based approach'*, [in:] *The New EU Competition Law*, Oxford 2023.

design and which errors or successes shaped them – is indispensable for designing effective future strategies.

The central aim of this study is to provide a critical analysis of the evolution and current configuration of Polish competition law and its enforcement system. It combines historical context, doctrinal analysis, and case-law examination to illuminate the key trends shaping the current legal landscape. This work does not aspire to be a handbook or statutory commentary. Instead, it adopts a developmental, problem-oriented perspective, focusing on distinctive institutional features and on areas that have received inadequate scholarly attention. Over the past decade, Polish competition law has undergone significant legislative and enforcement changes – many of which have not yet been subject to systematic or critical academic scrutiny. My goal is to address this gap and present a structured, contemporary study of Polish competition law and enforcement as of 2025. Special emphasis is placed on jurisdictional and institutional issues, which are often underestimated or undeveloped when analysis is limited to the substantive and procedural norms of competition law. Therefore, the 'enforcement' part of the book gains its proper visibility in the study.

Several interconnected research questions guide the inquiry. One concerns the motivations behind the institutional and procedural arrangements adopted in Poland and the extent to which these choices were coherent or normatively justified. Another examines the OCCP's institutional architecture and its relationship to enforcement outcomes. This raises the recurring question of formal independence: to what extent is the OCCP's independence – shaped by both domestic law and EU requirements – necessary or sufficient for effective enforcement? This highlights the relationship between independence and accountability, as well as the broader issue of how the OCCP legitimises its exceptional institutional position.

An additional line of inquiry concerns the absence of a coherent, publicly articulated competition policy in Poland and the OCCP's limited practice of priority-setting. This deficit has implications for predictability, enforcement, rationality, and institutional legitimacy. By tracing key developments in antitrust, merger control, and sanctions, I seek to identify the implicit strategic direction of Poland's enforcement.

The scope of the OCCP's jurisdiction has expanded significantly, placing a diverse array of regulatory tasks under a single authority. I therefore analyse the emergence of various 'non-orthodox' regulatory regimes – ranging from consumer protection and product safety to foreign investment screening and unfair trading practices in the food supply chain – which share superficial characteristics with competition law but differ in their aims and enforcement logic. This centralised model raises important normative and practical questions about its suitability for achieving the diverse policy objectives associated with both competition and non-competition regimes. Entrusting these tasks to the Polish NCA raises essential questions about institutional design, efficiency, and coherence, particularly when compared with other EU jurisdictions in which such responsibilities are distributed across multiple agencies or ministries. I consider how these additional competences affect the OCCP's core mandate to compete and explore what an optimal allocation of regulatory responsibilities entails. The analysis aims to contribute to broader academic debates on institutional design in post-transition economies and to inform potential future reforms.

The study offers a comprehensive and up-to-date examination of Polish competition law and enforcement, covering the jurisdictional, substantive, and procedural dimensions and providing a detailed exploration of how competition courts function. Earlier scholarship, though valuable, has often been outdated or confined to narrow doctrinal issues. Here, I integrate public and private enforcement perspectives, supplement the analysis with statistical data, and focus on the historical and political conditions that shaped the current framework. Particular attention is given to the 2023 implementation of the ECN+ Directive, which significantly altered the legal architecture of the Polish NCA. This study provides one of the first detailed assessments of the reform's implications for independence, accountability, and enforcement.

The analysis anticipates future developments in Polish competition law in light of a new wave of EU regulatory instruments, including the Digital Markets Act (DMA),[6] the Foreign Subsidies Regulation (FSR),[7] the Foreign Direct Investment Regulation (FDI),[8] and the emerging European Media Freedom Act (EMFA).[9] These instruments are part of a broader and more profound transformation of EU economic governance.[10] This transformation – often

6 Regulation (EU) 2022/1925 of the European Parliament and of the Council of 14.09.2022 on contestable and fair markets in the digital sector and amending Directives (EU) 2019/1937 and (EU) 2020/1828 (Digital Markets Act), OJ EU L 265, 12.10.2022.

7 Regulation (EU) 2022/2560 of the European Parliament and of the Council of 14.12.2022 on foreign subsidies distorting the internal market, OJ EU L 330, 23.12.2022.

8 Regulation (EU) 2019/452 of the European Parliament and of the Council of 19.03.2019, establishing a framework for monitoring foreign direct investment in the Union, OJ EU L 79I, 21.3.2019.

9 Regulation (EU) 2024/1083 of the European Parliament and of the Council of 11.04.2024 establishing a common framework for media services in the internal market and amending Directive 2010/13/EU (European Media Freedom Act), OJ EU L, 2024/1083.

10 This emerging system is rightly described as a 'spider's web' – I. Kokkoris, *A spider's web: regulatory oversight and the interplay between EU Merger Control, Foreign Direct Invest-*

incremental and without explicit political articulation – has initiated a structural shift in which regulatory competences are progressively concentrated at the EU level and enforcement is increasingly centralised within the European Commission and specialised EU bodies. The EU is thus moving beyond the classical model of decentralised, Member State-based enforcement towards a hybrid governance architecture in which NCAs operate within a more integrated, vertically coordinated system.

For national authorities such as the OCCP, this emerging architecture raises fundamental questions about institutional identity and strategic orientation. The key challenge for OCCP will be to position itself as an active contributor to the developing enforcement model rather than a passive recipient of EU-level mandates. Authority's continued relevance depends on its ability to remain subjects – actors capable of shaping enforcement practice and policy, rather than objects that merely absorb decisions taken elsewhere within the EU regulatory hierarchy.

The interplay between these new EU instruments and domestic law suggests that further transformation of the Polish competition regime is inevitable. Poland's institutional and legislative responses to these pressures will determine the orientation and character of its competition enforcement system over the next decade. What may be even more challenging is that most of those reforms, such as merger control, will take the form of soft-law developments. Yet this challenge coincides with a period in which strategic thinking in competition policy has been virtually abandoned. Over the past decade, the OCCP has increasingly relied on reactive, ad hoc enforcement tactics, operating without a clearly articulated policy vision, a priority-setting framework, or a long-term institutional strategy.

Such institutional stagnation places Poland at a disadvantage as EU-level reforms accelerate. Without a clear vision of how domestic enforcement should align with – or diverge from – the emerging EU governance architecture, Poland risks becoming increasingly peripheral to European competition policy debates. This situation underscores the urgent need to strengthen institutional capacity, rebuild a culture of strategic planning, and cultivate a mature culture of competition grounded in coherent policy objectives, transparent communication, and accountable governance. Only through deliberate institutional transformation can Poland ensure that its NCA remains capable of performing its core functions effectively (for the benefit of the Polish econ-

---

ment Screening (EU and National), and Foreign Subsidies Regulation, Yearbook of European Law, 2026, yeaf009.

omy and all the people living in Poland) while also engaging meaningfully with the developing EU system.

Finally, given the scarcity of English-language scholarship on Polish public economic law, I aim to address a critical research gap by making Polish doctrinal analysis, institutional debates, and empirical findings accessible to a wider international audience. By providing a structured and detailed account of the evolution, functioning, and prospective development of Polish competition law, this study seeks to enrich the broader European and global discourse on competition regulation. By integrating national and international perspectives, I hope to illuminate the distinctive characteristics of the Polish competition regime, identify the deeper structural factors shaping its trajectory, and demonstrate how its future will be intertwined with ongoing transformations within the European regulatory space. In doing so, the study contributes to a more comprehensive understanding of how post-transition legal systems in the CEE region negotiate their place within an increasingly centralised and integrated European economic governance framework.

2 Methods and Materials

This study relies primarily on dogmatic and doctrinal analysis, complemented by historical, empirical, and statistical methods. The dogmatic method serves as the principal analytical framework, enabling the systematisation of legal rules into a coherent structure and facilitating the evaluation of legislative and jurisprudential trends. It operates on two interrelated levels: the descriptive and the normative. The descriptive level concerns the reconstruction of the current state of the law and its dominant interpretations within the literature. The normative level involves evaluating the law, ranging from critical assessments of existing provisions to the formulation of legislative reform proposals.[11] Given that the core subject of inquiry concerns legal regulations and the institutional arrangements governing their application, the formal-dogmatic method is the primary research instrument in this book. It is equally well suited to analysing the legal forms of administrative action, including administrative decisions, soft law instruments, and administrative agreements. Its essence lies in a two-stage process: identifying the relevant sources of law and subsequently analysing and interpreting them. The method also

11 S. Taekema, *Relative Autonomy. A Characterisation of the Discipline of Law*, [in:] B. van Klink, S. Taekema (eds.), *Law and Method. Interdisciplinary Research into Law*, Tübingen 2011, 34–35.

necessitates a critical engagement with the existing literature to delineate the state of research, identify gaps, and situate the present study within the broader scholarly debate.[12]

Because this study's subject matter encompasses not only legal norms but also institutional design, enforcement culture, and the practical functioning of public authorities, the dogmatic method alone is not always sufficient. Consequently, dogmatic analysis is supplemented by insights from European and global administrative law, competition law theory, and political economy, particularly the extensive literature on independent regulatory agencies and their governance. These interdisciplinary inputs are essential in a field where purely doctrinal perspectives often fail to capture the broader drivers of institutional change and the non-legal rationales for adopting specific regulatory designs. This approach aligns with contemporary methodological debates in comparative administrative and regulatory scholarship, which emphasise combining doctrinal precision with contextual and empirical understanding to explain institutional variation across jurisdictions.

Historical inquiry is an integral part of the methodological framework. Given the rapid and uneven evolution of Polish competition law, interpreting the current institutional architecture requires tracing its historical development, including the motivations behind successive legislative amendments, the external influences shaping institutional choices, and the broader political and economic context in which these reforms were enacted. Historical analysis also plays an essential explanatory role in examining enforcement practice. Apparent enforcement deficiencies – such as inconsistent intervention rates or shifts in priority-setting – often become intelligible only when contextualised within earlier organisational reforms, leadership changes within the NCA, or evolving ideological orientations of government. Wherever possible, this historical analysis is supported by statistical data that help verify hypotheses concerning enforcement intensity, caseload dynamics, institutional output, and long-term trends.

The study draws on a comprehensive corpus of primary and secondary materials, including judgements of Polish courts and the Court of Justice of the European Union, administrative decisions of the OCCP, legislative preparatory documents, soft law instruments, press releases, annual activity reports, and formal statements or policy positions of the Polish NCA. Where essential information was missing from official publications – an increasingly common phenomenon in recent years – these gaps were addressed through

12 T. Hutchinson, *Doctrinal Research. Researching the Jury*, [in:] D. Watkins, M. Burton (eds.), *Research Methods in Law*, London 2017, 18.

requests submitted under the Public Information Act.[13] This ensured that the analysis rests on the most complete and reliable dataset currently available.

In addition to documentary research, the study benefits from the author's more than two decades of professional engagement with the Polish competition authority. While this experience does not in itself constitute empirical evidence, it provides valuable contextual insight into institutional culture, internal processes, and enforcement practices that cannot be reconstructed solely from official documents. It thus enhances the interpretative depth of the research's doctrinal and empirical components. To avoid personal bias, I have relied only on publicly available information (agency reports, decision and judgement registries, and official documents) or information obtained through public information requests. All tables are based on those two groups of sources. When collecting data, I aimed to extract data for the longest possible periods and present it in the most accessible form.

The book reflects the state of the law as at 1 February 2026. At the time of completion, only partial 2025 data were available, thereby limiting the scope of the quantitative analysis presented.

3 Structure of the Book

The study comprises 11 chapters, preceded by an introduction that outlines the conceptual framework, research questions, and methodological foundations of the inquiry. The opening chapter provides a historical account of the development of Polish competition legislation, tracing its evolution from the early post-transition period to the contemporary regulatory landscape. This is followed by a detailed examination of the 2007 Act on Competition and Consumer Protection, including subsequent amendments arising from the implementation of the ECN+ Directive and the legal adjustments necessitated by the DMA and the FSR.

The analysis then turns to the jurisdiction of the Polish competition authority, tracing its evolution from a specialised antimonopoly body into a multifunctional regulatory agency with an increasingly heterogeneous portfolio of competences. The subsequent chapter, devoted to the OCCP's regime, organisational structure, resources, and decision-making processes, completes the assessment of its institutional status and functional architecture. This institutional part of the study concludes with a chapter examining the courts com-

13 Act of 6.09.2001 on access to public information, JoL 2022, item 902.

petent to adjudicate competition matters, thereby providing a complete overview of the enforcement infrastructure.

The next chapter addresses competition policy and the OCCP's priority-setting practices (or, in recent years, the absence thereof), thereby offering an assessment of the strategic dimension of enforcement. The analysis then turns to substantive issues, beginning with anticompetitive practices and continuing with merger control, the two principal substantive pillars of competition law.

After examining substantive matters, the book turns to procedural issues. A comprehensive chapter scrutinises antimonopoly proceedings, followed by a discussion of the sanctioning regime applicable to infringements of the Competition Act.

The penultimate chapter explores the private enforcement of competition law in Poland, assessing both its current shortcomings and its potential for future development. The study concludes with a final chapter offering an integrated set of reflections and predictions concerning the further evolution of Polish competition law and its enforcement system, underscoring the thesis that Polish competition law remains, in many respects, an unfinished story.

4 Terminological Notes

The terminology employed throughout this study requires clarification, particularly given the interchangeable use – both in practice and in scholarship – of the adjectival terms 'competition' and 'antimonopoly'. Although these terms frequently refer to the same institutional structures or bodies of law, they carry distinct historical and conceptual connotations within Polish legal discourse. A notable illustration concerns the formal designation of the enforcement authority as the *President of the Office of Competition and Consumer Protection*. Polish administrative law follows a long-standing tradition of personifying administrative authorities, whereby the authority is identified with the office-holder and the administrative office is treated merely as *an* auxiliary apparatus serving that individual. This legal fiction means that, formally, all acts and decisions are attributed to the president personally, even though the Office's civil service staff perform the authority's jurisdictional functions on a day-to-day basis.

For the benefit of non-Polish readers, this study employs a simplified nomenclature. Repeated references to the 'President of the Office' would be cumbersome and could obscure rather than illuminate the institutional reality. Accordingly, the text adopts terms commonly used in Polish legal literature and administrative practice – including *competition authority*, *OCCP*, and *Polish NCA* – whichever best fits the analytical context.[14] A similar terminological duality applies to the governing statute. While its official name is the *Act on Competition and Consumer Protection*, it is still frequently referred to as the *Competition* or *Antimonopoly Act* because of historical usage. Throughout this study, the choice between these terms is guided by considerations of precision, clarity, and alignment with prevailing legal conventions.

For the sake of precision, this study follows the convention of specifying the year of enactment when referring to different versions of the Act. Where no year is stated, the reference is to the current text of the Act, in force since 21 April 2007, including its numerous subsequent amendments. This approach enables clear differentiation between the original statutory framework and the evolving regulatory landscape shaped by later reforms.

Clarification is also needed regarding the terminology used by market participants. References to 'persons' encompass both natural and legal persons unless otherwise indicated. Under Polish law, there is a distinction between *an entrepreneur* (*przedsiębiorca*) and *an undertaking* (*przedsiębiorstwo*).[15] An *entrepreneur* is the legal entity engaged in economic activity, whereas an *undertaking* refers to the organised set of assets or resources that constitute the operational basis for that activity.[16] To avoid ambiguity and ensure consistency with European and international competition law, this study uses the term 'undertaking' in its conventional English-language sense, referring to any entity engaged in economic activity, regardless of legal form.

The persistent use of the term 'antimonopoly' (*antymonopolowy*) in Polish discourse is rooted in historical naming conventions. Early legislation, administrative bodies, and specialised judicial units employed terminology closely associated with the antimonopoly model, and these linguistic patterns have endured. This is visible, for example, in the continued statutory use of 'antimonopoly proceedings' to describe administrative processes conducted before the competition authority. The terminology also reflects the influence of U.S. antitrust traditions during the early 1990s, when Poland received substantial technical assistance as it transitioned from a centrally planned to a market economy, and when American-style terminology entered the domestic legal lexicon.

---

14 The term 'Antimonopoly Authority' denotes the official name of the competition authority in the early 1990s and is used only in the historical context.

15 K. Zapolska, *Kształtowanie się pojęcia przedsiębiorcy i przedsiębiorstwa w prawie cywilnym oraz prawie gospodarczym w Polsce*, Miscellanea Historico-Iuridica 2024, no. 23(2).

16 I. Gancarz, *Pojęcie przedsiębiorstwa w świetle relacji pomiędzy unijnym i krajowym prawem konkurencji*, KPP 2011, no. 3–4.

Over the past three decades, however, the term *competition* has gradually displaced *antimonopoly* in much of Polish legal language. This shift mirrors Poland's progressive integration into the European Union and the harmonisation of domestic law with the *acquis communautaire*. It also corresponds to broader conceptual changes within the discipline: the shift away from the narrower structural focus of classical antimonopoly regulation towards a more comprehensive understanding of competition law as an element of modern economic governance. The increasing use of *competition,* therefore, signifies not merely a terminological update but a more profound transformation in legal doctrine, regulatory philosophy, and economic reasoning within the Polish competition law system.

5 Bibliographical Annotations

Polish competition law has generated a substantial and increasingly sophisticated body of scholarly literature.[17] Four principal commentaries on the Act on Competition and Consumer Protection are available. The most up-to-date are those by K. Kohutek and M. Sieradzka,[18] and the collective commentary edited by A. Jurkowska-Gomułka and A. Piszcz.[19] Earlier commentaries, now of primarily historical value, include those edited by C. Banasiński and E. Piontek,[20] and A. Stawicki and E. Stawicki.[21]

Several textbooks provide broader introductions to Polish competition law. Among the most influential are the classical works of S. Gronowski[22] and the textbook edited by Z. Brodecki,[23] as well as contribution by M. Stefaniuk.[24] More recent developments are captured in the textbook edited by C. Banasiński, which reflects contemporary legislative and enforcement practice.[25]

---

17 The section presents only basic literature limited to books. A comprehensive selection of relevant literature is presented throughout the book.

18 K. Kohutek, M. Sieradzka, *Ustawa o ochronie konkurencji i konsumentów. Komentarz*, Warsaw 2024.

19 A. Jurkowska-Gomułka, A. Piszcz (eds.), *Ustawa o ochronie konkurencji i konsumentów. Komentarz*, Warsaw 2024.

20 C. Banasiński, E. Piontek (eds.), *Ustawa o ochronie konkurencji i konsumentów, Komentarz*, Warsaw 2009.

21 A. Stawicki (ed.), E. Stawicki (ed.), *Ustawa o ochronie konkurencji i konsumentów. Komentarz*, Warsaw 2016.

22 S. Gronowski, *Polskie prawo antymonopolowe,* Warsaw 1998.

23 Z. Brodecki (ed.), *Konkurencja,* Warsaw 2004.

24 M. Stefaniuk, *Publicznoprawne reguły konkurencji,* Lublin 2005.

25 C. Banasiński (ed.), *Polskie prawo antymonopolowe. Zarys wykładu,* Warsaw 2018.

Certain substantive areas have attracted concentrated scholarly attention. Merger control, for example, has been examined in depth by D. Kostecka-Jurczyk,[26] D Aziewicz,[27] T. Skoczny,[28] J. Olszewski,[29] and M. Błachucki.[30] The principal monograph on cartel enforcement remains M. Król-Bogomilska's influential work.[31] Numerous studies have analysed particular categories of anticompetitive practices, including block exemptions,[32] vertical restraints,[33] refusal to deal,[34] the abuse of dominance,[35] franchising agreements,[36] and bid rigging.[37]

Several monographs address broader conceptual or cross-cutting issues in antimonopoly law. These include works on fines,[38] the rule of reason,[39] the notion of an undertaking,[40] leniency,[41] and the interaction between competi-

26 D. Kostecka-Jurczyk, *Koncentracja w formie wspólnego przedsiębiorstwa a ryzyko konkurencyjne w świetle prawa antymonopolowego*, Warsaw 2020.

27 D. Aziewicz, *Ocena siły rynkowej przedsiębiorcy w nadzorze nad horyzontalnymi koncentracjami przedsiębiorców*, Warsaw 2017.

28 T. Skoczny, *Zgody szczególne w prawie kontroli koncentracji*, Warsaw 2012.

29 J. Olszewski, *Nadzór nad koncentracją przedsiębiorców jako forma prewencyjnej ochrony konkurencji*, Rzeszów 2004.

30 M. Błachucki, *System postępowania antymonopolowego w sprawach kontroli koncentracji przedsiębiorców*, Warsaw 2012.

31 M. Król–Bogomilska, *Zwalczanie karteli w prawie antymonopolowym i karnym*, Warsaw 2013.

32 E. Kosiński, *Rodzaje i zakres sektorowych wyłączeń zastosowania ogólnych reguł ochrony konkurencji*, Poznań 2007 and A. Jurkowska, T. Skoczny (eds.), *Wyłączenia grupowe spod zakazu porozumień ograniczających konkurencję we Wspólnocie Europejskiej i w Polsce*, Warsaw, 2008.

33 R. Poździk, *Dystrybucja produktów na zasadzie wyłączności w Polsce i Unii Europejskiej*, Lublin 2006.

34 M. Kolasiński, *Obowiązek współpracy gospodarczej w prawie antymonopolowym*, Toruń 2009.

35 A. Brzezińska, *Zakaz nadużycia pozycji dominującej we wspólnotowym i polskim prawie antymonopolowym*, Toruń 2008, K. Kohutek *Praktyki wykluczające przedsiębiorstw dominujących. Prawidłowość i stosowalność reguł prawa konkurencji*, Warsaw 2012 or M. Szydło, *Nadużywanie pozycji dominującej w prawie konkurencji*, Warsaw 2010.

36 M. Sieradzka, *Porozumienia franczyzy w świetle prawa konkurencji*, Warsaw 2020.

37 G. Materna, *Zmowy przetargowe w prawie ochrony konkurencji i prawie karnym*, Warsaw 2016.

38 M. Król-Bogomilska, *Kary pieniężne w prawie antymonopolowym*, Warsaw 2001.

39 D. Miąsik, *Reguła rozsądku w prawie antymonopolowym*, Warsaw 2004.

40 G. Materna, *Pojęcie przedsiębiorcy w polskim i europejskim prawie ochrony konkurencji*, Warsaw 2009.

41 B. Turno, *Leniency. Program łagodzenia kar pieniężnych w polskim prawie ochrony konkurencji*, Warsaw 2003.

tion law and intellectual property rights.[42] Sector-specific analyses have examined the application of competition rules in agriculture,[43] energy,[44] and sport.[45]

Procedural aspects of Polish competition law have been the subject of three dedicated monographs by D. Sylwestrzak,[46] K. Róziewicz,[47] and M. Błachucki.[48] Additional studies address discrete procedural issues such as procedural fairness in antimonopoly proceedings,[49] the right to be heard,[50] evidence proceedings,[51] and the protection of business secrets.[52] The OCCP has published numerous books, monographs, and research reports[53] – some available in English[54] which provide valuable insights into administrative practice and institutional self-perception.

42 D. Miąsik, *Stosunek prawa ochrony konkurencji do prawa własności intelektualnej*, Warsaw 2012.

43 P. Popardowski, *Reguły konkurencji w rolnictwie w prawodawstwie Unii Europejskiej*, Warsaw 2019.

44 M. Kamiński, *Zastosowanie prawa ochrony konkurencji Unii Europejskiej w sektorze energetycznym*, Warsaw 2025.

45 W. Lewandowski, *Zakres ingerencji prawa konkurencji Unii Europejskiej w autonomię samoregulacyjną federacji sportowych*, Warsaw 2019.

46 D. Sylwestrzak, *Postępowanie przed Prezesem Urzędu Ochrony Konkurencji i Konsumentów*, Warsaw 2012.

47 K. Róziewicz-Ładoń, *Postępowanie przed Prezesem Urzędu Ochrony Konkurencji i Konsumentów w zakresie przeciwdziałania praktykom ograniczającym konkurencję*, Warsaw 2011.

48 M. Błachucki, *System.*

49 M. Bernatt, *Sprawiedliwość proceduralna w postępowaniu przed organem ochrony konkurencji*, Warsaw 2011.

50 K. Kowalik-Bańczyk, *Prawo do obrony w unijnych postępowaniach antymonopolowych – w kierunku unifikacji standardów proceduralnych w UE*, Warsaw 2012.

51 R.R. Wasilewski, *Postępowanie dowodowe przed Prezesem Urzędu Ochrony Konkurencji i Konsumentów*, Warsaw 2020.

52 P. Korycińska-Rządca, *Ochrona tajemnic strony postępowania antymonopolowego w sprawach praktyk ograniczających konkurencję*, Warsaw 2020.

53 For example M. Krasnodębska-Tomkiel, *Wspólnotowe prawo konkurencji. Skutki dla Polski*, OCCP, Warsaw 2006, C. Banasiński (ed.), *Ochrona konkurencji i konsumentów w Polsce i Unii Europejskiej (studia prawno-ekonomiczne)*, OCCP, Warsaw 2005 or C. Banasiński (ed.), *Prawo konkurencji – stan obecny oraz przewidywane kierunki zmian*, OCCP, Warsaw 2006. All available at www.uokik.gov.pl

54 M. Krasnodębska-Tomkiel (ed.), *Changes in Competition Policy over the Last Two Decades*, Warsaw 2010 or *Consumer Protection and Competition Policy – working together?*, Warsaw 2006.

Enforcement-related scholarship has been enriched by monographs on the independence of the competition authority,[55] the OCCP's discretionary powers,[56] and international cooperation in competition law enforcement.[57]

To complete this overview, it is essential to note the Yearbook of Antitrust and Regulatory Studies. This English-language academic journal publishes research on Polish, European, and comparative competition law and regulatory policy. Its accessibility to non-Polish readers makes it a particularly valuable resource in an otherwise predominantly Polish-language scholarly environment.[58]

6 Repository of Documents

This study draws on a broad and diverse body of sources on Polish competition law and its enforcement, including judicial decisions, administrative acts, legislative materials, soft-law instruments, policy statements, and historical documents. During the preparation of this book, it became apparent that a significant number of these materials have either fallen out of the public domain or become difficult to access through standard institutional or online channels. This problem affects not only older documents from the early stages of Polish competition enforcement but also more recent materials, particularly soft law instruments, internal policy documents, and archival versions of administrative decisions.

To address this deficit and facilitate future academic research on Polish competition law, the Centre for National and Economic Security Law of the Institute of Law Studies of the Polish Academy of Sciences has established an open repository of source documents, i.e. Competition Law Archive. The repository is an integral part of the Centre's broader research programme, which is dedicated to documenting and preserving the history and development of the legal regulations and enforcement practices analysed in the Centre's research.

The repository is conceived as a long-term archival resource. Its purpose is not merely to provide temporary access to selected materials, but to ensure the systematic preservation and availability of documents of enduring rele-

---

55 K. Rokita, *Niezależność krajowych organów regulacyjnych oraz krajowych organów konkurencji w świetle prawa Unii Europejskiej*, Wrocław 2017.

56 C. Banasiński, *Dyskrecjonalność w prawie antymonopolowym*, Warsaw 2015.

57 M. Błachucki, *International Cooperation, Competition Authorities and Transnational Networks*, London 2024.

58 Selected volumes are available at https://press.wz.uw.edu.pl/yars/.

vance for the study of Polish competition law and its institutional practice. By consolidating dispersed and, in some cases, otherwise inaccessible sources, the repository aims to support transparency, reproducibility of research, and cumulative scholarly inquiry in this field.

The repository will be available at: https://inp.pan.pl/en/scientific-centers-2/centre-for-national-and-economic-security-law/.

At the time of writing, the repository is under construction and is expected to become fully operational in early 2027.

7 Acknowledgements

This book summarises over two decades of my research on competition law and my experience applying it. I have had the privilege of engaging with many individuals – academics, practitioners, and enforcers from Polish and other national competition authorities across the European Union – who have taught me much and to whom I am deeply indebted. Since it is impossible to name everyone, I mention only those instrumental in completing this book.

I thank Professors Bartosz Majchrzak and Rafał Stankiewicz for reviewing the initial draft and for helping me plan a better monograph. I am also grateful to the anonymous reviewer, whose comments greatly improved the manuscript's structure and content.

Professor Marek Martyniszyn deserves endless appreciation for reading the final draft at a truly Stakhanovite pace. His insightful comments and suggestions were invaluable in shaping the book.

I also thank my Polish antitrust colleagues, who generously read and reviewed individual chapters. Their practical perspective led to a more balanced assessment of the issues.

My friend Jędrek Mikołaj offered invaluable assistance during the research process.

This book would not exist without Dr. Joanna Kurczab. She secured the publishing grant and provided steady support throughout the process. Her unique editorial skills united the book's parts into a coherent draft.

My thanks go to Karol Bieńkowski for assisting with the administrative aspects of the grant process.

I am grateful to my Brill editor, Ingeborg van der Laan, for her saintly patience and constant support throughout the publishing process. I also thank Kan Wai Min, whose efforts made immediate open access possible.

I hope this book helps everyone interested in the topic.

Any remaining errors are my own.

I dedicate this book to my aunt, Alice, who is very dear to me.

CHAPTER 2

The Development of Polish Competition Legislation

This chapter traces the historical development of Polish competition legislation, covering all six antimonopoly acts enacted so far. The importance of these acts in shaping Polish competition law varies significantly. While the Acts of 1933[1] and 1939[2] are historically notable, they had limited influence on the overall development of competition law in Poland. More focus is placed on the Acts of 1987,[3] 1990,[4] and 2000,[5] along with their later amendments.

The chapter aims to highlight key patterns in the evolution of Polish competition law and procedural methods, and to evaluate the effects of these legislative changes. This provides a thorough understanding of how Polish competition law has responded to changing economic and legal environments over time.

Additionally, this chapter briefly introduces the current Act of 2007 and its recent amendments. Although this section offers my overview of the Act's main features and updates, a detailed analysis of the current regulations will be provided in subsequent chapters. This approach ensures a comprehensive review of the development of Polish antimonopoly substantive and procedural rules within their wider legal and practical contexts.

1 Cartel Legislation in Years 1918–1939

Poland's regaining of independence in 1918 and its defence in the following years were monumental achievements,[6] yet they marked only the beginning of the effort to build a fully sovereign state. Unifying and adopting a cohesive

1 Act of 28.03.1933 on cartels, JoL No. 31, item 270.
2 Act of 13.07.1939 on cartel agreements, JoL No. 63, item 418.
3 Act of 28.01.1987 on counteracting monopolistic practices in the national economy, JoL No. 3, item 18.
4 Act of 24.02.1990 on counteracting monopolistic practices, JoL No. 14, item 88.
5 Act of 15.12.2000 on competition and consumer protection, JoL No. 122, item 1319.
6 S. Kutrzeba, *The Struggle for the Frontiers* [in:] W.F. Reddaway, J.H. Penson, O. Halecki, R. Dyboski (eds.), *The Cambridge History of Poland from Augustus II to Piłsudski (1697–1935)*, Cambridge 1941.

© 2026 THE AUTHOR(S) | HTTPS://DOI.ORG/10.1163/9789004754638-003
This is an open access publication distributed under the terms of the CC 4.0 license BY-NC-ND.

legislative framework were among the next critical steps. From the outset, cartels attracted governmental attention, though the approach to this issue was markedly different from contemporary standards. Not only were cartels permitted, but at certain times they were actively supported by the government.[7]

The first legislative act to address cartels indirectly was the Act of 2 July 1920 on war usury.[8] This act prohibited *participation in agreements or associations aimed at certain economic activities*. However, despite its explicit language, this provision was never applied to cartels. The political shift initiated by Józef Piłsudski's 1926 coup d'état ushered in a new era in Polish politics.[9] Initially, Marshal Piłsudski and his supporters sought the support of industrial and business elites, thereby delaying the implementation of cartel regulation. However, the economic crisis of the 1930s, coupled with growing public criticism of cartels, prompted the government to prioritise the issue. This culminated in the Polish parliament's adoption of the Act on 28 March 1933, marking the first normative regulation of cartels in the country's legal framework.

The Act of 1933 introduced comprehensive regulation of cartels in Poland, covering *all agreements, resolutions, and decisions involving mutual obligations aimed at controlling or regulating production, sales, prices, or conditions for exchanging goods in mining, industry, and trade* (Article 1). These agreements had to be in writing under penalty of nullity (Article 2) and notified to the Minister of Industry and Trade within 14 days of their conclusion. Notified cartels were then registered in a specialised cartel registry maintained by the Minister (Article 3).

The Minister of Industry and Trade was obligated to reject the registration of an agreement if its provisions or execution were deemed contrary to the public good (Article 4). In such cases, the Minister could file a motion with the Cartel Court to cancel the agreement (Article 5).[10] Besides procedural measures, the Act of 1933 included sanctions. The Minister of Industry and Trade could impose administrative fines for failing to meet notification obligations.[11] Penal sanctions were also provided, enforceable by regional courts, for the execution of invalidated agreements.[12] These provisions marked a significant

7 Z. Landau, *Rozwój ustawodawstwa kartelowego w Polsce międzywojennej na tle polityki kartelowej rządu*, Kwartalnik Historyczny 1972, no. 1, 72.

8 JoL No. 65, item 449.

9 He called it 'sanacja' (sanitation) of morals and politics.

10 The Cartel Court is discussed in detail in Chapter 5.

11 M. Król-Bogomilska, *Kary*, 42.

12 Several ordinances were adopted in the course of implementing the Act of 1933: Ordinance of the Minister of Justice, with the consultation of the Ministers of Industry and

step in formalising competition regulation and provided a legal framework to address cartel activity.

A scholar analysing the Act of 1933 often emphasises that it did little to alter the legal status of cartels. The primary innovation was the requirement to disclose cartel agreements.[13] However, this requirement signalled the Polish government's intent to increase oversight of cartel activities. Combined with the economic hardships of the time, the adverse effects of cartels on society became increasingly burdensome, prompting a shift in cartel policy.

The Minister of Industry and Trade began utilising the powers granted under the Act, filing several motions with the Cartel Court to invalidate cartel agreements. This plan showed the government's growing commitment to addressing the impact of cartels on people. The government's control over cartels was further enhanced through amendments to the Act of 1933.[14] A key change was the transfer of the authority to annul cartel agreements directly to the Minister of Industry and Trade. Under the amended provisions, the Minister's decision became final unless a party to the invalidated agreement filed a motion for review with the Cartel Court.[15]

To discourage frivolous appeals, the amendments introduced a significant financial deterrent: the losing party in any such court proceedings was required to bear all associated costs. This measure effectively dissuaded smaller undertakings from challenging the Minister's decisions, limiting their access to legal recourse. While this change streamlined enforcement, it also diminished the role and significance of the Cartel Court, weakening its position within the regulatory framework. The amendments also introduced new criminal sanctions (imprisonment), further intensifying the regulatory regime.[16] These sanctions underscored the government's intent to impose stricter controls on cartel behaviour, reflecting a decisive shift towards more robust oversight and enforcement of competition policy.

The 1935 amendment clearly signalled to the industrial sector that the government was committed to tightening its oversight of cartels. This intent was

Trade and of the Treasury, of 28.06.1933 on the execution of provisions of the cartel act in relation to the Cartel Court, JoL No. 33, item 381; Ordinance of the Minister of Industry and Trade of 4.07.1933 on reporting resolutions and decisions of cartels, JoL No. 33, item 382; and Ordinance of the Minister of Industry and Trade of 4.07.1933 on the registry of cartels, JoL No. 33, item 383.

13 Z. Landau, 80–81.

14 Decree of the President of Poland of 27.11.1935 on amending the Act on cartels of 28.03.1933, JoL No. 86, item 529.

15 C. Kosikowski, T. Ławicki, *Ochrona prawna konkurencji i zwalczania praktyk monopolistycznych*, Warsaw 1994 48.

16 M. Król-Bogomilska, *Kary*, 42.

soon put into action: in December 1935, the Minister of Industry and Trade invalidated 93 of 274 cartel agreements. Predictably, the number of appeals was minimal, likely because of the financial and procedural barriers put in place to discourage challenges.[17]

Despite these efforts, the government concluded that the existing cartel regulation remained insufficiently stringent. This realisation led to the drafting of a new act, which was enacted on 13 July 1939.[18] The Act of 1939 on Cartel Agreements maintained the legality of cartel agreements, provided they were adequately notified.[19] However, a significant new requirement was introduced: such contracts had to align with the interests of the national economy (Article 2). This stipulation expanded the Minister of Industry and Trade's discretionary authority, allowing for a broader interpretation of whether a cartel served the public good. A commentator referred to this approach as the 'socialisation' of cartels, as it effectively subjected cartel activities to state oversight aligned with national economic priorities.[20]

While the supervisory procedures and sanctions under the Act of 1939 remained essentially unchanged, the legislation itself represented a more comprehensive regulatory framework. Many provisions previously set out in secondary implementing regulations were incorporated directly into the main Act, thereby centralising and solidifying the legislative structure governing cartels.

Tragically, the potential impact of the Act of 1939 was never realised. Although it entered into force, the outbreak of World War II following the German, Slovak, and Soviet invasion of Poland in September 1939 meant that the law was never practically enforced. This abrupt end underscores the disruptive effect of historical events on legislative advancements during this period.

During the communist era, the anti-cartel legislation of the 1918–1939 period was harshly criticised, largely dismissed as a product of capitalist manipulation. A notable scholar of the time asserted that *pre-September*[21] *Poland, under the sway of capitalist interests, had supported and accelerated cartelisa-*

17 Z. Landau, 83.

18 The Act of 1939 was adopted on 13.07.1939, but formally came into force on 20.10.1939. It was never enforced as the war broke out in September 1939, followed by the occupation of the territory of Poland by Germany, Slovakia and the Soviet Union.

19 JoL No. 63, item 418.

20 Z. Landau, 84.

21 The expression ('pre-September Poland') was often used by communist propaganda and refers to 1.09.1939, when Germany and Slovakia invaded Poland, starting the Second World War.

tion from its inception... This perspective viewed the legislation on cartels as a glaring example of national and foreign capital exploiting state power for its own benefit.[22] However, such assessments were deeply rooted in ideological bias rather than a balanced evaluation of the legislation's intent or impact.

Despite their imperfections, the Acts of 1933 and 1939 marked a clear shift towards stricter government oversight and an anti-cartel stance. These laws reflected the state's growing awareness of the societal and economic harm caused by unchecked cartels. Nonetheless, the procedural rules established under these Acts were rudimentary and lacked the sophistication of a comprehensive administrative framework. The limited procedural provisions were technical and insufficient to address the complexities of antimonopoly enforcement.

Ultimately, the pre-1939 system of cartel regulation and substantive law did not directly shape the subsequent development of Polish antimonopoly law and procedure. For nearly five decades, the evolution of competition law in Poland was effectively halted under communist rule, reflecting the era's centralised, state-controlled economic policies. The antimonopoly legislation of 1918–1939, however, remains a valuable historical example of the early stages of competition law development. It highlights the contemporary understanding of the state's role in regulating the economy and the perception of cartels in the interwar period.[23]

2 Legislation under the Communist Regime

2.1 Rudimentary Legislation in Years 1945–1987

After World War II, Poland, under Soviet influence, transitioned to a communist regime with a centrally planned economy. In such totalitarian systems, genuine competition is effectively non-existent, and classical economic monopolies are absent. Instead, the national economy operates as a single institutionalised monopoly controlled entirely by the state. This centralised model left no room for antimonopoly legislation in the traditional sense, and the People's Republic of Poland was no exception.

---

22 J. Jończyk, *Prawo kartelowe,* [in:] F. Ryszka (ed.), *Historia państwa i prawa Polski 1918–1939*, Part I, Warsaw 1962, 414.

23 For the overview of that period, see D.J. Gerber, *Law and Competition in Twentieth Century Europe: Protecting Prometheus*, Oxford 1998, 115–164.

By the late 1970s, scholars observed that Polish law lacked any formal anti-monopoly provisions.[24] They argued that 'under socialism, the state directly orchestrated and regulated the activities of economic organisations', making competition law unnecessary. Moreover, the monopolies that existed were described as 'social monopolies' and ideologically justified.[25] These monopolies 'were expected to act in society's best interest, with the premise that their power was accompanied by an obligation to serve the public good'.[26]

However, these ideological justifications failed to address the realities of a centrally planned economy.[27] As economic crises deepened and the inefficiencies of the socialist model became more apparent, scholars began to critique the adverse effects of state monopolies. In cautious terms, they highlighted the need to address abuses of monopolistic power.[28] While no comprehensive competition law existed, some legal measures were identified as potentially helpful in mitigating monopolistic practices. For instance:

1) Civil Code Provisions:[29] Certain articles could be interpreted to counteract monopolistic behaviour indirectly.
2) State Economic Arbitration Commissions:[30] These bodies could address disputes involving economic organisations and, in limited ways, deal with monopolistic conduct.
3) Act on Prices:[31] Article 8 of this law prohibited vendors from exploiting monopolistic positions to secure profits exceeding the average.

24 S. Sołtysiński, J. Trojanek, *Proces koncentracji produkcji i usług a zagadnienie ochrony interesów konsumenta w PRL*, Studia Prawnicze 1978, no. 1, 23. However, such legislation was present in other communist states, e.g. Hungary or Yugoslavia – a brief presentation of this legislation is provided by I. Wiszniewska and A. Kawecki, *Problem legislacji antymonopolowej w systemie zreformowanej gospodarki*, PUG 1982, no. 10, 259.

25 J. Trojanek, *O potrzebie i ekonomiczno-prawnych sposobach przełamywania monopolistycznych praktyk w gospodarce uspołecznionej*, RPEiS 1973, no. 3, 50.

26 *Ibidem*.

27 J. Trojanek stated it clearly: 'theoretical presumption that the monopoly of socialistic company acts always in favour of social interest and that the more powerful it is, the more it should feel obliged in relation to the society… turned out to be idealistic and, in consequence, delusive and false'. J. Trojanek, *Ustawa antymonopolowa z 1987 roku. (Próba oceny podstawowych rozwiązań)*, RPEiS 1987, no. 4, 1.

28 It was characteristic that S. Sołtysiński and J. Trojanek did not criticise the principle of monopolisation of the economy but only some of the side effects of such an economic regime.

29 Act of 23.04.1964–Civil Code, JoL No. 16, item 93. It was possible thanks to the process of 'socialisation of civil law', which strengthened the position of the consumer in relations with 'socialised economic units' (J. Trojanek, *O potrzebie*, 61).

30 Act of 23.10.1975 on State Economic Arbitrage, JoL No. 34, item 183.

31 JoL No. 7, item 52.

Despite these provisions, the fragmented nature of these measures meant they lacked the coherence and effectiveness of a proper competition law framework.[32] They neither established mechanisms to foster competition nor provided robust consumer protection. These piecemeal regulations did not align with contemporary doctrinal understandings of competition law, which emphasise comprehensive and enforceable rules to prevent monopolistic practices and promote a healthy market economy. The absence of such a framework during the communist era underscored the systemic incompatibility between centralised economic control and the principles of competition law.

2.2 The Act of 1987

The real breakthrough, however, was yet to come. The adoption of the 1987 Act on Counteracting Monopolistic Practices in the National Economy marked a pivotal moment in Poland's economic and legal history, representing a significant shift towards market-oriented reforms even within the confines of a socialist system. This development was driven primarily by the martial law declared in 1981 and the subsequent systemic economic crisis.[33] These challenges forced the communist government to confront the inherent inefficiencies of the socialist economy and initiate substantial reforms.

The severe economic crisis exposed structural flaws in the socialist economic model, necessitating a programme of rationalisation and restructuring. As part of this broader reform agenda, the antimonopoly act became a cornerstone of efforts to modernise and correct the economy.[34] Among the key weaknesses targeted were the rigid, inefficient structures of the so-called 'groupings' (pl. *zrzeszenia*), which concentrated economic activity and stifled flexibility and innovation.[35]

Preparation of the antimonopoly act began in 1984 and 1985, signalling the government's recognition of the need for regulatory mechanisms to address monopolistic practices.[36] However, the political and bureaucratic inertia typ-

32 I. Wiszniewska, A. Kawecki, 260.

33 Z.M. Fallenbuchl, *The Polish Economy under Martial Law*, Soviet Studies 1984, no. 36, no. 4.

34 S. Sołtysiński, *O potrzebie ustawodawstwa zwalczającego praktyki monopolistyczne i nieuczciwą konkurencję*, PiP 1982, no. 12, 16–18.

35 I. Wiszniewska, *Kartelowe zagrożenia w działalności zrzeszeń przedsiębiorstw państwowych*, Part I and II, PUG 1983, no. 11 and 12, and K. Sobczak, *Niektóre aspekty grupowania przedsiębiorstw oraz ochrony antymonopolowej*, PUG 1986, no. 6.

36 E. Piontek, *Znaki zapytania*, Prawo i Życie 1986, no. 6.

ical of the time delayed formal adoption until 1987, when the Sejm finally passed the legislation. This delay underscores the tension between the communist regime's ideological commitments and the practical necessity of introducing market-oriented principles.

The 1987 Act acknowledged the need to address monopolistic structures and behaviours within the economy. It was part of a broader legislative package aimed at restructuring the socialist economy and mitigating some of its most glaring inefficiencies.[37] While still operating within the framework of a centrally planned economy, the Act signalled a shift in economic policy and governance.

This legislation was not merely symbolic; it was a practical step towards introducing regulatory oversight into areas previously dominated by state monopolies and rigid organisational hierarchies. It laid the groundwork for Poland's eventual transition to a fully market-based economy in the post-communist era, highlighting the importance of competition law in facilitating economic reform.

The Act did not outlaw monopolies. Their existence was neither forbidden nor subject to legal sanctions. Nonetheless, the Act prohibited specific monopolistic practices and agreements. It also established a system of supervision over mergers of so-called 'economic units' (undertakings) (Articles 17–19).

The 1987 Act introduced a foundational framework for addressing monopolistic behaviour in Poland's centrally planned economy. The Preamble emphasised its purpose: to protect the national market and its participants from monopolistic practices of economic units while fostering consumer protection and the creation and development of competition. This dual focus signalled a progressive step towards aligning with market principles, despite being implemented in a socialist economic context.[38]

The Act addressed both substantive and procedural issues, covering virtually all economic activities undertaken by legal and natural persons, regardless of ownership structure or size. However, its scope was limited by exclusions:

i. Article 3(1) exempted certain significant state monopolies and enterprises in sectors considered strategic during the communist regime from its scope. These included state-owned entities under the Ministers of Finance, National Defence, Justice, Internal Affairs, and Foreign Affairs, as well as those reporting to the President of the National Bank of

37 J. Kaliński, *What was the Direction of the Reform of the PRL (Polish People's Republic) Economy in the Eighties?*. Studia Historiae Oeconomicae 2020, no. 38, 93.

38 I. Wiszniewska, *Praktyki monopolistyczne w świetle ustawy antymonopolowej*, PiP 1987, no. 7, 33.

Poland. These exemptions demonstrated the central government's hesitance to completely relinquish control over vital parts of the economy.

ii. A Regulation of the Council of Ministers dated 24 October 1988 specified the list of entities excluded from the Act's purview, demonstrating a significant concession to the centrally planned economic framework.[39]

Despite its ambitions, the Act's effectiveness was limited by exemptions for major state monopolies and the socialist regime's framework, which constrained competition. The 1987 Act was a transitional law that balanced socialist principles with market reforms, paving the way for more comprehensive laws after Poland's shift to a market economy in the 1990s.

The 1987 Act did not follow the traditional distinction between anti-competitive practices and prohibited agreements, and between abuse of dominant position and other abuses. Instead, it listed monopolistic practices and banned agreements. Article 8 prohibited practices such as imposing unjustified contractual terms for an undue benefit, conditioning contracts on unrelated obligations, requiring exclusive dealings, and charging excessive prices. Article 11 banned practices such as market division, setting or restricting production or sales, and limiting market access or excluding economic units from agreements.

The Minister of Finance was designated as the antimonopoly authority, empowered to issue decisions and impose financial penalties. Additionally, the Council for Counteracting Monopolistic Practices was established as an advisory body to the Minister of Finance (Article 4). The Council served as a forum for discussion and the formulation of proposals to guide the Minister in shaping antimonopoly policy. The Council comprised representatives from public administration authorities, cooperatives, trade unions, and consumer organisations (Article 5). Its competencies and procedures were further detailed in the Administrative Ordinance of the Prime Minister of 30 December 1987, which outlined the Council's specific tasks, composition, and operating methods.[40]

Under the 1987 Act, the Minister of Finance was responsible for issuing administrative decisions. The APC applied with some exceptions. Proceedings could be initiated ex officio or on motion, but only certain groups could request proceedings: (i) Voivodeship national councils; (ii) economic units or their unions and associations affected by monopolistic practices; (iii) inspection bodies and institutions overseeing economic activities; and (iv) public

39 JoL No. 39, item 309.

40 MP of 1988 No. 1, item 3.

institutions protecting consumer interests where such interests might be infringed.

A motion to initiate proceedings had to be submitted in writing and adequately substantiated. Decisions issued by the antimonopoly authority were subject to appeal before the HAC. General principles of administrative-judicial procedure applied to such appeals.[41] However, there was one exception to these regulations: objections by the Minister of Finance to a notified merger of economic entities were governed by separate provisions. This specific appellate procedure was regulated under § 4 of the Regulation of the Council of Ministers of 23 December 1987 on the Conditions and Method of Notification of Intent to Concentrate Economic Units and the Procedure for Appealing Objections Raised by the Antimonopoly Authority.[42]

The Act of 1987 provided for sanctions for violations of its provisions, including civil, administrative, and criminal measures.[43] The primary sanction was invalidity, which applied to monopolistic practices and agreements as defined in the Act (Articles 10, 12, and 23). Additionally, the antimonopoly authority was empowered to impose administrative fines (Article 20). However, such penalties were not imposed automatically for violations of the Act itself but were instead levied for non-compliance with decisions issued by the antimonopoly authority prohibiting monopolistic practices (Article 20(1)). An interesting feature of the system was that fines were allocated to the Market Development and Trade Demonopolisation Fund.[44] Consequently, monopolists that breached the antimonopoly law effectively financed the liberalisation of the communist economy. In cases involving three prior infringements of the Act within the preceding three years, the Minister of Finance was authorised to order the division or liquidation of an economic entity (Articles 21–22). Criminal sanctions, including imprisonment, were prescribed for providing false information to the antimonopoly authority (Article 25).

From its inception, the Act of 1987 was the subject of considerable controversy. Some criticisms arose from significant liberalising amendments introduced by the Parliament, which rendered many provisions unclear.[45] However, the primary concern centred on sanctions. The Act's ambiguous wording

41 Act of 31.01.1980 on the Head Administrative Court and on amending the Act–Administrative Procedure Code, JoL No. 4, item 8.

42 JoL No. 41, item 242.

43 S. Sołtysiński, *Sankcje w ustawie o przeciwdziałaniu praktykom monopolistycznym w gospodarce narodowej,* RPEiS 1987, no. 4, 21.

44 C. Banasiński, *Ewolucja ustawodawstwa antymonopolowego,* 11.

45 Differences between the draft and the Act are presented by I. Wiszniewska, *Praktyki,* 33–44.

made it difficult to determine whether the monopolistic practices and agreements prohibited under Articles 8 and 9 were automatically null and void or subject to suspended invalidity, as was the case under Articles 11, 12, and 13.[46] The concept of suspended invalidity was considered an inappropriate mechanism within antimonopoly law, as it allowed enterprises to continue engaging in illegal monopolistic practices until a decision on nullity was issued. A critic argued that such practices should be declared illicit *ex lege*, without requiring additional procedural steps.[47]

Academics also criticised the criteria for imposing administrative sanctions. They argued that the frequency of violations of the Act was less significant than the overarching issue of market dominance. Consequently, the Act was perceived as disproportionately targeting small enterprises and partnerships rather than addressing major state monopolies.[48] Further criticism was directed at the procedure for imposing administrative fines. It was suggested that penalties should be imposed automatically for violations of the Act, rather than requiring a prior decision to prohibit monopolistic practices. This requirement was seen as an unnecessary watering-down that weakened the Act's preventive function.[49]

Besides its sanctions, a contentious aspect of the 1987 Act was the designation of the Minister of Finance as the authority for antimonopoly matters. The competition agency was situated within the Ministry of Finance's Department for Counteracting Monopolisation of the National Economy. This placement aimed to keep the competition agency under the influence of the price-control functions, which were seen as related.[50] As a result, the Minister faced a paradoxical legal role: on the one hand, he represented the interests of the State Treasury and was tasked with ensuring sufficient state revenues, often generated by state monopolies. On the other hand, the Minister was tasked with combating monopolistic practices and agreements involving those same monopolies.[51] A more effective solution would have been to establish an independent body directly subordinated to Parliament or the Council of State.[52]

The Act placed significant emphasis on consumer protection and the promotion of competitive markets, signalling a policy shift to balance state con-

46 Ibidem, 23–26.

47 J. Trojanek, *Ustawa*, 13.

48 S. Sołtysiński, *Sankcje w ustawie*, 34–36.

49 I. Wiszniewska, *Praktyki*, 41.

50 M. Martyniszyn, M. Bernatt, *Implementing a competition law system – Three decades of Polish experience*, 7, https://ssrn.com/abstract=3391298.

51 C. Kosikowski, T. Ławicki, 51.

52 J. Trojanek, *Ustawa*, 18–19.

trol with the benefits of competition. This dual role recognised the importance of protecting consumer interests while facilitating gradual economic liberalisation. Nevertheless, despite its innovative intentions, the Act of 1987 proved largely ineffective in addressing monopolistic behaviour in Poland's socialist economy. Its impact was constrained by structural, procedural, and economic challenges, as well as the broader context of a centrally planned economy, which was incompatible with the principles of effective competition law.

The ineffectiveness of the 1987 Act stemmed from several factors. First, enforcement activity was formally intense but substantively ineffective. Between January 1988 and April 1990, 220 administrative proceedings were initiated (52 in 1988, 134 in 1989, and 34 in 1990). During this period, the Minister of Finance issued 182 decisions, 101 of which identified monopolistic practices. However, the sole sanction available was an order to cease the infringing conduct. Appeals against these decisions were heard by the HAC, which reviewed 26 cases, upheld 25 decisions, and remitted only one for reconsideration.[53]

This record demonstrates a high level of enforcement activity that failed to produce any meaningful economic impact. Although the decisions formally addressed monopolistic practices, they focused predominantly on individual instances of abuse and neglected the more systemic and economically significant problems of the period – most notably monopolistic agreements involving market sharing, production restrictions, and sales limitations – which remained largely outside the reach of effective enforcement.[54] Next, ambiguities and vague provisions were present. Many parts of the Act were unclear and lacked the specificity needed for effective enforcement, leading to interpretive challenges and limiting the Act's usefulness. Additionally, the provisions were viewed as too lenient, allowing monopolistic practices to persist in crucial sectors without sufficient deterrence or corrective measures.[55] Lastly, structural limitations were present. The socialist economic model inherently supported monopolistic structures, making it difficult for the Act to challenge the status quo effectively. Exemptions for major state monopolies, as previously outlined, further curtailed the Act's scope and impact.

Despite its shortcomings, the 1987 Act played a vital role in the development of Polish competition law. It was the first post-war attempt to legally curb monopolies within a socialist economy, an unprecedented move in Pol-

---

53 A. Fornalczyk, *Pierwsze doświadczenia Urzędu Antymonopolowego* [in.] C. Banasiński (ed.), *Ochrona konkurencji i konsumentów w Polsce i Unii Europejskiej (studia prawno-ekonomiczne)*, Warsaw 2005, 26.

54 C. Kosikowski, T. Ławicki, p.52.

55 I. Wiszniewska, *Praktyki*, 32; J. Trojanek, *Ustawa*, 3.

ish legislative history. This marked a shift towards acknowledging the importance of competitive practices. The Act laid the groundwork for later legal reforms, introducing concepts and mechanisms that were further refined in the 1990 Act, better aligned with a transitioning free-market economy.

The procedural framework established by the 1987 Act influenced the 1990 Act's design, ensuring some consistency while allowing improvements. This suggests that, although the 1987 Act was inadequate for its era, it set the foundation for Poland's future competition law in a market-oriented context. Overall, the 1987 Act was an experimental effort to implement antitrust laws in a conflicted economic system. Its limitations highlighted the difficulties of regulating monopolies in a socialist economy, while also paving the way for transition to a free-market system in subsequent years.

3 Polish Antimonopoly Acts in the Years 1990–2007

3.1 The Act of 1990

The transition from a centrally planned economy to a market-based system would have been inconceivable without demutualisation and the systematic promotion of competition. These objectives necessitated adopting a coherent and effective legislative framework for competition law. The extent of monopolisation within the Polish economy in 1990 is evidenced by the fact that more than 70% of the total range of industrial products was produced by only 25% of state-owned enterprises.[56] This required a statutory response. Therefore, the 1990 Act served as the foundational regulation for the development of competition law during the first decade of Poland's economic transformation and was amended 12 times. The discussion of the 1990 Act begins with an overview of the fundamental principles of its original text. Subsequently, the key amendments are analysed. While not all changes were equally significant, the chapter focuses exclusively on the most important amendments.

The Act of 1990 was a semi-comprehensive piece of legislation that was significantly more restrictive than the 1987 Act. It addressed substantive, procedural, and enforcement matters, expanding the catalogue of monopolistic practices and narrowing the scope of exemptions from its application.[57] The Act was based on the 'effects doctrine', meaning its provisions applied to all

56 Activity report 1990, 1.

57 W. Rakoczy, *Podmiotowy zakres stosowania ustawy o przeciwdziałaniu praktykom monopolistycznym*, PPH 1993, no. 15, 14.

agreements that had effects within Polish territory, regardless of where the contracts were concluded. It introduced key concepts into Polish competition law, including 'dominant position', 'abuse of such position', and the 'rule of reason'.

According to its Preamble, the Act was adopted to foster competition, protect economic entities from monopolistic practices, and safeguard consumer interests. Although the Preamble articulated three distinct objectives, the preservation of free competition was the primary goal. In instances of conflict, this objective was intended to take precedence over the others, while the protection of economic entities and consumers remained important but secondary aims.[58]

In 1990, a separate Antimonopoly Authority was established as the principal enforcer. The Authority was a central state administration body subordinated to the Council of Ministers, which had the power to appoint and dismiss its President (Article 17). The Authority initially conceived its mandate as actively promoting competition through structural economic reforms. This approach encompassed two core elements: (1) creating conditions conducive to the emergence of new undertakings; and (2) preventing monopolistic practices detrimental to both consumers and economic operators. The underlying rationale was that promoting competition would lead to cost optimisation for undertakings by improving production quality and fostering more efficient management practices.[59]

The Act of 1990 introduced the term 'monopolistic practice' but did not provide a formal definition. Instead, it listed specific types of monopolistic practices. Unlike the provisions addressing the abuse of a dominant position, the list of anticompetitive agreements was exhaustive.[60] The 1990 Act banned certain agreements, including price fixing, market division, controlling production or sales volumes, excluding market participants, and setting contract terms among competitors.

The 1990 Act recognised other monopolistic practices, some of which were inherited from the 1987 Act. It continued to prohibit onerous contract terms and make contracts conditional on unrelated obligations. A new provision, the 'interdiction of competition', banned individuals from managing competing firms. Unlike the 2000 Antimonopoly Act, which saw interlocking direct-

58 W. Modzelewski, 13.

59 Activity report 1990, 2.

60 This was changed in 1995 when an open list of anticompetitive agreements was introduced.

orates as mergers, this approach treated them as illegal agreements, which was quite restrictive.

The second major monopolistic practice under the Act involved abusing a dominant position, defined as an economic entity with little competition, especially if its market share exceeded 40%. The Act listed abuses such as hindering competition, dividing markets, granting privileged sales, discriminating in transactions, and unfair price influence, including resale price fixing or below-cost selling to eliminate rivals.

All legal actions labelled as practices were null unless the entity proved their necessity and showed they didn't significantly restrict competition. The Act explicitly outlaws three monopolistic practices: limiting production or sales to increase prices, withholding sales to inflate prices, and imposing excessive prices, regardless of justification.

The 1990 Act introduced merger control provisions. Under the Act, economic units were required to notify the Antimonopoly Authority of their intention to merge or undergo a transformation that would result in the establishment of a new economic entity acquiring a dominant position. The Antimonopoly Authority had two months to issue a decision on the proposed transaction. If the Authority did not oppose the merger, transformation, or establishment of the new entity within this timeframe, the transaction could proceed. Obtaining explicit positive clearance from the Authority was not required to implement the operation.

The procedural framework largely remained unchanged, with the APC applying as before, with some modifications. Proceedings could commence either ex officio or upon motion. The entities authorised to request proceedings remained largely the same as under the previous regulations, including economic entities affected by monopolistic practices, their unions and associations, state and public inspection institutions, and public institutions protecting consumer interests where those interests might be infringed.

Interestingly, local authorities were deprived of the right to request the initiation of administrative proceedings. The most significant change introduced by the Act of 1990, however, concerned the appellate procedure. Decisions issued by the Antimonopoly Authority could, from that point onward, be appealed to a specialised court established under the Act – the Voivodeship Court of Warsaw, functioning as the antimonopoly court.[61] Proceedings before the Court were conducted under the Civil Procedure Code governing

61 Regulation of the Minister of Justice of 13.04.1990 on the establishment of the antimonopoly court, JoL No. 27, item 157.

economic cases.[62] Judgments of the Antimonopoly Court may be subject to extraordinary revision (pl. *rewizja nadzwyczajna*) by the Supreme Court. Notably, a party filing an appeal with the Antimonopoly Court did not have access to the legal remedies under the APC to revise final administrative decisions. Specifically, the party could not invoke measures such as resumption of proceedings, annulment, amendment, or an assessment of the invalidity of a final decision (Article 23).

Infringements of the Act were subject to sanctions imposed by the antimonopoly authority. The primary sanction was an administrative fine, which was levied for violations of the prohibitions outlined in the Act. This sanction was administrative in nature.[63] The fine could reach up to 15% of the revenue. It could be imposed for failure to comply with a decision of the antimonopoly authority or a judgment of the Antimonopoly Court. An even more severe sanction was introduced by Article 15. Under this provision, *state enterprises, cooperatives, and companies governed by Commercial Law that held a dominant position in the market could be subject to division or liquidation if they persistently restricted competition or obstructed the conditions necessary for its emergence.*

From the outset, the Act of 1990 was subject to criticism. While some authors acknowledged its positive aspects, they also highlighted problematic provisions that needed amendment.[64] Foremost, the formulation of the 'rule of reason' was ambiguous. Additionally, the regulation requiring merger notifications was seen as a potential source of problems because the notification threshold was subjective. It was also noted that the merger provisions should have included exemptions from the notification obligation. The absence of such exemptions led to the notification of transactions that had no impact on competition in Poland. Furthermore, other authors raised several concerns about the application of the 1990 Act.[65] Criticism was also directed at the absence of provisions governing appellate review of orders issued by the antimonopoly authority during antimonopoly proceedings. Commentators emphasised the significant role of the Antimonopoly Court in interpreting (and potentially creating) the legal norms of competition law.[66] Finally, the lack of essential

62 Act of 17.11.1964–Civil Procedural Code, JoL No. 43, item 296.

63 I. Wiszniewska, *Polska ustawa antymonopolowa z 1990 r.*, PUG 1990, no. 7–8, 130.

64 Ibidem, 131–132.

65 T. Gosztyła, *Wybrane problemy regulacji i orzecznictwa antymonopolowego*, Radca Prawny 1993, no. 2.

66 Ibidem, 24–25.

definitions (e.g. the concept of concentration) and the vagueness of several existing definitions (e.g. dominant position) were also criticised.[67]

3.2 The Amendments to the Act of 1990

The Act of 1990 represented a significant step forward in the history of Polish competition law. However, it was apparent from the outset that amendments were necessary for it to become an effective tool for the demonopolisation of the market.[68] The first change resulted from a fundamental shift in the political regime, i.e. the introduction of independent municipalities replacing state-controlled territorial district units.[69] The Act of 17 May 1990 on the division of tasks and competences, as set out in specific acts, between municipal authorities and government administration, and on amending various acts, granted municipal authorities the right to request the initiation of antimonopoly proceedings.[70] The next amendment was far more complex.[71] This amendment introduced changes to the Act that reflected a deliberate state policy, shaped by ongoing economic transformations and by new knowledge about the functioning of antimonopoly legislation.[72] The market share threshold for presuming a dominant position was raised to 40%. However, the most significant changes were to the antimonopoly procedure itself. The burden of proof was shifted to the party invoking the rule of reason. The antimonopoly authority was required to issue a decision within one year of the cessation of the monopolistic practice. The amendment also clarified the specific application of the principle of procedural economy in the antimonopoly procedure. If, based on the requested information and the data obtained by the Antimonopoly Authority, it was determined that the Act of 1990 had not been infringed, no administrative proceedings were to be initiated. The party submitting the request had to be informed of this decision and provided with a justification. However, if the party maintained its claim, the antimonopoly authority was required to initiate proceedings. Finally, antimonopoly liability was extended to cover individuals.

---

67 W. Szpringer, *Koncepcja 'przyjaznych' i 'wrogich' fuzji kapitałowych w prawie spółek i prawie rynku kapitałowego*, PPH 1993, no. 7, 15.

68 W. Rakoczy, *Zastosowanie instrumentów demonopolizacyjnych w restrukturyzacji gospodarki*, PUG 1993, no. 11, 24.

69 C. Banasiński, *Ewolucja*, 13.

70 JoL No. 24, item 198.

71 Act of 28.06.1991 on amending the Act on counteracting monopolistic practices, JoL No. 65, item 279.

72 C. Banasiński, *Ewolucja*, 13.

The subsequent amendment was of a systemic nature.[73] This was the most significant change since the Act was adopted in 1990. Firstly, new definitions were introduced, including those of 'competitor', 'average salary', and 'income'. Additionally, the definition of 'economic entity' was modified to include entities that organise or provide public utility services, which were not considered business activities under the Act of 23 December 1989 on Business Activity.[74] Secondly, the merger control provisions were almost entirely rewritten. Notably, new sanctions were introduced for violations of these provisions. The catalogue of monopolistic practices was also altered. In terms of antimonopoly procedure, the amending Act introduced a clear rule that the Antimonopoly Court could review the Antimonopoly Office's orders on appeal upon the filing of a complaint (pl. *zażalenie*). All economic entities and their associations were required to submit, upon request, all documents and data relevant to a case pending before the antimonopoly authority. New provisions were introduced to protect business secrecy during investigations.

However, the most significant changes to the antimonopoly procedure were introduced, making directly applicable the CPC provisions on evidence and costs. While this created several challenges, it was viewed as a step towards better aligning the antimonopoly procedure with the complexity of such cases.[75]

The subsequent two amendments concerned the reform of the so-called 'economic centre' of the government. The first amendment, the Act of 8 August 1996, which amended the Acts regulating the functioning of the economy and public administration, changed the name of the Antimonopoly Authority to the Office for Competition and Consumer Protection (OCCP).[76] In this instance, the purpose of the amendment was not only to rename the antimonopoly authority and clarify its position within the system of government administration, but also to place greater emphasis on consumer protection as a fundamental objective alongside competition protection.[77] A new definition of 'consumer' was introduced. The Act established rules to protect consumer interests, reflecting the authority's expanded role, which now encompasses both competition and consumer protection. To ensure the effective implementation of these rules, the Act broadened the antimonopoly author-

73 Act of 3.02.1995 on amending the Act on counteracting monopolistic practices, JoL No. 41, item 208.

74 JoL No. 41, item 324.

75 M. Król-Bogomilska, *Zasady procedury cywilnej w postępowaniu przed Urzędem Antymonopolowym cz. I*, Glosa 1995, no. 8, 5.

76 JoL No. 106, item 496.

77 C. Banasiński, *Ewolucja*, 15.

ity's responsibilities to safeguard consumer interests. It subordinated the Trade Inspection to the OCCP. The primary functions of the Trade Inspection are market surveillance and consumer assistance.[78]

The 1996 amendment was pivotal in shaping perceptions and the organisational structure of competition enforcement in Poland, initiating a shift from a specialised antimonopoly body to an authority with multiple functions. The legislator's heightened emphasis on consumer protection within the OCCP's mandate, accompanied by a change in the authority's name, marked the start of a gradual expansion of its competences. The OCCP began to exercise responsibilities that extended well beyond the traditional role of safeguarding the market against anticompetitive practices, encompassing powers only indirectly related to competition protection.[79]

The subsequent Act of 20 August 1997 – Provisions Introducing the Act on the National Judiciary Registry – replaced the term 'economic entity' with 'undertaking'.[80] The subsequent amending act introduced a more significant change – the Act of 24 July 1998 on Amending Certain Acts Regulating the Competencies of Public Administration Authorities, in connection with the reform of the state system.[81] The Act established a new institution – the authority for consumer policy, namely the local consumer ombudsmen. Their primary task is protecting consumer interests, with no bearing on competition policy. The amendment symbolically elevated consumer protection, as evidenced by the change in the title of the antimonopoly act.[82]

Equally important was the increased role of local government in competition policy, achieved by adding relevant provisions to the 1990 Act.[83] The change primarily affected the third chapter of the Act of 1990. The amendment aimed to streamline the merger control process by exempting mergers with a combined turnover below ECU 25 million from the notification requirement. Additionally, notification was not mandatory when an individual acquired stocks or shares in another undertaking, resulting in less than 10% of the votes at a general assembly or partners' meeting.

The 1998 amendments were warmly welcomed by scholars and practising lawyers, who highlighted the importance of the new provisions that enhanc-

78 See Art. 3 of the Act of 15.12.2000 on Trade Inspection, JoL 2001 No. 4, item 25.

79 C. Banasiński, *Ewolucja,* 16.

80 JoL No. 121, item 770.

81 JoL No. 106, item 668.

82 From then on, the official title was the Act of 24.02.1990 on counteracting monopolistic practices and protection of consumers' interests.

83 Act of 22.10.1998 on amendment of the Act on counteracting monopolistic practices and protection of consumers' interests, JoL No. 154, item 938.

ed consumer protection.[84] Many scholars and practitioners supported the changes to the merger notification procedure, arguing that these reforms would accelerate proceedings. They also positively evaluated the exclusion of privatisation and transformation of state-owned undertakings from the notification procedure. It was suggested that, given the advanced stage of Poland's economic transformation, such provisions were no longer necessary.[85] However, some academics disagreed with this opinion.[86] For these critics, the amendment could strengthen the monopolistic positions of state-owned undertakings. While they supported the introduction of consumer-oriented provisions, they argued that these measures were not comprehensive enough. They emphasised the need to develop consumer protection regulations further to ensure a more robust, well-rounded legal framework.[87] The new provisions on merger control expanded the subjective scope of applicability of the antimonopoly act, and these changes were evaluated positively.[88]

The institutional position of the President of the OCCP within the framework of government administration has also evolved. The previous subordination of the OCCP President to the Council of Ministers was replaced by supervision under the Prime Minister. This change could increase the OCCP's independence from current government policy.[89] The following years proved that this potential was only partially realised.

The last significant change to the Act of 1990 was made by the Act of 30 June 2000, which addressed the conditions for the admissibility and supervision of state aid for undertakings.[90] Under this Act, the OCCP was granted additional responsibilities for supervising state aid provided to undertakings. This change was a direct consequence of Poland's commitments arising from its accession to the European Communities.

The Act of 1990 is a prime example of the evolution of economic law in a transition economy. As the Act developed, its provisions expanded and became more complex. The OCCP has evolved further, from a former department of the Finance Ministry to a single central government agency with

---

84 S. Gronowski, *Zmiany w ustawie antymonopolowej*, MoP 1999, no. 2, 9.

85 Ibidem, 12.

86 J. Olszewski, *Uwagi o zmianach i propozycje dalszego reformowania prawa antymonopolowego*, Rejent 2000, no. 3, 78.

87 Ibidem, 82.

88 R. Pasiak, *Niektóre skutki ostatnich zmian ustawy o przeciwdziałaniu praktykom monopolistycznym dla spółek publicznych*, Prawo Spółek 1999, no. 6, 25–29.

89 C. Banasiński, *Ewolucja*, 16.

90 JoL No. 60, item 704.

expanding powers that extend well beyond competition law. The economy became increasingly liberalised, with the OCCP's oversight becoming more selective, subtle, and relaxed. This development offers a clear view of the ongoing legal reform process. The authority responded quickly when shortcomings of the 1990 Act became apparent, and Parliament addressed those problems swiftly. Such cooperation was essential for structural economic changes. From the mid-90s, the aim of European integration became apparent, influencing subsequent changes to competition, consumer, and state aid laws, all of which were enforced by the OCCP.

3.3 The Act of 2000: The First Modern Competition Act

Since the passage of the 1990 Act, Poland's economic and political landscape has undergone significant change. The establishment of a free-market economy and the country's close integration with the European Union provided strong impetus for adopting a new antimonopoly law. According to the Explanatory Memorandum,[91] the adoption of a new antimonopoly act was driven by several key factors:

1) Significant transformation of the Polish economy;
2) Rearrangement of Polish legislation following the adoption of the Constitution in 1997;[92]
3) The need for an effective legal instrument for competition protection;
4) Harmonisation of Polish law with EC standards.[93]

The Act of 2000 was intended to be a comprehensive regulation addressing both competition and consumer protection. However, it was truly comprehensive only in its competition protection provisions, which were well-developed and introduced several new rules. The consumer protection section of the Act was more selective, containing only institutional provisions. Therefore, the primary goal of the Act was to establish conditions that foster and protect competition. This was achieved by regulating practices that restrict competition and by measures countering anticompetitive concentrations of undertakings and their associations. The 2000 Act was markedly more comprehensive than its predecessor, primarily because the legislator, for the first time, sought to provide an exhaustive regulation of procedural rules governing

---

91 In Poland, all drafts of acts presented in parliamentary proceedings are accompanied by explanatory memoranda, in which the authors of the legislative proposal outline the objectives and anticipated impact of the proposed act.

92 JoL No. 78, item 483.

93 Explanatory memorandum, 44–45.

antimonopoly proceedings. Until then, such proceedings had been conducted predominantly under the general provisions of the APC.[94]

The 2000 Act consolidated and strengthened the trend towards establishing the President of the OCCP as an independent authority, insulated from contemporary political influence.[95] The OCCP gained greater independence through a revised appointment process for its President. The Prime Minister now appoints the President for a five-year term based on a competitive selection. Candidates must possess a university degree, especially in law, economics, or business administration, and show both theoretical understanding and practical experience in the market economy, competition, and consumer protection. This selection process is regulated by a Prime Minister-issued regulation and was unique as the only such procedure in Polish public administration at that time.[96] The Prime Minister had the power to recall the President of the OCCP, but only in specific, limited circumstances set out in an enumerated list. This regulation ensured the authority's formal independence and stability, thereby safeguarding the OCCP's impartiality.

The substantive provisions were significantly modified. The Act of 2000 prohibited two kinds of anticompetitive practices of undertakings (individual and collective) and anticompetitive concentrations. The Act of 2000 introduced the prohibition of collective competition-restricting practices. A new definition of 'agreement' and 'competition-restricting agreement' was added.

A significant portion of the substantive provisions of the new Act was modelled on European competition law.[97] Consequently, the wording of Article 5 of the Act, which prohibits agreements that restrict competition, aligns with that of Article 81 of the EC Treaty. Article 8 of the Act, which prohibits the abuse of a dominant position, mirrors the wording of Article 82 of the EC Treaty.[98] The Act of 2000 established a general prohibition on competition-restricting agreements, accompanied by an illustrative list of such practices. This list included both horizontal and vertical agreements, including distribution agreements. Compared with the European Union's competition law, the

---

94 M. Bychowska, M. Krasnodębska-Tomkiel, *Procedura antymonopolowa jako instrument ochrony konkurencji–refleksje dotyczące ustawy z 15.12.2000 r. o ochronie konkurencji i konsumentów* [in:] C. Banasiński (ed.), *Prawo konkurencji – stan obecny oraz przewidywane kierunki zmian*, Warsaw 2006, 26.

95 C. Banasiński, *Ewolucja*, 18.

96 Regulation of the Prime Minister of 29.06.2001 on the method and procedure for organising the contest for the office of the President of the Office of Competition and Consumer Protection, JoL No. 69, item 720.

97 R. Janusz, M. Sachajko, T. Skoczny, *Nowa ustawa o ochronie konkurencji i konsumentów*, KPP 2001, no. 3, 176.

98 C. Banasiński, *Ewolucja*, 19.

Act introduced two additional types of agreements: those aimed at limiting market access or eliminating competitors who are not parties to the agreement, and those involving the fixing of bid conditions in tenders.

There was, however, a significant exception to this general prohibition: agreements that had only an insignificant impact on the market were excluded from its scope. In addition, the Council of Ministers was authorised to issue block exemptions.[99] They reflected the Polish approach to harmonising national competition law with EU regulations while also addressing Poland's unique economic and market conditions at the time.

The 2000 Act's second category of practices that limit competition was the abuse of a dominant position. Unlike earlier legislation, the concept of a 'dominant position' was established as a single term, replacing the previous idea of a 'monopolistic position'. It describes a situation where an entity can hinder effective competition in the relevant market, regardless of competitors, contracting parties, or consumers. An entity is typically deemed dominant if it holds more than a 40% market share. Unlike the 1990 Act, which permitted certain justifications, the prohibition on abusing a dominant position under the new law was strict and could not be defended. This prohibition also extends to practices by groups of companies, introducing a ban on collective dominance. Although the law did not explicitly define 'abuse', it provided examples of practices that could be considered abusive.

The 2000 Act introduced a modern system of merger control, marking a significant shift from the previous regulatory framework. One key change in the Act of 2000 was the introduction of a broader definition of an 'undertaking'. This definition supplemented the basic definition established in the 1999 Law on Business Activity.[100] The expansion of this definition was significant because it allowed for a more comprehensive assessment of market participants, ensuring that mergers involving smaller or more complex entities could also be subject to scrutiny. This broader definition ensured that the author-

---

99 Regulation of the Council of Ministers of 30.07.2002 on exemption from the prohibition of competition-restricting agreements of certain categories of agreements concluded between undertakings engaged in insurance business activity, JoL No. 137, item 1151; Regulation of the Council of Ministers of 30.07.2002 on exemption from the prohibition of competition-restricting agreements of certain categories of agreements concerning transfer of technologies, JoL No. 137, item 1152; Regulation of the Council of Ministers of 13.08.2002 on exemption from the prohibition of competition-restricting agreements of certain specialisation agreements and research–development agreements, JoL No. 142, item 1188; Regulation of the Council of Ministers of 13.08.2002 on the exemption of certain vertical agreements from the prohibition of competition-restricting agreements, no. 142, item 1189.

100 JoL No. 101, item 1178.

ities could review a wide range of potential mergers, even those involving entities not traditionally considered large players in the market.

The Act of 2000 did not define 'concentration' but listed specific types of transactions that required notification, such as mergers, acquisitions, and joint ventures. The most controversial and often criticised[101] solution was mandatory notification in cases of 'quasi-concentrations', such as:

i. The acquisition of stocks or shares in another undertaking that results in the acquisition of at least 25% of the votes at a general assembly or partner meeting;
ii. The assumption by the same person of a position on the management or controlling body of competing undertakings;
iii. The initiation of exercising rights derived from stocks or shares acquired or taken over without prior notification.

The lack of clarity in defining 'concentration' led to a broader interpretation, potentially subjecting more transactions to scrutiny than necessary under EU competition law.[102]

The Act of 2000 established several exemptions from the obligation to notify concentrations. These exemptions applied where the concentration was deemed to have insignificant market relevance. Specifically, exemptions were granted in the following circumstances:

i. When the turnover of the undertaking did not exceed the equivalent of EUR 10 million in Poland;
ii. When the combined market share of the undertakings involved in the concentration did not exceed 20%;
iii. The parties to the concentration belonged to the same capital group.

The EUR 10 million turnover threshold was considered appropriately set for the Polish economy at the time. It was supposed to strike a balance between capturing concentrations with significant market impact and excluding smaller, less consequential transactions. The method for calculating turnover in these cases was defined in the implementing regulation.[103] This regulation provided a standardised approach to determine whether a concentration met the threshold for notification, ensuring consistent application of the law across cases. The 20% market-share threshold under the second exemption

101 R. Janusz, M. Sachajko, T. Skoczny, 190.

102 M. Rogala, *Kontrola koncentracji przedsiębiorców w nowej ustawie antymonopolowej*, Prawo Spółek 2001, no. 9, 47.

103 Regulation of the Prime Minister of 23.05.2001 on the calculation of turnover for undertakings participating in concentrations, JoL No. 60, item 611.

was criticised as being set too high.[104] The Act of 2000 also included three other exemptions, though these were of lesser practical importance.[105]

The procedural provisions of the 2000 Act were significantly more developed than those of the 1990 Act, accounting for two-thirds of the 2000 Act. However, the procedural framework became excessively complex. Antimonopoly proceedings were conducted under the rules set out in Section V of the 2000 Act. In matters not regulated by the 2000 Act, the APC applied, with two notable exceptions: evidentiary proceedings were governed by the CPC, and dawn raids were subject to the PPC. Consequently, the antimonopoly procedure evolved into a hybrid system combining elements of administrative, civil, and criminal procedures.[106] This intricate structure was subsequently retained in the 2007 Act.

The Act of 2000 defined two separate proceedings before the OCCP, as specified in Article 42: 1) explanatory investigations and 2) antimonopoly proceedings. While these proceedings were separate, the explanatory investigation could be conducted before initiating competition cases. The explanatory investigation was a new procedural tool introduced in Polish competition law, initiated automatically by the OCCP through an order and concluded with a subsequent order.

A notable feature of the Act of 2000 was that antimonopoly proceedings could be initiated not only ex officio but also upon motion. Even more strikingly, such a motion was, in principle, binding on the authority. This meant that the OCCP was obliged to consider motions filed by eligible parties, thereby giving private and public actors a concrete procedural role in triggering enforcement. Undertakings and their associations were treated as parties under substantive law, since their rights and obligations could be directly affected by the outcome. Local government authorities, inspection bodies, the consumer ombudsman, and consumer organisations were considered parties only in a procedural sense. Their standing was derived not from a substantive legal interest of their own, but from their role in defending the public interest within the process.

This dual model of party participation illustrates the balance the 2000 Act struck between private and public enforcement. On the one hand, undertakings were empowered to defend their legal interests in proceedings with direct

104 J. Olszewski, *Nowa ustawa o ochronie konkurencji i konsumentów cz. II*, MoP 2001, no. 15, 776.

105 For example, exemptions for financial institutions or transactions during insolvency proceedings.

106 M. Bychowska, M. Krasnodębska-Tomkiel, 27.

legal consequences. On the other hand, selected public and consumer bodies were granted procedural legitimacy to ensure that competition cases served broader societal goals.[107]

The Act of 2000 also changed the procedural rules for merger cases by creating a narrower definition of who could be a party. Only entities directly involved in the merger, such as the merging companies or the acquirer of shares, were recognised as parties. Other interested entities, like competitors, consumer groups, or broader market stakeholders, were not considered parties but could only participate as observers or submit views. This distinction had important effects: parties had full procedural rights, including influencing proceedings and challenging decisions, while participants played a more limited role, mainly providing input or information.

The rationale for narrowing party status in merger cases was twofold. On the one hand, it aimed to streamline proceedings by reducing procedural complexity and focusing the authority's attention on those entities most directly affected by the concentration. On the other hand, it curtailed procedural involvement by different stakeholders, particularly those representing public or consumer interests. The result was a more efficient but less participatory model of merger control.[108] The regulation of a party's legal status in merger cases has been criticised for being inconsistent and complex.[109]

The Act of 2000 introduced a new procedural category into Polish administrative law – the 'interested person' (*osoba zainteresowana*). Although novel in contemporary Polish law, it resembled an earlier institution regulated in Articles 9–14 of the 1928 Decree on administrative procedure.[110] Its modern shape, however, was primarily inspired by EU competition law.[111] An 'interested person' was broadly defined as anyone who either requested action from the antimonopoly authority or whose interests, even indirectly, were linked to its activities. While the institution broadened participation in proceedings, its limited procedural rights made it weaker than full party status.

The 2000 Act introduced the possibility of concluding administrative settlements during antimonopoly proceedings. The essence of an administrative settlement is an agreement between the parties to the proceedings, which is approved by the authority. The significance of this institution in OCCP practice was negligible, as undertakings showed little interest in it. Moreover, the

107 Z. Kmieciak, 35.
108 Ibidem, 309.
109 Z. Kmieciak, 35.
110 JoL No. 86, item 341.
111 R. Janusz, *Dostosowanie,* 308.

antimonopoly court also exhibited significant scepticism towards this institution.[112] No activity report of the OCCP recorded any administrative settlement ever concluded under the 2000 Act.

In the OCCP's own view, the administrative practice in conducting antimonopoly proceedings under the framework established by the 2000 Act demonstrated that the drafters' intentions (i.e. the OCCP) – to design a procedure constituting an effective instrument for competition law enforcement – were largely achieved. The OCCP was equipped with a modern, robust procedural mechanism tailored to the public-interest objective of detecting the most serious infringements of competition law. It may even be argued that certain procedural solutions incorporated in the 2000 Act were pioneering, exceeding the OCCP's institutional and operational capacity at the time. This is illustrated by the limited practical use of some advanced tools, such as search provisions, during the initial years following the Act's entry into force.[113]

3.4 The Amendments to the Act of 2000

The 2000 Act was adopted three years before Poland's accession to the EU and the entry into force of Regulation 1/2003. To align the Competition Act with the new framework introduced by the Regulation, Parliament subsequently enacted an amendment to the 2000 Act.[114] A further impetus for this legislative change stemmed from practical experience gained during the three years of implementing the Act.[115]

The 2004 amendment to the Competition Act explicitly incorporated Regulation 1/2003, designating the OCCP as Poland's national competition authority under Article 35. This reform significantly expanded the OCCP's powers, introducing two new types of rulings: interim measures and commitment decisions. Interim measures could be imposed to prevent serious and irreparable harm to competition pending final decisions, while commitment decisions allowed undertakings to offer remedies in exchange for closing proceedings without a finding of infringement or a fine.

Procedural changes further strengthened enforcement. Explanatory proceedings were subject to strict deadlines (30 days, extendable to 60 in complex cases), though market studies were exempt. Evidence rules were broad-

112 Antimonopoly Court judgments of 10.05.1993, XVII Amr 7/93, and of 27.02.1991, XV Amr 9/90.

113 M. Bychowska, M. Krasnodębska-Tomkiel, 27.

114 Act of 16.0.2004 amending the Act on Competition and Consumer Protection and certain other acts, JoL No. 93, item 891.

115 M. Bychowska, M. Krasnodębska-Tomkiel, 30.

ened: undertakings had to provide both information and documents, and written statements could now be submitted by any person. The OCCP's inspection powers were expanded to include searches authorised by courts, and it could also assist the European Commission in on-site inspections. Confidentiality rules were reinforced with a statutory definition of business secrecy and stricter limits on access to sensitive evidence.

The amendment also aligned Polish merger control with EU law by replacing the dominance test with the 'significant impediment to effective competition' test from Regulation 139/2004. The de minimis exemption for small concentrations was narrowed, ensuring greater scrutiny of transactions that strengthen local dominance. Institutionally, a short-lived 'Council for Good Economic Practices' was created to advise on policy but quickly proved ineffective.

Overall, the 2004 reform embedded Poland (i.e. the OCCP) in the ECN, ensuring harmonisation with EU standards and enhancing the OCCP's role in applying national and EU competition law. Yet the reform was largely derivative, with most changes driven by European requirements. National initiatives were limited, and persistent weaknesses – such as settlement procedures, third-party participation, and the review of quasi-concentrations – remained unresolved. The amendment thus illustrates the nature of EU-driven reform: it delivered stronger tools and integration but left underlying domestic deficiencies largely untouched.

4 The Act of 2007: The Overview of the Current Competition Act

The Act on Competition and Consumer Protection, in force since 21 April 2007, is the principal source of competition law in Poland. It provides a comprehensive framework for the institutional, substantive, and procedural dimensions of competition policy. The Act regulates proceedings before the President of the OCCP in four main areas: (i) anticompetitive agreements, (ii) abuse of a dominant position, (iii) merger control, and (iv) abuse of collective consumer rights.

Although each area is governed by specific rules, nearly two-thirds of the Act's procedural provisions apply across all cases, underscoring the centrality of procedure to Polish competition enforcement. The Act also authorises the Council of Ministers to issue implementing regulations and allows the OCCP to develop soft law instruments, such as guidelines and notices. Together, these legislative and non-legislative measures form a coherent framework for the effective application of competition rules in Poland.[116]

A characteristic feature of the Competition Act is that its procedural provisions are not exhaustive; numerous references to procedural codes and statutes are made for application accordingly. Three references are of crucial importance. Firstly, there is a general reference to the APC. This means that procedural aspects not directly regulated by the Competition Act are governed by the APC, unless otherwise provided in the Act. In particular, the regulation of evidence proceedings in the Competition Act is supplemented by the CPC's provisions on evidence, i.e. Articles 227–315. The procedure for search refers to the PPC. Multiple references of this kind create a rather complex procedural framework.

The Competition Act regulates only public competition enforcement.[117] It establishes a public authority competent to undertake such intervention. The Act defines a procedural framework and a substantive basis for OCCP's actions. The intervention is carried out in the public interest. The notion of the 'public interest' has been at the centre of doctrinal and judicial analysis, as it plays a jurisdictional role in determining which cases the authority should take. Private interests are protected only insofar as they serve the primary goal. It is assumed that the public interest is defined through the prism of the consumer welfare standard.[118]

The OCCP counteracts anticompetitive practices and supervises concentrations of undertakings that have or may have an impact in Poland, in accordance with the extraterritoriality principle.[119] In consequence, the authority may institute proceedings against any undertaking, irrespective of where the anticompetitive agreement was concluded, or a concentration will take place, provided that its effects are or may be detected in Poland.[120] Any foreign company may seek protection from the OCCP against any Polish company engaged in anticompetitive behaviour.[121]

116 All relevant legislation, together with soft law documents, is presented in the bibliography section.

117 Private enforcement is governed by a separate statute and discussed in detail in Chapter 11.

118 D. Miąsik, *Controlled Chaos with Consumer Welfare as the Winner–a Study of the Goals of Polish Antitrust Law*, YARS 2008, no. 1(1), 57.

119 R. Stankiewicz, *Zasada eksterytorialnego stosowania przepisów ustawy antymonopolowej do spraw z zakresu nadzoru nad procesami koncentracji przedsiębiorców*, Przegląd Prawniczy UW 2006, no. 1, 121.

120 PSC judgment of 10.05.2007, III SK 24/06.

121 CCCP judgment of 18.12.2002, XVII Ama 19/01.

The Competition Act recognises restrictions on competition allowed by separate statutes. Such restrictions preclude the OCCP from intervening.[122] The Competition Act explicitly provides exemptions for specific activities. The key exemptions include:

i. activities governed by the Act on games of chance and mutual bets;
ii. offset agreements related to a supply contract for state defence and security;
iii. certain mergers resulting from the Act on restructuring the iron and steel industry.

All these exemptions are interpreted narrowly to protect the fundamental objectives of competition regulation. None of the exemptions is absolute; each applies only within defined limits. Outside those limits, the Competition Act applies without any constraints.[123]

The Competition Act applies without prejudice to intellectual property rights. It recognises the existence of legal monopolies arising from statutory protections for inventions, utility models, industrial designs, semiconductor topographies, trademarks, geographical indications, copyright, and related rights. However, anticompetitive practices connected with IP rights – such as refusals to license or discriminatory licensing – fall within the scope of Polish competition law. Certain categories of technology transfer agreements benefit from exemption regulations, reflecting a balance between safeguarding innovation incentives and ensuring market access.[124]

The detailed presentation and analysis of the Competition Act's institutional, substantive, and procedural provisions are provided in the next chapters.

5 Amendments of the 2007 Act

5.1 First Amendments

In May 2012, the OCCP published its first draft proposals for changes. Following public consultations and intensive work within the government, the Polish parliament proceeded with the amendment, which was adopted on

122 CCCP judgment of 29.12.1993, XVII Amr 42/93.

123 CCCP judgment of 25.10.2000, XVII Ama 10/00.

124 Regulation of the Council of Ministers of 17.04.2015 on exemption from the prohibition of competition restricting agreements of certain categories of agreements concerning transfer of technologies, JoL 2015, item 585.

10 June 2014.[125] Together with the entry into force of the amending statute, three new implementing regulations were published in mid-January.[126]

According to the explanatory memorandum accompanying the amending statute, the OCCP has identified three areas as crucial to more effective competition protection. Accordingly, the amendment introduced several changes to Polish competition law:

i. A two-phase merger procedure, a limitation of the competition authority's merger jurisdiction;
ii. Stricter regulation of dawn raids and their separation from ordinary on-the-spot inspection activities;
iii. Remedies in antitrust cases;
iv. Liability of natural persons for antitrust infringements;
v. Leniency plus and changes to the leniency procedure;
vi. Settlement procedure.

The 2014 amendment was an important development with significant potential to invigorate enforcement. Unfortunately, apart from the merger control changes, the rest did not realise it. It was not a surprise, since the amendment was heavily criticised during the consultation process by the Supreme Court, academics, lawyers and their organisations, undertakings and their associations, and finally by the Government Legislation Centre.[127]

5.2 ECN+ Directive Implementation

The following substantial change to the Competition Act resulted from the implementation of the ECN+ Directive.[128] In justifying the adoption of the

125 Act of 10.06.2014 on amending the act on competition and consumer protection and the act – Civil Procedural Code, JoL 2014, item 945.

126 Regulation of Council of Ministers of 23.12.2014 on the mode of calculating the turnover of the undertakings engaged in the concentration, JoL 2015, item 79, Regulation of Council of Ministers of 23.12.2014 on the notification of the concentration of undertakings, JoL 2015, item 80, Regulation of Council of Ministers of 23.12.2014 on the mode and procedure of processing applications for immunity from and reduction of fines, JoL 2015, item 81.

127 All opinions are available at http://legislacja.rcl.gov.pl/lista/2/projekt/85314/katalog/85321.

128 For an overview of the ECN+ Directive and its implementation, please refer to W.P.J. Wils, *The European Commission's 'ECN+': Proposal for a Directive to empower the competition authorities of the Member States to be more effective enforcers*, Concurrences 2017, N° 4, and B. Van Rompuy, *Implementation of the ECN+ Directive in 23 Member States: An Introductory Overview*, CoRe 2021, no. 3.

ECN+ Directive, the Commission noted that there is untapped potential for NCAs to enforce EU competition rules even more effectively.[129]

This determined the scope of changes to the Competition Act. On 2 June 2023, the amendment entered into force in Poland.[130] While presenting the proposal for the implementing act, the OCCP noted that the amendment introduces a five-year term of office for the OCCP President. This solution, together with the determination of a closed catalogue of grounds on which the Prime Minister may dismiss the President of the OCCP, is intended to ensure greater independence for the President and to allow long-term planning of competition and consumer protection policy. The catalogue of grounds is closed and does not include any evaluative or undefined grounds (introducing such grounds into Article 29(4) of the Competition Act would be in apparent contradiction to the fundamental objective of the amendment – strengthening the guarantee of independence of the antimonopoly authority).[131]

In justifying the need to implement provisions on the authority's formal independence, OCCP stated that this is primarily to fulfil the obligation to transpose the ECN+ Directive into the Polish legal order. Moreover, according to the OCCP, 'the strengthening of the independence of the antimonopoly authority in Poland, as proposed in the above-mentioned scope, is the implementation of a demand repeatedly made in recent years by circles comprising persons academically or professionally related to the application of competition and consumer protection law [...] The introduction of a term of office will undoubtedly serve to make the President of the OCCP perform his statutory tasks more effectively.'[132] The OCCP didn't explain how formal independence was supposed to improve competition law enforcement. What is even more worrying is that the OCCP invokes important academic articles. Still, it treats them instrumentally, appealing only to their general conclusion about the legal obligation to guarantee the OCCP's formal independence. It completely ignores the details of how this independence should be constructed and enforced, and why factual independence plays an even more significant role.

---

129 Explanatory Memorandum to the Proposal for a Directive of the European Parliament and of the Council concerning the powers of the competition authorities of the Member States to ensure more effective enforcement of the competition rules and the proper functioning of the internal market, COM(2017) 142 final, 3, http://ec.europa.eu/competition/antitrust/proposed_directive_pl.pdf.

130 Act of 9.03.2023 on the amendment of the act on competition and consumer protection and other acts, JoL 2023, item 852.

131 Explanatory memorandum to the draft act amending the Act on Competition and Consumer Protection and certain other acts, Parliamentary Print No. 2990, 31.01.2023, 12.

132 Ibid, 11.

The 2023 amendment updated rules for dawn raids, inspections, private searches, and fines for non-cooperation or false info. Fines are now capped at 3% of the previous year's turnover, aligning with the ECN+ Directive, and include up to 5% daily penalties for delays. Changes to the leniency program exclude criminal liability for tender collusion when seeking penalty reductions, encouraging more cooperation. The amendment also broadens the scope of entities that must provide information to OCCP, now including more entities with procedural safeguards for individuals. Last but not least, the implementation of the ECN+ Directive enabled more effective cooperation among national authorities. The amendments to the Act provide, among other things, for the assistance of OCCP in EU NCAs' proceedings.

5.3 DMA, FSR, FDI Implementation

The most recent amendment[133] to the Competition Act reflects the need to align domestic law with the emerging EU system of economic governance, most notably through the DMA, the FSR, and the FDI Regulation.

5.3.1 DMA

The DMA, in force since November 2022, addresses the gatekeeping power of large digital platforms.[134] While enforcement rests primarily with the European Commission, national authorities play an assisting role. Article 14 introduces a novel notification obligation for gatekeepers involved in concentrations, regardless of whether they fall under EU or national merger control. Poland's 2025 amendment to the Competition Act aims to equip the OCCP with investigatory powers (including inspections, information requests, and cooperation with the Commission) to ensure the practical application of Articles 5–7 of the DMA. In contrast to the FSR's largely supportive national role, the DMA requires greater involvement from national authorities, thereby integrating Poland into a multi-level control system.

133 Act of 9.05.2025, amending certain acts to ensure the application of European Union law and improve the functioning of the internal market, JoL 2025, item 794.

134 For an overview of the DMA and its implementation, please refer to G. Colangelo, *DMA begins*, JAE 2023, no. 1(11), and G. Muscolo, A. Massolo (eds.), *Navigating the DMA: Application Across National Jurisdictions*, Concurrences 2025.

5.3.2 FSR

Applicable since July 2023, the FSR fills a regulatory gap by subjecting subsidies granted by non-EU states to scrutiny under existing EU merger and state aid rules.[135] It establishes an additional notification system for concentrations involving subsidised entities, requiring companies to monitor subsidies received over the past three years. The Polish 2025 amendment designates the OCCP as the competent national authority for cooperation with the Commission, transmission of information, and assistance with inspections. As in other CEE jurisdictions, this reform reflects the EU model of 'shared enforcement', in which Brussels leads while national authorities provide on-the-ground support.

5.3.3 FDI Regulation

Regulation (EU) 2019/452 established an EU-wide cooperation framework for foreign direct investment screening while leaving substantive decision-making powers at the national level.[136] Although the European Commission may issue opinions, final authority rests with Member States. Poland initially implemented the Regulation through a formally temporary regime that entrusted FDI screening to the OCCP. This institutional choice was exceptional, as it located investment control within an independent NCA rather than a ministerial structure. Following the 2025 amendment, the regime was made permanent and aligned with prevailing CEE models, under which FDI screening is exercised by ministries responsible for economic or industrial policy. This shift reflects the widely accepted view that FDI control is an inherently political function, ill-suited to technocratic competition authorities.

5.4 More Implementation to Come: DSA, AI Act, EMFA

The new amendments to the Competition Act, stemming from EU law, do not exhaust the scope of legislative changes that should be implemented. There

---

135 For an overview of the FSR and its implementation, please refer to K. Sideri, *Regulating foreign subsidies: legal implications under EU competition law*, ECLR 2023, no. 2(44), and T. Müller-Ibold, *The Draft Foreign Subsidies Regulation–Relationship with other Union Instruments–Some Thoughts on Multilevel Enforcement and Duplication of Efforts*, ZEuS 2022, no. 3.

136 For an overview of the FDI Regulation and its implementation, please refer to J. Velten. *Screening Foreign Direct Investment in the EU. Political Rationale, Legal Limitations, Legislative Options*, Cham 2022.

are other EU regulations (namely, the EMFA, the Digital Services Act (DSA),[137] and the AI Act[138]) that require implementation or adjustment of national rules.

5.4.1 EMFA

Adopted in September 2022, the EMFA introduces EU-wide safeguards for media pluralism and independence, including rules against political interference and surveillance, and a new pluralism test for media concentrations.[139] It establishes the European Media Services Council, which coordinates enforcement through national regulators. In Poland, draft reforms (prepared in 2024 by the Ministry of Culture)[140] foresee continued merger control by the OCCP, but with mandatory opinions from the National Broadcasting Council (NBC) on pluralism and editorial independence. By giving OCCP a central but shared role, Poland links competition law with non-economic criteria. One of them is media freedom – an area where institutional overlaps remain politically sensitive.

5.4.2 DSA

The DSA, in force since February 2024, aims to ensure safer online environments, combat illegal content, and increase platform transparency.[141] Enforcement is again Commission-led, but member states must designate national Digital Services Coordinators and empower sectoral authorities. In September 2025, the Polish government adopted a draft law assigning OCCP new

137 Regulation (EU) 2022/2065 of the European Parliament and of the Council of 19.10.2022 on a Single Market for Digital Services and amending Directive 2000/31/EC (Digital Services Act), OJ EU L 277, 27.10.2022.

138 Regulation (EU) 2024/1689 of the European Parliament and of the Council of 13.06.2024 laying down harmonised rules on artificial intelligence and amending Regulations (EC) No. 300/2008, (EU) No. 167/2013, (EU) No. 168/2013, (EU) 2018/858, (EU) 2018/1139 and (EU) 2019/2144 and Directives 2014/90/EU, (EU) 2016/797 and (EU) 2020/1828 (Artificial Intelligence Act), OJ EU L, 2024/1689, 12.7.2024.

139 More on EMFA, please refer to M. Sznajder, *European Media Freedom Act and its Implications for Both Merger Control and Media Pluralism: The Polish Perspective*, ELR 2024, no. 1(49).

140 European Media Freedom Act – concept of implementation into the Polish legal system, https://www.gov.pl/web/kultura/zalozenia-do-ustawy-medialnej.

141 More on DSA, please refer to A. Musil, *The Digital Services Act (DSA) and Its Possible Overlaps with Competition Law (December 05, 2025)*. Charles University in Prague Faculty of Law Research Paper No. 2025/III/5, http://dx.doi.org/10.2139/ssrn.5868864.

consumer protection and unfair practices competences vis-à-vis digital service providers.[142]

5.4.3 AI Act

The AI Act, adopted in 2024, regulates high-risk AI systems and introduces bans on certain practices.[143] At the EU level, it relies on national authorities for supervision and establishes a European AI Office within the Commission. In Poland, the Ministry of Digital Affairs has proposed establishing a new Commission for the Development and Safety of Artificial Intelligence, with the OCCP as a member and with enforcement cooperation duties.[144] The OCCP's role here focuses on consumer and market surveillance, supplementing the new AI body's sectoral expertise.

6 Conclusions

The evolution of Polish competition law illustrates how closely these rules are intertwined with the prevailing economic system. In many respects, competition law serves as a litmus test for the dominant economic paradigm of each era. In pre-war Poland, cartel legislation was introduced relatively late. It had limited practical impact, as cartels were then considered a lawful form of cooperation between undertakings, provided they were duly registered. These rules became entirely obsolete under the communist regime: in a centrally planned economy, where the state itself is the monopolist, antimonopoly regulation is structurally irrelevant. Only the gradual collapse of the communist system created space for new rules in 1987, though this was brief and limited in scope. It was the post-1989 political and economic transformation that enabled the adoption of modern antimonopoly legislation.

Polish competition law exemplifies how economic law evolves alongside economic transition. The initial Competition Act of 1990, enacted during a period of liberalisation, was brief yet impactful, establishing the basis for demerger and addressing new forms of illegal market practices. This legislation was mainly a domestic effort, with only slight influence from inter-

142 Draft law amending the law on the provision of electronic services and certain other laws, https://www.gov.pl/web/premier/projekt-ustawy-o-zmianie-ustawy-o-swiadczeniu-uslug-droga-elektroniczna-oraz-niektorych-innych-ustaw2.

143 More on AI Act, please refer to Th. Schrepel, *Decoding the AI Act: Implications for Competition Law and Market Dynamics*, JCLE 2025, no. 3(21).

144 Act of … 2024 on artificial intelligence systems, Draft of 15.10.2024, UC71.

national models. However, later amendments increasingly incorporated external influences. Technical aid from the United States, the OECD, and various European countries significantly shaped subsequent reforms. The enforcement experience in Poland contributed to the development of the legal framework at a later stage. Ultimately, Poland's accession to the EU became the most influential factor driving change.

The 2000 Competition Act was a significant step in this development, as it comprehensively regulated systemic, substantive, and procedural aspects for the first time, in line with the European model. The 2007 Act marked the culmination of harmonisation efforts: both the statute and its amendments contained progressively fewer domestic solutions and increasingly represented direct transfers of EU concepts. Unfortunately, this process was not always accompanied by adequate reflection. At times, the OCCP appeared to treat convergence as mere translation, overlooking the need to adapt EU mechanisms to the domestic legal and institutional context. This tendency became particularly visible in the amendments implementing the ECN+ Directive.

More recent amendments to the Competition Act have not only refined substantive and procedural rules but have also transformed the institutional landscape. This development is especially evident in Poland's response to new EU economic governance instruments. Together, the DMA, FSR, and FDI Regulation illustrate the EU's gradual move towards a layered governance model: Brussels takes the lead in agenda-setting and final decision-making (especially under the DMA and FSR), while relying on national authorities for information-gathering, monitoring, and enforcement support. Concentrating these additional tasks in the OCCP raises questions about institutional overload, capacity constraints, and the coherence of national enforcement structures.

Across the EMFA, DSA, and the AI Act, Poland exhibits a characteristic pattern: rather than establishing entirely new regulators, governments expand the mandates of existing competition authorities and supplement them with sector-specific bodies (e.g. the NBC in media regulation, the Digital Services Coordinator, or the proposed AI Commission). This hybrid model aligns with the EU's expectation of composite enforcement while reflecting administrative pragmatism, given limited resources, in which the competition authority becomes a natural institutional hub for new regulatory responsibilities. The downside, however, is the growing risk of institutional congestion and blurred boundaries of competence – developments that may ultimately challenge the effectiveness, independence, and strategic clarity of the enforcement system, as evidenced in the next chapter.

CHAPTER 3

Jurisdiction of the Polish NCA: From a Specialised Antimonopoly Authority to a Multitasked Agency

1 The Current Jurisdiction of the OCCP

The OCCP performs a wide range of tasks, most of which are only tangentially related – if at all – to competition policy. These competences include, in particular, consumer protection, market surveillance, the administration of state aid in Poland, the prevention of abuses of contractual advantage in the agri-food sector, combating excessive payment delays in commercial transactions, and, more recently, the screening of foreign direct investments,[1] as well as responsibilities as peculiar as safeguarding the correctness of the Polish language in advertising.

An analysis of the OCCP's jurisdictional trajectory reveals a profound structural shift. The balance between competition protection and consumer protection – together with other regulatory functions – has been seriously distorted. By 2026, it is difficult to regard the Polish NCA as a competition authority in the strict sense of the term. Instead, it should more accurately be described as a multitasked public economic authority, in which competition enforcement constitutes only one element of a significantly broadened and heterogeneous mandate.

The purpose of this chapter is to examine the evolution and progressive expansion of the OCCP's jurisdiction, to assess the normative justification for these changes, and to evaluate the coherence and efficiency of the current jurisdictional configuration.

2 Competition Protection

In Poland, the President of the OCCP serves as the central public administration body responsible for the public enforcement of competition law. The authority has exclusive jurisdiction over antitrust agreements, abuses of dominance, and merger control. It is also the designated authority to enforce EU competition law pursuant to Regulation 1/2003 and the ECN+ Directive, and

1 This competence was ultimately transferred to the Ministry of Development in 2025.

© 2026 THE AUTHOR(S) | HTTPS://DOI.ORG/10.1163/9789004754638-004
This is an open access publication distributed under the terms of the CC 4.0 license BY-NC-ND.

to cooperate with the European Commission in the application of the EUMR. The Polish NCA represents Poland in all international competition fora operating within international organisations such as UNCTAD and the OECD, as well as in informal networks such as the ECA and the ICN.[2]

Competition jurisdiction, together with the substantive and procedural dimensions of competition enforcement, will be analysed in the following chapters. This section focuses on the enforcement instruments used by the OCCP in exercising its competition powers.

2.1 Historical Scope of Competition Jurisdiction

When the Antimonopoly Authority was established in 1990, its jurisdiction was paradoxically at its most comprehensive precisely in relation to its principal and exclusive competence: the protection of competition. The authority's jurisdiction was extensive. Its primary mission was dismantling monopolies in the post-communist economy. It maintained a registry of dominant undertakings, conducted market surveys to measure concentration levels, and – based on these findings – could order deconcentration measures, including the breakup of undertakings, or propose legislative initiatives. It also pursued an intensive policy of price control and played an active role in government work related to economic transformation.

Over time, however, as market reforms stabilised and EU accession approached, this interventionist model gave way to a more restrained framework for competition enforcement aligned with European standards. In Poland, the competition authority was transformed into a multitasking market supervisory agency. The Antimonopoly Authority – later transformed into the OCCP – followed a specific trajectory: it abandoned its initial interventionist functions, expanded into consumer protection, with a snowballing effect on other competences, and adapted its enforcement approach to EU competition law. Thus, the initial 'era of competition omnipotence' was replaced by a gradual dilution of focus, driven by institutional expansion and the approximation of law to EU law.

2 For an overview and description of competition networks, please refer to M. Błachucki, *International Cooperation, Competition Authorities and Transnational Networks*, London, 2024.

2.2 Decisions

Decision-making constitutes the core competence of the OCCP. As a monocratic authority, it combines investigative and adjudicative functions. From the outset of Polish competition enforcement, the issuance of administrative decisions has been central to its role. In the context of the economic transformation of the 1990s, this institutional design enabled swift intervention and reflected the Polish administrative tradition, in which the issuance of decisions is regarded as the essence of administrative jurisdiction.[3]

The OCCP may issue a wide range of decisions, including interim and final decisions, infringement and commitment decisions, and decisions discontinuing proceedings on procedural or jurisdictional grounds. It may impose fines, adopt behavioural, structural, or contractual remedies, or merely declare an infringement without sanctions.

2.3 Non-executive Guidance

The strong tradition of equating administrative jurisdiction with decision-making is illustrated by the late introduction of non-coercive instruments. Non-executive guidance was introduced only in 2016.[4] Under Article 49a of the Competition Act, the OCCP may, without initiating formal proceedings, address an undertaking on matters relating to competition or consumer protection and invite it to submit its position.

In the official justification accompanying the introduction of Article 49a, the OCCP emphasised that the possibility of using 'soft' measures allows undertakings to cease potential infringements without initiating formal proceedings. The authority also stressed that, where doubts arise about the legality of a practice, it may first contact an undertaking and invite explanations before initiating proceedings. Non-executive guidance was presented as a preventive, proportionate, and resource-efficient tool, enabling the authority to respond to early warning signals while allowing undertakings to clarify the factual and legal background without the immediate reputational and procedural consequences of a formal investigation.[5]

---

3 For example, S. Kasznica, *Polskie prawo administracyjne*, Poznań 1946, 97, or J. Zimmermann, *Polska jurysdykcja administracyjna*, Warsaw 1996, 15.

4 Art. 49a added by Art. 1 item 13 of the Act of 5.08.2015, amending the Act on Competition and Consumer Protection and certain other acts, JoL 2015 item 1634.

5 Explanatory memorandum of the act on amending the Act on Competition and Consumer Protection and certain other acts, Parliamentary print No. 3662, 10.07.2015.

Initially, this instrument was criticised by some as unnecessary, on the assumption that the OCCP already possessed sufficient procedural tools to clarify any relevant circumstances – particularly through preliminary (formal) explanatory proceedings.[6] Such criticism, however, tends to perpetuate a formalistic view of administration, according to which public authorities should intervene exclusively through acts of administrative jurisdiction. It also overlooks the practical and institutional costs of formal proceedings. Explanatory investigations are burdensome for both the authority and undertakings: they require staff time, generate procedural duties, and may have reputational effects even when the matter ultimately proves inconsequential. Non-executive guidance offers a lighter-touch channel for obtaining information, correcting borderline conduct, and allocating enforcement resources more rationally.[7]

From the perspective of modern administrative governance, Article 49a therefore represents a genuine novelty. It gives the OCCP greater flexibility and facilitates the management of limited institutional capacity, particularly when the authority receives multiple signals that may not warrant immediate escalation to coercive instruments. The value of this tool has been most visible in consumer protection, where early contact and swift corrective action may be particularly effective. Over time, this instrument has also been extended beyond competition and consumer protection, strictly understood. It has been used in other areas of the OCCP's broadening jurisdiction, including unfair trading practices and payment backlogs. Annual reports indicate that the OCCP uses this tool with steady frequency, including in antitrust-related matters.

The authority's practice raises serious concerns about transparency, accountability, and the systemic effects of informalisation. First, the OCCP rarely discloses the scope, content, or outcomes of non-executive guidance. Analysing activity reports does not reveal whether such interventions led to changes in compliance, whether the authority considered the case resolved, or whether the guidance served merely as an information-gathering step preceding formal action. The OCCP presents only numbers, which it claims indicate its flexibility and effectiveness, but without any qualitative data to verify these claims (Table 3.1). This opacity prevents meaningful external evalu-

6 C. Banasiński, M. Bychowska, *Między efektywnością administracji a pewnością sytuacji prawnej przedsiębiorców (uwagi do ustawy z dnia 5 sierpnia 2015 r. o zmianie ustawy o ochronie konkurencji i konsumentów oraz ustawy – Kodeks postępowania cywilnego)*, IKAR 2015, no. 5, 70–71.

7 O. Brook, *Do EU and U.K. Antitrust 'Bite'?: A Hard Look at 'Soft' Enforcement and Negotiated Penalty Settlements*, The Antitrust Bulletin 2023, no. 68(3), 477–480.

TABLE 3.1 Number of non-executive guidance issued by the OCCP (Source: OCCP Activity Reports)

Year	Non-executive guidance (antitrust)
2016	N/A
2017	57
2018	77
2019	82
2020	63
2021	93
2022	52
2023	60
2024	76
2025	N/A

ation of efficiency and risks transforming non-executive guidance into an unreviewable 'shadow' enforcement channel.

Second, the increasing reliance on informal contact coincides with a broader decline in formal antitrust decisions.[8] While correlation is not necessarily causation, the institutional risk is clear: a tool designed to complement formal enforcement may begin to substitute for it. If undertakings learn that the OCCP frequently prefers informal engagement to authoritative intervention, the deterrent effect of competition enforcement may weaken. This is particularly problematic in antitrust matters, where credible deterrence depends on the visibility of enforcement outcomes and the predictability of consequences, including sanctions.

Third, non-executive guidance occupies a structurally ambiguous position within Polish administrative law. It is not a decision; it does not create formal rights or obligations; and it is not subject to direct judicial review. Yet it may exert real behavioural pressure, particularly when addressed to undertakings operating under regulatory or reputational constraints. This creates a tension between efficiency and accountability: the very features that make Article 49a attractive from the authority's perspective – speed, flexibility, informality – also weaken legal safeguards and public oversight.

8 Check against the table in Chapter 7 presenting the antitrust enforcement ratio.

In sum, non-executive guidance is a potentially valuable governance instrument, particularly in a system where formal proceedings are costly and slow. However, its value depends on disciplined use and minimum transparency standards. Without clearer disclosure of when and why the OCCP uses Article 49a, what outcomes follow, and how this tool relates to the formal enforcement strategy, the instrument risks undermining rather than strengthening the credibility of competition enforcement – by reinforcing perceptions of selective, informal, and weakly accountable intervention.

2.4 Soft Law

Soft law constitutes an integral element of contemporary competition enforcement.[9] In the Polish legal system, however, the use of soft-law instruments by the public administration – and by the OCCP in particular – has long been viewed with caution. This scepticism is rooted in historical experience, particularly the way guidelines and similar instruments operated under the administrative law of communist Poland.

During the People's Republic of Poland, public administration exercised pervasive control over economic and social life and operated within a rigid hierarchical structure. Alongside statutory provisions adopted by the legislature, administrative authorities issued internal normative acts – commonly labelled 'guidelines', 'directives', or 'ordinances'.[10] These instruments did not require an explicit statutory basis and were formally binding only on subordinate authorities.[11] However, they often produced external legal effects through what was described as their 'reflexive effect', as administrative decisions were routinely based on unpublished internal instructions.[12] This practice severely undermined procedural guarantees and transparency, depriving parties of knowledge of the rules governing their cases.

As a result, following the political transformation of 1989, Polish administrative law deliberately abandoned guidelines as an administrative instrument. The Constitution reinforced this shift by emphasising that administrative decisions must be based on statutory law (Article 7). Against this background, the re-emergence of soft law after Poland's accession to the European Union

---

9 For the concept of soft law and the meaning of competition law, please refer to O. Ştefan, *Soft Law in Court. Competition Law, State Aid and the Court of Justice of the European Union*, Netherlands 2013.

10 I. Lipowicz, *Pojęcie sfery wewnętrznej administracji państwowej*, Katowice 1991, 108–109.

11 W. Hoff, *Wytyczne w prawie administracyjnym*, Warsaw 1989, 22–23.

12 Z. Janowicz, *Zagadnienia legislacji administracyjnej*, Poznań 1978, 30.

marked a significant conceptual change. Soft law is an essential part of the EU legal order, particularly in competition law, and Polish authorities have gradually adopted similar instruments, including guidelines and explanatory notices.

In the Polish system, soft law is not regarded as a source of law.[13] Instead, it is understood as an official interpretation of statutory provisions or as non-binding guidance on their application. Such instruments are not binding on courts or undertakings, but they bind the issuing authority and any subordinate units. This internal binding effect is intended to promote consistency and predictability in enforcement.

The first Antimonopoly Act of 1990 did not provide a legal basis for issuing guidelines, and none were adopted in the 1990s. A legal basis was introduced only in the Antimonopoly Act of 2000 and retained in the Competition Act of 2007. The first guidelines appeared in 2003 and concerned merger control.[14] These initial documents were problematic: they were prepared by an external law firm, closely mirrored European Commission guidelines, and reflected little of the OCCP's own enforcement practice.

A more mature approach emerged in 2009, when the OCCP itself prepared guidelines on the calculation of fines[15] and on the leniency programme.[16] These documents were grounded in the authority's practical experience and addressed evident difficulties in applying statutory provisions. They marked the beginning of a more systematic use of soft law as an enforcement and information tool.

The legal basis for the OCCP's adoption of guidelines is set out in Article 31a of the Competition Act. Pursuant to this provision, 'the President of the Office may publish and announce explanations and interpretations of significant relevance for the application of legal provisions in matters falling within the scope of the President's competences. Explanations and interpretations shall be published in the Public Information Bulletin of the Office.' Notably, the legislature deliberately refrains from using the term 'guidelines', instead emp-

13 This approach aligns with practices in the EU. For the discussion of the nature and effects of soft law, refer to A. Ausfelder, A. Eick, M. Hartlapp, et al., *EU soft-law: Non-binding but enforceable,* ELJ 2024, no. 4(30).

14 Guidelines of the President for Competition and Consumer Protection Office on criteria of merger notifications, 2003 and Guidelines of the President for Competition and Consumer Protection Office on procedure of merger notifications, 2003.

15 Guidelines on setting fines for competition-restricting practices, of 01.01.2009.

16 Guidelines of the President of the Office of Competition and Consumer Protection on the Leniency Programme (the procedure of submitting and handling applications for immunity from or reduction of a fine – 'leniency applications'), of 24.02.2009.

loying the notions of 'explanations' and 'interpretations'. In functional terms, however, these instruments correspond to what is commonly understood as administrative guidelines, differing mainly in terminology rather than in substance or effect.

Article 31a grants the OCCP extensive discretion to decide whether and when to adopt soft law instruments. No statutory criteria delimit situations in which guidelines should be issued. The key formula – 'significant relevance for the application of legal provisions' – is inherently indeterminate and effectively leaves the assessment entirely to the authority. Equally, the Act does not prescribe any procedural framework for preparing or adopting such documents. In particular, there is no obligation to conduct public consultations or to involve stakeholders in a structured manner. The OCCP's approach has been inconsistent: in some instances, draft soft law documents have been subject to open public consultations;[17] in others, consultations have been limited to selected stakeholders, such as professional associations or academic experts;[18] and in several cases, guidelines have been adopted without any consultation at all.[19] The only explicit safeguard provided by the statute is the obligation to publish all explanations and interpretations, ensuring their formal accessibility and transparency.

Within this permissive framework, the OCCP has made relatively extensive use of soft law. At present, 11 general interpretations and guidelines concerning competition protection remain in force.[20] They address a wide range of issues, from procedural matters (such as access to files or settlement procedures) to substantive aspects of enforcement (including the assessment of con-

17 There is a dedicated section on OCCP's website for public consultation on guidelines: https://uokik.gov.pl/bip/projekty-wyjasnien. Unlike consultations during the governmental legislative process, the OCCP does not publish any responses received or provide any explanation for why a particular solution has been adopted instead of others.

18 It was a common practice in the first and second decades of the century: A. Piszcz, *Organy opiniodawcze i doradcze polskiego organu ochrony konkurencji* [in:] M. Bernatt, A. Jurkowska-Gomułka, M. Namysłowska, A. Piszcz (eds.), *Wyzwania dla ochrony konkurencji i regulacji rynku. Księga jubileuszowa dedykowana Profesorowi Tadeuszowi Skocznemu*, Warsaw 2017.

19 The last two revisions of the merger procedure guidelines were made without any prior consultations.

20 In the area of consumer protection, there are two additional guidelines: 1) Information on price reduction. Explanations by the President of the OCCP (8.05.2023). 2) Explanations concerning the fulfilment by the President of the Office of Competition and Consumer Protection of the obligation to provide the parties to consumer protection proceedings with information on the factual and legal grounds for allegations of violation of the provisions of the Act of 16.02.2007 on competition and consumer protection (28.05.2019, date of entry into force: 3.06.2019).

centrations and the calculation of fines for undertakings and managers). This body of documents illustrates not only the growing importance of soft law in the OCCP's enforcement practice but also the authority's tendency to use such instruments to structure and communicate its administrative policy.[21]

The diversity of these documents is striking. They differ in form, length, level of detail, scope of application, and the statutory provisions to which they relate. This heterogeneity confirms that soft law has become a flexible and evolving tool of the OCCP's information and advocacy policy rather than a coherent, codified system of guidance. It is also noteworthy that some explanations and interpretations simultaneously address competition and consumer protection issues. This overlap reflects the integrated nature of the Polish enforcement model and the fact that a significant part of the procedural framework under the Competition Act applies equally to both areas, making parallel interpretation both practical and, to some extent, inevitable.

Despite the central role that guidelines now play in the daily work of the Polish NCA, the regulatory framework governing their adoption and review remains underdeveloped.[22] There are no general rules concerning their amendment or withdrawal, nor any dedicated mechanisms for their administrative or judicial control. Judicial scrutiny is therefore only indirect and incidental.[23] The CCCP may assess the relevance or correctness of a guideline only when reviewing an individual decision, and only if the party explicitly raises this issue in its appeal. Even then, the limited statutory regulation of soft law instruments constrains the court's ability to exercise meaningful control over their content or use.[24]

As a result, while guidelines undeniably enhance predictability and coherence in the OCCP's enforcement practice, they also significantly expand administrative discretion. In the absence of clearer procedural safeguards and more robust review mechanisms, this discretion risks being insufficiently constrained, raising concerns about legal certainty, accountability, and the balance between flexibility and the rule of law in Polish competition enforcement.

---

21 All soft law documents available at https://uokik.gov.pl/bip/wyjasnienia.

22 M. Błachucki, *Stanowienie aktów tzw. prawa miękkiego przez organy administracji publicznej na przykładzie prawa antymonopolowego* [in:] M. Stahl, Z. Duniewska (eds.), *Legislacja administracyjna. Teoria, orzecznictwo, praktyka*, Warsaw 2012, 247–249.

23 In Poland, only guidelines on taxes and public levies may be directly scrutinised by administrative courts: B. Draniewicz, *Indywidualne interpretacje w zakresie prawa daninowego po nowelizacji*, PP 2009, no. 3.

24 M. Błachucki, *Judicial Control of Guidelines in Antimonopoly Fines in Poland*, 64.

2.5 *Amicus Curiae* Briefs

Pursuant to Article 31d of the Competition Act, where the OCCP considers it in the public interest, the President of the Office may submit to a court an opinion relevant to a given case in matters concerning competition or consumer protection. The 2015 amendment introduced this instrument into the Competition Act and explicitly refers to the institution of amicus curiae – the 'friend of the court'.

The concept of *amicus curiae* has a long pedigree, traditionally traced to Roman law, where it denoted lawyers appointed by the court to assist in matters beyond the court's expertise. Over time, this institution evolved into a broader mechanism that allows entities, not parties to the proceedings, to assist the court by submitting relevant information, analysis, or expertise. In contemporary legal systems, a friend of the court is understood as an impartial participant whose role is not to advocate for a particular party but to contribute to a more informed and comprehensive judicial assessment of the case.[25]

In the Polish legal system, *amicus curiae* briefs have traditionally been associated primarily with non-governmental organisations. These briefs typically present broader societal, economic, or constitutional perspectives and may include not only legal arguments but also empirical data, policy considerations, or the results of academic research. Their principal function is to broaden the factual and normative context in which a court adjudicates by introducing arguments and information that the parties themselves may not have raised.[26] An amicus curiae brief aims to enhance the court's understanding of the case rather than swaying the decision in favour of a specific litigant.

The admission of a public administration body – specifically, a competition authority – as a friend of the court is a significant novelty in Polish administrative and procedural law. Until recently, this role was almost exclusively reserved for social organisations (NGOs). However, the objectives pursued by social organisations acting as amici curiae differ from those underpinning the OCCP's participation. According to the Constitutional Tribunal, NGOs' opinions promote constitutional values.[27] The OCCP's involvement as a friend of the court is primarily functional and praxeological. Its purpose is not to

---

25 M. K. Lowman, *The litigating amicus curiae: When does the party begin after the friends leave?*, The American University Law Review 1992, no. 41, 1244.

26 A. Bodnar, B. Grabowska, P. Osik, *"Opinie przyjaciela sądu"* (*amicus curiae*) *w postępowaniu przed Trybunałem Konstytucyjnym w praktyce Helsińskiej Fundacji Praw Człowieka* [in:] K. Budziło (ed.), *Ewolucja funkcji i zadań Trybunału Konstytucyjnego–założenia a ich praktyczna realizacja. Księga XXV-lecia Trybunału Konstytucyjnego*, Warsaw 2010, 145.

27 Constitutional Tribunal judgement of 16.1.2006 r., SK 30/05.

represent societal interests in the abstract, but to assist courts in the correct and uniform application of complex competition and consumer protection rules and to help clarify any public interests involved.

The OCCP's introduction of *amicus curiae* briefs is closely linked to European Union law. Even before the 2015 amendment, both the OCCP and the European Commission were formally entitled, under Article 15(3) of Regulation 1/2003, to submit observations to national courts in cases concerning the application of Articles 101 or 102 TFEU. However, there is no evidence that this power was exercised in Poland before 2015. The amendment to the Competition Act significantly broadened this competence, allowing the OCCP to submit opinions in all proceedings involving elements of competition and consumer protection, including purely national cases. This solution is clearly inspired by EU competition law and mirrors the European Commission's role in national judicial proceedings.[28]

As in the EU framework, the rationale for empowering the OCCP to act as amicus curiae is twofold. First, it is intended to promote consistency between administrative enforcement and judicial interpretation of competition and consumer protection rules, thereby reducing the risk of divergent approaches. Second, it aims to support the development of private enforcement by providing courts and litigants with authoritative guidance on complex economic and legal issues. In principle, this instrument could strengthen the coherence and effectiveness of the Polish competition law system. Its practical significance ultimately depends on how often and transparently the OCCP exercises this competence, and on whether it maintains the required neutrality when acting as a 'friend' rather than an enforcer. As the Table 3.2 suggests, the OCCP's use of *amicus curiae* briefs remains sporadic and has not yet gained real momentum in practice.

2.6 Market Surveys

In addition to its decision-making and quasi-normative functions, the OCCP conducts proactive investigations to identify potential competition concerns in specific sectors or areas of economic activity. The primary objective of these initiatives is to collect market data, analyse market structures and conduct, and detect practices that may justify initiating antimonopoly proceedings. In principle, the findings of such activities may serve as a basis for launching

28 K. Wright, *European Commission Opinions to National Courts in Antitrust Cases: Consistent Application and the Judicial-Administrative Relationship*, CCP Working Paper 2024, no. 8, 3–4.

TABLE 3.2 Number of *amicus curiae* briefs issued by the OCCP (Source: PI request)

Year	*Amicus curiae* briefs	
	Antitrust	Mergers
2016	0	0
2017	0	0
2018	0	0
2019	0	0
2020	0	0
2021	0	0
2022	0	0
2023	2	0
2024	5	0
2025	0	1

formal enforcement actions. However, they are more often used for advocacy, including informing public debate, supporting legislative initiatives, or signalling the authority's enforcement priorities. Importantly, market surveys conducted by the OCCP do not constitute a 'New Competition Tool'[29] in the Polish sense, as the authority lacks the power to intervene against problematic market structures or powerful undertakings absent a proven infringement of competition law in antimonopoly proceedings.

Since its inception, the OCCP has conducted market research in Poland to support subsequent actions in both the judicial and advocacy spheres. Market surveys have traditionally been regarded as an auxiliary instrument supporting enforcement and policy-oriented activities.[30] The OCCP conducts investigative proceedings as market studies, in particular to assess market structure, competition, and concentration. According to the authority, 'the publication of information on the results of such studies – carried out under established principles – forms part of the Office's mission to pursue an active policy of promoting competition. Market studies serve to generate and systematise

29 For the concept of NCT–B. Vesterdorf, K. Fountoukakos, *A New Competition Tool into Old Bottles? Considerations on the Legal Design of the European Commission's Proposed NCT*, JECLP 2021, no. 4.

30 OECD, Market Studies Guide for Competition Authorities, Paris 2018, 7.

knowledge concerning individual markets, thereby enhancing the transparency of economic activity and providing stakeholders with an authoritative reference point on prevailing conditions.'[31] However, the reference to 'established principles' is largely declaratory and effectively leaves the OCCP with full discretion as to both the conduct of surveys and the manner, scope, and timing of publication of their results.

Historically, market surveys were an essential element of the OCCP's competition enforcement activity. In particular, during the early 1990s, the results of these studies played a significant role in supporting the authority's actions to dismantle monopolistic market structures inherited from the centrally planned economy and in justifying broader structural reforms promoted by the government.[32] At that stage, market surveys were closely aligned with enforcement priorities and often led to concrete administrative or legislative initiatives.

At present, the OCCP officially refers only to a limited number of market studies, covering, in particular, the beer and hop market, various segments of the waste management sector (including medical and municipal waste), the operation of apple collection points and processing plants, and the market for newspaper printing services.[33] Additional reports, partial findings, and survey-related information may be found scattered throughout the 'news' section of the OCCP's website.[34] This approach to dissemination creates the impression of a fragmented, incoherent information policy, undermining the considerable organisational and analytical effort invested in conducting market studies and preparing reports.

The current framework governing the conduct and publication of market research has several systemic shortcomings. First, there is no comprehensive or coherent body of publicly available information. The OCCP does not publish an annual or multiannual plan for market surveys, nor does it maintain an exhaustive, easily accessible list of completed studies. Second, research results are often published with a significant delay, typically two or three years after the underlying analysis is completed. While qualitative observations may

31 *Badania rynku*, https://uokik.gov.pl/badania-rynku.

32 Each year, a dozen or more surveys were conducted, and their results were utilised in the authority's daily work: Activity Report 1992, 4–5; Activity Report 1993, 2 and 9; Activity Report 1994, 14–16; Activity Report 1995, 29–34; Activity Report 1996, 9–14, or Activity Report 1997, 30–37.

33 Badania rynku, https://uokik.gov.pl/badania-rynku.

34 For example *Krajowy rynek słodu do produkcji piwa. Raport UOKiK*, https://uokik.gov.pl/krajowy-rynek-slodu-do-produkcji-piwa-raport-uokik, or *Analiza UOKiK: Rynek detalicznej sprzedaży leków*, https://archiwum.uokik.gov.pl/aktualnosci.php?news_id=11636.

retain some relevance in identifying long-term trends, quantitative data rapidly lose their practical value and become of limited use for ongoing investigations, private enforcement, or regulatory debate. A telling example is the report on rail passenger transport in Poland, which analysed the years 2019–2023.[35] Although completed in October 2024, it was not published until September 2025. Such delays are not exceptional but rather illustrative of broader deficiencies in the OCCP's approach to transparency and enforcement support. Finally, there is no consistent policy specifying which elements of market studies should be disclosed, in what form, and at what stage, further weakening predictability for market participants and other stakeholders.

A comparative perspective demonstrates that more structured and transparent practices are both feasible and desirable. The European Commission, for instance, conducts sector inquiries pursuant to Article 17 of Regulation 1/2003, enabling it to collect extensive market data where competition concerns arise.[36] These inquiries are accompanied by publicly available questionnaires, interim reports, and final reports, all published within defined timeframes.[37] The Commission also announces planned inquiries in advance through annual management plans, thereby ensuring transparency and legal certainty. Importantly, the outcomes of sector inquiries are not merely descriptive, but often serve as a basis for subsequent enforcement actions, legislative proposals, or soft law instruments.

The OCCP's current practice appears fragmented and largely reactive, with weak links between market research, enforcement priorities, and policy outcomes. The introduction of clearer procedural standards for initiating, conducting, and disseminating market studies – whether inspired by the European Commission's practice or by the OCCP's own more structured approach in the 1990s – could substantially enhance the practical relevance of this instrument. Timely publication of results, combined with stakeholder engagement and clearly articulated follow-up actions, would not only strengthen competition enforcement but also reinforce the OCCP's credibility as a central institution responsible for safeguarding competition in Poland.

35 *Time to Change Tracks: UOKiK report on rail passenger transport*, https://uokik.gov.pl/en/time-to-change-tracks-uokik-report-on-rail-passenger-transport.

36 OECD, Methodologies for Conducting Market Studies–Note by the European Union, DAF/COMP/WP3/WD(2017)20.

37 Sector inquiries, https://competition-policy.ec.europa.eu/antitrust-and-cartels/sector-inquiries_en.

2.7 Domestic and International Cooperation

Cooperation constitutes an essential dimension of the OCCP's enforcement activity, both at the domestic and international levels.[38] From its inception, the authority benefited from substantial foreign assistance, most notably from the US Department of Justice, the Federal Trade Commission, and the OECD, including material support and technical expertise. Subsequently, further know-how was provided by Germany, Sweden, the United Kingdom, and the European Commission. As a result, cooperation has become a natural and enduring element of Polish competition enforcement.

The current Competition Act expressly provides for international and domestic cooperation, with particular emphasis on Poland's obligations under EU and international law. Within the EU, the OCCP participates in the work of the Council of the EU, its preparatory bodies, and specialised working groups. It cooperates closely with the EC, particularly DG Competition, primarily through the ECN and the ECA forum. At the global level, the OCCP is active within the International Competition Network, as well as in the committees and working groups of the OECD and UNCTAD, complemented by various regional and bilateral initiatives.[39]

Domestic cooperation, though less visible, is equally significant. It may be mandatory, arising from statutory obligations, or voluntary, reflecting the OCCP's past policy priorities. Formal cooperation exists with sectoral regulators, notably in the fields of electronic communications,[40] energy,[41] and railways,[42] where ex ante regulatory competences are combined with the OCCP's ex post competition enforcement.[43] All decisions by OCCP and sectoral regulators are subject to judicial review before a single specialised forum, the CCCP in Warsaw. Statutory cooperation is also expressly provided for with bodies such as the Financial Supervision Authority[44] and the Public Procurement Office (PPO).[45]

38 The significance of international cooperation and foreign assistance is emphasised from the very beginning of the authority, as evidenced by the very first activity report and subsequent reports. To name the first few reports: Activity Report 1990, 5–6; Activity Report 1992, 16–17; Activity Report 1994, 17–19; Activity Report 1995, 38–41; Activity Report 1996, 29–32, or Activity Report 1997, 46–51.

39 Foreign cooperation, https://uokik.gov.pl/en/foreign-cooperation.

40 Article 21 of the Act of 16.07.2004 – Telecommunication Law, JoL 2018, item 1954.

41 Article 23(2)(14) of the Energy Law.

42 Article 13(3a)(2) of the Railway Transport Act.

43 PSC judgement of 19.10.2006, III SK 15/06.

44 Act of 29.07.2005 on Capital Market Supervision, JoL 2017, item 1480.

45 Act of 11.09.2019 – Public Procurement Law, JoL 2024, item 1320.

Alongside these formal arrangements, the OCCP also collaborates informally with various public institutions such as the Internal Security Agency, the Prosecutor General, the Supreme Audit Office, and the PPO.[46] This cooperation typically involves sharing non-protected information, joint training and education, attending conferences or thematic events, and collaborating on legislative projects. Importantly, many of these activities emphasise consumer protection and market oversight rather than traditional competition enforcement, underscoring OCCP's expanding role beyond its conventional antitrust responsibilities.

2.8 Advocacy and Information Policy

From its inception, advocacy and information policy have been integral to the OCCP's jurisdiction and mission. The authority played a significant role in Poland's political and economic transformation, with competition policy forming one of its essential components.[47] The adoption and implementation of the Antimonopoly Act of 1990 were among the first tangible steps towards establishing a market economy. Equally important was ensuring that the regulatory environment and legal framework did not create unjustified restrictions on competition. In parallel, a fundamental challenge was to educate entrepreneurs and consumers, many of whom initially associated the concept of antimonopoly more with the former state alcohol monopoly than with promoting free and fair competition in the Polish economy.

In its inaugural annual report, the OCCP highlighted its ongoing efforts to combat monopolistic practices enforced by state administrative bodies. It pointed out that many of these authorities still operated under regulations that had become outdated due to evolving economic conditions. The Office also emphasised the need for its demonopolisation program to be closely aligned with the broader economic policies of the government. Consequently, by the end of 1990, the Antimonopoly Office had submitted the *Government Programme for the Development of Competition* to the Economic Committee of the Council of Ministers.[48] Throughout 1992, the Office actively helped shape the foundations of state economic policy, including creating competitive mar-

46 The complete list is provided in M. Błachucki, *Ponadnarodowe sieci organów administracji publicznej oraz ich wpływ na krajowy porządek prawny (na przykładzie ponadnarodowych sieci organów ochrony konkurencji)*, Warsaw 2019, 118.

47 W.M. Orłowski, *Piętnaście lat walki z monopolem – kilka uwag z perspektywy makroekonomicznej* [in.] C. Banasiński (ed.), *Ochrona konkurencji i konsumentów w Polsce i Unii Europejskiej (studia prawno-ekonomiczne)*, Warsaw 2005, 39.

48 Activity Report 1990, 6–7.

ket conditions, co-developing pro-market restructuring programmes for key sectors, and drafting legal acts promoting pro-competitive solutions.[49]

Over time, the focus and role of advocacy within the OCCP have evolved considerably. While the Office still engages in the legislative process – drafting legislation and holding consultations – the emphasis has shifted mainly towards consumer protection. Consumer laws are broader, more politically significant, and more media-friendly, offering the OCCP President greater exposure and recognition opportunities. Consequently, advocacy has gradually shifted from embedding competition principles in public policy to promoting consumer-focused or politically sensitive initiatives.

Information policy remains vital to the OCCP's work but is less dynamic than in the 1990s and early 2000s. The Office continues to run public campaigns and share information with stakeholders. Notably, it publishes decisions, judgements, and updates on merger cases, as well as books and informational materials.[50] The online database of decisions, available since 2000, contains all decisions issued since then.[51] Additionally, the OCCP releases several books annually on various jurisdictional topics, complemented by leaflets and brochures.[52]

In summary, although the OCCP's advocacy and informational activities have changed significantly since the early 1990s, they remain crucial for influencing market behaviour and shaping public views on competition in Poland. The systematic publication of decisions, reports, and educational content has strengthened the authority's legitimacy and visibility. These efforts also support the OCCP's broader goals of recognition, the use of soft law, and public outreach, which are explored further in the next chapter.

3 Consumer Protection

Consumer protection became part of the OCCP's jurisdiction in 1995, when the authority's competencies were significantly expanded, and it was entrusted with a central role in shaping and implementing government consumer policy. This reform was part of a broader reconfiguration of Poland's economic administration and was actively endorsed by the OCCP's leadership. According to the authority's 1995 activity report, the expansion was 'dictated by the

49 Activity Report 1992, 12.
50 Public Information Bulletin of the OCCP, https://uokik.gov.pl/bip.
51 Decision database, https://decyzje.uokik.gov.pl/bp/dec_prez.nsf.
52 Publications, https://uokik.gov.pl/publikacje.

need to stimulate and coordinate activities aimed at developing a consumer protection system in Poland and harmonising it with European standards', including the creation of a comprehensive legal framework, the transposition of EU directives, and the establishment of effective consumer redress mechanisms. The report further argued that integrating pro-competitive and pro-consumer policies, together with the Office's interministerial position, justified assigning it a leading role.[53] Notably, none of these arguments appeared in the legislative materials accompanying the statutory amendments, underscoring a disconnect between the administrative rationale and the parliamentary justification.

Unlike later jurisdictional expansions, the 1995 transfer of consumer protection competences was preceded by relatively thorough institutional preparation. In late 1996, the OCCP initiated the transfer of consumer-related documentation from the dissolved Ministry of Industry and Trade and systematically collected comparative materials on consumer protection systems across EU Member States. It also commissioned the Polish Consumer Association to prepare a study – Model of Legal Consumer Protection – based on EU consumer rights catalogues, identifying areas requiring urgent legislative intervention. Parallel cooperation with domestic consumer organisations was also established.[54] The absence of comparable preparatory effort in subsequent expansions of the OCCP's mandate suggests either that the 1995 reform was exceptionally well planned or, more plausibly, that later extensions of the mandate were adopted with far less institutional reflection.

Polish consumer protection legislation emerged relatively early, but specialised enforcement structures developed much later – Poland being a paradigmatic case of delayed institutionalisation. A distinctive feature of the Polish model is its high degree of fragmentation. Alongside the central authority, numerous local bodies are active, and many functions are delegated to civil society organisations. This pluralistic, multi-level design contrasts sharply with the highly centralised architecture of competition enforcement.[55]

Substantively, the OCCP's consumer jurisdiction focuses on two core areas: protecting collective consumer interests and controlling standard contract terms. In addition, the authority supervises the Trade Inspection and participates in consumer counselling schemes. In collective interests cases, the OCCP may order the cessation of unlawful practices (Article 26), impose

53 Activity Report for 1995, 8.

54 Activity Report for 1996, 3.

55 M. Błachucki, *Razem czy osobno? Specjalizacja i integracja organów antymonopolowych, ochrony konsumentów i regulacyjnych w Polsce i krajach Unii Europejskiej*, KPP 2017, no. 3.

fines (Article 106), accept commitments (Article 28), and issue public warnings where there is a risk of imminent and irreversible harm (Article 31c). It also possesses investigative tools unavailable in antimonopoly proceedings, most notably mystery shoppers.[56]

In the field of contract terms, the President of the OCCP assesses the unlawfulness of clauses and may order their withdrawal, accompanied by corrective measures (Article 23b). These decisions bind only the undertaking concerned. Prior to 2016, however, the control over abusive clauses lay with the CCCP, whose judgements had an *erga omnes* effect upon their entry into a public register. The 2016 reform shifted this competence from the judiciary to the administration, prioritising speed and regulatory efficiency over individual access to justice.

Yet this change raises significant concerns. The shift away from judicial control weakens procedural safeguards for consumers. Under the former model, any consumer could initiate judicial review of a clause; under the current framework, enforcement depends entirely on the OCCP's discretion. Crucially, no legal remedy exists against the authority's refusal to act. The Polish system thus illustrates a fundamental tension between administrative efficiency and accountability, even if it remains formally EU-compliant and regionally consistent.[57]

Consumer jurisdiction encompasses all tools mentioned earlier.[58] In this area, the OCCP is a decision-making authority. Institutionally, consumer protection has become the OCCP's most active and visible domain. The authority issues far more consumer decisions than antitrust decisions, and in some periods, consumer fines have exceeded those imposed for competition infringements.[59] Consumer enforcement is also markedly more fragmented, involving sectoral regulators (communications, energy, railways, finance), district consumer ombudsmen, and the Financial Ombudsman (FO), with parallel proceedings being common.

In 2020, the OCCP President actively campaigned to strengthen his consumer-protection jurisdiction. The most prominent example was his personal

56 E. Mandrosz, *'Tajemniczy klient' jako nowe narzędzie w zakresie pozyskiwania dowodów praktyk naruszających zbiorowe interesy konsumentów*, iKAR 2016, no. 1, 52.

57 C. Banasiński, M. Bychowska, *Między*, 60.

58 S. Kaczorowska, A. Kurzyńska-Lipniewicz, *Prawne aspekty ochrony konsumenta w Polsce i w Unii Europejskiej*, Legnica 2009, p. 17.

59 M. Martyniszyn, M. Bernatt, 24.

and zealous attempt to liquidate and absorb the FO.[60] The Financial Ombudsman was established to assist customers in disputes with financial market entities, providing advice, intervention, amicable resolution, and assistance with court proceedings. It is an institution of around 200 employees. The OCCP's basic argument was to strengthen consumer protection.[61] In reality, the OCCP President was eager to increase his staff by more than 30%, add new competencies, and manage a significant education fund managed by the FO.[62] Needless to say, the OCCP provided no analysis of how these new competencies fit within the existing consumer-protection framework or, more importantly, within the OCCP's competition jurisdiction. The OCCP President lacked broader political support, and the project ultimately failed; nevertheless, it demonstrated the ambition and long-term perspective of the OCCP's current leadership regarding the authority's development and enforcement priorities.

The OCCP also plays a leading role in consumer policy-making, defining its core elements.[63] It prepares and implements the government's Consumer Policy. In 2015, competition and consumer policies were formally combined into a single strategic document. However, the OCCP has not consistently followed this integrated policy, nor has it provided systematic explanations for this divergence. Soft law instruments are also used in consumer matters, though less frequently than in competition law.

International cooperation in consumer protection remains less developed than in antitrust, reflecting the localised nature of most consumer disputes. Nevertheless, the OCCP participates in global networks such as ICPEN, the CPC Network, ECC-Net, the OECD Consumer Policy Committee, and UNCTAD's Expert Group on Consumer Law and Policy.

Consumer education and information campaigns constitute another central pillar of OCCP activity. While NGOs are contracted to provide individual counselling, the OCCP focuses on broader awareness initiatives. This combination of enforcement, research, and education underscores the authority's hybrid role as both regulator and system coordinator.

60 Prezes UOKiK: Po stronie konsumenta powinna stać jedna, silna instytucja publiczna, https://biznes.gazetaprawna.pl/artykuly/1491731,chrostny-prezes-uokik-konsumenci-kredyty-banki-konkurencja-piramidy-finansowe.html.

61 Ibidem.

62 In 2023, the fund was worth around 200 mln PLN, see *Fundusz Edukacji Finansowej rusza po pięciu latach,* https://www.inforlex.pl/dok/tresc,I02.2023.206.000000602,Fundusz-Edukacji-Finansowej-rusza-po-pieciu-latach.html.

63 M. Lissowska, *Polityka konsumencka–podstawy teoretyczne, cele i narzędzia*, Gospodarka Narodowa 2010, no. 10, 68.

The OCCP's communication profile further confirms the dominance of consumer protection in its operational priorities.[64] Press releases – an indicator of both enforcement activity and institutional self-presentation – show a consistent asymmetry between competition and consumer-focused communication. Between 2020 and 2024, the OCCP issued between 59 and 30 competition-related press releases annually, with a clear downward trend (from 59 in 2020 to 34 in 2024). Consumer-protection and consumer-education topics generated substantially higher output, ranging from 81 to 100 press releases in 2020–2023, and only declining in 2024 (to 54), though still exceeding the volume of competition-related communication. Market surveillance and product-safety issues generated a steady but comparatively modest number of press releases (between 27 and 46 per year), reflecting their stable but secondary place within the OCCP's activities. Communication on payment-backlog matters remained marginal throughout the period, with only 3–6 press releases annually.[65]

Taken together, these figures reinforce the broader picture that consumer protection – particularly consumer education and information campaigns – has become the most visible and communicatively prioritised field within the OCCP's mandate. They also align with the budgetary and organisational trends previously identified, confirming that the integrated model has shifted the authority's external focus and public messaging decisively towards consumer-facing activities, often at the expense of classical antitrust enforcement.[66]

The pattern is also reflected in the commissioning of social surveys.[67] Between 2020 and 2024, the OCCP commissioned five surveys, only one of which addressed competition protection (in 2021). The remaining surveys – conducted in 2020, 2022, 2023, and 2024 – focused exclusively on consumer protection issues. This distribution confirms the institutional shift towards consumer-oriented evidence-gathering and policy design. Social research, which plays a marginal role in classical antitrust analysis, has become increasingly central to the OCCP's consumer protection strategy. The near-absence of competition-related research not only illustrates the asymmetry of priorities within the integrated authority but also underscores how consumer protection has come to shape the authority's epistemic and analytical agenda.

Consumer protection attracts substantial media attention, a fact the president of the OCCP appears particularly willing to exploit. Consumer-related

64 Data in this paragraph was received from the OCCP upon a public information request.
65 Source: OCCP PI request.
66 M. Martyniszyn, M. Bernatt, 24.
67 https://uokik.gov.pl/badania-spoleczne.

press releases dominate the authority's public communication strategy and have become a central element of its political marketing. A significant number of initiatives formally framed as consumer protection campaigns display a clear political orientation and appear to serve short-term political interests rather than long-term regulatory objectives.

The implementation of the ECN+ Directive and the introduction of formal guarantees of independence and impartiality have not curtailed this form of political activism in any meaningful way. A recent and illustrative example is the OCCP's campaign against banks – particularly foreign-owned banks. The current president of the OCCP has publicly called for introducing a tax on excess bank profits, mechanisms to limit the payment of dividends abroad, and measures to encourage banks to retain profits domestically, to strengthen the financial sector's stability and support investment in the Polish economy.[68] Irrespective of the substantive merits of such proposals, this form of public advocacy is incompatible with the technocratic, neutral, and apolitical model of an independent national competition authority. It blurs the line between regulatory enforcement and economic policymaking, positioning the OCCP as a political actor rather than an impartial administrative authority.

Moreover, this practice exposes the structural tensions inherent in the institutional integration of competition and consumer protection. Rather than generating the promised synergies, the dominance of consumer-oriented political messaging tends to crowd out competition policy and instrumentalise the authority's public profile for political purposes. Ironically, this phenomenon constitutes the most tangible 'synergy' produced by the integration of competition and consumer protection within the OCCP – one that operates to the detriment of both regulatory neutrality and effective competition enforcement.

4 Market Surveillance and Trade Inspection

A particularly significant extension of the OCCP's consumer protection mandate was the conferral of market surveillance powers, coupled with the subordination of the State Trade Inspection Authority. Between 2000 and 2003, within the framework of consumer policy, the OCCP laid the legal and institu-

68 *Szef UOKiK-u chce zmian w bankach. 'Spijają śmietankę z polskiego rynku'*, https://businessinsider.com.pl/finanse/wielkie-zyski-bankow-pod-lupa-pomysl-ograniczenia-dywidend-i-nowego-podatku/kog1k5s.

tional foundations for a national market surveillance system based on the Act on General Products Safety[69] and the Act on the Conformity Assessment Systems.[70] The system became fully operational upon Poland's accession to the EU.

Market surveillance in Poland is institutionally complex. It involves a wide range of specialised authorities – such as labour inspectors, telecommunications and railway regulators, construction supervision bodies, environmental protection authorities, maritime offices, and metrology authorities – alongside the OCCP, which serves as the general market surveillance authority. Unlike the specialised bodies, the OCCP is not assigned to any specific sector. Instead, it operates horizontally across the system and, uniquely, performs a coordinating and monitoring role vis-à-vis other market surveillance authorities. It may request inspections, demand reports and copies of final decisions, and serve as Poland's liaison authority to the European Commission, handling surveillance plans, safeguard notifications, and reporting obligations.

The OCCP lacks formal powers to intervene directly in inspections or proceedings conducted by specialised authorities.[71] Effective enforcement, therefore, depends on informal cooperation, largely structured through bilateral agreements with sectoral regulators. While such soft coordination may be pragmatic, it remains legally fragile and heavily reliant on goodwill rather than on enforceable competence.

In substantive terms, the OCCP directly supervises non-food products under Regulation (EU) 2023/988 on general product safety. It may initiate administrative proceedings to eliminate threats to health and safety, impose sanctions, and monitor voluntary notifications submitted via the Safety Business Gateway. These instruments are designed to deter non-compliance and to encourage proactive risk management by undertakings.

The OCCP presents this institutional model as a deliberate policy choice. According to the authority, placing market surveillance within the competition authority should enhance the coherence of economic regulation and create synergies between competition and consumer protection.[72] However, such synergies remain largely rhetorical. Neither annual reports nor public communications provide evidence of cases in which market surveillance activities have been meaningfully integrated with competition enforcement. Even wit-

69 Act of 12.12.2003 on general product safety, JoL 2021 item 222 (initially the Act of 22.01.2000 on general product safety).

70 Act of 30.08.2002 on the conformity assessment systems, JoL 2023 item 215.

71 A. Sadkowska, *Model nadzoru rynku w systemach oceny zgodności*, Warsaw 2022.

72 Produkty i nadzór rynku, https://uokik.gov.pl/produkty-i-nadzor-rynku.

hin the broader consumer protection sphere, the parallel or joint application of market surveillance and consumer law remains exceptional.

Instead, the arrangement has generated systemic dysfunctions. Market surveillance decisions are adopted under statutes separate from the Competition Act and therefore fall within the jurisdiction of administrative courts. Nevertheless, the CCCP and the Court of Appeal in Warsaw have sought to assume jurisdiction over such cases, despite their statutory competence being limited to decisions issued under the Competition Act.[73] This practice creates jurisdictional uncertainty, undermines legal certainty, and weakens judicial protection for undertakings subject to market surveillance measures.

In mid-2025, the current president of the OCCP announced plans to transfer market surveillance competences, supervision of the Trade Inspection Authority, and responsibility for combating payment gridlocks to a new authority subordinated to the Ministry for Development, with entry into force envisaged for early 2027. According to the president, the reform would enable the new authority to pursue national economic interests more effectively while allowing the OCCP to refocus on competition and consumer protection enforcement. He further claimed to have requested inclusion of these proposals in the official List of Legislative and Programme Work of the Council of Ministers.[74]

Several months after this announcement, no such entry appeared on the List. On the contrary, a proposed amendment to the General Product Safety Act – sponsored by the OCCP itself – explicitly retained the authority's existing market surveillance competences.[75] The Ministry of Development has issued no official statement on the matter. This discrepancy between public declarations and legislative practice undermines the credibility of the OCCP's leadership and casts serious doubt on the political feasibility of any meaningful reconfiguration of its jurisdiction.

Poland's decision to centralise market oversight within the OCCP appears to be an unusual structural move. Rather than serving as a model of effective cooperation, it acts as an experiment that has caused conflicts not seen elsewhere. The costs involved – in legal clarity, judicial consistency, and account-

---

73 M. Błachucki, *Glosa do postanowienia Sądu Apelacyjnego w Warszawie z 30 listopada 2016 r., VI ACz 2293/16*, OSP 2017, no. 10.

74 Inspekcja Handlowa zmieni zwierzchnika. UOKiK: Powinna działać w ramach polityki rządu, https://www.bankier.pl/wiadomosc/Inspekcja-Handlowa-zmieni-zwierzchnika-UOKiK-Powinna-dzialac-w-ramach-polityki-rzadu-8969095.html.

75 UC53 – Draft General Safety Act, https://www.gov.pl/web/premier/projekt-ustawy-o-ogolnym-bezpieczenstwie-produktow.

ability – seem to outweigh any purported benefits, underscoring the need to reevaluate this jurisdictional setup.

5 State Aid Monitoring

EU institutions, particularly the Commission and EU courts, are key players in overseeing state aid. This centralisation reflects the fact that the legal framework for state aid is established at the EU level and primarily enforced by the Commission.[76] Since Poland's accession to the EU on 1 May 2004, any new state aid measure – whether an aid scheme or an individual grant – must be notified to the Commission. Even before accession, Poland introduced a national framework to align domestic practice with EU state aid rules and to restrict and monitor the granting of aid.[77]

Despite the Commission's central role, national authorities remain key to implementing state aid policy. Member States retain discretion to designate the national authority responsible for state aid monitoring and coordination. In Poland, the Act of 30 June 2000 on the admissibility and supervision of state aid for undertakings assigned these functions to the OCCP as part of Poland's accession preparations.[78] This institutional choice was preserved upon accession and remains in force. The current legal basis – the Act of 30 April 2004 on proceedings in matters concerning state aid – assigns the OCCP responsibility for: (a) monitoring state aid; (b) preparing notifications of aid schemes, individual aid, and restructuring aid in cooperation with aid-granting authorities; (c) representing Poland before EU courts in state aid cases; and (d) monitoring the recovery of unlawful aid, except for agricultural aid.[79]

The legislator justified this concentration of competences by reference to the OCCP's prior involvement in state aid supervision and its intermediary role between national authorities and the Commission.[80] This justification is unconvincing. The OCCP's prior performance of specific tasks does not, in itself, provide a convincing institutional rationale for conferring exclusive and permanent competence in this politically sensitive area.

---

76 For an overview of the EU state aid framework, see C. Quigley, *European State Aid Law and Policy*, Oxford 2022.

77 A. Werner, *Przepisy Komisji Europejskiej dotyczące pomocy publicznej i ich transpozycja do regulacji polskich*, PUG 2002, no. 2, 4.

78 JoL No. 60, item 704.

79 JoL 2007 No. 56, item 404.

80 Explanatory memorandum of the act on proceedings in matters concerning public aid, Parliamentary print No. 2636, 8.03.2004.

Legal doctrine has often viewed the Polish solution favourably, emphasising the conceptual link between state aid control and competition policy.[81] It has also been argued that placing state aid coordination within an independent authority, rather than a line ministry, fosters a competition-oriented perspective and shields the process from narrow departmental interests.[82] These arguments, while plausible in the abstract, underestimate the structural tensions inherent in this arrangement.

Critics have rightly pointed out that concentrating state aid coordination within the competition authority risks politicising the OCCP's role. In most EU-15 Member States, responsibility for state aid lies with ministries of finance or economy, which are institutionally and politically equipped to design and defend economic policy measures.[83] Poland assigned these functions to the NCA. As a result, the OCCP is placed in a structurally contradictory position: it is required to safeguard competition while facilitating the notification of measures that, by definition, distort competition in pursuit of economic or social objectives.

This dual role has caused difficulties. Tasks such as enforcing the standstill obligation and managing unlawful aid recovery clearly align with the OCCP's competition mandate. However, other activities do not. Helping to prepare and defend aid notifications essentially transforms the OCCP into a supporter of government industrial policy, despite the fact that the political responsibility and benefits of Commission approval rest with the ministries that create the aid programs. Representation before EU institutions further requires not only technical expertise but also elements of political advocacy, a function ill-suited to an authority whose legitimacy rests on independence and technocratic neutrality.[84]

With two decades of experience, it is hard to see meaningful synergy between state aid supervision and the OCCP's core functions. State aid work remains separate from competition enforcement and burdens the OCCP with politically sensitive responsibilities, conflicting with its role as an independent enforcer. This issue has worsened since the ECN+ Directive emphasised the

---

81 S. Dudzik, *Współpraca państw członkowskich i instytucji wspólnotowych w sprawach pomocy państwa dla przedsiębiorstw. Zagadnienia podstawowe*, PUG 2004, no. 1, 7.

82 M. Błachucki, *Rola instytucji krajowych w zakresie kontroli udzielanej pomocy publicznej–na przykładzie Polski* [in:] B.T. Bieńkowska, D. Szafrański (eds.), *Problemy prawa polskiego i obcego w ujęciu historycznym, praktycznym i teoretycznym*, Part 3, Warsaw 2011, 44.

83 A. Werner, *Polskie postępowanie notyfikacyjne dotyczące udzielenia pomocy publicznej*, Glosa 2004, no. 9, 7.

84 Ibidem, 8.

independence of NCAs. While centralising state aid in the OCCP may have seemed practical during accession, long-term practice questions its suitability. Merging competition enforcement with state aid coordination blurs the line between regulatory enforcement and economic policy, weakens the OCCP's mandate, and offers little benefit for competition in Poland.

6 Counteracting the Abuse of Market Power in Contractual Relations in the Food Sector

A further and particularly consequential expansion of the OCCP's jurisdiction occurred on 12 July 2017, with the entry into force of the Act on Counteracting the Unfair Use of Contractual Advantage in the Trade in Agricultural and Food Products (the UTP Act).[85] The declared objective of the legislation was to improve the functioning of the food supply chain – ostensibly including food safety – by addressing unfair trading practices (UTPs). These practices are understood to arise primarily from structural asymmetries in bargaining power between economically strong, concentrated market actors (notably large retailers and processors) and weaker, fragmented counterparts, especially farmers and small suppliers.

The Polish initiative was not isolated. It mirrored broader developments at the EU level, which ultimately culminated in Directive (EU) 2019/633 on unfair trading practices in business-to-business relationships in the agricultural and food supply chain.[86] As the Directive went beyond the scope of the original Polish statute, the latter was replaced by a new Act adopted on 17 November 2021. Both the 2016 and the 2021 statutes designated the OCCP as the competent enforcement authority.

What is striking, however, is the complete lack of justification for this institutional choice. Neither the explanatory memorandum to the 2016 Act[87] nor

85 Act of 15.12.2016 on counteracting the unfair use of contractual advantage in the trade in agricultural and food products, JoL 2017, item 67.

86 Directive (EU) 2019/633 of the European Parliament and of the Council of 17.04.2019 on unfair trading practices in business-to-business relationships in the agricultural and food supply chain, OJ L 111, 25.4.2019.

87 Explanatory memorandum of the act on counteracting the unfair use of contractual advantage in the trade in agricultural and food products, Parliamentary print No. 790, 25.07.2016.

that accompanying the 2021 Act[88] offered reasons why enforcement should be entrusted to NCA rather than to the Ministry of Agriculture or another sectoral authority. During consultations on the 2016 draft, stakeholders explicitly raised concerns about the regulation's vague scope, its sector-specific nature, and the appropriateness of the OCCP as the enforcer.[89] Yet the designation of the OCCP was accepted without discussion.[90] This silence is particularly revealing, given that the bill was sponsored by the Ministry of Agriculture, which appeared unwilling to assume the political and distributive risks of direct enforcement, effectively outsourcing them to an independent authority.

Although initially sceptical, the OCCP gradually embraced its new role and actively shaped the procedural architecture of the UTP regime. The procedural provisions of the Act largely mirror those of the Competition Act, creating a familiar yet derivative framework. As a result, the OCCP became the central enforcement authority. The Agricultural Market Agency was assigned only marginal ancillary tasks, primarily related to compliance with EU obligations regarding written contracts under Regulation (EU) No. 1308/2013.

The institutional design of enforcement raises serious doubts. Initially, competence to apply the UTP Act was concentrated in the OCCP's small regional office in Bydgoszcz – an unprecedented arrangement in the authority's history. This office, with around 10 staff, was responsible for both competition and consumer protection matters and tasked with enforcing a major new regulatory regime. Plans to establish a dedicated department of 40 positions within the OCCP's headquarters never materialised due to a lack of funding.[91]

In 2023, a small six-person department was finally established at headquarters, creating parallel enforcement structures in Warsaw and Bydgoszcz. However, this arrangement did not improve outcomes. Enforcement indicators deteriorated further. The ratio of explanatory proceedings and complaints to final decisions worsened, indicating a growing gap between investigatory activity and decisive enforcement as evidenced by the Table 3.3. The OCCP's

88 Explanatory memorandum of the act on counteracting the unfair use of contractual advantage in the trade in agricultural and food products, Parliamentary print No. 1502, 04.08.2021.

89 See: https://legislacja.rcl.gov.pl/projekt/12286400.

90 For the compilation of the comments received during public consultations on the draft Act, see https://legislacja.rcl.gov.pl/docs//2/12286400/12357779/12357780/dokument231732.pdf.

91 Explanatory memorandum of the act on counteracting the unfair use of contractual advantage in the trade in agricultural and food products, Parliamentary print No. 790, 25.07.2016.

TABLE 3.3 OCCP enforcement activities regarding UTPs (Source: OCCP Activity Reports)

Year	Decisions (fines/ commitments)	Explanatory proceedings	Formal investigations	Dawn raids	Complaints	Non-executive guidance	*Amicus curiae* briefs
2017	–	10	–	4	19	13	–
2018	1 (0/1)	11	6	7	57	26	–
2019	5 (1/4)	19	1	1	58	40	–
2020	5 (2/3)	36	6	2	54	10	–
2021	3 (2/1)	5	3	2	52	8	–
2022	3 (3/0)	17	4	1	72	14	1
2023	6 (1/5)	11	2	0	42	18	1
2024	1 (0/1)	11	2	2	29	31	2

reliance on non-coercive instruments – such as non-executive guidance and, more recently, amicus curiae briefs – grew markedly. These soft tools are increasingly being used in place of binding decisions, raising doubts about whether UTP enforcement has become mainly symbolic rather than substantive.

The initial attempt in 2023 to strengthen UTP enforcement by establishing a dedicated department within the OCCP's headquarters proved short-lived. Faced with declining enforcement outcomes and a growing reliance on non-coercive measures (as shown in the table), the department was liquidated, and its competencies were transferred back to the OCCP's small branch office in Bydgoszcz. These organisational changes are difficult to justify. At best, they reflect a managerial miscalculation; at worst, they reveal a lack of a coherent enforcement strategy.

The Act creates a framework to counter unfair contractual advantages in the agricultural supply chain, applying broadly to farmers, producers, intermediaries, wholesalers, distributors, and retailers, targeting both buyers and suppliers. Although officially framed as a measure to protect product quality and food safety, the Act primarily serves to improve trading conditions for producers. This raises the question of whether the OCCP will gradually evolve into a quasi-regulatory or even a quasi–price–control authority in the food sector, rather than maintaining a competition-oriented perspective.

Institutionally, the OCCP's designation remains controversial. Enforcement by a small regional office signals limited political and financial commitment and further strains an authority already burdened by competition and consumer protection, market surveillance, and state aid responsibilities. From a functional perspective, the Ministry of Agriculture might appear a more 'natural' enforcer. Yet, precisely because of its close ties to the sector, it would be particularly vulnerable to lobbying and capture. In principle, the OCCP's relative independence could ensure greater objectivity. Hence, entrusting the OCCP with this task reflects a political compromise rather than a functional necessity.

7 Combating Delayed Payments in Commercial Transactions

In 2019, the Polish Parliament adopted the Act amending certain acts on reducing payment gridlocks, presented by the government as a response to what it identified as one of the most serious structural problems of the Polish economy.[92] Empirical surveys indicated that more than 80% of Polish entrepreneurs experienced late payments, often triggering cascading liquidity problems that impaired their ability to meet obligations towards contractors, employees, and financial institutions. According to the government, payment backlogs undermined business liquidity, increased dependence on costly external financing, and exerted a systemic drag on economic performance. The declared objective of the reform was therefore to shorten payment deadlines and introduce sanctions against the largest and most persistent debtors.[93]

The Act introduced a hybrid enforcement model that combines civil law, tax, and administrative instruments. Statutory payment deadlines were shortened: public entities must now pay within 30 days (or 60 days for medical institutions), and in transactions where small or medium-sized enterprises are creditors vis-à-vis larger debtors, payment periods may not exceed 60 days. The statutory interest rate for late payments was also increased, strengthening creditors' financial claims.

The most controversial innovation, however, was the decision to entrust the OCCP with enforcement powers in this area.[94] The OCCP may initiate proceedings ex officio where overdue payments exceed PLN 5 million within a three-month period (a threshold reduced to PLN 2 million in 2021). During investigations, the OCCP may examine payment practices from the preceding two years, request documents, and conduct dawn raids. The OCCP is authorised to issue non-executive guidance, intended to induce behavioural change

92 The Act of 19.07.2019 on amending certain acts on reducing payment gridlocks, JoL 2019 item 1649.

93 Explanatory memorandum of the act on amendments to the Act on combating excessive delays in commercial transactions and the Act on public finances, Parliamentary print No. 2620, 19.09.2022.

94 The Act of 8.03.2013 on combating excessive delays in commercial transactions, JoL 2023 item 1790.

without recourse to formal proceedings.[95] The legislative memorandum justified this soft instrument by reference to efficiency and reduced procedural burdens, reflecting a broader trend in Polish administrative governance.[96]

From an institutional perspective, justifying the allocation of these competences to the OCCP is challenging. Virtually all relevant data on payments and arrears are held by the tax administration, which is structurally better placed to detect, verify, and assess payment delays. Yet the explanatory memorandum offered no substantive reasoning for assigning enforcement to the NCA. The decision appears to have been driven more by institutional and political dynamics than by functional considerations, including the ambitions of the OCCP's leadership and the promise of additional resources that accompanied the new mandate.

The Act requires the OCCP to submit annual enforcement reports to the Prime Minister. These reports, however, remain confidential. Only fragmented and aggregated information is disclosed in the Office's general activity reports, where – tellingly – combating payment delays is subsumed under the heading of competition policy. This lack of transparency significantly undermines public accountability.

Enforcement officially began on 1 July 2020. The outcomes so far have been underwhelming. Despite significant legislative focus and resource allocation – including three departments set up within OCCP headquarters – the number of cases and sanctions remains limited, and the decision-making process has faced challenges, as shown in the table.

The OCCP's performance in this area, especially in 2024, has been marked by pronounced inefficiency and inconsistency, further aggravated by opaque reporting practices. The Table 3.4 illustrates a fundamental problem: the OCCP's persistent inability – or unwillingness – to deliver noticeable enforcement outcomes. Particularly striking is the reaction of the current president of the OCCP, who publicly announced in a press interview his intention to relinquish the Office's competences in this area.[97] This situation highlights a significant failure of managerial responsibility and institutional governance, compounded by a lack of personal accountability for years of problematic enforcement and the misuse of public resources.

---

95 P. Dolniak [in:] *Przeciwdziałanie nadmiernym opóźnieniom w transakcjach handlowych. Komentarz,* LEX/el. 2025, Art. 13(ca).

96 Explanatory memorandum of the act on amendments to the Act on combating excessive delays in commercial transactions and the Act on public finances, Parliamentary print No. 2620, 19.09.2022.

97 *Inspekcja Handlowa zmieni zwierzchnika. UOKiK: Powinna działać w ramach polityki rządu,* https://www.bankier.pl/wiadomosc/Inspekcja-Handlowa-zmieni-zwierzchnika-UOKiK-Powinna-dzialac-w-ramach-polityki-rzadu-8969095.html.

TABLE 3.4 OCCP enforcement activities regarding financial backlogs (Source: OCCP Activity Reports)

Year	Proceedings pending	Proceedings initiated	Decisions issued	Undertakings fined	Non-executive guidance
2020	100	100	0	0	n/a
2021	108	8	21	7	n/a
2022	88	n/a	35	13	n/a
2023	85	30	52	28	165
2024	n/a	31	1	1	79

The payment backlog regime thus provides a paradigmatic example of negative synergy. Rather than strengthening competition policy, the addition of this competence has led to jurisdictional atrophy: an economically important task has never received genuine institutional recognition within the OCCP. The president's public disavowal of the competence effectively confirms its marginalisation.

Yet despite this explicit admission of failure, neither the government nor Parliament has taken steps to redesign the institutional framework or reassign responsibility. The result is regulatory limbo: enforcement remains formally vested in an authority that has openly signalled its reluctance to exercise it, and there is no political will to correct the structural error. Poland's experience shows that assigning payment-backlog enforcement to an NCA lacking both functional affinity and institutional commitment creates systemic inefficiencies and undermines regulatory credibility.

8 Foreign Investment Screening: A Temporary Experiment with Lasting Damage

The most recent – albeit initially temporary – competence entrusted to the OCCP concerned the screening of foreign direct investments (FDI). In 2020, an amendment to the Act on the Control of Certain Investments ('FDI Act') conferred upon the OCCP powers to review transactions involving Polish undertakings deemed essential to public order, public security, or public health.[98] From that point onward, investments resulting in (i) the acquisition of control, (ii) the attainment of a significant shareholding (20% or more), or (iii) the acquisition or lease of assets of a protected undertaking by entities established outside the EU and OECD were subject to OCCP scrutiny.

The official justification invoked the COVID-19 pandemic and the alleged risk of hostile takeovers of strategically critical Polish companies, which were weakened by declining liquidity. On this basis, the screening mechanism was incorporated into the so-called Anti-Crisis Shield.[99] Formally, the amendment was presented as an exceptional and temporary response to pandemic-related threats. In reality, however, it was closely linked to the transposition of Regulation (EU) 2019/452, which establishes a permanent framework for screening foreign direct investments into the EU.[100] For purely pragmatic legislative reasons, to ensure the matter could proceed smoothly, it was included in the temporary anti-crisis legislation. It should not come as a surprise that the Polish regime – originally set to last 24 months[101] – was first extended to 60 months and ultimately made permanent in July 2025.[102]

Despite this evolution, Article 12a of the amended FDI Act still characterises the system as a pandemic-related measure. The amendment created a dual and incoherent investment control system. Under the pre-existing regime, the Council of Ministers established a closed list of protected undertakings, and transactions were reviewed by the Ministry for Development, assisted by an inter-ministerial Consulting Committee comprising representatives of intelligence and security services (but not the OCCP).[103] The new regime relied on a broad catalogue of strategic sectors and transactions that trigger notification obligations and designated the OCCP as the competent authority. Strikingly, the legislative justification for this choice was rudimentary: the explanatory memorandum merely stated – without analysis – that 'the screening authority will be the President of the Office of Competition and Consumer

98 The Act of 24.07.2015 on the control of certain investments, JoL 2020 item 2145.

99 Act of 19.06.2020 on subsidies for interest on bank loans granted to entrepreneurs affected by COVID-19 and on simplified proceedings for the approval of arrangements in connection with COVID-19, JoL 2022, item 2141.

100 OJ L 79I, 21.3.2019, 1–14.

101 Art. 6 of the Act of 12.05.2022, amending the Act on Tax on Goods and Services and certain other acts, JoL 2022, item 1137.

102 Art. 2 of the Act of 9.07.2025, amending the Act on the control of certain investments and the Act on subsidies for interest on bank loans granted to entrepreneurs affected by COVID-19, and on simplified proceedings for the approval of arrangements in connection with COVID-19, JoL 2025, item 973.

103 Regulation of the Council of Ministers of 18.12.2024 on the list of entities subject to protection and the competent control authorities for them, JoL 2024, item 1892.

Protection'.[104] The Regulatory Impact Assessment referred to pandemic-related economic risks but offered no explanation of why an NCA should administer a politically sensitive security instrument.[105]

The institutional and organisational arrangements were far from satisfactory. The amendment provided no additional resources for the OCCP to exercise its new functions.[106] Moreover, the Ministry for Development retained its role as the contact point for the European Commission under the FDI Regulation and continued to handle international coordination.[107] This created a dysfunctional duality: the Ministry was responsible for negotiating the framework rules and managing European-level strategic and day-to-day cooperation, while the OCCP was charged with enforcing them domestically, despite lacking both experience and political legitimacy in the FDI sphere. Assessing mergers under the SIEC test and screening them against national security threats requires distinct evidence and separate analysis, not to mention that the final decision under the FDI mechanism is political *par excellence*.

The substantive and procedural provisions of the amended FDI Act were also poorly drafted. Vagueness in protected sectors led to interpretative uncertainty.[108] The notification obligation was extended beyond reasonable limits, covering even intra-group transactions that posed no plausible threat to national security or public order. The measure did not achieve its intended purpose, as indicated in the explanatory memorandum, of deterring takeovers by Russian or Chinese investors; instead, the few notifications concerned mostly Ukrainian or Arab investors.

Between 2020 and 2025, the OCCP received only 27 notifications. Of these, 12 resulted in decisions: eight refusals to initiate control proceedings, three discontinuances on grounds of irrelevance, and one discontinuance due to the OCCP's loss of competence; and 12 notifications were deemed unnecessary

---

104 Explanatory memorandum of the draft act on subsidies for interest on bank loans granted to ensure financial liquidity to entrepreneurs affected by the effects of COVID-19 and on amending certain other laws, Parliamentary print No. 382, 22.05.2020, 40.

105 Regulatory Impact Assessment of the draft act on subsidies for interest on bank loans granted to ensure financial liquidity to entrepreneurs affected by the effects of COVID-19 and on amending certain other laws, Parliamentary print No. 382, 22.05.2020, 2.

106 To contrast, the FDI screening ministerial unit consists of seven individuals.

107 Regulation of the Minister of Development, Labor, and Technology of 8.10.2020 on the contact point for the implementation and application of the regulation establishing a framework for monitoring foreign direct investment in the Union, JoL 2020 item 1762.

108 K. Czapracka, M. Gac, J. Gubański, I. Małobęcki, *Kontrola inwestycji zagranicznych – wstępna ocena polskiego ustawodawstwa i praktyki w kontekście europejskich i światowych trendów*, iKAR 2022, no. 4, 24.

because the statutory thresholds had not been met.[109] This statistical outcome illustrates the system's ineffectiveness and the confusion it generates: nearly one-third of notifications were redundant due to unclear drafting of the legislation.

Ultimately, in 2025, the Ministry for Development promoted a further amendment to the FDI Act, transferring screening competence from the OCCP to itself. The accompanying memorandum stated that 'the competence of the minister responsible for economic affairs in foreign investment control in Poland should be a permanent solution',[110] suggesting that the regime's temporary element was not the screening mechanism itself but the OCCP's jurisdiction over it. The justification remains unconvincing and underscores the arbitrary nature of both the original entrustment of competence to the OCCP and its subsequent withdrawal. The complete arbitrariness and the absence of any discernible rationale in the competence-appointing process are further evidenced by the fact that, although the OCCP served as the principal authority responsible for FDI control over the past five years, it is now not even a member of the Consulting Committee – composed of 23 central government bodies – which issues opinions on notified FDI transactions.

The Polish experiment of entrusting an NCA with FDI screening was ill-conceived from the outset. The only comparable example in the EU was Romania, which has already begun to retreat from such an arrangement. Assessing FDI is inherently political, requiring consideration of security, foreign policy, and strategic industrial priorities – factors outside the remit of a technocratic competition authority. The OCCP lacked the political legitimacy and institutional capacity to exercise such powers. Moreover, between 2020 and 2025, the OCCP's dual role, which simultaneously assessed concentrations under competition law and investments under the FDI regime but according to different criteria, created an incoherent and contradictory enforcement framework.

The political nature of FDI control was highlighted by the high-profile case of the OCCP's no-objection decision[111] regarding the Saudi Arabian Oil Company's acquisition of control of three Lotos Group subsidiaries. When the new government was installed in autumn 2023, the OCCP's decision prompted

---

109 Explanatory memorandum of the draft act on the amendment of the act subsidies for interest on bank loans granted to ensure financial liquidity to entrepreneurs affected by the effects of COVID-19 and on amending certain other laws, Parliamentary print No. 1383, 20.06.2025, 5.

110 Ibidem, 3.

111 OCCP decision No. DKK-201/2022.

intervention by the political police, underscoring that FDI screening is not a matter of technocratic law enforcement but of political judgement.[112]

In this context, entrusting the OCCP with such competences not only risked politicising an independent authority but also undermined the credibility of competition enforcement in Poland. The episode thus serves as a cautionary example of the dangers of conflating competition policy with strategic investment control. The eventual transfer of competence from the OCCP to the Ministry for Development corrected this institutional misfit, but only after five years, during which the system's dysfunctions became evident. The episode underscores the risks of conflating competition enforcement with strategic investment control and illustrates why, across Europe, FDI screening is treated as a political, not a technocratic, task.

9 Other Competences

The powers outlined above constitute the OCCP's principal jurisdiction as an administrative authority. However, certain ancillary competences may also be identified. For instance, pursuant to the Polish Language Act, the OCCP is entrusted with monitoring the use of the Polish language in consumer transactions.[113] This has been described as the 'forgotten competence' of the OCCP: in its first decade, the authority actively enforced this Act, whereas in the last decade it has been substantially neglected.[114]

It should also be noted that the President of the OCCP has the authority to delegate representatives to other public bodies, including the Financial Supervision Authority, the Financial Education Council, and the supervisory boards of Special Economic Zones.[115]

10 Enforcement and Prospects for Development

At present, there are no credible indications that the scope of the OCCP's jurisdiction will be modified in the near future. Although the current presi-

112 Standpoint of President of UOKiK, https://uokik.gov.pl/en/standpoint-of-president-of-uokik.

113 Art. 7b of the Act of 7.10.1999, on the Polish language, JoL 2024, item 1556.

114 T. Bagdziński, *Język polski w obrocie, reklamie i marketingu, czyli parę słów o zapomnianych kompetencjach Prezesa UOKiK* [in:] M. Bernatt, A. Jurkowska-Gomułka, M. Namysłowska, A. Piszcz (eds.), 745–752.

115 Art. 7 of the Act of 20.10.1994 on special economic zones, JoL 2023, item 1604.

dent of the OCCP has publicly announced his intention to separate market surveillance and payment-backlog enforcement into a new authority,[116] these declarations have not been followed by corresponding legislative action. The OCCP's conduct within the government's legislative programme contradicts these announcements, significantly undermining their credibility.

Beyond the limited political capital of the current OCCP leadership and its weak legislative effectiveness, any structural reallocation of competences appears fiscally unrealistic. Given the prevailing budgetary constraints, it is highly unlikely that the Minister of Finance would support the creation of a new authority requiring additional administrative structures, staffing, and funding. If anything, what may attract attention at the ministerial level is the demonstrated inefficiency in using public funds currently devoted to adjudicating matters that the OCCP itself now seeks to abandon – an inefficiency well documented in the preceding analysis.

Accordingly, no substantial reconfiguration of the OCCP's jurisdiction should be expected. Instead, future developments are more likely to take the form of incremental strengthening or weakening of existing competences (depending on their enforcement), particularly in the core areas of competition and consumer protection. As discussed in the previous chapter, Poland remains obliged to implement several major EU legislative instruments, notably the EMFA and the AI Act. These measures will inevitably expand the OCCP's operational responsibilities. However, given the OCCP's disputable effectiveness, it is unclear how this will affect enforcement. With the EMFA, this expansion will primarily affect merger control in the media sector, while the AI Act is likely to reinforce the OCCP's role in consumer protection and market oversight within the digital economy.

The precise contours of these future competences remain uncertain. In particular, the Polish draft implementing legislation for the AI Act has been widely criticised as poorly conceived and institutionally incoherent.[117] Given the controversy surrounding this proposal, it is difficult to predict whether it will be adopted in its current form, substantially revised, or abandoned altogether. This uncertainty, together with the history of OCCP jurisdictional development, further reinforces the conclusion that, rather than embarking on ambitious institutional reforms, the Polish legislature is more likely to rely

116 Refer to fn 97.

117 M. Błachucki, *Sąd Ochrony Konkurencji i Konsumentów jako sąd właściwy w sprawach systemów sztucznej inteligencji, czyli droga donikąd* [in:] G. Sibiga (ed.), *Wpływ Aktu w sprawie sztucznej inteligencji na funkcjonowanie administracji publicznej*, Warsaw 2025, 434.

on incremental adjustments that leave the OCCP's fundamentally problematic jurisdictional structure intact.

11 Conclusions: The OCCP as a 'Competence Dumpster' Rather than a Rational Institutional Design

The chapter demonstrated that the OCCP has experienced an unprecedented expansion of its mandate. The authority has been entrusted with functions that are only tenuously connected – if connected at all – to the public-law protection of competition, including enforcement of the UTP regime, combating delayed payments in commercial transactions, and FDI screening. This institutional trajectory does not appear to result from a coherent design choice. Rather, it reflects political convenience and, to some extent, the personal ambitions and policy preferences of the last two Presidents of the OCCP.

What is particularly striking is that successive expansions of the OCCP's portfolio have proceeded without meaningful justification, as the analysis of the explanatory memoranda makes clear. Neither the sponsors of the relevant amendments nor the Sejm have offered a serious explanation for why the OCCP – rather than another administrative body – should assume these additional responsibilities. A review of the explanatory memoranda accompanying amendments to the Competition Act, as well as the statutes conferring new competences on the OCCP, reveals a conspicuous absence of analysis of: (i) the functional relationship between the new tasks and the authority's original mandate; and (ii) the institutional rationale for locating heterogeneous regulatory functions within the competition authority. Legislative choices were therefore made without any visible assessment of systemic consequences, administrative capacity, or the trade-offs inherent in building a multipurpose agency. As the chapter proved, the ill-conceived jurisdiction amendments led to ineffective enforcement outcomes.

11.1 Crowding Out of Competition Enforcement

The research conducted for this study indicates that, over time, consumer protection has come to dominate the OCCP's operational profile.[118] Immediately after the OCCP replaced a specialised antimonopoly authority, consumer protection remained marginalised, and competition enforcement was still presented as the core function – an assessment confirmed by annual activ-

118 Similarly: M. Martyniszyn, M. Bernatt, 23–24.

ity reports from 1995 to 2024. Yet as the OCCP's competences expanded, institutional priorities shifted progressively. This change is reflected in a marked decline in antitrust decisions, accompanied by an inverse rise in consumer-protection rulings.[119] A similar trend is evident in the allocation of financial and human resources: consumer-protection units, particularly those responsible for collective consumer interests, have grown in importance relative to competition departments.[120] Even the symbolic ordering of annual reports since 2014 – where consumer protection is often presented before competition enforcement – signals a reorientation of institutional identity and administrative attention.[121]

The OCCP's resource structure illustrates the scale of this shift. In 2024, competition protection accounted for only 28.8% of total expenditure (including 19.8% for anticompetitive practices, 5.3% for merger control, and 3.7% for abuse of contractual advantage). By contrast, consumer protection – along with market surveillance, the Trade Inspection, and laboratories – accounted for 49.9% of the budget. State aid activities represented 7.0%, payment-backlog enforcement 14.0%, and EU Presidency-related tasks a marginal 0.7%.[122] Notably, no funds were allocated to foreign investment screening, indicating that this competence remains largely nominal rather than operational.

11.2 The 'Synergy' Narrative as Institutional Self-Justification

The president of the OCCP continues to defend the integrated model, arguing that combining competition and consumer protection creates synergies and that effective competition policy depends on a strong consumer-protection foundation.[123] This position is difficult to reconcile with the empirical picture: a dynamic rise in consumer decisions and a parallel decline in antitrust decisions suggest not synergy but displacement. Moreover, the examples offered by the president as evidence of synergy – namely that antitrust enforcement benefits consumers and that market liberalisation increases the need for con-

119 Decisions in the field of merger control are excluded from this analysis, as merger proceedings are application-based and their volume does not depend on the intensity or effectiveness of enforcement activity by the NCA.

120 Refer to Section 7.6.

121 This should be regarded as significant yet entirely understandable, since in the field of consumer protection the OCCP was able to demonstrate tangible and politically salient achievements, whereas no comparable record could be presented with respect to its commitment to antitrust enforcement.

122 Refer to Section 4.3.2.6.

123 OECD, Roundtable on changes in institutional design of competition authorities: Note by Poland, DAF/COMP/WD(2014)90, 4.

sumer protection – do not demonstrate synergy arising from institutional integration.[124] Those effects would also arise if competition and consumer protection were administered by separate authorities. What is illustrated instead is a conceptual slippage: the president appears to treat any consumer benefit produced by antitrust enforcement as proof of institutional synergy, when it is simply a feature of competition law's welfare logic.

This defensive posture is understandable in institutional terms. As the doctrine notes, the initial determination of an administrative authority's structure tends to shape the entire regulatory architecture built upon it; reversing that foundational choice is politically and legally 'revolutionary' because it triggers a chain of procedural and substantive adjustments.[125] In Poland, the 1995 merger of competition and consumer protection became a foundational solution – an 'original sin' of the current architecture. Yet path dependency cannot shield an arrangement from critical evaluation. A structure that may have been justifiable in 1995 now appears to produce predominantly negative effects, particularly for competition enforcement. On that basis, the separation of competition and consumer protection emerges as a principal conclusion of this research, together with the need to remove functions unrelated to competition enforcement from the competition authority.

11.3 Independence, Technocracy, and Internal Contradictions

These design deficiencies become more problematic following the implementation of the ECN+ Directive. The OCCP was granted formal guarantees of independence, which presuppose a technocratic, impartial enforcement role. Yet many of the additional competences now hosted within the OCCP – consumer campaigns, state aid oversight, payment-backlog enforcement, and especially FDI control – are inherently political or distributive in character. They place the authority in the role of an advocate for particular economic and social objectives, often requiring value-laden choices. The resulting contradiction is difficult to manage institutionally: the same authority is expected to act as a neutral enforcer of competition rules while simultaneously engaging in politically charged initiatives in adjacent domains. If, for example, the president publicly campaigns against foreign banks and advocates taxation measures aimed at 'excess profits', it becomes institutionally implausible to claim

124 Ibidem, 2–3.

125 E.M. Fox, *Antitrust and Institutions: Design and Change*, 4Loyola University Chicago Law Journal 2010, no. 41, 474.

that the same authority will appear fully neutral when those banks are parties in antimonopoly proceedings.

11.4 Modern Instruments without Modern Accountability

Paradoxically, the OCCP has become a pioneer in using modern governance tools: soft law (guidelines), market studies, non-executive guidance, public positions, and amicus curiae briefs. In consumer protection, the toolkit is even broader, including mystery shoppers, public warnings, and registers of prohibited conduct. These instruments can enhance flexibility and responsiveness, but they also require robust guarantees of transparency, methodological discipline, and accountability. In a multipurpose 'competence dump', such guarantees are harder to ensure across the entire portfolio – particularly because stakeholder groups diverge and sometimes conflict across competition, consumer, industrial policy, and security-related domains. The result is a risk of inconsistent use of quasi-normative tools, opaque selection criteria, and limited evaluability of effects – producing legal uncertainty for market participants.

11.5 Final Remark: The Need for Legislative Redesign

The history of the OCCP's expanding jurisdiction reveals the force of political inertia, reinforced by successive leaders' ambitions: broader competences justify larger budgets, larger management structures, and greater institutional visibility. Although this expansion has sometimes introduced modern procedural instruments into the OCCP's administrative practice, it has not been accompanied by corresponding reforms in accountability and transparency. More importantly, the broadening of the OCCP's portfolio has contributed to the authority's drift from its original mission – transforming the Polish NCA into a multi-tasked market-surveillance authority at the expense of effective competition enforcement.

CHAPTER 4

Polish Competition Authority: Regime, Organisation, Resources, and Decision-Making Process

Effective implementation of competition law requires not only a robust legal framework but also an efficient and coherent organisational structure. The preceding chapters on jurisdiction and institutional history have outlined the evolution of the OCCP's competence. To provide a complete understanding of competition law enforcement in Poland, it is essential to examine the OCCP's internal organisation and decision-making mechanisms.

This chapter presents the institutional framework governing the public enforcement of competition rules in Poland. It analyses in detail the OCCP's regulatory regime, organisational structure, human and financial resources, and decision-making processes. The authority's current position and jurisdiction are the culmination of more than three decades of institutional development and adaptation.

The evolution of the OCCP's institutional and internal framework provides a revealing case study of how the organisational design of a public authority may reflect broader political and administrative dynamics of a given period. These include shifts in government priorities, concerns about the concentration of executive power, and the enduring imperative to ensure transparency, accountability, and professional integrity in public administration.[1]

This chapter also examines the evolution of staffing within the OCCP, covering both managerial and non-managerial staff, as well as the Office's budgetary framework and the principles governing its formulation and execution. To date, no comprehensive study within Polish legal scholarship has undertaken a detailed analysis of the OCCP's internal organisation.[2] Accordingly, this examination seeks to fill a significant gap in the literature by providing a systematic assessment of the institution's internal structure, management practices, and financial governance.

---

1 J.L. Selin, *What Makes an Agency Independent?*, American Journal of Political Science 2015, no. 4, 984.

2 Some aspects of the OCCP's internal design were discussed like international unit composition–M. Błachucki, *Służba publiczna wobec umiędzynarodowienia administracji* (*na przykładzie administracji antymonopolowej*), Annales UMCS Sectio G (Ius) 2017, no. 64, 2, or advisory bodies: A. Piszcz, *Organy*, 359–378.

© 2026 THE AUTHOR(S) | HTTPS://DOI.ORG/10.1163/9789004754638-005
This is an open access publication distributed under the terms of the CC 4.0 license BY-NC-ND.

More broadly, analyses of the internal organisation of NCAs remain scarce. This research gap is particularly noteworthy, as organisational design and administrative practice can decisively influence the effectiveness of competition law enforcement.[3] The experience of the OCCP illustrates a clear correlation between suboptimal organisational arrangements and the overall effectiveness of its enforcement activity. This observation underscores the importance of institutional structure and management in determining the practical success of competition policy implementation.

1 Evolution of the Institutional Regime of the OCCP

The first body entrusted with competition law enforcement in Poland was the Minister of Finance. This arrangement existed only briefly, from 1987 to 1990, during the final years of the communist regime. Under this model, competition enforcement functions were exercised by a politically appointed government member, subject to dismissal at any time and bound to implement the government's general policy objectives. As a result, the authority lacked any formal guarantees of institutional or functional independence. Competition enforcement was carried out by a single organisational unit within the ministry – the Department for Counteracting the Monopolisation of the National Economy. This department served as the core administrative and human resources base for establishing the first independent Antimonopoly Authority in 1990. Upon its creation, all staff members of the former department were given the opportunity to transfer to the new authority, and most chose to do so, ensuring some institutional continuity despite the profound systemic change.[4]

The Antimonopoly Authority was established as a central body of state administration. It was subordinated to the Council of Ministers, with its chairperson appointed and dismissed by the Prime Minister. The founding legislation did not prescribe any specific professional qualifications for appointment, nor did it provide safeguards against the arbitrary dismissal of the authority's chairperson. Consequently, despite its formal organisational separation from ministerial structures, the Antimonopoly Authority lacked the

3 To name the most relevant: E.M. Fox, *Antitrust and Institutions: Design and Change*, 41 Loyola University Chicago Law Journal 473 (2010); W. Kovacic, M. Mariniello, *Competition Agency Design in Globalised Markets*, E15Initiative. Geneva 2016; A. Ottow, *Market and Competition Authorities. Good Agency Principles*, Oxford 2015 or D.A. Crane, *The Institutional Structure of Antitrust Enforcement*, OUP, Oxford 2011. More works are referred to in the book.

4 M. Martyniszyn, M. Bernatt, 16.

essential attributes of institutional independence. From the outset, the authority was organised around a central office in Warsaw, supported by a network of regional offices. In 1996, its institutional remit was expanded to include protecting consumer interests, and it changed its name to the OCCP.

The 2000 Act introduced significant changes to the authority's structure and functions. Article 24(2) provided that the Prime Minister shall appoint the OCCP President for a term of five years, following a competitive selection process. The Act introduced significant provisions to ensure the authority's independence and to provide legal guarantees for its operation.

The years 2006–2007 were a complex and turbulent period in the OCCP's institutional history. First, with the enactment of the Act of 24 August 2006 on State Personnel and High State Positions, the OCCP was stripped of all statutory guarantees of independence.[5] This change was systemic and did not result from any negative assessment of the authority's functioning; rather, it reflected a broader reconfiguration of public administration governance.[6] Second, the Competition Act of 2000 was replaced by the currently binding Act of 2007, which formally reverted to the concept of an independent NCA. In particular, Article 29 of the 2007 Act restored the OCCP's independence, closely modelled on the provisions in the 2000 Act. Third, a subsequent amendment reinstated the provisions introduced by the Act on State Personnel and High State Positions, effectively removing the OCCP's formal independence once again.[7] These rapid and contradictory legislative changes were the direct consequence of intense political tensions within the governing coalition at the time.[8] Competition law legislation became an instrument reflecting the shifting balance of power within the Polish government, rather than a product of a coherent institutional or policy-oriented assessment of the role and independence of the NCA.

Between 2007 and 2023, the OCCP did not operate as a formally independent authority. The President of the OCCP was appointed by the Prime Minister for an indefinite term. Although candidates were required to meet several statutory eligibility criteria – requirements that, in their core elements, remain

5 JoL No. 170, item 1217.

6 The government at the time decided that civil service in the traditional sense was unnecessary, as were all independent administrative agencies. More on this law: K. Działocha, A. Łukaszczuk, *Nowa ustawa o służbie cywilnej (Aspekt prawno-konstytucyjny)*, PiP 2006, no. 11.

7 Act of 13.04.2007 amending the Act on Competition and Consumer Protection and the Act on State Human Resources and High State Positions, JoL No. 99, item 660.

8 The Competition Act came into force on 21.04.2007, and the provisions establishing the authority's independence expired on 20.06.2007.

largely unchanged – the appointment framework offered no effective guarantees of independence. In particular, the Prime Minister retained the power to dismiss the President of the OCCP at any time, without any statutory obligation to provide reasons for such a decision. Dismissals were typically made without formal justification, as illustrated by the removal of former Presidents Małgorzata Krasnodębska-Tomkiel and Adam Jasser.

This institutional model changed only with the implementation of the ECN+ Directive, which introduced formal safeguards intended to strengthen the independence of national competition authorities.

2 The Current Position of the OCCP President

2.1 The Legal Status

The legal position of the OCCP is set out in Article 29(1) of the Act. Pursuant to this provision, the President of the OCCP serves as the NCA in Poland. This central public administration authority is responsible for enforcing competition and consumer protection law. The activities of the OCCP are subject to the Prime Minister's supervision.

The Competition Act designates a single authority – the OCCP – to enforce the Act. Consequently, the OCCP enjoys exclusive jurisdiction over matters regulated by the Act. Unlike in certain other jurisdictions, no additional public authority in Poland shares competence for the public enforcement of competition law. For example, in the United States, enforcement is divided between the Department of Justice and the Federal Trade Commission,[9] while in the United Kingdom, the Competition and Markets Authority operates alongside sectoral regulators such as Ofcom, Ofgem, and Ofwat.[10]

The OCCP's mandate includes enforcing competition and consumer law. The authority's name, together with the scope of the Competition Act, indicates that its jurisdiction extends to public enforcement of competition and consumer protection rules.[11] This, however, does not preclude civil courts from adjudicating private actions for damages arising from infringements of competition law. The OCCP operates as a monocratic authority. The President

---

9 For an overview of the US system: K. H. Anker, *Best Frenemies: Evaluating the Dual Jurisdiction of the Federal Antitrust Agencies*, Boston College Law Review 2022, no. 1(63).

10 For an overview of the UK system–OECD, Interactions between competition authorities and sector regulators–Contribution from the United Kingdom, DAF/COMP/GF/WD (2022)25.

11 Refer to Chapter 2 for discussion on OCCP powers.

formally embodies the institution, while the Office of Competition and Consumer Protection performs auxiliary and administrative functions in support of the President's decision-making.

The OCCP is a central government authority, and this status entails two principal consequences. First, the authority's territorial jurisdiction extends throughout the Republic of Poland, without prejudice to the potential extraterritorial application of Polish competition law. As Poland is a unitary state, the OCCP's regional offices, although located outside its Warsaw headquarters, are considered integral internal units of the authority. Second, there is no administrative appeal instance above the OCCP. In Poland, central government agencies and ministries typically constitute the highest administrative instance, and appeal mechanisms within such bodies are exceptional.

The Prime Minister exercises administrative supervision over the OCCP (Article 29(1)). Within the hierarchical structure of public administration, such supervision is a standard mechanism for ensuring legality and efficiency in the operation of public authorities. From an organisational perspective, the OCCP's direct supervision by the Prime Minister underscores its special status, as most central agencies are subordinate to individual ministries. The Prime Minister, acting as a supervisor and not an appellate authority, may not interfere directly in the OCCP's decision-making process and may intervene only where explicitly authorised by statute. Following the implementation of the ECN+ Directive, the scope and intensity of administrative supervision over the OCCP have become significantly limited.

2.2 Appointment and Dismissal of the OCCP President

Since 1996, the process for appointing the OCCP President has remained consistent. The Prime Minister appoints the President from candidates chosen through an open, competitive recruitment process. The recruitment process is governed by specific provisions in the Competition Act. Information about this process must be publicly posted on the Chancellery of the Prime Minister's official website, including the mandatory details and a submission deadline at least 10 days after the announcement. In the last two appointments, this minimum deadline was adhered to. A selection committee, appointed by the Head of the Chancellery on behalf of the Prime Minister, conducts the recruitment. The committee, consisting of at least three knowledgeable and experienced members, evaluates each candidate's professional background, relevant expertise, and managerial skills.

However, the transparency of the recruitment procedure is undermined by the lack of disclosure regarding the composition of the selection committee.

In the case of each of the last three appointments of the OCCP President, the Head of the Chancellery of the Prime Minister declined to make the composition of the committees public.[12]

Following the assessment, the committee selects up to three candidates and submits their names to the Head of the Chancellery of the Prime Minister, together with a report summarising the recruitment process. Unfortunately, these reports are not made publicly available. The outcome of the recruitment procedure is announced by publishing a brief notice on the Chancellery of the Prime Minister's website. As a result, it is impossible to verify the basis for selecting particular candidates, whether other applicants participated, or how the final recommendation was determined. Publicly available information about the candidates is limited to informal, unverified reports.[13]

Although the procedure may appear transparent on the surface, its practical implementation raises serious concerns. The process described as 'open and competitive' does not guarantee genuine competition among candidates. The statutory requirements guarantee only that the vacancy information is public and that any qualified person may apply. Beyond that, the Act provides no mechanism to ensure the selection of the most competent candidate.

The Prime Minister retains full discretion to appoint any candidate, irrespective of the committee's recommendation. The composition of the selection committee and the minutes of its proceedings remain undisclosed, precluding meaningful public scrutiny of its members' qualifications and the selection criteria. This opacity makes it impossible to verify whether the candidate ultimately appointed was indeed the most suitable.

The Prime Minister's unfettered discretion in appointments was confirmed in the highly controversial case concerning the 2006 appointment of the president of the telecommunications regulator.[14] During judicial review proceed-

12 In response to my PI request, the Chancellery provided only selected casting announcements, claiming no other information is available.

13 Some press speculations from previous selection: *10 kandydatów w ponownym konkursie na szefa UOKiK,* https://www.wnp.pl/rynki/10-kandydatow-w-ponownym-konkursie-na-szefa-uokik,269656.html; *Drugi konkurs na szefa UOKiK. Dziesięciu kandydatów,* https://tvn24.pl/biznes/z-kraju/uokik-dziesieciu-kandydatow-w-ponownym-konkursie-na-szefa-ra628078-ls4468446.

14 In March 2006, the Prime Minister announced an open competition for the position of President of the Office of Electronic Communications (OEC). Twenty-five candidates applied, and nine qualified for the second stage of the recruitment process. A. Streżyńska was not among them, as she did not meet the formal eligibility criteria. On 24.04.2006, the selection committee adopted a resolution recommending three other candidates for appointment to the position. On 9.05.2006, the Prime Minister appointed A. Streżyńska as President of the OEC.

ings, both the administrative courts[15] and the CCCP[16] held that they lacked competence to examine either the legality of the competition procedure for the position of president or the correctness and legitimacy of appointing a particular individual to that post. This precedent establishes that the Prime Minister may appoint virtually any applicant to the position, even if that person does not meet the formal eligibility requirements or was not recommended by the selection committee. No court has the legal authority to annul or review such an appointment. The same principle applies, by analogy, to the procedure for selecting and appointing the President of the OCCP.[17]

In this context, the government's actions following the ECN+ Directive's implementation are particularly contentious. Rather than conducting a new recruitment process consistent with the Directive's objective of strengthening NCAs' independence, the Polish government simply allowed the previously appointed president to remain in office and enjoy the benefits of tenure. It is stressed that the automatic assumption of the first term of office by the holder of the authority at the time of entry into force of the amendments to the Act is not reflected in the provisions of the ECN+ Directive and raises serious doubts about the real objectives of the amendment.[18] Circumventing the obligation to conduct a recruitment process appears inconsistent with both the spirit and the objectives of the ECN+ Directive, further weakens the institutional legitimacy of the OCCP's leadership, and raises serious concerns about the credibility of the independence framework.

---

15 In its judgment of 11.02.2009 (II GSK 771/08), the HAC held that the examination of the correctness or legality of the appointment of a person serving as the head of a public authority falls outside the jurisdiction of administrative courts.

16 In its judgment of 6.07.2007 (XVII Amt 30/06), the CCCP expressly held that the President of the OEC may lawfully exercise his powers and issue decisions despite the controversial circumstances surrounding his appointment. The Court stated that it was not competent to review the procedure by which the authority had been appointed. Furthermore, the Court observed that even if procedural irregularities had occurred during the appointment, such defects would not invalidate the decisions subsequently issued by the President of the OEC.

17 K. Jaroszyński [in:] T. Skoczny (ed.), *Ustawa o ochronie konkurencji i konsumentów. Komentarz*, Warsaw 2014, Art. 29, Nb 21.

18 M. Kozak, *Raz, dwa, trzy, niezależny będziesz ty… O konieczności szerszego spojrzenia na niezależność polskiego organu antymonopolowego w świetle dyrektywy ECN+*, iKAR 2019, no. 6, 35.

2.3 Personal Requirements

The Competition Act sets out formal eligibility criteria for appointment to the position of President of the OCCP. A candidate must:

i. hold a master's degree or equivalent qualification;
ii. be a Polish citizen;
iii. enjoy full public rights;
iv. have no criminal conviction for an intentional offence or an intentional fiscal offence;
v. possess managerial skills;
vi. have at least six years of professional experience, including three in a managerial role;
vii. possess education and knowledge relevant to matters within the OCCP's competence; and
viii. not have served, worked, or collaborated with the communist-era state security authorities.

The master's degree requirement is consistent with expectations for the head of a specialised central authority. Approximately half of the OCCP Presidents have strong academic profiles. The first two – Professor Anna Fornalczyk and Professor Andrzej Sopoćko – were economists; Cezary Banasiński and Małgorzata Krasnodębska-Tomkiel held doctoral degrees in law. By contrast, the current President, Tomasz Chróstny, completed doctoral studies but did not obtain the degree. His repeated public emphasis on this fact, despite limited professional achievements, has been interpreted as signalling a lack of substantive qualifications and has been criticised in scholarly literature.[19]

Polish citizenship is a standard and uncontroversial requirement for public office, and dual citizenship is not prohibited.

The requirement that the candidate 'enjoy full public rights' means there are no penal measures that deprive an individual of voting rights, eligibility for public office, the right to hold state honours, or participation in the administration of justice. Such deprivation is reserved for offences warranting significant moral censure.

A candidate must not have been convicted of an intentional criminal or fiscal offence; unintentional offences or misdemeanours do not constitute grounds for exclusion.

The statutory requirement of 'managerial skills' is vague and grants the appointing authority wide discretion. Given that the OCCP employs roughly

19 J. Menkes, *Sped-Pro S.A. przeciwko Komisji Europejskiej–studium przypadku i jego kontekst*, PPP 2023, no. 4, 53.

600 staff, managerial competence is undeniably essential, yet its assessment is almost entirely subjective.

The condition of six years of professional experience, including three in a managerial position, is verifiable but its application remains ambiguous. The Act does not define what constitutes a 'managerial position', leaving room for flexible, potentially inconsistent interpretations.

Similarly, the requirement that the candidate possess 'education and knowledge' relevant to the OCCP's fields of competence is drafted in deliberately broad terms. When the Competition Act was first adopted, the law required that the candidate preferably hold a degree in law, economics, or management and 'stand out in terms of theoretical knowledge and experience in market economy and competition and consumer protection'. Remarkably, this qualitative requirement was removed in an amendment adopted only three months later. The change was widely viewed as lowering the threshold for appointment and enabling the selection of candidates lacking specialised expertise.[20]

Despite this relaxation, seven of the eight individuals who have led the agency held degrees in law or economics. The exception was Adam Jasser, whose background in journalism sparked significant controversy over compliance with statutory qualification requirements.[21] Nonetheless, he remained in office until dismissed by the next Prime Minister. Because judicial review of such appointments is excluded, the courts have consistently held that any irregularities in the appointment process do not invalidate the OCCP's subsequent administrative actions.[22]

The Prime Minister's Chancellery, which conducted a quasi-competitive selection process for the OCCP presidency, sought to raise qualification standards by imposing additional non-statutory criteria. The legality of these requirements is doubtful, particularly after the formal strengthening of the OCCP President's independence following the transposition of the ECN+ Directive. Nonetheless, the requirements sought to set modestly higher expectations.

In 2014, the selection announcement required additional competencies, including experience in managing complex organisations, knowledge of state economic policy, public- and private-sector managerial experience, and English-language proficiency sufficient for international representation. The selected candidate met these requirements.

20 J. Menkes, 53.

21 M. Martyniszyn, M. Bernatt, 12.

22 Fn 16 and 17.

In the 2016 procedure, only three of these additional requirements remained. Even these proved too demanding: the candidate ultimately appointed – Marek Niechciał – was selected only after 'knowledge of state economic policy' was removed.[23] The current President, Tomasz Chróstny, similarly met only the reduced 2019 requirements.[24] Paradoxically, the criteria for deputy presidents – who share the same statutory requirements as the president – were significantly higher in the 2023 competition, including mandatory expertise in EU competition and consumer law, experience in public administration, and a defined set of analytical and communication competencies.[25] These requirements were plainly unlawful, as they lacked a statutory basis and were not derived from the ECN+ Directive.

The arbitrary inflation and reduction of qualification criteria across successive competitions reveal the highly discretionary – and at times politically tailored – nature of the appointment process. The absurd result is that deputy presidents have been selected under more stringent qualification criteria than the president himself. In this context, it is less surprising that OCCP directors may be expected to possess lower substantive competence than regular case handlers, a structural inconsistency explored later in this chapter.[26]

Finally, the 2023 amendment introduced an additional negative requirement, prohibiting the appointment of anyone who was involved with communist-era state security authorities (Article 29(3a)(8)). Although symbolically significant, this criterion is practically irrelevant today, given that more than three decades have passed since the fall of the communist regime.

In sum, the statutory personal requirements for the OCCP presidency are neither controversial nor demanding. They establish only minimal eligibility thresholds, leaving substantial room for subjective assessment and political discretion. The recurring problem is not the text of the law but its implementation: the wide interpretive leeway afforded to the Prime Minister, coupled with the use of quasi-competitive procedures, has facilitated the appointment of individuals whose suitability remains unverifiable.

---

23 *UOKiK ma wreszcie prezesa*, https://tvn24.pl/biznes/pieniadze/premier-beata-szydlo-powolala-marka-niechciala-na-szefa-uokik-ra643220-ls4472296.

24 Ogłoszenie o naborze na stanowisko Prezesa Urzędu Ochrony Konkurencji i Konsumentów, https://uokik.gov.pl/download/14647.

25 Ogłoszenie o naborze na stanowisko Wiceprezesa Urzędu Ochrony Konkurencji i Konsumentów, https://www.gov.pl/attachment/8694f71d-99a6-4346-8a58-2ffd4c18908e.

26 Refer to Section 8.4.

3 Regulation of the OCCP Independence

Independence is central to the institutional design of modern competition law enforcement. The independence of NCAs was a key issue and primary objective underpinning the adoption of the ECN+ Directive. Likewise, numerous international organisations and fora – such as the OECD,[27] UNCTAD,[28] and the ICN[29] – emphasise independence as a fundamental prerequisite for establishing an effective and credible competition administration.

The topic also continues to provoke vigorous debate in academic and policy circles.[30] On the one hand, calls for independence are often used to critique politically driven arrangements deemed detrimental to impartial enforcement.[31] On the other hand, it has been argued that the contemporary emphasis on independence has evolved into a form of administrative orthodoxy – an 'obsession' that risks detaching competition authorities from their original policy objectives and democratic accountability.[32]

Given the normative importance and doctrinal complexity of independence, this issue warrants separate and detailed consideration.

3.1 Personal Independence

The implementation of the ECN+ Directive substantially altered and strengthened the legal position of the OCCP President. The 2023 amendment to the

---

27 *Independence of competition authorities. From designs to practices,* https://www.oecd.org/en/publications/independence-of-competition-authorities-from-design-to-practice_ea9749e1-en.html.

28 Model Law on Competition – Revised chapter IX. TD/B/C.I/CLP/L.2, 2010, 10.

29 *An Assessment of Institutional Machinery. Methods Used in Competition Agencies and What Worked for Them,* https://www.internationalcompetitionnetwork.org/wp-content/uploads/2018/09/AEWG_CPIInstitutionalMachinery2007.pdf.

30 From Polish literature on the topic, the following examples may be cited: M. Banasik, *Administracyjnoprawne formy działań regulacyjnych niezależnych organów administracji publicznej,* Warsaw 2019, K. Rokita, *Niezależność krajowych organów regulacyjnych oraz krajowych organów konkurencji w świetle prawa Unii europejskiej,* Wrocław 2017, W. Hoff, *Prawny model organu regulacyjnego sektorowej,* Warsaw 2008, or M. Przybylska, *Pozycja ustrojowa funkcje organów regulacyjnych,* Warsaw 2012.

31 W.P.J. Wils, *Competition Authorities: Towards More Independence and Prioritisation?–The European Commission's "ECN+" Proposal for a Directive to Empower the Competition Authorities of the Member States to Be More Effective Enforcers,* Paris, Concurrences 2017, np. 4, Art. N° 84881, 73.

32 J. Gersen, *Designing Agencies. Public Choice and Public Law* [in:] D. Farber, A. O'Connell (eds.), *Research Handbook In Public Law And Public Choice,* Cheltenham 2010, 346 ff.

Competition Act introduced extensive provisions to ensure greater personal independence for the leadership of the Polish competition authority.

3.1.1 Fixed Term of Office

Under the new Article 29(3) of the Competition Act, the President of the OCCP is appointed by the Prime Minister for a five-year term. The term expires only upon the President's death or dismissal. Furthermore, the same individual may not serve more than two terms as President. Upon the expiration of a term, the incumbent continues to perform their duties until a successor is formally appointed. The rationale for this change was to 'ensure greater independence for the OCCP and enable long-term planning of competition and consumer protection policy'.[33]

This formulation introduces several important novelties, though certain interpretative doubts remain. In particular, it is unclear whether the restriction to two terms applies to two consecutive terms or to any two terms. By analogy with other Polish statutes governing fixed-term appointments, it appears that the legislature intended to impose a limit of two consecutive terms, even though the provision does not expressly state this.

3.1.2 Closed List of Dismissal Grounds

The 2023 amendment also introduced a closed and exhaustive list of grounds that may justify the premature dismissal of the President of the OCCP. Under the new Article 29(3a)(8) of the Competition Act, the Prime Minister may dismiss the president only in the following cases:

i. conviction by a final judgment for an intentional criminal or fiscal offence;
ii. deprivation of public rights;
iii. resignation;
iv. loss of Polish citizenship;
v. a medical condition or other obstacle permanently preventing the performance of duties, confirmed by a medical practitioner;
vi. violation of prohibitions specified in the Act on Restrictions on Conducting Business Activities by Persons Holding Public Functions (of 21 August 1997);

33 Explanatory memorandum to the draft act amending the Act on Competition and Consumer Protection and certain other acts, Parliamentary Print No. 2990, 31.01.2023, 17.

vii. violation of the prohibition on holding incompatible employment (other than academic posts) or engaging in other gainful activities;
viii. submission of a false lustration declaration, confirmed by a final court decision.[34]

Although limited, this list largely reflects international practice and is broadly consistent with earlier Polish legislation, particularly the 2000 Competition Act. The accompanying Article 29(4a) reiterates that the term of office ends only upon death or dismissal, thereby reinforcing the OCCP President's stability and security of tenure.

3.1.3 Guarantees of Personal and Jurisdictional Independence

Of particular importance are the provisions introduced by the newly inserted Article 34a(1) of the Competition Act, which establish explicit guarantees of personal and jurisdictional independence. Pursuant to this provision, the president, vice-presidents, and employees of the OCCP:

i. exercise their powers and perform their duties independently of political or other external influences;
ii. may neither seek nor accept instructions from any government authority or from public or private entities in the performance of their duties;
iii. are required to refrain from any actions that could give rise to a conflict of interest.

This provision marks a major normative breakthrough in Polish competition law. It formally removes the Prime Minister's authority to issue guidelines or instructions to the OCCP and clearly bans any external interference. Additionally, it introduces a general duty of integrity and impartiality for all members of the authority, including rules addressing potential conflicts of interest.

However, the introduction of these guarantees exposes a surprising and difficult-to-justify legislative omission: the lack of any prohibition on political party membership for the OCCP President. From a systemic perspective, this omission seriously undermines the credibility of the independence guarantees.[35] Unlike many other independent authorities in Europe, the Polish legal framework does not require the OCCP's leadership to be politically neutral.

---

34 The lustration declaration pertains to the disclosure of any cooperation with the security services of communist-era Poland.

35 Unfortunately, this reflects a systemic issue. A weak political culture leads to party ties influencing appointments to roles meant to be politically neutral, like the head of public television, the data protection authority, or Constitutional Tribunal judges. Often, individuals are appointed to these positions mainly because of their party connections

Historically, the politicisation of the office is evident. The first OCCP Presidents were politically active figures – some during the communist period (e.g. Andrzej Sopoćko), others during the post-1989 liberal transformation (e.g. Anna Fornalczyk, Tadeusz Aziewicz). Except for Małgorzata Krasnodębska-Tomkiel, whose entire professional career was spent within the OCCP, all subsequent Presidents were high-ranking government officials appointed directly from the political sphere (Cezary Banasiński, Adam Jasser, Marek Niechciał, Tomasz Chróstny). As noted in the doctrine, it is therefore difficult to argue that the OCCP presidency has ever been insulated from partisan influence. Even today, the combination of minimal statutory requirements and quasi-competitive selection procedures effectively guarantees the appointment of the Prime Minister's political nominee.[36]

The obligation to avoid conflicts of interest is another pillar of personal independence, yet compliance with this requirement has been uneven. In the early 1990s, doubts surrounded the alleged irregularities in compliance with the Act of 5 June 1992 on restrictions on business activities by persons performing public functions,[37] particularly regarding simultaneous public office and membership on public company management bodies.[38]

More recently, and paradoxically, following the formal strengthening of independence guarantees after the implementation of the ECN+ Directive, serious concerns have arisen about the current OCCP President. Publicly available information indicates that he accepted invitations worth several thousand euros to events organised by a foundation linked to one of the wealthiest and most influential Polish businessmen and his family, while companies within that business group were simultaneously under OCCP investigation. The OCCP defended this conduct by claiming that the president was merely 'building dialogue with business' and that such practices were 'normal'.[39] Neither the acceptance of such benefits nor the authority's justification appears convincing in light of Article 34a(1) and the basic standards of public integrity.

This situation underscores the importance of the newly introduced conflict-of-interest provisions, yet it also exposes their fundamental weakness.

rather than in spite of them, which erodes the institutional independence these roles should uphold.

36 M. Martyniszyn, M. Bernatt, 12.

37 JoL No. 56, item 274.

38 Głos Katolicki, no. 40, 13.11.1994.

39 W. Ferfecki, *Prezes UOKiK na balu u żony Rafała Brzoski. Twierdzi, że był tam tylko służbowo*, https://www.rp.pl/polityka/art42598761-prezes-uokik-na-balu-u-zony-rafala-brzoski-twierdzi-ze-byl-tam-tylko-sluzbowo .

Despite their strong declaratory character, these rules lack an effective mechanism for the President of the OCCP to enforce them. While OCCP employees are subject to disciplinary liability under civil service regulations, the president – who is not part of the civil service – is effectively shielded from disciplinary accountability. Only in extreme circumstances could a breach of Article 34a(1) constitute the criminal offence of abuse of power under Article 231 of the Criminal Code.[40]

As a result, the combination of strong irrevocability guarantees and the absence of disciplinary or administrative accountability produces a paradoxical effect. Provisions designed to safeguard independence may, in practice, leave the president unaccountable for non-criminal violations of independence and integrity standards. Because dismissal is possible only after a final criminal conviction, even serious breaches of Article 34a(1) may have no practical consequences.

This structural weakness is particularly striking given the OCCP's institutional history, which shows that the absence of clear, enforceable accountability mechanisms has repeatedly undermined both the authority's effectiveness and its legitimacy. Independence without accountability risks becoming not a safeguard of impartial enforcement but a source of systemic dysfunction.

3.2 Institutional and Jurisdictional Independence

In addition to personal guarantees for the President of the OCCP, the institutional and organisational dimensions of independence are equally significant. Although the OCCP is a monocratic authority, in practice, competition enforcement is carried out by its administrative apparatus – the Office itself. Consequently, the OCCP's institutional and organisational independence is a decisive factor in the effective and impartial exercise of its competition jurisdiction.

3.2.1 Organisational Separation

The OCCP enjoys full organisational independence within the framework of Polish public administration. Between 1987 and 1989, the functions of the antitrust authority were performed by the Minister of Finance, but since 1990, the OCCP has operated as a distinct administrative body.[41] It has its own assets, a

40 Act of 6.06.1997 – Criminal Code, JoL 2024, item 17.

41 Analysed in Chapter 2.

separate budgetary allocation, and dedicated civil service staff, enabling it to perform its statutory duties autonomously.

3.2.2 Independent Decision-Making and Jurisdictional Autonomy

The OCCP enjoys complete decision-making autonomy in exercising its administrative jurisdiction. There is no appellate or supervisory authority empowered to interfere with, modify, or annul OCCP decisions. Likewise, no public administration body in Poland may compel the OCCP to initiate proceedings, undertake specific actions, or direct the taking of evidence.

As noted earlier, under Article 34a of the Competition Act – introduced following the ECN+ Directive – neither the President of the OCCP nor any of its officials may seek or accept instructions from any public or private entity in the exercise of their powers. This ensures that decisions on competition enforcement are taken independently and exclusively within the OCCP, in accordance with both national law and EU Regulation 1/2003, which requires the independent application of Articles 101 and 102 TFEU.

3.2.3 Policy-Making Independence

Policy-making independence is more complex.[42] While competition enforcement falls entirely within the OCCP's exclusive jurisdiction, competition policy – in the broader sense – is formally determined by the Council of Ministers. This arrangement reflects the multi-sectoral nature of competition policy, which involves not only the OCCP but also other public institutions that influence market regulation and competitive conditions.

However, in practice, the OCCP plays a decisive role in shaping or stalling competition policy. It is responsible for drafting the national Competition Policy, which the government then adopts. The most recent such document was approved in 2015 but is now long forgotten.

3.2.4 Employment Policy and Civil Servants

The OCCP enjoys a relatively high degree of independence in setting its employment policy. However, this independence is subject to two categories of constraints: general legal constraints arising from public service legislation and financial constraints linked to the state budget. The first limitation does not apply to the OCCP's managerial staff, whose employment and compos-

42 Analysed in detail in Chapter 6.

ition are determined solely at the discretion of the President of the OCCP, subject only to budgetary limits.

At present, the OCCP is a large authority as evidenced by the Table 4.1. It has evolved alongside new competences.

The legal status of public officials serving in the OCCP is governed by general legislative acts applicable across the entire public administration. Employment matters within the civil service are primarily regulated by two statutes:

i. The Civil Service Act[43] and
ii. The Act on State Officials.[44]

The latter is a remnant of the communist era and, despite its anachronistic nature, remains in force – despite having originally been intended only for transitional purposes.[45]

The Civil Service Act implemented constitutional guidelines, in particular those set out in Articles 153 and 60 of the Constitution, and introduced modern principles grounded in the constitutional right of every Polish citizen to serve the state. It establishes a professional, apolitical, and merit-based system of public employment. Recruitment into the civil service is carried out through open and transparent competitions, and the results are made public. The Act defines in detail the rights and obligations of civil servants, including remuneration, leave entitlements, and disciplinary liability.

This system was designed to safeguard meritocracy and prevent employment for political or personal reasons. Consequently, a professional and politically neutral civil service enhances rather than limits the independence of the OCCP, as it supports the integrity and continuity of the authority's operations.

However, the intended reform was undermined by transitional provisions that allowed the continued application of the Act on State Officials to preserve existing employment relationships. What was meant to be a temporary measure has, in practice, become a means of circumventing the competitive recruitment system. The use of this outdated law allows appointments without open competition, transparency, or salary restrictions. Employees hired under this regime are governed primarily by individual employment contracts and are not subject to disciplinary responsibility, as they fall outside the civil service corps.[46]

---

43 Act of 21.11.2008 on civil service, JoL 2024, item 409.

44 Act of 16.09.1982 on state officials, JoL 2025, item 1459.

45 S. Płażek, *Zbyt długi żywot ustawy o pracownikach urzędów państwowych*, Studia z zakresu Prawa Pracy i Polityki Społecznej 2024, no. 4, 293.

46 W. Drobny, *O prawnych i pozaprawnych powodach odstąpienia od publicznoprawnego modelu służby cywilnej,* Studia Iuridica no. 92, 2022, 117.

TABLE 4.1 Number of OCCP employees (Source: OCCP activity reports)

Year	1990	1991	1993	1996	1997	1999	2001	2004	2005	2008	2010	2013	2015	2018	2021	2024
Employed	43	105	120	169	183	192	222	264	280	296	457	472	464	489	568	656

TABLE 4.2 Number of OCCP employees outside the civil service (Source: PI request)

Year	Non-civil service employees
2024	19
2023	14
2022	7
2021	16
2020	13
2019	2

Unfortunately, this practice has also been employed by the OCCP. Table 4.2 illustrates the scale of employment outside the civil service.

This trend demonstrates an increasing reliance on non-civil service staff, thereby weakening the transparency and merit-based character of the OCCP's human resources policy.

Employment at the OCCP is also constrained by budgetary limits, as the number of available positions is determined by the state budget's limits on salary funds. The initial number of posts is set at the authority's creation and may later be adjusted to reflect changes in workload or the expansion of the OCCP's competences. Ideally, any extension of the OCCP's powers should be accompanied by a corresponding increase in the number of civil service positions.[47] However, such adjustments are often subject to political bargaining within the government and parliament, particularly regarding the Minister of Finance's fiscal policy.

Table 4.3 illustrates the allocation of new positions corresponding to the expansion of the OCCP's powers.

Additionally, the annual Budget Act sets limits on salary funding for OCCP civil service positions. The authority may employ staff outside the civil service, provided that limits are not exhausted and there are unfilled civil service posts. The OCCP maintains a permanent number of vacancies, enabling the president to employ individuals outside the statutory civil service framework (Table 4.4).

This practice reveals a pattern of maintaining flexibility by deliberately leaving certain positions unfilled within the civil service structure.

The analysis demonstrates that the OCCP enjoys broad discretion in shaping its employment policy, particularly regarding managerial and contractual

47 M. Martyniszyn, M. Bernatt, 23–24.

TABLE 4.3 Number of OCCP employees allocated to new competences (Source: OCCP Activity Reports and PI request)

Year	New area of competence	Number of posts allocated
1990	Competition protection	106
1996	Consumer protection	24
2000	Market surveillance	10
2001	State aid monitoring	27
2017	Counteracting unfair trading practices	0
2020	Combating payment delays	109
2021	FDI screening	0

TABLE 4.4 Number of unfilled civil service positions (Source: OCCP PI request)

Year	Unfilled positions
2024	23
2023	51
2022	70
2021	70
2020	77
2019	28

staff. The constraints arising from the Civil Service Act are objective and serve to ensure professionalism and integrity in public administration. However, these safeguards are frequently circumvented through employment contracts outside the civil service framework, undermining the OCCP's transparency and accountability.

While this practice may reflect a form of de facto independence of the OCCP President, it is, in substance, a distortion of the ECN+ Directive's objectives, which aim to strengthen institutional independence in a manner consistent with good governance and merit-based recruitment.

Ultimately, the OCCP's autonomy in employment matters remains vulnerable to fiscal and political constraints, primarily stemming from the Minister of Finance's budgetary policy and parliamentary negotiations. These external factors, combined with internal circumvention of civil service standards, pose a serious challenge to the OCCP's integrity and professionalism.

3.2.5 Competence to Determine Internal Organisation

The ability to determine its internal organisation is an important aspect of the OCCP's independence. Although internal arrangements do not formally affect the administrative jurisdiction of the Polish NCA, they are crucial to its operational efficiency. Given the breadth of its competences, the capacity to design an appropriate organisational structure is essential to the OCCP's effective functioning.

The OCCP's independence in shaping its internal structure is subject to two principal limitations. First, certain elements of its internal system are prescribed directly by the Competition Act. Second, the OCCP's fundamental organisational framework is set out in its Charter, which is issued by the Prime Minister.

With respect to the first limitation, the 2019 amendment to the Competition Act substantially strengthened the OCCP's institutional autonomy.[48] Prior to this reform, Article 33 of the Act provided that the Office comprised the Headquarters in Warsaw and regional branches in Bydgoszcz, Gdańsk, Katowice, Cracow, Lublin, Łódź, Poznań, Warsaw, and Wrocław. Branch directors were authorised to issue decisions on the OCCP's behalf, while the Prime Minister retained the power to determine the branches' territorial and material jurisdiction by regulation.[49]

Since 2020, the Competition Act has provided that the Office comprises the Headquarters in Warsaw, regional branches, and laboratories supervised by the OCCP President. According to the explanatory memorandum accompanying the amending act, the objective was 'to introduce greater flexibility in the creation and allocation of tasks by the President of the Office to the local units of the Office, i.e., the regional branches'.[50]

This change was both significant and necessary, as there was no longer any justification for enshrining the specific locations of OCCP delegations in statute. Nonetheless, certain presidents of the OCCP had previously taken a liberal approach to the former provision. For example, in 2017, the then president effectively discontinued the operation of the Warsaw branch office – a step

---

48 Act of 4.07.2019 amending the Act on Competition and Consumer Protection and certain other acts, JoL 2019 item 1667.

49 Such a regulation was issued – Regulation of the President of the Council of Ministers of 1.07.2009 – on the territorial and material jurisdiction of the regional branches of the Office for Competition and Consumer Protection, JoL 2017 item 816.

50 Explanatory memorandum for the draft act amending the Act on Competition and Consumer Protection and certain other acts, Parliamentary Print No. 3542, 12.06.2019, 3–4.

that was unlawful under the Competition Act at the time but subsequently legitimised through legislative amendment. Since 2020, the number and location of the OCCP's regional offices have been determined solely by its Charter.

The process by which the OCCP's Charter is issued constitutes the second constraint on its organisational autonomy. The Charter is granted by the Prime Minister through a regulation.[51] Although the Competition Act does not expressly set out the procedure, in practice, the OCCP prepares draft statutes and any amendments, which are then submitted to the Prime Minister for approval. Formally, however, this competence rests exclusively with the Prime Minister, who is not obliged to accept the OCCP President's organisational proposals.

As regards content, the Competition Act merely requires that the Charter define the Office's organisation, tasks, and the location of its regional branches. Pursuant to paragraph 15 of the Charter, the internal organisation, detailed allocation of responsibilities, and working procedures of both the headquarters and regional offices are set out in the organisational regulations issued by the President of the Office at the request of the Director General.

3.2.6 Financing of the OCCP

The OCCP lacks genuine financial independence. Its budget is prepared under the general rules applicable to all central government administrative authorities, making it heavily dependent on decisions by the Ministry of Finance, and, ultimately, by the Council of Ministers and Parliament.

Each year, the Finance Minister collects draft revenue and expenditure estimates from ministries and other central institutions, including the OCCP. The OCCP prepares its own draft budget and submits it to the Finance Ministry. However, the Minister may modify these proposals without any obligation to consult the OCCP or provide justification. Importantly, there is no mechanism in the Polish public administration that allows individual authorities to challenge or appeal the draft state budget once it has been amended by the Finance Ministry.

After the Minister finalises the draft budget, it is submitted to the Council of Ministers for approval and then adopted by the Parliament (Sejm). In the past, there have been instances – though not directly concerning the OCCP – where the Finance Ministry significantly reduced the budgets of other public bodies, including constitutional institutions such as the media regulator or the Con-

51 Regulation No. 272 of the President of the Council of Ministers of 20.12.2019 on granting a Charter to the Office of Competition and Consumer Protection, MP 2025, item 362.

stitutional Tribunal.[52] This practice illustrates the potential vulnerability of independent institutions to political or fiscal discretion.

The OCCP does not generate or retain any revenue of its own. All financial penalties imposed by the authority, together with fees related to its proceedings – such as notification fees in merger control cases – form state budget income, not OCCP income (Articles 94(5) and 112(2)). Consequently, the OCCP's financial resources are entirely disconnected from the scale, intensity, or effectiveness of its enforcement activity.

While this rule aligns with the general model used by most regulatory and enforcement authorities in Poland, it limits the OCCP's operational autonomy. The authority's financial standing depends exclusively on allocations from the central state budget, which may vary from year to year depending on fiscal priorities, political decisions, or macroeconomic conditions (Table 4.5).

Comparable arrangements apply to other Polish regulators, such as the ERO and the OEC, which likewise lack independent revenue streams. The only notable exception is the Financial Supervision Authority.[53] Although formally included in the state budget, the FSA is financed primarily through mandatory contributions from supervised entities – banks, insurers, and investment firms – rather than general taxation. This funding model affords the financial regulator a substantially higher degree of stability and de facto autonomy than the OCCP enjoys.

The absence of independent financial resources exposes the OCCP to budgetary pressure and indirect political influence, undermining its institutional independence in practice. Although the ECN+ Directive emphasises the need for competition authorities to be adequately resourced, the Polish system pro-

TABLE 4.5 OCCP general budget (PLN million) (Source: OCCP activity reports)

Year	2001	2003	2005	2008	2010	2013	2015	2018	2021	2024
Budget	21,2	22,2	25,3	29,7	47,8	55	64,7	76,5	108	174,5

52 *Polityczny pat wokół budżetu. Chodzi o finansowanie tzw. świętych krów*, https://www.bankier.pl/wiadomosc/Polityczny-pat-wokol-budzetu-Chodzi-o-finansowanie-tzw-swietych-krow-8873585.html, or *Sejm. "Święte krowy" będą miały ścięte budżety. Na liście KRRiT i Kancelaria Prezydenta*, https://next.gazeta.pl/next/7,151003,30597528,swiete-krowy-beda-mialy-sciete-budzety-wiemy-kto-straci-najwiecej.html.

53 S. Peszkowski, *System finansowania kosztów nadzoru nad rynkiem finansowym*, Warsaw 2016.

TABLE 4.6 OCCP budget structure in 2024 (percentage allocation) (Source: OCCP PI request)

Year	Total budget	Competition protection: total	Antitrust	Merger control	Consumer protection	Payment gridlocks	State aid	UTP	EU presidency	FDI control
2024	174,5	25,1%	19,8%	5,3%	49,9%	14%	7%	3,7%	0,7%	0%

TABLE 4.7 Fines paid by competence area (PLN million) (Source: OCCP PI request)

Year	Competition protection	Consumer protection	Market surveillance	Payment gridlocks	UTP	Total
2024	7,8	121,8	1,4	4,8	0,3	136,3
2023	6,2	178,3	1,2	5,7	1,3	192,8

vides no specific safeguards against arbitrary budget reductions or structural underfunding.

As a result, the OCCP's enforcement capacity and strategic planning remain vulnerable to external fiscal decisions, revealing a persistent tension between formal guarantees of independence and the realities of budgetary dependence.

Although fines do not constitute OCCP revenue, the distribution of fines actually paid is nonetheless illustrative of enforcement priorities (Table 4.7).

These figures highlight a pronounced asymmetry between the OCCP's formal mandate and its practical enforcement priorities. Although the protection of competition lies at the core of the authority's statutory mission, consumer protection generates both the highest fiscal returns and the most visible enforcement outcomes. Within the OCCP's integrated budgetary framework, this dynamic results in a structural crowding out of competition enforcement.

Consumer protection thus offers the OCCP President a distinct 'double dividend': strong public visibility and substantial budgetary inflows. This, in turn, exposes a paradox in Polish enforcement discourse. Competition-law fines are frequently portrayed as severe, quasi-criminal sanctions requiring heightened procedural safeguards, whereas consumer-protection fines – often significantly higher in aggregate – are treated as benign and purely administrative. In practice, consumer protection, rather than competition enforcement, has become the OCCP's primary source of both publicity and revenue, shaping enforcement incentives and, ultimately, budgetary outcomes as evidenced by the Table 4.6.

4 Supervision over the OCCP

The independence of the Polish NCA does not preclude supervision; however, such oversight is limited and strictly defined by statute. Supervision concerns the legality of actions undertaken by the authority and may be exercised internally – by public administration authorities – or externally by independent or judicial entities.

4.1 Administrative Supervision: The Prime Minister and the Government

The OCCP remains subject to limited supervision by the Prime Minister, who may order audits of either the Office itself or broader governmental activity. The Prime Minister determines the scope, subject, and methodology of the inspection, and inspectors are entitled to access documents and request explanations. To date, there is no public record of individual audits of the OCCP. Available data also suggest that any control exercised under the Law on Control in Government Administration[54] remains marginal.[55]

As head of the civil service, the Prime Minister exercises general oversight of civil servants, including those employed by the OCCP, though these powers have not been used in practice and would be exceptional.

Financial supervision is exercised by the Minister of Finance. The OCCP lacks budgetary autonomy, as explained earlier. While this could theoretically influence the authority's actions, there is no evidence that the Minister uses this mechanism to exert pressure.

4.2 Supervision by the Supreme Audit Office (SAO)

Oversight is also exercised by the SAO, the state's supreme control authority reporting to Parliament. The SAO audits the legality, economy, and efficiency of the financial and administrative activities of public authorities.[56] The SAO's influence over independent authorities is limited to issuing findings or notifying competent bodies of legal infringements.

Between 2014 and 2024, the OCCP was audited 31 times, with 10 audits limited to routine budgetary scrutiny. Only one audit focused exclusively on competition protection, and another addressed it partially. The 2024 audit sparked controversy due to discrepancies between the OCCP's public communication and the SAO's official position. The OCCP President characterised the audit as a comprehensive review of the Office's operations and equated the positive findings with a form of *absolutorium*.[57] The SAO, however, explicitly rejected this interpretation, clarifying that the audit covered only selected aspects of infringement detection and that, under the Act on the Supreme

54 Act of 15.07.2011 on control in government administration, JoL 2020, item 224.

55 M. Błachucki, *Ponadnarodowe sieci organów administracji publicznej oraz ich wpływ na krajowy porządek prawny* (*na przykładzie ponadnarodowych sieci organów ochrony konkurencji*), Warsaw 2019, 556.

56 Act of 23.12.1994 on the Supreme Audit Office, JoL 2017, item 524.

57 Pozytywna ocena NIK dla UOKiK, https://uokik.gov.pl/pozytywna-ocena-nik-dla-uokik.

Audit Office, a positive assessment cannot be regarded as an *absolutorium* for the authority's overall activity.[58]

4.3 External Supervision: The Ombudsman and the Prosecutor

Both the Ombudsman and the Public Prosecutor's Office may review administrative activities, but have limited jurisdiction over the OCCP's international functions. The prosecutor may intervene in administrative proceedings under Article 182 of the Administrative Procedure Code to remedy unlawful acts. Similarly, the Ombudsman may act under Article 14(6) of the Act on the Ombudsman in cases involving violations of civil rights.

More troubling, however, is the OCCP's current practice of obstructing or significantly limiting cooperation with the Ombudsman. This became particularly evident in the politically sensitive PKN Orlen/Polska Press merger case, which raised fundamental concerns about media pluralism and the potential instrumentalisation of competition law for political purposes. In response to numerous public complaints, the Ombudsman sought to exercise oversight by reviewing case files. Despite the Ombudsman's constitutional authority to examine any criminal, civil, or administrative proceedings, the OCCP refused access, citing business confidentiality.[59]

As a result, the Ombudsman was forced to appeal the decision without access to the evidence, undermining both the effectiveness and the very purpose of this supervisory mechanism.[60] This episode reveals a dangerous precedent: an administrative authority shielding its actions from constitutional oversight by selectively invoking trade secrecy without conducting a proportionality analysis or considering partial-disclosure mechanisms.

The implications are significant. First, it severely weakens external accountability mechanisms that should serve as checks on highly independent authorities such as the OCCP. Second, it signals a shift towards an antagonistic stance towards constitutional bodies designed to protect fundamental rights and republican governance. Third, it risks normalising institutional opacity in pol-

---

58 SAO information from 12.11.2025, KRR.0141.9.2025.

59 *Prezes UOKiK nie udostępni akt sprawy zakupu Polska Press przez PKN Orlen – mimo interwencji Rzecznika. (EDIT) T. Chróstny: "To tajemnica przedsiębiorstwa"*, https://bip.brpo.gov.pl/pl/content/prezes-uokik-nie-udostepnia-rpo-akt-sprawy-zakupu-polska-press-przez-orlen.

60 *Zakup Polska Press przez PKN Orlen. Rzecznik o zagrożeniach dla wolności słowa*, https://bip.brpo.gov.pl/pl/content/rpo-o-zagrozeniach-wolnosci-prasy-po-kupnie-polska-press.

itically salient cases, thereby eroding public trust and reinforcing concerns about the politicisation of competition enforcement.

4.4 Judicial Review

Judicial control applies when OCCP actions affect the parties' rights. Such control cannot be initiated ex officio and falls within the jurisdiction of civil courts – primarily the CCCP, the Court of Appeal in Warsaw, and the Supreme Court – and administrative courts. Civil courts hear appeals against OCCP decisions, while administrative courts retain residual competence, including complaints against the OCCP's inaction.[61]

4.5 Parliamentary Supervision

Parliamentary control over administrative authorities in Poland remains underdeveloped. The Sejm exercises constitutional oversight primarily over the Council of Ministers (Article 95(2) of the Constitution) and certain central authorities whose heads it appoints. The expansion of the number of central authorities appointed by the Sejm results from the influence of European law and the need to strictly preserve the independence of certain public administration authorities.[62] Committees of the Sejm conduct inquiries, request reports, and may involve the SAO.[63] Individual deputies exercise oversight through interpellations and inquiries, though these typically concern only politically relevant matters.

Although parliamentary oversight could play an important role in compensating for the broad independence granted to authorities such as the OCCP – especially after the implementation of the ECN+ Directive – this potential remains largely unrealised. Effective scrutiny would require genuine political interest, procedural continuity, and a minimum level of substantive literacy in competition law and policy. Instead, Parliament's influence is largely indirect, exercised through its control of the budget or through amendments to the legislative framework governing the authority. It does not – and cannot – interfere with individual administrative decisions, but it could, in theory, hold the OCCP accountable for the broader strategic direction – or its absence.

61 Judicial review is discussed in Chapter 5.

62 W. Odrowąż-Sypniewski, *Funkcja kontrolna Sejmu na tle zagadnienia rozdziału władzy publicznej i zasady nadrzędności konstytucji*, Przegląd Sejmowy 2008, no. 3(86), 14–15.

63 M. Habowski, *Funkcje kontrolna i kreacyjna Sejmu w kształtowaniu polityki zagranicznej Rzeczypospolitej Polskiej w latach 1997–2004*, Warsaw 2019, 231–291.

The events of 2020 illustrate how illusory this oversight has become. In response to mounting public controversy surrounding several high-profile proceedings, members of Parliament attempted to scrutinise the OCCP's actions. Yet the authority provided minimal cooperation, refused access to essential documents, and effectively neutralised the inquiry.[64] This episode revealed two structural weaknesses: the absence of enforceable mechanisms to compel independent authorities to cooperate with parliamentary committees, and a lack of political will to insist on such cooperation. The result is an oversight framework that is constitutional in theory but hollow in practice.

4.6 Social Supervision

Citizens and civil society organisations may exercise social control over public administration primarily under the Act on Access to Public Information and, to a lesser extent, under the Administrative Procedure Code. The former guarantees public access to all official information, including the OCCP's activities. The latter allows social organisations to participate in administrative proceedings if justified by their statutory objectives and the public interest, though such participation remains rare in competition cases. Despite its potential, social oversight of administrative authorities, including the OCCP, remains underutilised, and transparency regarding the OCCP's many activities is limited.

4.7 Superficial Supervision

Supervision of the OCCP is formally multi-layered – administrative, financial, judicial, parliamentary, and social – but in practice limited. The Prime Minister and the Finance Minister exercise minimal administrative and fiscal control; the SAO and the Ombudsman have theoretical powers that are rarely exercised; judicial review remains confined to individual decisions; and parliamentary and social oversight lack effective mechanisms. Consequently, while the OCCP's independence is institutionally safeguarded, the broader supervisory system for its activities remains weak and largely declaratory.

64 *Orlen przejmuje prasę lokalną, a prezes UOKiK pod presją*, https://www.prawo.pl/biznes/orlen-przejmuje-prase-lokalna-rpo-i-poslowie-pytaja-prezesa,505321.html

5 Accountability Measures

The concept of accountability is rarely discussed in Polish literature on administrative law. The reasons for this can be found in Polish legal culture, which has long emphasised the formal rules governing public administration's liability.[65] Meanwhile, the flip side of independence is accountability, even if the OCCP focuses mainly on the former.[66] Accountability is often described as one of the key values that administrative law is intended to uphold.[67] The essence of accountability boils down to the obligation to explain and justify one's actions and encompasses a number of institutionalised mechanisms through which entities can be held accountable ex post by a forum.[68] Accountability is an obligation that can be either absolute, required by law, or voluntary, a conscious choice by the person responsible for providing information and justifying their actions (the holder of a public office), usually in order to improve their legitimacy.[69]

The accountability of OCCP has rarely been analysed in the literature and even less frequently consciously implemented by OCCP.[70] However, it is worth gathering legal instruments from general administrative law, as well as those specific to Polish competition law, which together form the basis for OCCP accountability. It is worth highlighting the accountability measures introduced by the ECN+ Directive to assess whether they align with the guarantees of OCCP independence.

5.1 Existing Measures

Polish administrative law contains regulations and institutions that create a certain degree of accountability for Polish public administration bodies, inc-

---

65 R. Kusiak-Winter, *Odpowiedzialność administracji publicznej. Struktura odpowiedzialności z perspektywy determinantów prawnych*, Wrocław 2019, 50–51.

66 M. Dębicki, A. Jaxa-Dębicka, *W poszukiwanie good governance* [w:] J. Boć, A. Chajbowicz (red.), *Nowe problemy badawcze w teorii prawa administracyjnego*, Wrocław 2009, 198.

67 P. Craig, *UK, EU and Global Administrative Law: Foundations and Challenges*, Cambridge 2015, 15.

68 M. Bovens, *Two Concepts of Accountability: Accountability as a Virtue and as a Mechanism*, 2010 West European Politics 33(5), 948.

69 M. Busuioc, M. Lodge, *The Reputational Basis of Public Accountability*, 2016 Governance 29(2), 253–255.

70 M. Kozak, *Raz*, 23, M. Błachucki, *Niezależność organów administracji publicznej na przykładzie ewolucji statusu prawnego Prezesa UOKiK*, AUWrP 2019, no. 329, 271, A. Piszcz, *Niezależność Prezesa Urzędu Ochrony Konkurencji i Konsumentów a dyrektywa Parlamentu Europejskiego i Rady (UE) 2019/1*, PUG 2022, no 10, 12.

luding the OCCP. Although these instruments were not designed to introduce accountability for administrative bodies into the Polish legal system, their nature and objectives allow them to be understood in this way.

5.1.1 General Rules on Impartiality

We can identify three groups of provisions that establish the framework for accountability of Polish public administration bodies. First, there are procedural provisions in the Administrative Procedure Code. Second, there are systemic provisions under the Civil Service Act. Third, there are provisions on the financial transparency of persons performing public functions.

Under the APC, accountability elements are in the Code's principles and provisions, excluding employees or agencies from cases. Noteworthy principles include:

i. Trust in public authorities – authority conducts proceedings that inspire trust, guided by proportionality, impartiality, and equal treatment, avoiding deviation from established practice without good reason (Article 8).
ii. Information – authorities must provide parties with adequate, comprehensive information affecting their rights and obligations, and ensure they are not harmed by ignorance of the law, offering explanations and guidance (Article 9).
iii. Criticism – authorities allow parties to assess the activities of their offices and employees (Article 14a).

The APC introduces Chapter 5: Exclusion of an employee and an authority, detailing when an employee or authority must be excluded due to conflicts of interest.[71] These conflicts may occur if the case involves the rights and obligations of the employee or the authority's president, close relatives as parties, prior involvement in a decision that was appealed, or if a party holds a position of professional superiority. There is also a clause for removing an employee if other circumstances raise doubts about impartiality. Both parties and employees can request exclusion.

The systemic provisions on the civil service also introduce accountability elements. In particular, this is reflected in the duties of civil servants. These include reliability and impartiality in the performance of assigned tasks (Article 76.1.4), a prohibition on being guided by individual or group interests, a prohibition on publicly expressing political views, and a prohibition on combining employment in the civil service with a local councillor's man-

71 B. Majchrzak, *Wyłączenie pracownika organu administracji publicznej w świetle przepisów k.p.a.*, KPP 2002. No. 4, 155.

date (Article 78). Interestingly, directors, director generals, or even the president of the OCCP, as well as regular civil servants, may be party members.[72]

The third set of rules comes from the Act on Restrictions on Business Activities by Persons Performing Public Functions. Article 7(1) states that senior government officials, civil servants, and managerial staff – such as director generals, department heads, and their deputies – may not work for entrepreneurs involved in decisions affecting them within a year of leaving their position. The Prime Minister's commission may, in justified cases, approve employment before this period ends.

5.1.2 Specific Transparency Measures

The Competition Act introduces several specific provisions to enhance transparency in the authority's activities and improve access to information on the OCCP's functioning and enforcement of competition law.

Article 31, which defines the scope of the OCCP's activities, stipulates that these include:

i. submitting periodic reports to the Council of Ministers on the implementation of government programmes concerning the development of competition and consumer policy;
ii. developing and publishing educational materials and programmes promoting knowledge of competition and consumer protection; and
iii. collecting and disseminating case law on competition and consumer protection, in particular through the publication of decisions of the OCCP on the Office's website.

The extent to which these obligations are fulfilled varies considerably. Competition policy will be discussed in a subsequent chapter,[73] but it may already be observed that the OCCP generally neither implements nor reports on competition policy, as there is effectively nothing to report. The most recent report concerns the implementation of the Competition Policy for 2008–2010, published in 2011. There is no available information on the implementation of subsequent competition policies.

The OCCP performs far better in relation to its information policy and the dissemination of materials designed to popularise knowledge of competition law. Each year, the OCCP publishes a number of master's theses, and occasionally doctoral dissertations, which have previously been recognised in its annual competition for the best student and doctoral works. These publica-

72 Refer to Section 3.1.3.

73 See Chapter 6.

tions are notably more regular and accessible than other NCAs.[74] There has been a visible decline in this regard in recent years, and the OCCP adopted a confusing policy that limits access to past publications.[75] Informational brochures are published rather infrequently.

The OCCP also effectively performs its third transparency task. This is facilitated by Article 31b of the Competition Act, which reiterates the OCCP's obligation to publish all decisions. Although this provision arguably duplicates Article 31 and is therefore redundant, it nonetheless reinforces the transparency requirement. Decisions are published, except for parts containing trade secrets, and it is indicated whether the decision is final. However, there is no procedure for agreeing on the contents of the public version of a decision with undertakings, leaving the OCCP with considerable discretion. The OCCP publishes all decisions concluding proceedings across its entire jurisdiction on its website, and it does so efficiently. At present, the list of published decisions includes all those issued since 2010.[76] The scope and regularity of this publication practice are unique not only among Polish administrative authorities but also within the European NCA network. In addition, the OCCP publishes court judgments issued following appeals against its decisions.[77]

The OCCP also issues the Official Journal of the OCCP. Until 2015, its legal basis was Article 32 of the Competition Act; it is now based on separate provisions governing the publication of legal acts by administrative authorities.[78] Whereas the journal previously contained decisions and judgments, it now primarily includes internal legal acts concerning the OCCP's functioning and organisation, as well as internal procedures.[79] It must be observed, however, that the OCCP President retains wide discretion to determine which materials are published, and no transparent criteria are established for this purpose.

Since its inception, the OCCP has issued soft law instruments, as discussed in greater detail in Chapter 2. It now has an explicit legal basis for this activity under Article 31a of the Competition Act. The preparation of such instruments is a discretionary competence of the OCCP, but it is accompanied by an absolute obligation to publish them – an approach still uncommon in Polish administrative practice.[80] Certain guidelines, following the European law model,

---

74 List of publications, https://uokik.gov.pl/publikacje .

75 The accessibility criteria are unknown.

76 Registry of decisions, https://decyzje.uokik.gov.pl/bp/dec_prez.nsf.

77 Registry of judgments, https://decyzje.uokik.gov.pl/bp/wyroki.nsf.

78 Act of 20.07.2000 on the publication of normative acts and certain other legal acts, JoL 2019, item 1461.

79 Access to official journals, https://dziennikurzedowy.uokik.gov.pl/actbymonths.

80 Registry of soft law documents, https://uokik.gov.pl/bip/wyjasnienia.

provide procedural guarantees that go beyond those in Polish law, thereby enhancing transparency in antimonopoly proceedings and decision-making. Examples include guidelines on calculating fines or communicating competition concerns. While these undoubtedly strengthen the legal position and legal certainty of undertakings, they are also, in part, legally questionable, as they regulate issues that should arguably be governed by statute.

The above analysis does not exhaust the range of information made available by the OCCP. It also maintains a register of all notified concentrations, including a description of each transaction and the case's current procedural status.[81]

5.2 Post ECN+ Directive Measures

5.2.1 Professional Impartiality Guarantees for the OCCP President

There are two sets of professional impartiality guarantees for the OCCP President. The first concerns impartiality during decision-making and policy-making. The second concerns the 'cooling-off' period after leaving the office.

The 2023 amendment introduced guarantees of the OCCP's personal impartiality, addressing both the financial and jurisdictional aspects of its authority. Impartiality in the decision-making and policy-making processes has already been discussed.[82] Under the newly added Article 29(3aa) of the Competition Act, the President and Vice-Presidents of the OCCP may not hold any other position, except for a teaching, research, or combined teaching and research position at a university, the Polish Academy of Sciences, a research institute, or any other entity engaged in scientific activities, or a lecturing position at the National School of Public Administration. Furthermore, they may not engage in any other gainful occupation that conflicts with their duties as President or Vice-President of the OCCP. This provision is typical of independent entities, as scientific activity within academic institutions is traditionally permitted for judges or other independent officials. Moreover, the provision allows for additional income, albeit in a limited and function-specific manner. This is reasonable, as the OCCP President may serve on various public bodies or State Treasury entities, which could involve additional personal income.

---

81 Registry of notified mergers, https://uokik.gov.pl/bip/koncentracje.

82 Refer to Section 5.2.

What is particularly new is Article 34a(2) of the Competition Act, which prohibits the President, Vice-Presidents, and employees of the OCCP who participated in the issuance of a decision from participating in the same case for three years after leaving office or employment with the OCCP. This is a substantial increase from one to three years, compared with the general provisions mentioned earlier. However, the prohibition is quite narrow, as it applies only to cases concluded by an administrative decision in which the person participated in its issuance. One might question how the term 'participation in issuing the decision' should be interpreted. It appears to refer to case handlers, individuals from support units who provided internal advice, and all executive personnel whose approval was necessary for procedural actions in a case ultimately closed by an administrative decision. While ethically questionable, this provision does not prohibit former employees or the OCCP President from participating in cases that have not resulted in an administrative decision, even if they concern long-term investigations.

The illusory nature of these restrictions is evident in the controversial practice of post-tenure activities among former OCCP Presidents. With the exception of Andrzej Sopoćko, Tadeusz Aziewicz, and Marek Niechciał, most former office-holders established consultancy firms or boutique law practices shortly after leaving office. These entities often employed former mid- and senior-level OCCP officials and provided advisory services on competition matters. Such career trajectories raise legitimate concerns about revolving-door dynamics, institutional capture, and the blurring of boundaries between public enforcement and private advisory roles.

5.2.2 Reporting Obligation

The 2023 amendment introduced an obligation to publish reports on the OCCP's activities. Under the new Article 31aa(1) of the Competition Act, the OCCP must submit, by 30 April each year, a report to the Prime Minister detailing its activities for the preceding year. This report must include, in particular, the following information:

i. The implementation of the OCCP's tasks and their outcomes, categorised by the various areas of activity;
ii. The names of the President and Vice Presidents of the OCCP who were in office during the relevant calendar year;
iii. The resources available to the OCCP during the relevant calendar year, along with information regarding any changes in these resources compared to previous years.

The OCCP is required to publish this report on its website. However, this provision does not introduce significant changes. Historically, the OCCP has published annual reports, all of which are available on the authority's website. The primary changes introduced by this amendment are the establishment of a clear deadline for publication (previously, reports were often released in the third or fourth quarter of the year) and possibly a more detailed report (though it is difficult to assess whether this will occur in practice, as the provisions are general and do not contain any mechanism to ensure sufficient detail in the report). This is the only provision that introduces some accountability mechanisms for the OCCP. Public reporting plays a crucial role in public administration as a fundamental tool for accountability. Furthermore, given the diminished media coverage of public administration, the obligation to publicly report on public affairs becomes even more important, serving as a primary means of direct accountability.[83]

The OCCP published such reports even without an explicit legal obligation to do so. In fact, it has published them since its inception in 1990. They used to be available in full, but now only those from the period when the current President has been working at the OCCP, i.e. since 2018, are made available. In this respect, it was an exception among other public administration bodies in Poland – currently, this reporting obligation is becoming increasingly common. Paradoxically, the provision itself narrowed the OCCP's information obligation, which previously presented a wider range of information in its annual reports than is currently required by the Competition Act.

It is impossible not to notice that annual reports are less informative. The number of photos, including those of the president of the Office, is increasing, while the content itself is decreasing. Another problem is the late publication of the reports themselves, which usually appear in the third quarter of the following year, which reduces their informational value.

Finally, it should be noted that, under separate regulations, the OCCP publishes reports, e.g., on the enforcement of the UTP Act or on counteracting payment backlogs.

83 M. Lee, *Intersectoral differences in public affairs: the duty of public reporting in public administration*, Journal of Public Affairs 2002, no. 2, 40.

5.3 Past Institutional Accountability Attempts: Advisory and Expert Bodies

In the past, the OCCP undertook various initiatives to enhance its accountability and institutional capacity by establishing advisory bodies. During the communist era, the first advisory and consultative body to the Minister of Finance was the Council for Counteracting Monopolistic Practices, established by the 1987 Act. However, the Council's significance was limited, and there is no data suggesting any visible activity of the Council.[84] Under modern antimonopoly legislation, only the Competition Act 2000 made a one-off attempt to institutionalise such a body by providing a statutory foundation for its operation. In other instances, advisory or expert bodies were created without any express legal basis and operated with varying degrees of formality.

In its early years, the OCCP made extensive use of external expertise. In 1992, the then-president of the Polish competition authority appointed several expert teams comprising OCCP officials and external specialists, mainly from academia. These included: (1) a drafting team responsible for preparing the Act on Combating Unfair Competition, which subsequently guided the bill through governmental and parliamentary stages; and (2) a number of harmonisation teams tasked with aligning Polish legal regulations concerning horizontal agreements, exclusivity clauses, licensing, mergers, state aid, and energy law with the corresponding EEC framework.[85]

In 1995, the next president also appointed a team of advisors. However, there is no available information on its objectives or outputs, and the team appears to have operated for only one year.[86]

A decade later, in March 2003, the then-president of the OCCP established the *Council for Competition and Consumer Protection*. The Council was conceived as a forum for dialogue among undertakings, non-governmental organisations, academic experts, and public institutions, with the overarching goal of promoting consumer awareness and safeguarding consumer interests. One of its primary tasks – consistent with contemporary EU policy priorities – was to support the development of sectoral codes of good market practice. The Council organised a conference in 2003, held in cooperation with the OCCP.[87]

---

84 A. Piszcz, *Organy*, 359–378.
85 Activity Report of 1992, 2–3.
86 Activity Report of 1995, 7.
87 Activity Report of 2003, 56–57.

In 2004, the Council was transformed into the *Council for Good Economic Practices*, following an amendment to the 2000 Competition Act, enacted in preparation for Poland's accession to the EU.[88] This transformation was intended to strengthen the Council's institutional position as an advisory body to the OCCP President.[89] Its composition comprised specialists in competition and consumer law, together with representatives of business and consumer organisations. As stated in the explanatory memorandum accompanying the amendment, 'the composition of the Council will reflect a combination of theoretical and practical expertise in competition and consumer protection law'.[90] The Council began its work at the end of 2004 and met twice in 2005, addressing issues of self-regulation, the interface between consumer and competition policy, and the implementation of the Unfair Commercial Practices Directive in Polish law. No information is available on its activities in 2006, which coincided with the end of the then-President's term of office.

The next advisory body was established on 9 May 2014 by Order No. 2/2014 of the President of the OCCP.[91] This Advisory Council was an internal, informal unit attached to the OCCP President. Its functions included issuing opinions on key legislative acts and draft government strategies in the areas of competition and consumer protection, recommending amendments to these documents, and fostering cooperation with external experts and academia. The OCCP noted that the Council's establishment was intended to enhance the transparency of the authority's operations.[92] The Council comprised nine members, primarily academics. However, no public record exists of its activities or achievements. It is difficult to overlook that the Council's creation coincided with attempts to strengthen the legitimacy of the then President of the OCCP, whose appointment had been criticised for failing to meet statutory educational requirements.

In January 2016, President Adam Jasser was dismissed from office, and the Council subsequently ceased to function effectively. On 24 May 2017, it was

88 Act of 16.04.2004, amending the Act on Competition and Consumer Protection and certain other acts, JoL No. 93, item 891.

89 Activity report for 2004, 181.

90 Explanatory memorandum of the draft act amending the Act on Competition and Consumer Protection and certain other acts, Parliamentary Print No. 2561, 20.02.2004, 9; Report on activities for 2005, 198–199.

91 Order No. 2/2014 of 9.05.2014. President of OCCP on the establishment of the Advisory Board to the President of the Office for Competition and Consumer Protection.

92 Activity Report of 2014, 13.

formally dissolved without public explanation.[93] Since then, no subsequent OCCP President has sought to establish a comparable advisory or expert body.

The experience of the OCCP shows that such advisory bodies can be valuable instruments for enhancing the effectiveness and legitimacy of competition authorities – provided they operate transparently and independently of the authority's decision-making functions. The European Commission's Competition Commissioner, for example, has at times convened expert panels to advise on emerging challenges, such as those posed by the digital economy.[94]

A review of the OCCP's advisory initiatives shows that their establishment and operation depended entirely on the incumbent president's initiative. Of all presidents, only the first appears to have made full use of the potential offered by expert bodies. Later efforts were sporadic and produced limited, if any, measurable results. The 2014 initiative was a commendable step towards improving accountability, but subsequent leadership did not sustain it.

Although the legal basis for such informal advisory bodies may be debatable, their existence arguably enhanced the OCCP's organisational culture and accountability by enabling limited participation by external stakeholders in policy formation. Regrettably, this practice has since been abandoned. The increase in institutional independence following the implementation of the ECN+ Directive has not been accompanied by a corresponding effort to strengthen accountability or legitimacy. In this respect, the monocratic character of the OCCP presidency continues to dominate its institutional design and operational philosophy.

6 Organisation and Resources of the OCCP

6.1 Management and Personnel of the OCCP

Although the OCCP is a monocratic authority, practical considerations require a collegial approach to management. Accordingly, the President of the OCCP is assisted by Deputy Presidents, who are responsible for specific areas of administrative jurisdiction, and by the Director General, who oversees organisational matters and the day-to-day functioning of the Office.

---

93 Order No. 12/2017 of the President of the OCCP on the abolition of the Advisory Council to the President of the Office of Competition and Consumer Protection.

94 Shaping competition policy in the era of digitisation, https://competition-policy.ec.europa.eu/about/europes-digital-future/shaping-competition-policy-era-digitisation_en.

The OCCP formally considers these positions to constitute its entire management structure. However, this interpretation is not entirely accurate. More precisely, the President, the Deputy Presidents, and the Director General together form the senior management of the OCCP. The middle management level comprises directors, deputy directors, and unit heads.

The legal position of the President of the OCCP has been analysed in the preceding section.[95] The following sections will examine the roles and functions of the remaining members of the OCCP's management.

6.2 Deputy Presidents of the OCCP

The second-highest position in the OCCP hierarchy is the Vice President of the Office. This position is similar to that of the OCCP President in terms of the legal basis for employment and the duties performed. The main difference is that the OCCP President constitutes the public administration authority, not the Vice Presidents. In the sphere of administration, only the President possesses legal personality. The Vice Presidents, as part of the Office's senior management alongside the President, act solely within the scope of the authorisations granted to them. This means they do not have statutory powers of their own but may exercise only powers delegated by the President within the limits of such authorisations. In this respect, they perform acts on behalf of and for the benefit of the President. They are subject to the President's direction and control, who may issue them official instructions and guidelines and define their specific responsibilities. As with other employees of the Office, the President may grant Vice Presidents written authorisations to handle matters on his or her behalf within a defined scope, including the issuance of decisions, rulings, and certificates.[96]

The 2023 amendment set eligibility criteria for OCCP Vice Presidents similar to those for the President, with regulations mostly mirroring. There's a debate about whether Vice Presidents should undergo a quasi-competitive process. While justified for the NCA President, it seems unnecessary for Vice Presidents, as the NCA President should freely select deputies with complementary skills to form the core decision-making group. A quasi-competition would be a formality since the President, a political appointee of the Prime Minister, likely approves Vice President appointments informally. Legally, Vice Presidents depend on the President's discretion, who alone defines their powers and acts on their behalf.

95 Refer to Section 2.

96 K. Jaroszyński [in:] T. Skoczny (ed.), Art. 30, Nb 1.

Historically, Presidents of the OCCP have always appointed two deputies: one responsible for departments dealing with competition in the broad sense and the other for consumer affairs. This arrangement persisted for more than two decades. However, between mid-2020 and November 2023, the President of the OCCP served without any Vice Presidents. In November 2023, a single Vice President was appointed. Under this structure, the President directly supervised 15 key departments and eight regional delegations, while the Vice President oversaw only three departments: market supervision, laboratories, and trade inspection.[97] This configuration marked a pronounced centralisation of authority in the President's hands and a corresponding diminution of the Vice President's functional role.

6.3 Director General

The Director General is a member of the OCCP's senior management, yet her role differs fundamentally from that of the President and Vice Presidents. One does not exercise administrative jurisdiction, including in competition enforcement. Instead, the Director General serves as the OCCP's highest-ranking civil servant and is primarily responsible for the organisation and day-to-day functioning of the Office.

Four bureaus are directly subordinate to the Director General: the Human Resources and Organisation Bureau, the Finance Bureau, the Administration Bureau, and the Information Technology and Security Bureau. Through these structures, the Director General oversees personnel management, budgetary and financial planning, administrative services, and the institution's digital and physical security.

In this capacity, the Director General acts as the principal coordinator of the OCCP's internal operations, ensuring that the organisational framework supports the effective performance of the Office's statutory functions. Although she is part of the Office's senior management, her role remains administrative rather than jurisdictional, reflecting the broader principle of separating managerial oversight from the substantive exercise of public authority.

The original legislative intention was that the office of Director General would constitute an element of institutional stability, independent of changes

---

97 Ordinance of the President of the Office for the Competition and Consumer Protection of 7.01.2025, on the division of powers within the Management of the Office for the Protection of Competition and Consumer Rights.

in government or the President of the agency.[98] Accordingly, under the former Civil Service Act,[99] Directors General of central government agencies and ministries were appointed by the Prime Minister. Even under the current Civil Service Act of 2008,[100] there remains a provision (Article 17(1)) stating that the Head of the Civil Service performs the tasks specified therein with the assistance of the directors general of the offices.

The significance of this provision has been curtailed. The Director General of the OCCP is currently appointed and dismissed directly by the President of the OCCP, at the President's sole discretion and without any statutory conditions limiting that discretion. Each of the last two Presidents, beginning in 2016, appointed and dismissed Director Generals in this manner. None of the appointees had any prior connection with the OCCP. The OCCP's attainment of formal independence following the implementation of the ECN+ Directive did not alter this position.

Consequently, within the current legal framework, the Director General can no longer be regarded as a representative of an independent and professional civil service. Instead, the office has effectively become a position of employment within the personal gift of the President of the OCCP, held by an individual who is not required to have civil service experience and who remains fully dependent on the President.

Formally, however, the office of Director General remains a key position within the OCCP's internal organisation. Under the Civil Service Act, the Director General holds exclusive responsibility for matters including the announcement of competitions, the recruitment of staff, the organisation of work, budget management, and the administration of the OCCP's internal operations. He is also charged with supervising the organisational aspects of the timely preparation of the draft budget and the implementation of the executive budget in respect of the OCCP; managing the OCCP's property, including the commissioning of services and the procurement of supplies; ensuring the proper maintenance of records of the OCCP's assets; and representing the Office.[101]

---

98 E. Ura [in:] K.W. Baran (ed.) *Ustawa o służbie cywilnej. Komentarz*, Warsaw 2021, Art. 25.

99 Act of 8.2006 on civil service, JoL 2006, item 1218.

100 Act of 21.11.2008, on civil service JoL 2024, item 409.

101 C. Banasiński, E. Piontek (eds.), Art. 34.

6.4 Directors

Department Directors play a central role in the OCCP's operations. Although the OCCP President may occasionally determine specific actions or set strategic priorities, the day-to-day operations of the Office are carried out by its departments under the leadership of their respective Directors. Department Directors (and equivalent heads of organisational units) report directly to the President of the OCCP, except for functions expressly entrusted by the Civil Service Act to the Director General. In view of the current system of appointment, it may reasonably be concluded that the autonomy of Directors is, in practice, negligible.

The heads of departments (and equivalent organisational units – bureaus[102]) occupy senior management positions comparable to that of the Director General, within the meaning of Article 52 of the Civil Service Act. Under the former Civil Service Act, such positions were intended to be filled by highly qualified professionals selected through open and competitive recruitment procedures. Since 2016, however, this principle has been abandoned. The change was introduced for explicitly political reasons: it led to the dismissal of all directors and deputy directors in government administration and enabled the newly ruling party to fill these posts with politically loyal appointees.[103] In the longer term, the objective of the reform was to dismantle the civil service as a professional public service corps and fully politicise it, particularly at the senior and middle management levels.[104] Directors are now appointed and dismissed directly by the Director General, at his sole discretion and without any statutory constraints on the exercise of that power. The same legal framework applies to deputy directors.

Formally, Directors are employed by the Director General. Nonetheless, given his subordination and practical dependence upon the President of the OCCP, it is evident that the President may, in effect, exercise decisive influence over such appointments. Prior to 2016, Directors and Deputy Directors were appointed through competitive selection processes, whereas at present

102 Bureaus are organisational units that do not conduct administrative proceedings and often have a supporting role. They are often created instead of departments. The status of departments and bureaus is identical, and they are managed by directors with the same formal status.

103 B. Springer, *Stan i perspektywy służby cywilnej po nowelizacji ustawy o służbie cywilnej w 2015 roku*, Studia Polityczne 2023, no. 4, 141.

104 A. Banaszkiewicz, *Zmiany wprowadzane w roku 2015/2016 w Ustawie z dnia 21 listopada 2008 roku o służbie cywilnej–refleksje wybrane*, Studia Administracyjne 2016, no. 8, 151.

such procedures apply only to non-executive civil servants.[105] Although the Civil Service Act, as amended in January 2016, no longer requires competitive recruitment for Director-level positions, it still permits such procedures on a voluntary basis. In practice, however, neither of the last two Presidents of the OCCP has chosen to use that option. Between 12 May 2016 and September 2025, a total of 46 Directors and 68 Deputy Directors were appointed, none of whom were selected through a public or open competition. The OCCP's acquisition of formal independence following the implementation of the ECN+ Directive did not alter this position.

6.5 Heads of Units

Heads of units constitute the middle-management level within the OCCP. Departments or bureaus may be subdivided into units, each led by a Head of unit. A Head oversees several staff members, or in some cases, a dozen or more. The appointment of a Head of unit is not mandatory – the Director may personally manage the department's internal units. It must be explicitly stated in the department's internal statute that a Head position exists. The key departments responsible for competition enforcement – the Department of Competition Protection and the Department of Concentration Control – include internal units where such positions are formally established.

These positions do not belong to the senior civil service; therefore, only civil servants may be appointed as Heads of units. Unlike directors or the Director General, a Head must demonstrate the requisite training, expertise, and experience in public administration to perform his or her duties effectively. Heads of units do not have formally appointed deputies. In their absence, their responsibilities are temporarily assigned to another departmental staff member, or the matter is referred directly to the Director or Deputy Director.

The legal status of Heads of units is only vaguely defined in the implementing regulation to the Civil Service Act.[106] Officially, the position is described as coordinating rather than managerial. However, in OCCP practice, Heads of units perform clear managerial functions and represent a genuine middle-management layer. Some Heads supervise units comparable in size to small departments. This practice reflects the President of the OCCP's broad discre-

105 This is shown by information about current and archived completed selection processes, https://archiwum.uokik.gov.pl/wyniki_naboru.php#faq5045.

106 Regulation of the President of the Council of Ministers of 29.01.2016 on the determination of civil service positions, required professional qualifications, civil service grades, multipliers for determining remuneration, and detailed rules for determining and paying other benefits to which members of the civil service are entitled, JoL 2025, item 670.

tion in shaping the Office's internal organisation, including the establishment of units and the appointment of their heads.

The appointment of a Head of unit formally falls within the competence of the Director General. Although such appointments may be made through an open competition, the established practice in the last decade has been to promote experienced career civil servants already employed within the relevant department.

6.6 Case Handlers, Civil Servants, and Other Employees of the OCCP

As previously discussed, OCCP personnel may include members of the civil service as well as employees outside the civil service employed under the Act on State Officials.[107] The civil service comprises two categories: regular and nominated. Nominated civil servants are intended to constitute the most experienced and best-qualified segment of the civil service. Any regular civil servant may be nominated, provided they meet the requisite experience criteria and pass a dedicated examination. Each year, the state budget sets the limit for such appointments. As of the end of 2024, there were 1,742 offices in Poland employing 121,559 civil servants, of whom 7,652 were nominated officials.[108]

Nominated civil servants enjoy certain additional rights – including extended leave entitlements, salary supplements, and enhanced protection against dismissal – but they are also subject to stricter obligations, such as non-standard working hours, possible transfers to other offices, and prohibitions on striking or joining political parties.

Civil servants are recruited through open competitions, whereas other employees are engaged at the President of the OCCP's discretion, often through entirely non-transparent procedures. The qualifications of candidates for civil service posts are duly verified, while those of other employees are not subject to any formal verification process. Civil servants are also subject to special disciplinary liability, whereas other employees are covered only by the general provisions of labour law.

The organisational units directly responsible for competition enforcement are composed predominantly of civil servants, which ensures the professional competence of case handlers. Paradoxically, however, the qualifications required for case-handling positions and the recruitment process itself are consid-

107 Refer to Section 3.2.4

108 Civil service in numbers, https://www.gov.pl/web/sluzbacywilna/dane-i-statystyki.

erably more demanding and rigorous than those applicable to the OCCP's senior management.[109]

Civil servants in competition-related departments of the OCCP perform a wide and complex range of tasks. Beyond their core duties in applying competition law – such as conducting administrative proceedings, preparing draft decisions, and analysing market behaviour – they are also deeply involved in shaping and implementing European competition policy. As a member of the ECN, the Polish NCA participates in the broader EU competition enforcement system, which increasingly requires not only the application but also the co-creation of European competition law. This entails substantive involvement in drafting and commenting on policy papers, legislative initiatives, and guidelines prepared at the EU level, as well as in joint investigations and case cooperation with the European Commission and other national authorities.

Doctrinal research suggests that civil servants involved in application of the EU law need a combination of technical expertise, strategic insight, and diplomatic skill.[110] However, the highly centralised, formalistic, and hierarchical management model that characterises the OCCP does little to foster these competencies. It discourages initiative, limits autonomy, and restricts the flow of ideas within the institution. As a result, civil servants – despite their expertise – often function as passive executors of decisions made at the top rather than active participants in shaping European administrative cooperation. This structural rigidity weakens the OCCP's ability to contribute meaningfully to EU-level policy debates and reduces Poland's influence within the ECN.

7 The Internal Organisation of the OCCP

The internal organisation of the OCCP has evolved in parallel with the progressive expansion of its jurisdiction. The personal preferences and administrative philosophies of successive Presidents have significantly influenced the OCCP's institutional design, as reflected in the structure and scope of its organisational units.

109 Refer to Section 6.1.

110 J. Jakubek-Lalik, *Procesy koordynacji polityki europejskiej w polskiej administracji rządowej. Studium administracyjnoprawne*, PhD thesis, Warsaw 2016, 164.

7.1 Origins and Early Development

Established in 1990, the Antimonopoly Authority – predecessor to the OCCP – was a newly created institution that had to build its organisational identity from the ground up. Reflecting the broader transformation of the Polish administrative system during the political transition, a traditional model was adopted: a single-person central authority supported by regional delegations. Initially, the Office's human resources were drawn from a small unit within the Ministry of Finance, yet within a few years, it grew into an organisation of over a hundred employees. Over time, as new competences were added, its staff expanded sixfold.

In its early phase (1990–1992), the Polish competition authority operated within a simple, flat structure composed of two departments: (1) the Antitrust Adjudication Department and (2) the Antitrust Policy Department.[111] In 1992, a more refined tripartite division was introduced, distinguishing between (1) market structure and merger control, (2) anti-competitive agreements, and (3) abuses of dominance and natural monopolies. Auxiliary units were also established, including an IT Team, a Foreign Cooperation Team (an innovative solution at the time, justified by extensive international aid and the need to align with EEC law), and a Legal Department that provided comprehensive legal support to the Office.[112]

7.2 Structural Expansion (1995–2004)

The first major reorganisation occurred in 1995, following a change in leadership. The reform reflected the growing complexity of the Polish economy and the expanding international obligations arising from cooperation with the European Union, OECD, and WTO. A sectoral model was introduced, comprising three adjudicative departments covering industrial goods, agricultural products and services, and infrastructure sectors. Supporting departments were also expanded to include the President's Office, Legal Department, Foreign Competition Department, and newly established Press and IT Teams.[113]

In 1996, the President's Office was formalised as a back-office unit, incorporating administrative, personnel, control, and financial functions. That same year, the Trade Inspection was subordinated to the OCCP, consolidating consumer policy under a single authority. The following year, a Consumer Policy

111 Activity Report of 1990, 2.

112 Activity Report 1992, 2–3.

113 Activity Report 1995, 6.

Department was created, and international cooperation structures were reorganised into the Department of European Integration and Foreign Cooperation, reflecting Poland's growing engagement with EU competition policy.[114]

7.3 Consolidation and Functional Division (2004–2024)

In 2004, the OCCP consolidated its adjudicative functions into a single Competition Protection Department, merging the previously sectoral divisions. This department became responsible for both anti-competitive practices and merger control, with shared competence between headquarters and regional delegations. In 2007, the functions were again separated, with the re-establishment of the Merger Control Department – a structure that remains in place today. The reasons for these shifts were never officially explained, though they likely reflected administrative pragmatism and internal policy preferences.

Significant organisational reforms of the OCCP were introduced under President Adam Jasser in 2015. The Office was restructured into two core divisions – competition protection and consumer protection – supported by cross-cutting departments for legal affairs, economic analysis, and communications. The reform aimed to enhance the quality and consistency of decision-making, primarily by strengthening the role of economic analysis in both antitrust and consumer matters. Within the competition department, operational and investigative units were separated from the strategic and analytical unit, reflecting a more modern enforcement model. The changes also introduced an internal evaluation system, including review committees that assess the quality of the Office's actions. This institutional innovation was intended to improve both the coherence of case law and the timeliness of proceedings, marking a shift towards evidence-based and efficiency-oriented approaches to enforcement.[115] In contrast, the Merger Control Department experienced no structural changes and continued to operate under its pre-reform framework.

A short-lived structural experiment occurred in 2020 with the establishment of the Department for Combating Bid Rigging.[116] Despite assuming responsibility for numerous antitrust proceedings, it was abolished in 2024,

114 Activity Report 1997, 4–5.
115 Activity Report 2015, 15.
116 Activity Report 2020, 8–9.

presumably due to its limited effectiveness and the negligible number of final decisions.[117]

7.4 Regional Structure and Decentralisation

Since its establishment, the OCCP has operated as a partially decentralised institution. From the outset, it was assumed that effective competition enforcement required action not only at the central level but also at the regional – and often even local – levels. Accordingly, a central headquarters was established in Warsaw, complemented by regional offices operating across the country. Importantly, the decision to create regional offices rather than independent authorities carried significant administrative consequences. In the Polish system of public administration, regional offices of central authorities function as internal organisational units of those authorities, whereas regional authorities are independent first-instance bodies, functionally subordinate to the regional representative of the government (*wojewoda*). Decisions issued by regional authorities can be appealed to a higher-level central body. The chosen model, therefore, ensured internal cohesion and enabled the President of the OCCP to manage the entire system uniformly, while retaining hierarchical control over the regional offices.

When the OCCP (then the Antimonopoly Authority) was created in 1990, six regional offices were established, with an intended target of eight, located in the main cities representing Poland's macroregions.[118] In 1992, the seventh office was created, and in 1994, the eighth. Initially, regional offices were empowered to initiate administrative proceedings at the request of parties and to conduct preventive control of structural changes in local markets. From 1994 onward, their competences were extended to include the power to initiate proceedings *ex officio* within their territorial jurisdiction. From the outset, regional offices reportedly cooperated closely with the headquarters on control activities and enforcement coordination.[119]

The final division of territorial jurisdiction was established in 1999, following the administrative reform that reduced the number of provinces from forty-nine to sixteen. The territorial and material competences of the nine regional offices of the OCCP were formally defined in the Prime Minister's Regulation of 20 January 1999 on the determination of the local and material

117 The Activity Report for 2024 does not report the existence of this department and provides no explanation for why it disappeared.

118 Activity Report 1990, 1.

119 Activity Report of 1994, 3.

jurisdiction of the delegations of the OCCP. This structure remained largely stable for over two decades. However, in 2020, the Warsaw branch was officially closed – its operations had, in practice, been suspended as early as 2018, reportedly without a clear legal basis. The OCCP offered no detailed justification, stating only that the Warsaw delegation's duties had been transferred to the headquarters' departments responsible for competition and consumer protection.[120]

The decentralised structure of the OCCP is characteristic of Poland's competition protection system. The division of tasks between the headquarters and regional offices was designed to balance efficiency with local responsiveness.[121] The headquarters focuses on cases concerning anti-competitive practices of national or cross-regional scope, as well as all merger control proceedings, which have been centralised since 2007. Regional offices, in turn, are responsible for enforcing competition and consumer protection law at local and regional markets.[122] Their work includes monitoring compliance by undertakings, conducting investigations, and initiating proceedings in matters within their territorial competence. Regional offices also handle cases referred to them by the OCCP President. The President may delegate, reassign, or take over cases at any stage, and disputes regarding competence between regional offices or between regional and central units are resolved directly by the President.[123]

This model of flexible decentralisation has proven effective in maintaining consistency in law enforcement while enabling the OCCP to address regional market issues. However, in recent years, there has been a discernible trend towards centralisation, with regional offices increasingly handling cases referred from the headquarters rather than initiating their own proceedings. As a result, the local enforcement function originally envisioned in the early 1990s has been gradually weakened, and regional offices now play a more auxiliary role in nationwide enforcement strategies.[124]

120 Activity Report of 2020, 6.

121 M. Krasnodębska-Tomkiel, *Perspektywy polityki konkurencji w Polsce–w 20. rocznicę powstania UOKiK* [in:] M. Krasnodębska-Tomkiel (ed.), *Zmiany w polityce konkurencji na przestrzeni ostatnich dwóch dekad*, Warsaw 2010, 537.

122 Ibidem.

123 C. Banasiński [in:] A. Jurkowska-Gomułka, A. Piszcz (eds.), Art. 34.

124 It's based on the evidence of the recent decisions delivered by the regional offices, which concern more national than local markets.

TABLE 4.8 OCCP units and staff (Source: OCCP PI request)

Internal unit	Number of employees
President's Bureau	15
Human Resources, Training and Organization	21
Finance	28
Administrative	23
International Cooperation	23
IT and Security	20
Consumer Signal Analysis	0
Evidence Analysis	0
Communication	21
Legal	34
Market Analysis	35
Competition Protection	46
Merger Control	17
State Aid Monitoring	33
Contractual Advantage	6
Protection of Collective Consumer Interests	54
Market Supervision	33
Trade Inspection	21
Laboratories	52
Analysis Development	15
Proceedings in Payment Backlog Cases	39
Support for Proceedings in Payment Backlog Cases	15
Bydgoszcz branch	15
Gdańsk branch	9
Katowice branch	11
Kraków branch	10
Lublin branch	10
Łódź branch	9
Poznań branch	11
Wrocław branch	11

7.5 The Current Organisation of the OCCP

At present, the OCCP comprises its headquarters in Warsaw and eight regional offices (Bydgoszcz, Gdańsk, Katowice, Kraków, Lublin, Łódź, Poznań, and Wrocław). The headquarters comprises seven bureaus and fourteen departments.

The internal organisation, as well as the territorial and substantive jurisdiction of the OCCP's regional offices, is determined by a Prime Ministerial regulation that grants the Office its Charter.[125] Departments are subdivided into internal units according to subject-matter criteria, while the Trade Inspection Authority remains institutionally subordinate to the President of the OCCP. The detailed internal subdivision and the activities of these units are determined by an internal order of the President of the OCCP.[126]

The staffing structure shows that competition enforcement functions represent only a small share of the organisation's overall capacity, while support, coordination, and administrative activities account for a disproportionately large share of personnel. When staff are considered holistically, it is clear that the institutional centre of gravity lies outside core competition enforcement as evidenced in the Table 4.8.

Although the Competition Protection Department employs 46 people, this number does not place it in a dominant position within the organisation. Several units approach or exceed this level of staffing, and, taken together, support, analytical, inspection, and administrative functions substantially outweigh competition protection. This indicates that competition protection is one policy area among many, rather than the principal operational focus.

The limited role of merger control is even more pronounced. The Merger Control Department employs only 17 staff, a figure marginally higher than the President's Office (15 employees) but significantly lower than the Communications Department (21 employees) and the International Cooperation Office (23 employees). From a resource-allocation perspective, such a configuration strongly suggests that merger control does not occupy a central place in day-to-day institutional priorities.

Taken together, the staffing data support the conclusion that, under the current leadership of the OCCP, competition protection – particularly merger control – plays a comparatively limited role in practice. The prominence of the President's Office, communications, and international cooperation relative to merger control, combined with the strong expansion of support func-

---

125 See fn 53.

126 Order of the President of the OCCP of 27.12.2024 on the adoption of organisational regulations for the OCCP, JoL OCCP of 2024 item 16.

tions, demonstrates that competition enforcement capacity is not the primary beneficiary of staffing decisions. The organisation's human resources allocation, therefore, points to a strategic emphasis on coordination, visibility, and support activities rather than on strengthening core competition enforcement functions.

7.6 Units of the OCCP Responsible for Competition Enforcement

Among the departments operating at the headquarters, competition enforcement is the exclusive responsibility of the Department of Competition Protection and the Department of Merger Control, with analytical and economic support provided by the Department of Market Analyses, which performs functions typically assigned to a chief economist unit. The Department of Competition Protection handles anti-competitive practices of nationwide relevance, while regional offices deal with similar practices at the local level. Since 2007, all merger control proceedings have been centralised and remain the sole competence of the Department of Merger Control.

The Department of Competition Protection is managed by a Director, two Deputy Directors, and five Heads of Units. It comprises the following internal units:

1. Industry, Energy and Services;
2. Telecommunications, Media and Financial Services;
3. New Technologies;
4. Strategy, Analysis and Regulation;
5. Investigation Division;
6. Position for Competition Policy;
7. Position for Legal Advisor;
8. Secretariat.

The first three divisions are adjudicative and organised along sectoral lines. The New Technologies unit, the newest of the three, reflects the growing importance of digital markets and technological innovation to competition policy. The Strategy, Analysis and Regulation unit conducts preliminary assessments of complaints and notifications of potential infringements, analyses incoming information from consumers and businesses, and coordinates with sectoral regulators. The Investigation unit prepares and conducts inspections and searches in suspected violations. The independent competition policy and legal advisor positions provide horizontal support by ensuring consistency in case law, legal representation, and policy analysis. This structure ensures the department's jurisdictional self-sufficiency – it has its own units for preliminary verification, investigation, adjudication, policy evaluation, and litigation.

The Department of Merger Control operates under a streamlined structure, managed by a Director, one Deputy Director, and two Heads of Division. It comprises three internal units:

1. Industry and Trade;
2. Financial Institutions, Services and Media Division;
3. Secretariat.

This simpler structure reflects the narrower scope of the units' responsibilities compared with the broader field of anti-competitive practices. The department's units handle adjudicative tasks and administrative and legislative cooperation in merger control. However, unlike the Department of Competition Protection, it lacks dedicated analytical, policy, or legal representation units. This structural asymmetry suggests a weaker position for the Merger Control Department within the OCCP's internal hierarchy. It also reflects the relatively lower institutional priority accorded to merger control by the Office's current leadership, as indicated by resource allocation and staff size.

More on the role of the Market Analysis and Legal Departments in the next section.

8 The Decision-Making Process

The above considerations indicate that the OCCP is a monocratic and highly hierarchical authority. This is not unusual, as the Polish public administration adheres to hierarchical and single-person management.[127] Media coverage, especially of the current President, is dominated by messages about personal decision-making at the OCCP. For this reason, some believe that the OCCP President formally determines the content of all competition decisions. Case handlers, economic and legal support units, or high-level management (directors) have a subsidiary role to the President of the OCCP.[128] Although, in theory, every administrative decision is issued by the OCCP President, this is a legal fiction, and the President's actual involvement in individual decisions varies. Given that the President has ordered that he must approve every deci-

127 Collegial authorities exist in the Polish central administration, but only as an exception rather than the rule – this is the case, for example, with the financial markets regulator (the Financial Supervision Authority) or the television and radio regulator (the National Broadcasting Council). In both cases, the collegial nature of these authorities was determined primarily by political and historical factors, rather than by any justified consideration.

128 P. Podrecki, M. Mroczek, K. Menszig-Wiese, *O potrzebie zastąpienia Prezesa UOKiK kolegialnym organem ochrony konkurencji*, iKAR 2019, no. 6, 15.

sion, it is difficult to reasonably assume that each of the several hundred decisions issued solely in the area of competition enforcement is even read by him, let alone analysed. Therefore, such a simplified picture of reality overlooks many important factors, and it is worth analysing what the OCCP's decision-making process actually entails.

Statutory provisions rarely regulate the internal decision-making process, and each OCCP President may shape it freely through internal regulations (within the general limits of the Competition Act). Each president has introduced modifications, some of which have proved permanent. The internal decision-making procedure has also evolved as the OCCP's jurisdictional portfolio has expanded – although the number of cases has increased, there is still only one president. Each new category of cases has required adjustments to internal regulations, making it difficult to speak of a uniform internal decision-making process; rather, there have been many variations of a single process. Differences are noticeable even in competition protection cases – different decision-making challenges arise in antitrust, merger, infringement, or market study cases.

Pursuant to § 2 of the OCCP Charter, the president exercises authority with the assistance of vice-presidents, the Director-General, directors of the Office's delegations, and directors of organisational units. Merger cases are handled by the Department of Merger Control, whereas antitrust cases are handled by the Department of Competition Protection and, to a lesser extent, by regional offices. The directors of these units handle cases referred to them by the president or vice-president, or taken up on their own initiative, and assign them to department heads, who in turn distribute them among case handlers. As a rule, cases are handled by individual case handlers. Sometimes two, and very rarely teams, are assigned to handle a case.

In addition to the aforementioned adjudicative departments, the Market Analysis Department, the Legal Department, and the internal review committee are involved in the decision-making process.

Throughout the history of the OCCP, the Legal Department has played a key role in decision-making. In the first decade of the OCCP's operation, the Legal Department conducted antitrust proceedings, provided legal advice on complex issues, and performed comparative legal analyses. Currently, the Legal Department's main focus is legal representation and consultation on infringement decisions. For over a decade, the department has not been conducting any legal analyses, preparing summaries of case law or publications, or issuing alerts on legal changes for case handlers, as it did in the past. This means that although the first presidents of the OCCP granted the Legal Department a position similar to the Legal Service in the Commission, the department's importance is now limited and its role is purely instrumental.

The Market Analysis Department has been operating since 2003, established in the wake of the implementation of European practices and as an expression of the growing importance of economic analysis in law.[129] Initially, the Department assisted the adjudicative departments with economic analysis. Between 2005 and 2010, it was also responsible for competition enforcement (antitrust and mergers) in financial markets. Its role grew significantly in 2015, when the then-President referred to it as the Chief Economist Unit, and the director was often treated as an informal member of the OCCP top management.[130] This practice had no legal basis, but it reflected the will of the then-President. Currently, the Department's status is based solely on regulations, yet its role in the decision-making process is crucial. The history of this department shows how arbitrary, rather than rational, the OCCP's internal organisation can be, shaped by the President's personal preferences.

There are two key moments in the decision-making process: 1. initiation of proceedings. 2. resolution/closure of the case. In cases initiated upon request, the OCCP is bound by the entity's request, and the proceedings are initiated by operation of law. This only applies to merger control cases. Antitrust and infringement cases are initiated *ex officio*, and the OCCP has discretionary powers.[131] It is therefore worth examining these two decision-making paths separately. The internal drafting and consultation process is governed by the President of the OCCP under the internal regulations.[132]

Antitrust cases are handled by the Department of Competition Protection and its regional offices. Antitrust cases are handled by individual case handlers, sometimes in pairs, with one leading and the other assisting. All draft documents are reviewed by the unit head, the deputy director, and finally the director. In antitrust cases, the decision-making process is more lengthy, as it involves Market Analysis, the Legal Department, and consultations with the internal review committee. All major draft documents in those cases are reviewed and consulted by the Market Analysis and Legal Department, and then again by the committee. Whenever necessary, there is a parallel process of informing and consulting the EC and NCAs when EU competition rules

129 Activity Report of 2003, 9.

130 Activity Report of 2015, 1.

131 Refer to Section 6.2.1.

132 Regulation No. 7/2008 of the President of the Office of Competition and Consumer Protection of 8.05.2008 on internal rules for conducting antitrust proceedings at the Office of Competition and Consumer Protection and rules for using the 'Monopol' database.

apply. As a result, the decision-making process in antitrust cases is rather lengthy.

Since 2015, internal evaluation committees have operated within the OCCP. Initially, they played a broad role in competition enforcement, but now their scope is limited to antitrust cases. The Competition Committee includes top management of the OCCP. The Committee's tasks include assessing the legitimacy of proceedings, draft decisions, appeals, amicus curiae briefs, and press release recommendations. These are discussed after the Legal Department's opinion, with decisions made collectively or by the President in disputes. Office units must implement the Committee's recommendations.

Merger cases have a simpler decision-making process. After notification of a concentration, the director transfers the case to the relevant unit, and the head of the unit assigns it to a case handler. Cases are handled by a single person. Internal regulations require that all draft letters in the case be prepared by the case handler and approved by the unit head and the director. The Department of Market Analysis must be consulted in the event of moving to the second phase, preparing a market survey, drafting a statement of objections, and making the final decision. This consulting role is decisive. There is no effective procedure for resolving disputes during the consultation process. The most problematic issue is that the consultation is obligatory even in straightforward cases with no reportable markets. It prolongs merger proceedings by days, if not weeks. Draft acts for the second phase, SO, and all decisions are verified and accepted by the President of the OCCP. There are no exceptions to this rule. As a result, the President himself verifies more than 300 merger draft decisions each year. It is open to speculation as to the extent to which such verification is effective or whether it is merely a formal, time-consuming exercise. In merger infringement cases, in addition to the Market Analysis Department, the Legal Department consults on initiating proceedings and drafting the final decision.

Neither in regular merger cases nor in infringement-related merger proceedings is the OCCP's internal review committee currently involved. This marks a sharp departure from the practice established during President Adam Jasser's tenure, when merger cases were routinely subject to internal consultation and quality control. Subsequent presidents abandoned this mechanism, significantly diminishing institutional oversight and the internal deliberative process.

The 2018 decision to formally exclude merger cases from the evaluation committee's remit had even more serious systemic consequences. It resulted in the effective loss of access to the only comprehensive internal database – Monopol – which contained detailed information on all antitrust and merger cases spanning more than two decades.[133] Since merger cases are no longer fed into or processed through the committee system, no parallel database has been created for at least 8 years. Case handlers in the Department of Merger Control now have only fragmentary or ad hoc access to historical files.

This degradation of institutional memory is not accidental; it is the direct outcome of decisions by the last two OCCP presidents. It is difficult to identify a clearer example of wasteful mismanagement of public resources, nor one that more starkly contradicts the notion – often emphasised in international best-practice documents – that a competition authority should function as a learning organisation capable of cumulative expertise, institutional continuity, and evidence-based policy development.[134] The disappearance of an accessible record of merger precedents undermines internal consistency, weakens decision-making quality, and diminishes accountability both within and outside the institution.

OCCP's decision-making process is highly centralised and rigid. This rigidity is further reinforced by similar arrangements across other areas of OCCP enforcement. However anachronistic and dysfunctional (especially given the much larger number of decisions from the other fields within its administrative jurisdiction), the OCCP's decision-making system, as it stands, makes the President of the OCCP a central figure (or bottleneck) in Poland's enforcement competition regime. This makes the importance of this person's actual competence and actual independence all the more fundamental. In the past, it has been argued that this centralised approach allows the OCCP to achieve homogeneity and coherence in its decisions, as well as legal and economic balance. This position is naturally accurate when it refers to the consistency of the authority's actions and the substantive predictability of its decisions.[135]

However, the system is unpredictable in its duration, which is particularly frustrating in most merger cases. Such a complex decision-making system often makes it very difficult for case handlers to manage cases. Their independence and ability to make procedural arrangements with the parties to the proceedings are often illusory. The consultation process often takes an extremely long time, and in the absence of an effective internal dispute reso-

---

133 The OCCP reported in 1995 that it had begun establishing this database (1995 Activity Report, 6).

134 *The Optimal Design, Organisation and Powers of Competition Authorities, OECD Competition Policy Roundtable Background Note*, 5, http://www.oecd.org/daf/competition/the-optimaldesign-organisation-and-powers-of-competition-authorities-2023.pdf.

135 M. Krasnodębska-Tomkiel, *Procedural Fariness. OECD Working Party No. 3 on Cooperation and Enforcement 16 February 2010. Prezentacja. UOKiK*, https://www.uokik.gov.pl/aktualnosci.php?news_id=1934.

lution mechanism, this puts the departments consulting on draft documents in a privileged position. At each significant stage of the decision-making process, the need for approval by the President of the OCCP introduces significant uncertainty about timing and, to some extent, substance. Such a complex internal decision-making system blurs responsibility for a case's outcome, which is not conducive to effective decision-making.

Another issue concerns case management. The OCCP generally follows a traditional approach, with one case handler per case. For simple actions or straightforward matters, this arrangement may suffice. However, for complex antitrust or merger cases, it is inefficient. It adversely affects the execution of the investigation plan, task coordination, monitoring of correspondence, and file management. Although all these actions may be done by one person, they are likely to be more prompt and less error-prone when handled by the case team. More importantly, if the substantive side of the investigation is undertaken by the team, it may lead to a more complex assessment and simply better decisions. There are no internal guidelines for case management, and it largely depends on the initiative of departmental executives. However, it should be the president who breaks old administrative habits and adopts a new management attitude, given that he appoints directors solely at his discretion, without any public procedures, and may choose whoever suits him best.

Internal regulations governing the decision-making process, together with the absence of effective time limits for consultations, make it difficult to align internal decision-making with statutory deadlines, particularly in merger cases. It is also difficult not to notice that merger control is the lesser brother of competition enforcement. The consultation process is extremely incomprehensible: in antitrust cases involving penalties of several hundred thousand zlotys, consultations are conducted within the internal review committee, but fines of millions of zlotys for merger infringements are not consulted.

9 Legal Status of the President of the OCCP and Cooperation within the European Administrative Space

Before turning to conclusions, one further issue must be examined: the institutional position of the Polish NCA and its capacity to cooperate with the European Commission and other EU NCAs within the ECN. This question acquired particular significance following the General Court's judgment in

Sped Pro,[136] which for the first time considered whether systemic rule-of-law deficiencies in a Member State may influence the determination of the authority 'best placed' to handle a competition complaint.

In Sped Pro, the General Court annulled the Commission's decision dismissing a complaint against PKP Cargo – a state-controlled undertaking – alleging abuse of dominance in the Polish rail freight sector. The core issue was whether rule-of-law concerns in Poland prevented the Commission from relying on the OCCP as the competent authority under Regulation 1/2003. To resolve this, the Commission applied, by analogy, the two-step *LM* test developed in the context of the European Arrest Warrant (Case C-216/18 PPU).[137] That test requires, first, the identification of systemic or generalised deficiencies affecting judicial independence in the Member State concerned, and, second, an assessment of whether, in the specific case, there is a real risk of a breach of the right to a fair trial. The General Court accepted that, although the EAW mechanism and competition enforcement differ in nature, the underlying logic of safeguarding fundamental rights could justify the analogical application of *LM* to determine whether a complaint should be handled by the Commission or directed to a national authority.

Nevertheless, the Court found that the Commission had failed to conduct a thorough examination of several pieces of circumstantial evidence presented by the complainant. These included the state's control over PKP Cargo, the OCCP President's dependence on the executive, the involvement of PKP Cargo's parent company in organisations advocating controversial judicial reforms, the OCCP's allegedly lenient enforcement history vis-à-vis PKP Cargo, interventions by the Prosecutor General in OCCP proceedings, and allegations concerning the lack of independence of the courts competent to review OCCP decisions. Crucially, the General Court did not conclude that the OCCP lacked independence; instead, it criticised the Commission for failing to adequately assess the matter.[138]

The *Sped Pro* judgment predates the 2023 amendments to the Polish ECN+ Directive, which introduced formal guarantees of the OCCP President's independence. Several caveats must be emphasised. The appointment procedure was not reformed, so the President in office – appointed under a system lacking objective selection criteria – automatically acquired the new independent

136 Judgment of the General Court of 9.02.2022, T-791/19, Sped-Pro v. Commission, EU:T:2022:67.

137 ECLI:EU:C:2018:586.

138 M. Woźniak-Cichuta, *Badanie przez sądy krajowe niezależności organu ochrony konkurencji–uwagi na tle wyroku Sądu z 9.02.2022 r., T-791/19, Sped-Pro przeciwko Komisji Europejskiej*, EPS 2022, no. 12, 39.

status. Formal guarantees, however, do not produce actual independence; genuine independence depends on political culture, institutional practice, and the personal integrity of officeholders rather than on legal provisions alone. Moreover, the OCCP President's earlier grant and subsequent withdrawal of independent status demonstrate that legal classifications are fragile and reversible.

From the perspective of the *Sped Pro* test, the 2023 amendment may appear decisive. In substantive terms, however, it brings little change to the way the OCCP operates or to the processes through which its president is selected and supervised. The judgment thus highlights a structural tension in EU administrative law: the tendency to conflate formal guarantees with actual independence. Although the ECN+ Directive codifies minimum institutional safeguards for NCAs, these safeguards cannot address deeply embedded issues of political culture, informal pressures, or deficiencies arising from the mode of appointment. Paradoxically, Sped Pro accentuates this tension. If independence is formally assessed, Poland now fully complies with ECN+ requirements. If independence is assessed substantively, the ECN+ framework is insufficient. This raises a broader constitutional question: whether EU administrative law should treat independence as a formal legal status or a sociopolitical reality. The General Court declined to address this issue directly, leaving the enforcement community in uncertainty.

Some commentators have argued that *Sped Pro* obliges EU NCAs and the Commission to verify the independence of partner authorities whenever cooperation occurs.[139] This interpretation is difficult to reconcile with the ECN's practical functioning. It is unclear, first, at which procedural stage such verification would be required – whether at the referral stage, during evidence exchange, when inspections are conducted at another authority's request, or in the context of working groups and informal discussions.

Second, cooperation within the ECN does not occur at the level of NCA presidents. The Court's reasoning would require case handlers, administrative units coordinating referrals, and Commission case teams to assess potential rule-of-law deficiencies when deciding whether to reject complaints. These actors lack both the mandate and the expertise to evaluate issues such as state capture, threats to judicial independence, or structural institutional weaknesses. Imposing such expectations effectively judicialises political asse-

139 J. Mainardi, *Co wyrok Sped-Pro oznacza dla kontroli koncentracji w Unii Europejskiej?*, EPS 2022, no. 12, 31, or P. Bogdanowicz, *O niektórych trudnościach związanych z testem LM w prawie konkurencji – uwagi na tle wyroku Sądu z 9.02.2022 r., T-791/19, Sped-Pro przeciwko Komisji Europejskiej*, EPS 2022, no. 12, 16.

ssments and transforms ordinary administrative cooperation into a form of constitutional oversight – an approach that Regulation 1/2003 does not support and that is incompatible with the ECN's practical design.

Third, according to information provided by the OCCP, neither the EU NCAs nor the Commission has ever conducted an independence assessment of the OCCP before or after the introduction of ECN+ guarantees. The OCCP continues to participate actively in the ECN, the ECA, and the merger working groups. Taken literally, therefore, the *Sped Pro* framework would impose obligations that are both unworkable and inconsistent with the established practice of EU administrative cooperation. It would also generate legal uncertainty by raising questions about the type of evidence required, the extent to which NCAs must monitor political developments in partner Member States, and whether they should evaluate each other's appointment procedures, budgetary structures, or potential exposure to political pressure. EU administrative structures are not designed to undertake such assessments, and *Sped Pro* offers no practical guidance on how to conduct them.

Although the OCCP now formally meets the ECN+ independence criteria, doubts remain about its substantive independence.[140] Yet such doubts do not automatically generate *Sped Pro*-style consequences within the ECN. If treated as binding, the *Sped Pro* test would function as a mechanism for ad hoc 'micro-sanctions', applied inconsistently across procedures and authorities. Systemic problems, however, require systemic solutions,[141] not procedural substitutes imposed on EU competition enforcement.

10 Conclusions: Towards Caesarism of the President of the OCCP

The evolution of the regime governing the OCCP shows a trajectory marked by oscillation between institutional extremes. Over time, the Office has shifted from formal independence to complete dependence, from competitive recruitment to overt political appointments, and from sectoral to horizontal internal specialisation. Its current configuration is not necessarily the result

140 M. K. Kolasiński, *Odmowa wszczęcia postępowania antymonopolowego przez Komisję Europejską po wyroku Sądu w sprawie Sped-Pro*, PPH 2023, no. 4, 13.

141 B. Grabowska-Moroz, *Naruszana praworządność i niewzruszone zaufanie–uwagi na kanwie wyroku Sądu z 9 02.2022 r., T-791/19, Sped-Pro przeciwko Komisji Europejskiej*, EPS 2022, no. 12, 22.

of deliberate institutional design by the Polish legislature; rather, it reflects the consequences of implementing the expanding OCCP portfolio, the ECN+ Directive within a broader administrative context, or, most especially, the personal preferences of presidents. As part of the central government administration, the OCCP follows a monocratic and hierarchical model typical of Polish administrative bodies. What distinguishes it from most of them is the statutory guarantees of independence – protections otherwise reserved only for specialised regulators such as telecommunications, financial, or media authorities.

Although the OCCP's legal regime was shaped by legislation, its internal organisation has largely evolved in response to its expanding competences. Throughout this process, particularly in the 1990s, the influence of foreign technical assistance and the requirements of EU accession were clearly visible. Many organisational reforms were justified by reference to the needs of integration. The decisive role of successive OCCP presidents cannot be overlooked. Many of them sought to assert their authority through organisational restructuring, the merits of which can be debated, but which were certainly easier to implement than substantive policy changes. In this respect, the current President's approach is especially illustrative.

OCCP lacks financial independence. The Polish NCA combines strict budgetary dependence with a highly fragmented and expanding mandate, without any compensatory safeguards to ensure stable or adequate funding for core competition tasks. There are no informal conventions, earmarking mechanisms, or medium-term budgetary commitments that would protect the OCCP against politically motivated or fiscally driven underfunding. This combination magnifies the structural risk: competition enforcement must compete internally for resources not only with consumer protection, but also with politically salient regulatory tasks that attract funding and visibility. In this sense, while the fiscal dependence of NCAs is a broader CEE phenomenon, the Polish model represents an extreme case. The OCCP's lack of financial autonomy, combined with its unusually broad jurisdictional portfolio, exacerbates the crowding out of competition enforcement and further weakens the practical effectiveness of the formal independence guarantees introduced by the ECN+ Directive.

Formally, the OCCP's institutional and jurisdictional independence is well established. The authority is structurally distinct, jurisdictionally autonomous, and legally shielded from direct political interference in its decision-making. However, these guarantees are not matched by commensurate transparency and accountability mechanisms. Since their introduction, neither the government nor the current OCCP President has treated the independence guarantees as instruments to strengthen the effectiveness and impartiality of the NCA. Instead, they have been understood – and openly presented – as a means of ensuring the irremovability of political appointees. The government accepted the president's proposal to refrain from establishing a legal basis for a transparent and competitive selection process, and even from organising a nominal 'competition' under the existing rules. The political appointee was simply granted a fixed five-year term, ostensibly to facilitate long-term planning of competition and consumer protection policy. In reality, neither the government nor the OCCP President has implemented the existing competition policy, developed a new one, or articulated the authority's priorities.

Particularly troubling is the OCCP's illusory accountability. Statutory oversight mechanisms are weak, and their practical implementation is even weaker. Poland's administrative system has swung from one extreme to another: it now complies with ECN+ requirements on independence, yet provides no corresponding safeguards for accountability. External control is extremely limited. The current president has, in some cases, refused access to documents requested by members of parliament and, more alarmingly, has effectively obstructed oversight by the Polish Ombudsman, the state body charged with protecting civil rights and with guaranteed full access to administrative files. The refusal was justified on the grounds of business secrets. Although the Supreme Audit Office still exercises supervisory powers, the OCCP President has misrepresented its findings, portraying partial audit results as general endorsements of his leadership.

The OCCP's institutional difficulties also stem from the fact that although the ECN+ Directive conferred on NCAs the authority to set enforcement priorities, neither the current nor the previous OCCP presidents have shown interest in exercising this authority. Neither has articulated priorities, even informally. The absence of formalised procedures for defining and publishing priorities undermines the predictability, legitimacy, and strategic coherence of the OCCP's work. Thus, while organisational and jurisdictional autonomy reflect a central purpose of the ECN+ reform, the Polish implementation exemplifies a distortion of the Directive's aims: independence without accountability, resulting in a governance model that is formally compliant yet substantively deficient.

In this context, the OCCP's current legal status may be characterised as a caricature of the ECN+ Directive. Although the 2023 amendments formally granted the President of the OCCP independence, there is little evidence that this has translated into improvements in the quality or intensity of competition enforcement. This paradox is particularly apparent when the OCCP is assessed against the independence tests developed by the EU courts. Comparative experience shows that even far-reaching institutional reforms rarely eliminate structural tensions between politics and administration, autonomy and control, centralisation and decentralisation, or market efficiency and competing public values such as security, openness, and the rule of law.[142] Granting formal independence to an authority is therefore not a panacea for systemic deficiencies in public administration or the state. Its effects are inherently uncertain and difficult to evaluate in a clear-cut manner. The recent evolution of the OCCP provides a telling illustration of these limits.

Some shortcomings are general rather than specific to the OCCP. One such systemic issue is the erosion of the Polish civil service. Because qualifications and competitive recruitment apply only to lower-level staff, while senior management positions are filled through political appointments, neither a civil service ethos nor administrative professionalism can take root. Although the OCCP President did not create this legal framework, he makes vigorous use of it. Whether such an environment can support an independent and technocratic NCA is a rhetorical question.

The OCCP's organisational evolution is shaped not only by the expansion of its competences but also by the personal preferences of its president. A telling example is the cyclical reorganisation of the Competition Protection Department: structures organised by practice type have repeatedly been replaced by sectoral divisions, only to be restored to their previous form. Most OCCP presidents begin their terms with similar reorganisations. These changes are implemented rapidly, yet the speed with which they are introduced tends to be inversely proportional to their strategic justification. Publicly, they are accompanied by rhetoric of innovation and success; failures, by contrast, disappear without explanation. The short-lived Tender Collusion Department established by the current president – announced with great fanfare and quietly dissolved after only a few years – illustrates this dynamic well.

The staffing data point to an even clearer conclusion about the declining role of antitrust enforcement, the marginal role of merger control, and the institutional emphasis on visibility-oriented functions under the current President of the OCCP. When viewed objectively, the allocation of human resources sends a strong signal about real priorities, irrespective of formal mandates. The prominence of the President's Office, the Communications Department, and

142 T. Christensen, P. Lægreid, *Regulatory Agencies. The Challenges of Balancing Agency Autonomy and Political Control*, Governance: An International Journal of Policy, Administration, and Institutions 2007, no. 3, 518.

the International Cooperation Bureau is telling. Together, these units form a staffing cluster oriented towards executive positioning, propaganda, and international exposure. Their combined weight, especially when contrasted with the modest size of merger control, suggests a deliberate emphasis on personal visibility, institutional branding, and international presence. The organisation appears structurally aligned to support the public profile and external engagement of the current president rather than to maximise enforcement capacity in technically demanding areas of competition law. This interpretation is reinforced by the broader expansion of support and process-driven departments across the organisation. Significant personnel resources are devoted to procedural handling, auxiliary support, and administrative execution, while enforcement-intensive competition tools – most notably merger control – remain thinly staffed. The cumulative effect is an institution that prioritises visibility, coordination, and managerial oversight over substantive competition enforcement. In sum, the staffing configuration provides strong empirical support for the conclusion that antitrust enforcement is in decline, while merger control is institutionally sidelined, and that under the current presidency of the OCCP, organisational resources are disproportionately aligned with personal publicity, communications, and international visibility, rather than with strengthening the core enforcement functions that define an effective competition authority.

Over the past decade, the pattern of creating and abolishing internal units has closely followed leadership changes. These organisational experiments have not improved the effectiveness of enforcement or the Office's functioning. More concerning still is the diminishing role of regional offices. From the OCCP's inception, regional offices have played a crucial role in shaping competition culture, addressing local infringements, and developing case law. The current tendency to shift nationally significant cases to regional offices while simultaneously reducing their autonomy and centralising decision-making power in the president's hands threatens to undermine the long-term effectiveness of enforcement. The consequences are already visible in the declining number of antimonopoly proceedings initiated and concluded, notwithstanding the high volume of merger cases, which results solely from turnover thresholds that have remained unchanged for nearly two decades.

Decision-making processes further illustrate the concentration of power. These processes appear designed less to ensure high-quality outcomes than to enable the president to exercise control over each significant stage of an antitrust proceeding. Although case handlers are formally responsible for investigations, their role is curtailed by continuous consultations and hierarchical interventions. Under such conditions, efficient case management is impossible, and responsibility for outcomes becomes dangerously dispersed.

In the case of the OCCP, the independence mechanism has produced a Caesarist form of competition governance. A seemingly powerful office has emerged, but it reflects not administrative strength but rather the weakness of the state and civil society.

CHAPTER 5

Courts Competent in Competition Matters

This chapter examines judicial jurisdiction in competition cases against the background of its historical evolution and the development of case law. The establishment of the Antimonopoly Office and the Antimonopoly Court in 1990 constituted an important institutional response to the profound economic transformation following the political changes of 1989. The creation of a specialised competition authority and a court designation was a natural corollary of Poland's transition to a market economy and the adoption of a public-law model of competition protection. Over time, the jurisdiction and function of the antimonopoly court evolved.

The chapter traces the sequence of these legislative and institutional changes, together with the justifications advanced by their sponsors. It identifies the principal features of the judicial system established for competition cases and highlights the difficulties arising from this distinctive regulatory framework. Finally, it provides a critical analysis of the court structure and its competence in competition matters.

1 Cartel Court (Register) 1933–1939

The Cartel Court was established in 1933. Until this year, there was no legislation in Poland that comprehensively regulated cartels.[1] The adoption of the Cartel Act of 1933 was preceded by numerous debates, and several draft laws were also introduced, providing various systemic solutions for the then antimonopoly court.[2] The function and position of the Cartel Court were significantly influenced by the Act's basic assumption that the conclusion of cartel agreements was not prohibited, but that their legality was conditional on official registration of the cartel. Cartel agreements had to be notified to the Minister of Industry and Trade, who kept a register of cartels. Should the Minister refuse, he must submit a request to the Cartel Court for annulment of the cartel agreement. The Cartel Court operated within the Supreme Court, but,

1 On the origins of antimonopoly legislation in Poland around the world, see R. Piotrowski, *Cartels and Trusts: Their Origin and Historical Development from the Economic and Legal Aspects*, London 1933.

2 It is discussed in detail by A. Podolska-Meducka, *Projekty ustawy kartelowej w Polsce międzywojennej*, CzPH 2002, no. 2.

© 2026 THE AUTHOR(S) | HTTPS://DOI.ORG/10.1163/9789004754638-006
This is an open access publication distributed under the terms of the CC 4.0 license BY-NC-ND.

despite its organisational ties, it was a separate court that adjudicated in review proceedings.[3] Pursuant to Article 6 of the Act, the court was composed of five members: three Supreme Court judges, one of whom was the chair, and two members appointed from a list of persons with special knowledge of economic relations and other qualifications required of commercial judges. It was therefore a lay court with a predominance of legal elements, modelled on the German Cartel Court.[4] The Cartel Court was a single-instance court, which ruled as a court of first instance or as an appellate court. Its rulings were final, and no appeal could be lodged against them.

The Cartel Court played a limited role in combating certain cartels in Poland during the interwar period. With the intensification of centralist tendencies in the Polish economy, its role gradually diminished, as reflected in the adoption of an amendment to the Act on 27 November 1935,[5] and then the adoption of a new Act on Cartel Agreements on 13 July 1939.[6] The pre-war model of antimonopoly jurisdiction reflected prevailing views on competition law at the time and, as such, did not influence the further development of this jurisdiction after the war.[7]

2 Communist Poland: 1945–1990

During the communist era in Poland, there was no need for specialised antimonopoly courts, as antimonopoly legislation did not exist until 1987. Under the Act of 1987, jurisdiction in antimonopoly cases was conferred upon the HAC, which was authorised to hear complaints against decisions issued by the antimonopoly authority – the Minister of Finance. Proceedings were conducted pursuant to the Act of 31 January 1980 on the Head Administrative Court and the amendment to the APC.[8] The 1987 Act itself did not introduce

3 A. Podolska, *Polska ustawa kartelowa w II Rzeczypospolitej*, CzPH 2000, no. 1–2, 173.

4 A. Podolska-Meducka, *Sąd Kartelowy w Polsce i jego orzecznictwo w latach 1933–1935*, CzPH 2001, no. 2, 86.

5 JoL No 86 item 529.

6 JoL No 63 item 418. In view of Germany's aggression against Poland and the outbreak of World War II, this law was never implemented in practice.

7 The excellent and comprehensive analysis of the phenomena of cartel registers is provided in the collective volume edited by S. Fellman and M. Shanahan, *Regulating Competition. Cartel registers in the twentieth-century world*, London 2016.

8 JoL No 8.

any substantive modifications to the rules of administrative court proceedings in competition cases.[9]

The jurisprudence of the HAC under the 1987 Act remained limited, owing both to the short period of the Act's operation and to the sparse decision-making activity of the antimonopoly authority. In its judgments, the Court most frequently addressed the absence of a legal basis empowering the competition authority to shape the content of civil law agreements, noting that the authority was limited to declaring void contractual provisions contravening the Act.[10] In addition, the Court emphasised the need to take the 1987 Act into account in the registration of cooperatives[11] and in concession proceedings.[12]

The jurisprudence of the HAC under the 1987 Act reflects the broader context of a transforming economy and the gradual adaptation of both entrepreneurs and the judiciary to the emerging discipline of antimonopoly law. In its form, however, this case law remained firmly rooted in the traditional model of administrative judicial review, without developing the distinctive features that later characterised competition law adjudication in Poland.

3 Establishment of the Antimonopoly Court in 1990

The change in Poland's political and economic system after 1989 was accompanied by a fundamental reorganisation of the model of judicial review in competition cases. The 1987 Antimonopoly Act had proven ill-suited to demonopolise the economy and introducing effective competition rules. Its limited scope and reliance on the HAC for review reflected the pre-1989 system rather than the needs of a rapidly liberalising economy. This made its amendment both urgent and inevitable.

On 5 December 1989, the government presented a draft Law on Counteracting Monopolistic Practices, together with an explanatory memorandum.[13] The draft formed part of a wider legislative package designed to lay the institu-

9 The only exception concerned proceedings in a merger control case, when the Minister of Finance filed an objection. Please refer to § 4 of the Regulation of the Council of Ministers of 23.12.1987, on the conditions and procedure for notifying the intention to merge business entities and the appeal procedure in the event of an objection by the antimonopoly authority, JoL No. 41, item 242.

10 Judgments of the HAC of 9.10.1989, II SA 935/89, of 11.01.1990, II SA 1231/89, and 31.05.1990, II SA 291/90. The Supreme Court expressed a similar opinion–Resolution of the Supreme Court of 20.09.1990, III AZP 8/90.

11 Judgment of the HAC of 5.12.1989, II SA 1169/89.

12 Judgment of the HAC of 29.01.1990, II SA 1287/89.

13 Parliamentary print No 112, 5.12.1989.

tional and legal foundations of a market economy. A significant innovation concerned the system of judicial review. Article 8 of the draft provided that decisions of the newly created Antimonopoly Authority – issued under Article 6(1) and (3) and Article 7 – could be appealed to the provincial court on grounds of illegality within two weeks of delivery. This was a radical departure from the earlier model: instead of administrative judicial review by the HAC, competition cases would now be adjudicated by ordinary civil courts.

The CPC was amended to include specific provisions on competition cases. Article 479(36) effectively empowered the provincial courts not merely to review the authority's decisions but also to act as courts of substitution, capable of issuing a binding decision on the merits of a competition case. Such a model was unusual in the Polish legal system, where judicial review of administrative action typically took the form of annulment rather than substitution.

The explanatory memorandum to the draft law emphasised that the rationale for its submission lay in the insufficient resources of the existing competition authority to counteract anti-market practices and the accelerating concentration of economic power.[14] To address these shortcomings, the draft envisaged the creation of a separate, independent central body of state administration – the Antimonopoly Authority. A reform of judicial review accompanied this institutional change. The draft proposed that the competent courts to hear challenges against decisions of the Antimonopoly Authority would be the provincial (economic) courts, with the parties being entitled to lodge an 'appeal' to such courts.[15]

The drafters explicitly acknowledged that this reform might prolong the adjudication of antimonopoly cases. However, they justified the measure by reference to the need to ensure legality and judicial oversight of the competition authority's decisions. To balance the potential delays, the draft also provided for the possibility of rendering antimonopoly decisions immediately enforceable. Courts retained the power to suspend enforcement under general principles, where necessary to prevent irreparable harm to the complainant. A new provision was expected to accelerate the proceedings, allowing the authority itself to uphold an appeal when it considered the appellant's allegations justified, thereby avoiding unnecessary litigation.[16]

14 Ibidem, 1.

15 Describing this legal remedy as an appeal may suggest that it is similar to the appeal against a decision provided for in the APC. However, this similarity is only in name, as this remedy is, in fact, a civil action. Refer to A.G. Harla, *Postępowanie sądowe w sprawach antymonopolowych*, Palestra 1991, no 5–7, 36.

16 Parliamentary print No. 112, 5.12.1989, 1–2.

According to the explanatory memorandum, the legislative model for this system drew inspiration from the CPC governing social security cases. However, unlike in social security disputes, antimonopoly cases were to be examined on their merits, with the provincial courts empowered not merely to annul administrative decisions but to substitute them with substantive rulings. Judgments of provincial courts would be subject to extraordinary review by the Supreme Court.[17]

These proposals were subsequently modified during the Sejm's legislative deliberations. In particular, Members of Parliament advocated for the establishment of a single specialised commercial court – the Antimonopoly Court – constituted as a division of the Provincial Court in Warsaw. In supporting this change, the rapporteur[18] of the Parliament committee stressed that the reform aimed to reinforce the effectiveness and authority of decisions issued by the antimonopoly authority.[19] The creation of a specialised forum exclusively dedicated to antimonopoly cases was considered essential to ensure consistency and expertise.

In justifying the new solution, the rapporteur further noted its inspiration, particularly the American model, where adjudicative functions in competition matters are reserved for courts.[20] It was argued that the proposed Polish system, whereby a central government administrative authority would adopt decisions and a specialised court with the status of a provincial court would hear appeals, was fully compatible with the principle of the rule of law. Moreover, by analogy with patent law, judgments of the Antimonopoly Court would be subject to extraordinary appeal before the Supreme Court, thereby safeguarding judicial oversight at the highest level.[21]

Parliament adopted the Act as proposed by the committees. The Act of 24 February 1990 on Counteracting Monopolistic Practices[22] provided in Article 10(1) that decisions of the Antimonopoly Office could be appealed to the Provincial Court in Warsaw – designated as the Antimonopoly Court. The Antimonopoly Court was established pursuant to Article 20 of the Act of 20 June 1985 – the Law on the Organisation of Common Courts,[23] and by the

17 Ibidem, 6.

18 The MP was Anna Dynowska.

19 Stenographic Report from the 22nd session of the Sejm of the Republic of Poland on 22–24.02.1990, 372.

20 This statement is somewhat simplistic. For example, on the American system, see W.P.J. Wils, *Principles of European Antitrust Enforcement*, Oxford 2005, 155.

21 Stenographic Report, 372–373.

22 JoL No 14, item 88.

23 JoL 1994, No. 7, item 25.

Regulation of the Minister of Justice of 13 April 1990 on the establishment of the Antimonopoly Court.[24] From an institutional perspective, therefore, the Antimonopoly Court was a common court, formally constituted as the 17th Antimonopoly Division of the Provincial Court in Warsaw. Its jurisdiction covered the examination of legal remedies against administrative acts adopted by the Antimonopoly Office.

The establishment of a dedicated Antimonopoly Court within the common courts to hear appeals against the Antimonopoly Authority's decisions was unique at the time. It constituted a clear and largely unjustified departure from the standard model of judicial review of administrative action exercised by administrative courts, introducing an atypical mechanism for reviewing administrative decisions within the common judiciary. A hybrid institutional model was thus created, combining the application of civil procedural rules with a degree of sectoral specialisation. This solution reflected the transitional legal culture of the early 1990s. Nevertheless, like many arrangements adopted during the transformation period, it became permanent, illustrating the persistence of institutional inertia and the difficulty of revisiting provisional design choices once they become embedded in the legal system.

4 Discussion of the 1990 Jurisdictional Change

When assessing the rationale for transferring jurisdiction from the administrative courts and establishing a specialised antimonopoly court within the common court system, it becomes evident that the arguments advanced were neither well-founded nor conceptually coherent. They were, to a large extent, based on a misunderstanding of the nature of administrative cases and of the very essence of administrative justice. This was particularly visible in the original draft of the act, which envisaged that an appeal to a common court could be lodged solely on the ground of illegality of the contested decision, yet the court would nevertheless issue a substantive ruling. This interpretation clearly demonstrated a lack of understanding of the differences between administrative and common courts: if the appeal was based solely on allegations of unlawfulness, the reviewing court could not logically make its own decision on the merits.

Although this obvious defect was eventually corrected during the legislative process, the official justification for the changes remained limited and vague. The claim that referral to a common court would guarantee the legality

24 JoL No 27, item 157.

of antimonopoly decisions was hardly valid, since administrative judicial review already served precisely this purpose. Likewise, the assertion that creating a separate division of the provincial court, entrusted with competition jurisdiction, would enhance the effectiveness of the Antimonopoly Authority's decisions lacked any evidentiary basis. There is no demonstrable causal link between the reviewing court's structural location and the practical effectiveness of administrative enforcement. If the goal had truly been to strengthen legality and judicial oversight, this could have been achieved within the HAC framework without depriving it of jurisdiction.

Equally unconvincing was the reference to American models. The fact that in the United States, antimonopoly jurisdiction is exercised primarily by civil and criminal courts does not demonstrate compatibility with the Polish constitutional or judicial system. In the US, courts are the principal decision-makers in antimonopoly law, whereas in Poland, the Antimonopoly Authority was intended to act as the central government decision-making body, with the courts limited to review and, in certain cases, modification. The reliance on such a foreign model – without adapting it to Polish legal realities – only underlines the superficiality of the argumentation.

The legislative history itself suggests that haste rather than careful design drove the reform. As the rapporteur of the Parliament committee candidly admitted, 'the pace is generally fast... lawyers cannot work in such chaos, and in the long run, none of us can work like this'.[25] This frank observation points to the randomness of the adopted solutions and the lack of deeper reflection at the drafting stage.

The academic literature, too, has seldom engaged with the justification for the change. Where explanations have been offered, they appear more like post hoc rationalisations than genuine motivations.[26] It has been argued, for instance, that administrative courts, acting as courts of cassation, could review only legality, whereas the common court – recast as an Antimonopoly Court – could also assess expediency.[27] Another oft-cited reason was the alleged 'missteps' in the HAC's early jurisprudence.[28] Yet these claims collapse under scru-

25 Stenographic Report, 370.

26 S. Gronowski, *Sądownictwo z zakresu ochrony konkurencji w Polsce (wybrane problemy)* [in:] C. Banasiński (ed.), *Prawo konkurencji – stan obecny oraz przewidywane kierunki zmian*, Warsaw 2006, 15.

27 See W. Modzelewski, *Nowa ustawa o przeciwdziałaniu praktykom monopolistycznym. Podstawowe zagadnienia*, Warsaw 1990, 6; S. Gronowski, *Ustawa antymonopolowa. Komentarz*, Warsaw 1996, 182 and E. Modzelewska-Wąchal, *Ustawa o ochronie konkurencji i konsumentów. Komentarz*, Warsaw 2002, 269–270.

28 W. Modzelewski, 12.

tiny. The empirical basis for such criticism was extremely thin, as the HAC had issued only a handful of judgments under the 1987 Act. Moreover, the court was still developing its case law and becoming acquainted with the novel field of competition law. To form categorical conclusions about judicial inadequacy after merely three years was premature at best and misleading at worst.

In conclusion, the 1990 change lacks any convincing justification, either in its contemporary legislative rationale or in later doctrinal accounts. The reform appears to have been the product of legislative haste, conceptual misunderstanding, and political expediency rather than of a reasoned attempt to design a coherent judicial system for competition law.

5 Legislative Changes Regarding the Jurisdiction and Procedure of the Antimonopoly Court

The Antimonopoly Act of 1990 vested the newly created Antimonopoly Court with jurisdiction to hear appeals against decisions of the Antimonopoly Authority and its regional delegations. In subsequent years, the court's competence gradually expanded to include a review of decisions issued by sectoral regulators: the energy regulator (1997 – President of the Energy Regulatory Office),[29] the rail transport regulator (2001 – President of the Office of Rail Transport),[30] the telecommunications regulator (2001 – President of the Office for Telecommunications Regulation and Post, now the President of the Office of Electronic Communications),[31] the postal regulator (2003 – President of the Office for Telecommunications Regulation and Post),[32] and finally the water regulator (2017 – Director of the Regional Water Management Board of the Polish Waters authority).[33]

29 Article 58(1) of the Act of 10.04.1997 – Energy Law, JoL No. 54, item 348.

30 Article 5(1) of the Act amending the Act on Higher Education, the Act on Higher Vocational Schools, the Act on Railway Transport and the Act on Tourist Services, as well as the Act – the Civil Procedure Code, the Act – the Law on the System of Common Courts and the Act on Departments of Government Administration – in relation to adaptation to the law of the European Union of 8.12.2000, JoL. No. 122, item 1314. It should be added here that these provisions were dead until the appointment of the President of the Railway It should be added that these provisions remained effectively dormant until the appointment of the President of the Railway Transport Office, i.e. until 1.06.2003.

31 Article 126(1) of the Act of 21.07.2000 – Telecommunications Law, JoL No. 73, item 852.

32 Art. 71 item 3 of the Act of 12.06.2003 – Postal Law, JoL No. 130, item 1188.

33 Art. 27f of the Act of 7.06.2001 on collective water supply and collective sewage disposal, JoL 2017, item 328.

Until the entry into force of the 2000 Competition Act on 1 April 2001, proceedings in both competition and regulatory cases followed the same procedural framework set out in a single chapter of the CPC. The 2000 reform amended the Code, creating four separate procedures for appeals against the administrative rulings of four distinct regulators.[34] Further expansion of the Antimonopoly Court's jurisdiction was granted. The court was entrusted with:

1. adjudicating cases declaring provisions of model contracts unlawful;[35]
2. hearing appeals in cases of practices infringing collective consumer interests;[36] and
3. reviewing decisions of the OCCP imposing fines in state aid proceedings.[37]

In state aid matters, however, the legislator failed to amend the CPC accordingly, leaving only the general indication that such cases fell within the competence of the Antimonopoly Court and were to be adjudicated under the provisions on competition cases.[38]

Originally, judgments of the Antimonopoly Court were final and unappealable, rendering the proceedings effectively single-instance. Only an extraordinary review or a cassation appeal could challenge its rulings. This framework was struck down by the Constitutional Tribunal, which held that Article 479(31) of the CPC, establishing the finality of Antimonopoly Court rulings, violated Articles 78 and 176 of the Constitution.[39] The Tribunal emphasised that proceedings before the Antimonopoly Court were first-instance proceedings and therefore subject to appeal under the principle of two-instance judicial review. Consequently, Article 479(31) lost force, and the Act of 2 July 2004 amended the CPC to provide for appeals to the Court of Appeal in Warsaw.

In 2002, the court's official name was changed to the District Court in Warsaw – Court of Competition and Consumer Protection.[40] A further significant

---

34 In 2017, the fifth separate procedure was established for the water regulator.

35 Article 19 of the Act of 2.03.2000 on the protection of certain consumer rights and liability for damage caused by a hazardous product, JoL No. 22, item 271.

36 Article 1 of the Act of 5.07.2002 amending the Act on Competition and Consumer Protection, the Civil Procedure Code and the Act on Combating Unfair Competition, JoL No. 129, item 1102.

37 Art. 48 (1) of the Act of 27.07.2002 on the conditions of admissibility and supervision of public aid for entrepreneurs, JoL No. 141, item 1177.

38 Since the adoption of this legislation, no case of this type has yet come before the Antimonopoly Courts.

39 Judgment of CT of 12.06.2002 (P 13/01), OTK-A 2002 No 4, item 42.

40 Act of 5.07.2002 amending the Act on Competition and Consumer Protection, the Act – Code of Civil Procedure and the Act on Combating Unfair Competition, JoL No. 129, item 1102.

change occurred in 2011 when the Act on the financial liability of public officials for gross violations of law amended the CPC. The amendment required the CCCP, in every case, to determine whether the decision under appeal had been issued without legal basis or in gross violation of the law. This expanded the court's supervisory role well beyond traditional appellate review, obliging it to investigate substantive and procedural legality even *ex officio*. Interestingly, this far-reaching shift was not discussed in the legislative justification, demonstrating again the often accidental nature of reforms in this area.

Subsequent changes further broadened the CCCP's competence. The 2014 amendments[41] to the Competition Act allowed the court to review complaints concerning searches, inspections, and procedural irregularities, codifying existing case law.[42] The OCCP initially proposed an even broader general clause, but the proposal was rejected. This clause would have given the CCCP jurisdiction over all OCCP decisions and actions, but it was deemed incompatible with the strictly defined scope of common court adjudication.

In contrast, the 2015 reform marked the first significant narrowing of the court's remit, transferring cases concerning abusive clauses in standard form contracts from judicial to administrative adjudication.[43] This change was particularly important for the OCCP, as the court had become severely congested with such cases. Between 2010 and 2016, more than 80% of all cases brought before the court each year concerned abusive contract clauses, with a peak in 2013, when over 41,000 such cases were filed, accounting for almost 99% of the court's caseload that year.[44] The reform thus partially rebalanced the court's previously expanding jurisdiction.

A new extension of the CCCP's competence followed in 2016, when the Act on counteracting the unfair use of contractual advantage in the trade in agri-

41 Act of 10.06.2014 amending the Act on Competition and Consumer Protection and the Act – Code of Civil Procedure JoL 2014, item 945.

42 The issue of the court's jurisdiction to consider legal remedies in relation to search activities has given rise to the question of the delimitation of the jurisdiction of criminal and civil courts. In the decisions of the District Court in Warsaw of 28.09.2011, in cases II Kp 1711/11, 1712/11, 1713/11 and 1714/11, as well as the decision of the CCCP of 6.10.2011, XVII Amz 44/1 l/A, judicial jurisprudence has unanimously held that Article 236 of the Code of Criminal Procedure is inapplicable to antimonopoly proceedings, that criminal courts have no jurisdiction in these cases, and that civil courts have exclusive jurisdiction in this respect.

43 Article 2 of the Act of 5.08.2015 amending the Act on Competition and Consumer Protection and certain other acts, JoL 2015, item 1634.

44 M. Martyniszyn, M. Bernatt, 50.

cultural and food products conferred on the court jurisdiction to review OCCP decisions adopted under that statute.[45]

The most likely development reflects the proposed Polish implementation of the EU Artificial Intelligence Act (Regulation 2024/1869).[46] The government's October 2024 draft law designates the CCCP as the competent court for AI-related cases.[47] Yet the justification fails to explain why this court, already burdened with a wide and diverse docket, should be the appropriate forum for such novel and technically complex matters. This lack of reasoning perpetuates the long-standing tradition of expanding the CCCP's jurisdiction ad hoc, without regard for coherence, functionality, or judicial specialisation.[48]

At present, only a small minority of cases – approximately 20% – brought before the CCCP concern appeals against decisions and orders issued by the OCCP, and less than half of these relate to competition enforcement. The statistical data, therefore, demonstrate that the overwhelming majority of cases heard by the CCCP now concern regulatory matters and consumer protection. Because of the progressive expansion of the OCCP's jurisdiction, the CCCP has effectively developed from an antimonopoly court into a generalist court, whose docket is no longer centred on competition law but on public economic law (Table 5.1).

6 The Court of Competition and Consumer Protection: Jurisdiction Fragmentary by Design

The jurisdiction of the CCCP expanded as it absorbed more appeals from sectoral regulators. Yet from the outset, it remained fragmented: the CCCP did not oversee all OCCP decisions, nor did it exercise full control over regulatory authorities. This reveals a systemic inconsistency and a visible randomness in

45 Act of 15.12.2016 on counteracting unfair use of contractual advantage in trade in agricultural and food products, JoL 2017, item 67.

46 Regulation (EU) 2024/1689 of the European Parliament and of the Council of 13.06.2024, on the establishment of harmonized rules on artificial intelligence and amending Regulations (EC) No. 300/2008, (EU) No 167/2013, (EU) No 168/2013, (EU) 2018/858, (EU) 2018/1139 and (EU) 2019/2144 and Directives 2014/90/EU, (EU) 2016/797 and (EU) 2020/1828 (Act on Artificial Intelligence), OJ EU L of 12.07.2024.

47 Act of ... 2024 on artificial intelligence systems, Draft of 15.10.2024, UC71.

48 M. Błachucki, *Sąd*, 412–439.

TABLE 5.1 CCCP statistics (appeals + complaints) (Source: CCCP reports)

Year	Cases (total)	OCCP (competition and consumers)	Consumers (contract clauses)[a]	UTP	Energy	Telecommunications	Railways	Water and sewage
2024	814	118 + 99		4	325	34	6	113+1
2023	706	99+131		1	280	26	10	25+5
2022	640	85+97			240	52	37	22+2
2021	627	85+34	4		279	59	7	97+7
2020	1 103	94+24	1		327	127	4	175+294
2019	766	42+37	4		349	237	8	29
2018	843	52+64	10		432	173+1	9	3+1
2017	938	56+19	269		380	42+1	22	
2016	2 327	69+30	1 859		186	60+1	22	
2015	2 409	73+34	1 968		193	62+5	15	

a Until 2016 anyone could file for declaration of abusive character of the contract clause and decision of the OCCP was necessary.

the solutions adopted for judicial protection, undermining coherence and predictability in the review system.

The second chapter outlined the wide scope of the OCCP's competences. Judicial control over its decisions is divided between two judicial tracks. In four core areas – competition protection, consumer protection, contractual advantage in the food sector, and state aid[49] – OCCP decisions fall under the jurisdiction of the CCCP. In other fields, such as market surveillance, payment backlogs, and, until recently, foreign investment control, jurisdiction lies with the administrative courts.

This dualism is even more evident with regulatory authorities for telecommunications, railways, and the water and sewage market. For these authorities, the default jurisdiction of administrative courts has been retained as the rule,[50] with the CCCP competent only for certain enumerated decisions.[51]

An analysis of the narrative memoranda to the relevant statutes reveals no logical justification for such a differentiated approach to judicial jurisdiction, whether regarding the OCCP or sectoral regulators. This supports the conclusion that the CCCP's jurisdiction is fragmentary by design. There is no internal logic in this fragmentation. The ill-considered legislative practice of the Polish Parliament exacerbates the selectivity of the CCCP's jurisdiction.

7 The Role of the CCCP in Light of Recent Supreme Court Case Law

According to part of the legal doctrine, the legislator's intention in transferring competition jurisdiction to the CCCP was to entrust appeals against administrative decisions to a court that would examine them on the merits as a first-instance court, rather than merely review the legality of the authority's deci-

49 However, the OCCP never issued any decision regarding state aid proceedings, and therefore no case in this area was ever referred to the CCCP.

50 Act of 30.08.2002 – Law on proceedings before administrative courts, JoL 2023, item 1634.

51 See Electronic Communications Office–Article 12(3) of the Act of 23.11.2012 – Postal Law, JoL 2023, item 1640, and Article 206(2aa) of the Act of 16.07.2004 – Telecommunications Law, JoL 2022, item 1648; Railways Transport Office – Articles 13b and 13c of the Act of 28.03.2003, on rail transport, JoL 2023, item 1786; State Water Management Authority Polish Waters: Art. 27f(1) of the Act of 7.06.2001, on collective water supply and collective sewage disposal, JoL 2023, item 537.

sion in the manner typical of cassation or administrative court proceedings.[52] In line with this rationale, the CCCP was not to limit itself to assessing procedural errors committed by the OCCP, but to adjudicate the case anew, disregarding purely procedural objections raised in the appeal.

This approach was confirmed in one of the first Supreme Court rulings, which held that filing an appeal against a decision of the competition authority initiates first-instance proceedings governed by adversarial principles.[53] The Court emphasised that the formal requirements of an appeal resemble those of a lawsuit, and that exhaustion of administrative proceedings serves only as a condition of admissibility. On this basis, the Antimonopoly Court was tasked not only with legality review but also with assessing the legitimacy and expediency of OCCP decisions. The Supreme Court further excluded the possibility that the CCCP could annul an OCCP decision and remand it for reconsideration; instead, the court was to issue a substantive ruling. Nonetheless, case law was not entirely uniform on this point.[54]

In more recent judgments, the Supreme Court has reaffirmed this substantive role. It held that the protective function of judicial review requires courts to verify both the factual findings and the legal assessment made by the OCCP in competition cases. Where the evidentiary basis does not confirm all the prerequisites for an infringement, the CCCP must issue a reformatory judgment either altering or annulling the OCCP's decision. In such cases, procedural errors committed by the authority are irrelevant, since the CCCP is not a cassation court but one entrusted with making independent factual and legal determinations.[55]

However, a recent Supreme Court ruling could mark a shift in this model. The Court held that appeals against OCCP decisions may legitimately include charges of procedural irregularities committed by the authority.[56] If these are substantiated, the CCCP may accept the appeal and annul the OCCP decision without ruling on the substantive competition infringement. Contrary to the Court's assertion that this does not represent a departure from established jurisprudence, this ruling significantly alters the traditional model. It equips the CCCP not only with reformatory powers but also with cassatory control over the administrative procedure. This dual role raises doubts as to its con-

52 S. Gronowski, *Ustawa o przeciwdziałaniu praktykom monopolistycznym*, Warsaw 1994, 102, E Modzelewska–Wąchal, *Ustawa o ochronie konkurencji i konsumentów. Komentarz*, Warsaw 2002, 269.

53 Judgment of the PSC of 29.05.1991, III CRN 120/91.

54 Example, the resolution of the PSC of 24.09.1993, III CZP 92/93.

55 PSC judgement of 12.04.2013, III SK 28/12.

56 PSC judgement of 3.10.2013, III SK 67/12.

sistency with the legislator's original intent to entrust the CCCP with merit-based adjudication rather than procedural review.

The problem becomes particularly acute in penalty cases. The Supreme Court has accepted that the CCCP is fully entitled to reassess the imposition of administrative fines, even where the OCCP has correctly applied statutory prerequisites and followed its penalty guidelines.[57] In practice, this strips the OCCP of the ability to implement a coherent penalty policy, since the CCCP retains the authority to substitute its own assessment of the fine's purpose and proportionality.[58] The result has been significant judicial activism: common courts often reduce penalties arbitrarily, without providing the detailed reasoning typically found in OCCP decisions.[59] This combination of activism and lack of transparency undermines the system's predictability, making it difficult to establish a consistent fining policy in competition enforcement.

8 Judicial Control of Administrative Acts of the OCCP in Competition Cases

Administrative acts (decisions and orders) issued by the OCCP constitute the core of its legal activity and can interfere with rights and freedoms in the most far-reaching manner. The OCCP has the power to issue many administrative acts in competition cases. It is therefore appropriate to classify these acts and examine their contestability.

There are three categories of contestable decisions.[60] Appeals against these decisions are heard by the CCCP. However, one cannot accept the claim that

---

57 PSC judgement of 16.04.2015, III SK 24/14.

58 M. Bernatt, *Między pełną kontrolą sądową a poszanowaniem polityki karania organu administracji–o sądowej kontroli kar nakładanych w sprawach konkurencji,* EPS 2016, no. 9, 24.

59 Vide judgments in cases of anti-competitive practices e.g. judgments of the CCCP of 27.01.2011, XVII AmA 73/10, of 11.08.2014, XVII AmA 84/13, of 21.11.2013, XVII AmA, of 1310.2014, XVII AmA 127/13, of 7.08.2015, XVII AmA 50/14, of 7.11.2023. XVII AmA 12/20, or judgments of the Court of Appeal in Warsaw of 17.06.2015, VI ACa 1475/14, of 10.06.2015, VI ACa 1477/14, of 19.12.2012, VI ACa 752/12, of 14.08.2015, VI ACa 1223/14, of 9.11.2010, VI ACa 383/10, of 23.05.2013, VI ACa 1451/12, and merger control, e.g. judgment of the CCCP of 6.12.2012, XVII AmA 43/11, or judgment of the Court of Appeal in Warsaw of 17.05.2016, VI ACa 630/15.

60 Under the Competition Act, the OCCP can issue decisions in competition cases: (1) Antitrust: declaring practices restrictive, commitment decisions, revoking obligations or commitments, recognising managerial infringements, interim measures, and settlement decisions. (2) Concentration cases: granting, conditionally granting, or prohibiting

a *numerus clausus* applies and that the CCCP is not competent to consider appeals against any other decisions of the OCCP.[61] Such an approach disregards Article 83 of the Antimonopoly Act, which expressly states that the procedural regulations contained in the Act are not exhaustive and that, to the extent not regulated, the general provisions of administrative procedure shall apply.

When analysing the APC, it becomes evident that the OCCP may issue decisions on its basis in the following situations:

i. discontinuance of antimonopoly proceedings pursuant to Article 105;
ii. amendment or annulment of decisions under the extraordinary procedures regulated in Articles 145–163.

Regarding the first situation, Article 81 of the Competition Act should be emphasised, and the CCCP shall examine an appeal against such a decision. This issue has not, so far, given rise to controversy in the jurisprudence.[62]

In antimonopoly proceedings, decisions may also be issued under the APC. In this respect, particular attention should be drawn to the appealable decisions regulated in Articles 97 and 98 of the Code, concerning the suspension of proceedings. A similar principle applies to decisions correcting or clarifying earlier decisions (Articles 111 §1 and 113 §§1–2 of the Code) and to decisions refusing to issue a certificate (Article 219 of the Code). All such decisions are subject to an ordinary legal remedy – a complaint – which should be examined by a common court. The jurisdiction of administrative courts is excluded in these cases, as confirmed by the clear wording of the relevant provisions and the Antimonopoly Court's case law, which has expressly recognised its competence to examine complaints against decisions clarifying the content of a decision.[63]

The CCCP hears complaints against contestable orders. Non-appealable orders, by contrast, may be subject to indirect judicial review by a common court only if there is an appeal against the final decision in the case. However, the use of a non-appealable order under the Competition Act to discontinue antimonopoly proceedings raises serious doubts. The adoption of non-appealability for such an administrative act is highly controversial in light of the constitutional right to a court guaranteed under Article 45(1) of the Constitution. A decision discontinuing proceedings brings the case to an end with-

---

concentration, and related remedies or extensions. (3) Fines: penalties for infringements of competition or procedural rules, including managerial or individual penalties.

61 M. Sieradzka, *Sądowa weryfikacja decyzji i postanowień wydanych przez Prezesa Urzędu Ochrony Konkurencji i Konsumentów* (*cz. I i II*), Rejent 2007, no. 10, 101.

62 For example, see the judgment of the CCCP of 9.08.2010, XVII AmA 83/09.

63 Orders of the CCCP of 16.12.2010, XVII Amz 41/10 and of 11.02.2014, XVII Amz 38/13.

out a legally binding determination of the rights or obligations of the party to the proceedings. Given the far-reaching legal consequences of such an act, the addressee of the decision should be able to seek judicial protection, as provided for in Article 77(1) of the Constitution.

9 The Course of Actions before the CCCP

The CCCP conducts judicial review of decisions and orders issued by the OCCP. Court proceedings are initiated when a party challenges an OCCP decision or order. The statutory time limits for filing are strict: one month for decisions and seven days for orders. Failure to comply with these deadlines results in the appeal being disregarded by the court, and the time limits cannot be extended by either the authority or the court itself.[64] In exceptional cases, however, the court may restore the time limit upon request, provided that the party demonstrates significant justification.[65]

The grounds for appeal typically concern alleged defects in the legal reasoning or factual findings that underpin the OCCP's decision. A party may challenge the decision in whole or in part and may object not only to the operative part (the ruling itself) but also to the reasoning. This possibility is particularly relevant when the reasoning includes adverse statements or assessments that could harm the undertaking's reputation or impede its business activities. In such cases, the party may seek judicial review even if the operative part of the decision is not directly contested.[66] The appeal must comply with all formal requirements set out in the Civil Procedure Code and be accompanied by payment of the appropriate stamp fee.[67] Importantly, the appeal must be submitted through the OCCP rather than directly to the court. If lodged directly with the court, it has no legal effect, and the appellant risks missing the filing deadline. The CPC, in particular Articles 479(28)–479(35), governs the procedural framework for these cases.

Under the CPC, all relevant evidence that is not contrary to law may be admitted. The evidentiary system is open – there is no hierarchy among means of proof. However, the court relies predominantly on evidence collected during the administrative proceedings before the OCCP. It rarely commissions expert opinions, even in cases requiring economic analysis, a notable

64 The order of the CCCP of 4.04.2000, XVII Amo 5/99.
65 The order of the CCCP of 11.06.1997, XVII Ama 26/97.
66 The order of the CCCP of 22.06.1994, XVII Amr 45/93.
67 The order of the CCCP of 9.09.1992, XVII Amr 25/92.

limitation in complex competition matters. As a result, evidentiary proceedings before the CCCP are typically confined to an exchange of arguments and the interpretation of documentary evidence already gathered by the OCCP. Witness testimony is admitted upon motion of the parties, where justified by the circumstances of the case.

The CCCP is required to review the case on its merits, not merely to assess the legality of the OCCP's decision. The court may not limit itself to a purely formal review.[68] Nevertheless, the scope of adjudication is determined by the content of the appeal[69] – the court may only rule within the boundaries of the issues challenged and may not extend the subject of the case beyond the matters decided by the OCCP.[70] Importantly, the court must take into account any changes in fact or law that occurred after the issuance of the contested decision, as well as any new evidence presented during the proceedings.

Following its examination, the Antimonopoly Court may issue one of three types of judgments:

i. Disregard the appeal – when it is inadmissible (e.g., filed after the deadline or by an unauthorised person);
ii. Dismiss the appeal – when it finds the OCCP's decision justified and well-grounded;
iii. Annul or amend the decision when it reaches a different conclusion from the OCCP, in which case the court must rule on the merits and replace the contested decision with its own judgment.

When rendering its decision, the court is also obliged, ex officio, to consider whether the OCCP's decision was issued without a legal basis or with a manifest legal error. Such findings may constitute grounds for the affected party to seek compensation for damages caused by the defective decision.

The court provides written reasoning for its judgment ex officio within two weeks of its announcement. A party seeking a copy must request it within one week of the judgment's pronouncement. Judgments of the CCCP are appealable before the Court of Appeal in Warsaw. This court does not have a specialised division for competition or regulatory matters. Subsequently, the Court of Appeals' rulings may be challenged before the Supreme Court through a cassation appeal, an extraordinary legal remedy. Cassation appeals may be brought only on strictly defined grounds, and the Supreme Court retains broad discretion in deciding whether to admit them for hearing.

---

68 The judgment of the CA of 21.06.2006, VI ACa 142/06.

69 The judgment of the Court of Appeal of 24.07.2008, VI ACa 12/08.

70 The order of the CCCP of 9.01.2002, XVII Ama 11/01.

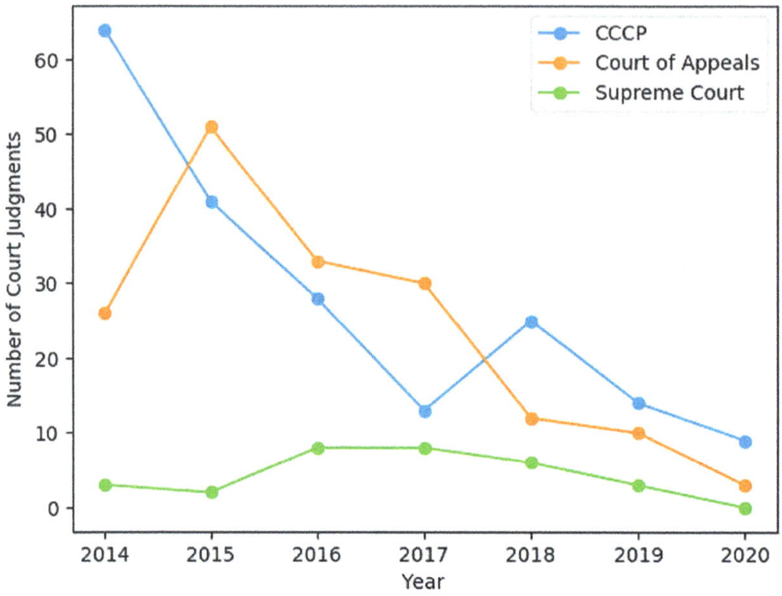

GRAPH 5.1 Court judgments in general (2014–2020)

The Graph 5.1 presents the statistics of civil court judgments in competition judgments delivered in 2014 and 2020.[71]

The majority of cases concern vertical agreements and abuse of dominance. On the other hand, merger cases are not common; hardly any have reached the Supreme Court.

When analysing the substance of those judgments, it turns out that, in most cases, courts uphold the OCCP's decisions (Table 5.2).

Statistical data indicate that the vast majority of decisions issued by the President of the OCCP are upheld by the courts. Historically, the rate of successful appeals has remained moderate, reflecting the judiciary's deferential approach towards administrative authority. Recent research shows that for the period 2004–2021, 67% of appeals were fully dismissed, 14% were fully successful, and 18% were partially successful.[72] In recent years, the probability of success when challenging OCCP decisions has remained broadly similar.

71 Data taken from the annual report of OCCP's activity. Unfortunately, after 2020, the OCCP no longer provides such data.

72 M. Bernatt, M. Janik, *Poland Report* [in:] B. Rodger, O. Brook, M. Bernatt, F. Marcos, A. Outhuijse (eds.), *Judicial Review of Competition Law Enforcement in the EU Member States and the UK*, Alphen aan den Rijn 2024, 654.

TABLE 5.2 Courts' intervention ratio in competition cases in the periods 2011–2016,[a] 2017–2018, and 2022–2024[b]

Type of judicial intervention	2011	2012	2013	2014	2015	2016	2017	2018	2022	2023	2024
Abrogation of the OCCP decision	3	3	3	6	7	2	6	22	5	3	2
Change of the decision of the OCCP	11	10	7	17	8	1	2		0	1	3
Upholding the challenged decision of the OCCP	44	47	61	41	26	25	5	18	17	14	14

a Data taken from the annual report of OCCP's activity. Unfortunately, after 2016, the OCCP no longer provides such data.
b Data taken from the OECD's Annual Report on Competition Policy Developments in Poland. Unfortunately, the OCCP does not provide uniform or consistent statistics for particular years. The OCCP's policy on providing public information on court statistics is deeply worrying. Compared with OCCP activity reports from the 1990s, there's a drastic decrease in the demonstration of how courts intervene against authorities' decisions. It's another symptom of the OCCP's declining accountability despite the implementation of the ECN+ Directive.

This has been accompanied by stagnation in the quality of judicial reasoning or the depth of substantive economic analysis in the judgments.

A further, and arguably more pressing, problem concerns the excessive duration of proceedings before the Antimonopoly Court. On average, it takes approximately two years for the court to hold the first hearing in a case. According to court statistics in 2024, of 55 cases, 1 was handled in 3 to 6 months, 10 in 6 to 12 months, 12 in 12 months to 2 years, 1 in 2 to 3 years, 8 in 3 to 5 years, and 1 in 5 to 8 years.[73] Based on my estimates, proceedings before the Court of Appeal typically last between nine and eighteen months, and if a cassation appeal is admitted by the Supreme Court, the case may take several additional months – sometimes years – before a final ruling is issued. However, as evidenced in Chapter 7, the most complex cases, such as cement or bank cartels, may take decades to reach a final resolution. This protracted timeline severely undermines the right to effective judicial protection, as guaranteed by both the Polish Constitution and Article 47 of the Charter of Fundamental Rights of the EU.

The consequences of these delays are particularly acute in merger control cases. When the Antimonopoly Court delivers a judgment two years after the OCCP's decision prohibiting a concentration, such a judgment often ceases to have any practical significance. In most cases, the transaction will already have been abandoned or become commercially unfeasible due to elapsed time, changes in market conditions, or expired contractual obligations. As a result, even a successful appeal that overturns a prohibition decision does not constitute an effective remedy in the sense of restoring the undertaking's rights or market opportunities.

Last but not least, staffing is a structural challenge. Empirical research has highlighted persistently high turnover among judges, for whom service at the CCCP often serves only as a transitional stage in their judicial careers before returning to general civil adjudication. After several years on the bench and the acquisition of valuable expertise, many judges leave to pursue higher-remunerated positions in legal practice. Budgetary constraints prevent the formation and retention of a stable, highly qualified judicial cohort.[74]

A further difficulty is the absence of systematic, specialised training in competition law. Judges appointed to the CCCP or the Court of Appeal often begin

73 MS-S19k Sprawozdanie w sprawach z zakresu ochrony konkurencji, regulacji energetyki, telekomunikacji i transportu kolejowego za rok 2024 r., https://bip.warszawa.so.gov.pl/artykul/488/374/dane-statystyczne.

74 M. Martyniszyn, M. Bernatt, 51.

their tenure with limited prior experience in competition matters.[75] This should not be understood as an individual failing but as a consequence of the structural features of the Polish judiciary, which traditionally favours a generalist model over judicial specialisation.

These systemic inefficiencies raise serious questions about the effectiveness of judicial protection in Polish competition law. The excessive duration of proceedings, coupled with the insufficient analytical reasoning of judgments, undermines confidence in the judicial review process and the predictability of competition enforcement more broadly. It therefore seems essential to consider institutional and procedural reforms to streamline judicial review, particularly in merger cases where time is a critical factor.

10 Administrative Courts and Competition Cases

Contrary to a popular but overly narrow reading of the Competition Act or even the CPC, judicial control over the OCCP's actions in antimonopoly proceedings rests on a dual-jurisdiction model.[76] On the one hand, common courts – the CCCP, the Court of Appeal in Warsaw, and, ultimately, the Supreme Court – exercise review. On the other hand, administrative courts also play a role, reflecting the dualistic nature of OCCP oversight.

Administrative courts in Poland consist of two instances: the Voivodship Administrative Courts (VACs) and the Head Administrative Court (HAC). The VACs hear all complaints unless jurisdiction is expressly reserved to the SAC. The HAC examines appeals from VAC rulings, issues resolutions to clarify complex legal questions, and resolves jurisdictional disputes between public authorities.

Administrative courts review challenged decisions or acts solely through the prism of the principle of legality. They may issue only cassation rulings – either upholding or setting aside the contested act. In this way, they serve as guarantors of legality, not as bodies for substantive re-decision of administrative cases. Administrative courts review all public administration activities and address complaints about decisions, orders, or actions affecting rights, local laws, supervision acts, or failures to act. They also resolve jurisdiction disputes between authorities, exercising comprehensive control.

---

75 Ibidem, 48.

76 This is how, for example, it is accepted by M. Sieradzka, *Glosa do postanowienia NSA z dnia 11 lutego 2009 r., II GSK 749/08*, LEX/el.

An earlier analysis of the CCCP's jurisdiction shows that it may hear appeals only against decisions and orders of the OCCP (and its predecessor). Other acts or omissions of the authority remain within the competence of the administrative courts. Thus, in competition matters, administrative courts are competent to examine complaints against:

1. failures to act by the OCCP, such as ignoring notifications of potential anticompetitive behaviour or failing to transmit files to the Antimonopoly Court,
2. excessive prolongation of explanatory or antimonopoly proceedings,
3. certain forms of discontinuance of antimonopoly proceedings,
4. return of merger notification filings.

However, administrative courts have been reluctant to exercise this jurisdiction.[77] In some situations, it is unclear which court should decide – for instance, who controls the transmission of appeal and case files to the Antimonopoly Court. Administrative courts have declined to exercise jurisdiction in such cases, while the Antimonopoly Court lacks the legal authority to intervene, leaving parties without effective judicial protection.[78] However, administrative courts have acknowledged jurisdiction over the OCCP's failures to act in competition matters.[79] This is a significant achievement in securing legal protection for any addresses of the OCCP's inactions.

All complaints concerning the actions or omissions of the OCCP fall within the exclusive jurisdiction of the VAC in Warsaw. Judgments from this court can be appealed to the HAC. However, proceedings in administrative courts are more efficient than those in civil (competition) courts. Typically, the VAC in Warsaw schedules the first hearing about 6 months after the complaint is filed.[80] Appeals to the HAC for cassation can add an average of 19 months.[81] As a result, the combined process often takes 2–3 years, diminishing the effectiveness of judicial protection and, at times, rendering it merely symbolic.

Administrative courts have issued relatively few judgments in competition cases. The majority involve access to case files under the Act on Access to

---

77 Order of VAC of 17.02.2009, VI SAB/Wa 91/08, and resolution of the HAC of 24.02.2010, II GPS 6/09.

78 For detailed discussion see M. Błachucki, *System*, 412.

79 The orders of the HAC of 22.05.2012, II GSK 620/12, and of 17.02.2014, II GSK 1804/12.

80 Information on the activities of the Voivodeship Administrative Court in Warsaw in 2024, 10, https://bip.warszawa.wsa.gov.pl/1392/informacja-o-dzialalnosci-wsa-w-warszawie-w-2024-r.html.

81 Information on the activities of administrative courts in 2024, Parliamentary Print 1164, 27.03.2025. 1.

Public Information, with only a few addressing the OCCP's inaction or the lengthy duration of proceedings.[82]

One illustrative case involved a third-party motion seeking access to the merger notification form submitted by an undertaking under investigation. Access was denied by the OCCP, which claimed the notification form was not 'public information' because it was created by a private entity and only appended to the case file. The VAC disagreed, ruling that documents forming part of administrative case files are covered by the concept of public information, irrespective of their author.[83] Following the OCCP's appeal, the HAC later reversed the lower court's decision, concluding that although the notification form itself was not a public document, certain portions of it could contain public information. The case was remitted to the VAC with instructions to determine which sections of the form could lawfully be disclosed to third parties.[84] However, in the subsequent judgment, the HAC held that the notification form and supporting documents are private and not accessible to the public.[85]

A similar issue arose in a case in which a third party sought access to contracts collected during an antimonopoly investigation. This time, the HAC held that any document collected during an administrative investigation and forming part of the case file falls within the notion of public information.[86] Similarly, the HAC ruled that the internal memo containing the findings of explanatory proceedings, as well as the correspondence with the European Commission during this investigation, is not accessible.[87]

Another public information case involved a third party's request to access an expert opinion forming part of the case file. The OCCP denied the request, arguing that the file had already been transferred to the CCCP for judicial review and that the authority was therefore no longer in possession of the requested document. The VAC upheld this position, affirming that a public authority is obliged to provide access only to public information in its possession at the time of the request.[88]

The second category of administrative court cases concerns failing to act or the excessive duration of antimonopoly proceedings. In one significant judgment, the VAC held that conducting a competition investigation for more

82 Act of 6.09.2001 on the access to public information, JoL No. 112, item 1198.

83 VAC judgment of 29,03.2012, II SAB/Wa 485/11.

84 HAC judgment of 25.10.2012, I OSK 1696/12.

85 HAC judgment of 01.10.2015, I OSK 1872/14.

86 HAC judgment of 11.06.2011, I OSK 490/11.

87 HAC judgment of 08.03.2017, I OSK 1435/15 or of 08.12.2017, I OSK 2957/15.

88 VAC judgment of 11.10.2012, SAB/Wa 310/12.

than five years constitutes an obvious violation of both the statutory time limits set out in the Competition Act and the general principles of administrative procedure. The court found that the OCCP's prolonged inactivity amounted to a manifest violation of procedural law, thereby confirming the possibility of judicial review of the OCCP's inactivity under administrative jurisdiction.[89] This judgment was upheld by the HAC.[90] Both rulings are of particular importance, as it definitively settled the previously disputed question of whether administrative courts are competent to adjudicate on cases involving the OCCP's failure to act.

Overall, while administrative courts offer a supplementary mechanism of judicial protection in competition matters, lengthy proceedings and a formalistic approach to procedural rights often undermine the remedial value of this avenue. Nonetheless, these proceedings play an important role in delineating the procedural boundaries of the OCCP's authority and in safeguarding participants against administrative inertia or denial of access to information.

11 Civil Courts and Private Enforcement

Public enforcement of competition law in Poland is now complemented by private enforcement. The adoption of the Damages Directive (2014/104/EU) paved the way for harmonised rules on compensation claims for victims of anticompetitive practices.[91] With a certain delay, Poland successfully implemented the Directive through the Private Enforcement Act,[92] which provides a stronger legal basis for victims to seek damages from undertakings engaging in cartels, abuse of dominance, or other anti-competitive practices. From the perspective of judicial organisation, an important feature of the Polish model is that the legislator did not entrust private enforcement cases to the CCCP or any other specialised court. Instead, such claims are adjudicated by the gen-

89 The judgment of the VAC of 07.08. 2012, VII SAB/Wa 134/12.

90 The judgment of the HAC of 17.02.2014, II GSK 1804/12.

91 Directive 2014/104 EU of the European Parliament and of the Council of 26.11.2014 on certain rules governing actions for damages under national law for infringements of the competition law provisions of the Member States and of the European Union Text with EEA relevance, OJ EU L 349, 5.12.2014, 1–19, hereinafter the 'Damages Directive' or the 'Directive 2014/104'.

92 The Act on Claims for Compensation for Damage caused by a Breach of Competition Law of 21.04.2017, JoL 2017, item 1132, hereinafter the 'Private Enforcement Act'. It entered into force on 27 June 2017.

eral civil courts. The detailed analysis of this issue and of private enforcement is provided in Chapter 11.

12 Conclusions

Judicial protection in Polish competition cases is available through two distinct paths: proceedings before the Antimonopoly Court (CCCP) and proceedings before the administrative courts. Each serves a different function within the system of legal remedies available to parties affected by the OCCP's decisions or actions.

The CCCP, operating within the Warsaw Regional Court, is the principal body responsible for reviewing the legality and merits of OCCP decisions. Its proceedings are governed by civil procedure rules and allow a full re-examination of both facts and law. Although the vast majority of OCCP decisions are upheld, the lengthy proceedings provide at least some temporal relief. However, the fundamental weakness of this review remains its unpredictability and the quality of reasoning in many judgments, both of which undermine legal certainty. Equally problematic is the excessive duration of proceedings – often exceeding two years at first instance and up to five years on appeal including cassatory proceedings before the Supreme Court – rendering judicial protection ineffective, particularly in merger cases where timeliness is essential.

Administrative courts provide a supplementary form of judicial protection, limited to complaints against the OCCP's inaction or prolonged conduct, as well as disputes concerning access to public information contained in administrative files. Although their jurisdiction in such matters has been confirmed, administrative court proceedings are also lengthy and often formalistic, offering limited practical redress. Their jurisprudence remains inconsistent, particularly regarding access to documents, which weakens the transparency of the competition enforcement process.

The undertaken analysis suggests that the legislator made an exception by excluding competition law matters from administrative court jurisdiction and empowering a common civil court (the CCCP) to review certain administrative decisions. This exceptional transfer raises multiple difficulties: disputes over the proper character and competence of the civil court, uncertainty about its jurisdictional boundaries, and even situations amounting to a denial of judicial protection.

The court's jurisdiction in competition cases was a topic of academic discussion more than a decade ago, but no consensus was reached.[93] Draft amendments to the CPC proposed abolishing the CCCP and restoring the powers of administrative courts in competition cases, but they were never adopted.[94] Additionally, the Supreme Court's developing jurisprudence has influenced perceptions of the CCCP's role and jurisdiction in competition cases. Simultaneously, administrative courts have continued to refine their case law in selected aspects of competition matters, contributing to a certain stabilisation of judicial approaches. Taken together, these developments provide a comprehensive view of the current state of competition law jurisprudence in Poland regarding the delimitation of judicial jurisdiction.

When analysing the evolution of the CCCP's competence, it should be noted that this court ceased to be exclusively an Antimonopoly Court in the strict sense of the word, and its competence was broadened to include the recognition of regulatory and public law consumer protection cases. These changes were reflected in the CPC's separation of distinct chapters, creating four new categories of proceedings. Significantly, the extension of the CCCP's competence covered both cases of an essentially administrative nature (appeals against decisions of sectoral regulators) and cases of a substantive civil nature (control of abusive clauses in consumer contracts).

Observing the evolution of the CCCP's cognition, it is also apparent that the legislator has adopted a flawed approach to determining this jurisdiction, as evidenced by Article 479(28) of the CPC. On the one hand, this provision provides a general indication of the CCCP's jurisdiction to hear appeals from OCCP decisions; on the other hand, it lists specific provisions or actions that may be appealed to the CCCP. This way of defining jurisdiction is incorrect, as it may suggest the universality of the CCCP's cognition regarding the OCCP, arising from the CPC.[95] This translates into an expansive interpretation of the formally casuistic complaints recognised by the CCCP.[96]

---

93 For example, B. Turno, *Model sądowej kontroli decyzji Prezesa Urzędu Ochrony Konkurencji i Konsumentów, PiP* 2012, no. 10, 33–47. and M. Bernatt, *W sprawie kontroli sądowej postępowania przed Prezesem UOKiK,* PiP 2013, no. 3, 89–99; M. Błachucki, *Właściwość sądów administracyjnych i sądów powszechnych w sprawach antymonopolowych,* [in.] M. Błachucki, T. Górzyńska (eds.), *Aktualne problemy rozgraniczenia właściwości sądów administracyjnych i powszechnych,* Warsaw 2011.

94 They are discussed by. R. Stankiewicz, *Likwidacja procedur hybrydowych–krok w dobrym kierunku czy szkodliwy dogmatyzm?* [in:] ibidem, 159.

95 This is e.g. adopted by M. Sieradzka, *Glosa.*

96 An example is the order of the Court of Appeal in Warsaw of 30.11.2016, VI ACz 2293/16. Commentary by M. Błachucki, *Gloss to order of the Court of Appeal in Warsaw of 30.11.2016, VI ACz 2293/16,* OSP 2017, no. 10.

Despite the gradual expansion of the CCCP's jurisdiction and its being entrusted with an increasing number of new types of cases, the legislator did not decide to make the CCCP a court exercising universal jurisdiction over all activities of the OCCP and its regulatory bodies. From the outset, the jurisdictional dualism between the administrative courts and the Antimonopoly Court in relation to the said administrative bodies was apparent. Significantly, this dualism concerned not only different types of cases dealt with by a given authority,[97] but also could occur within the same case.[98] In addition, situations arose where it was difficult to determine the jurisdiction of the competent court.[99]

The courts are in favour of maximising the judicial protection afforded to the addressees of the OCCP's actions, which is undoubtedly a good sign (especially in the context of the earlier tendency to avoid adjudication and to concentrate on procedural aspects of the case[100]). It is hoped that the courts will develop competition case jurisprudence, thereby increasing legal certainty for undertakings and raising the standard of antimonopoly proceedings.

In this context, it is worth stressing that the CPC was never designed to verify the correctness and legality of administrative decisions. Its application in this field, therefore, generates persistent procedural difficulties. On the one hand, this weakens the legal protection available to the addressees of such decisions; on the other hand, it causes, at the dogmatic level, the progressive disintegration of civil procedure itself. As a result, cases concerning administrative decisions – such as those involving competition protection – bear no substantive connection with ordinary civil disputes, and the CPC does not provide an adequate procedural framework for their adjudication.

For these reasons, the current model of administrative decision review performed by the CCCP requires amendment. Specifically, provisions relating to competition and consumer protection, as well as decisions in the fields of energy, telecommunications and postal services, rail transport, and the water and sewage market, should be removed from the CPC and transferred to the

97 For example, the OCCP has jurisdiction over competition cases and general product safety cases. For the first type of cases, the CCCP has jurisdiction to hear appeals from decisions; for the second type, the standard administrative and judicial-administrative review procedures apply.

98 For example, in one case, the administrative court considers a complaint for inaction, and the CCCP considers legal remedies against administrative acts issued.

99 Vide the order of the CA in Warsaw of 30.11.2016, VI ACz 2293/16.

100 M. Martyniszyn, M. Bernatt, 53.

jurisdiction of administrative courts.[101] Such a reform would bring coherence to judicial protection and eliminate the inconsistencies of the present fragmented framework. This solution has long been advocated in administrative law doctrine and appears to represent the most rational and ultimate direction for systemic reform.[102]

101 Ł. Błaszczak, *Model sądowej kontroli decyzji administracyjnych (na przykładzie spraw z zakresu ochrony konkurencji i konsumentów oraz postępowań regulacyjnych). Postulaty de lege ferenda*, „Gdańskie Studia Prawnicze" 2022, no. 5, 275–276. Among others, the following academics advocated such changes: W. Broniewicz, *Czy potrzebny jest nowy kodeks postępowania cywilnego?*, PiP 2004, no. 4, 15; K. Weitz, *Czy nowa kodyfikacja postępowania cywilnego?*, PiP 2007, no. 3, 25, M. Manowska, *Postępowanie sądowe w sprawach gospodarczych*, Warsaw 2008, 237, T. Ereciński, *O uwarunkowaniach, potrzebie oraz zakresie nowego kodeksu postępowania cywilnego*, PPC 2010, no. 1, 18.

102 R. Stankiewicz, *Likwidacja*, 159., M. Błachucki, *Sądownictwo antymonopolowe w Polsce–historia i ustrój*, Warsaw 2011, 17, B. Turno, *Model*, 46. Opposite views by: T. Skoczny, *Instytucjonalne modele wdrażania reguł konkurencji na świecie–wnioski dla Polski*, RPEiS 2011, no. 2, 98 or M. Bernatt, *Sprawiedliwość proceduralna w postępowaniu przed organem ochrony konkurencji*, Warsaw 2011, 280.

CHAPTER 6

Competition Policy in Poland

In Polish legal scholarship, the concept of competition policy remains strikingly underdeveloped. The overwhelming majority of academic work on competition issues focuses almost exclusively on the legal, doctrinal, and procedural dimensions of competition law enforcement, while the broader strategic, economic, and policy-oriented aspects of state intervention in markets receive negligible attention.[1] Even when the notion of competition policy is invoked, it is typically discussed through the prism of the European Union's legal framework – particularly the evolution of EU competition rules, the decisional practice of the European Commission, or the jurisprudence of the EU courts.[2] By contrast, the specifically Polish perspective tends to collapse competition policy into its narrowest component: the enforcement of competition law.[3] In effect, the legal execution of statutory provisions is treated as synonymous with the entire field of state action in support of competitive markets.

This conceptual impoverishment reflects two mutually reinforcing phenomena. First, Polish legal and administrative sciences have long lacked a developed tradition of analysing public policy as a distinct field of governance.[4] Unlike in many EU jurisdictions – where 'policy' encompasses not only legal norms but also strategic objectives, administrative practices, and regulatory design – Polish legal discourse remains heavily text-oriented, focusing on statutes, procedures, and judicial interpretation.[5] Strategic governance,

1 Notable examples are S. Gronowski, *Polskie prawo antymonopolowe*, Warsaw 1998, M. Stefaniuk, *Publicznoprawne reguły konkurencji*, Lublin 2005, or C. Banasiński (ed.), *Polskie prawo antymonopolowe. Zarys wykładu*, Warsaw 2018.

2 For example, T. Korbutowicz, *Polityka konkurencji Wspólnoty Europejskiej i Unii Europejskiej w latach 1962–1997*, Kraków 2004, T. Jarocki, Ewolucja polityki konkurencji we Wspólnocie Europejskiej, Kielce 2008, or A. Zabłocka, *Polityka konkurencji Unii Europejskiej wobec koncentracji przedsiębiorstw*, Gdańsk 2008.

3 Refer to Z. Jurczyk, *Wybrane zagadnienia polityki konkurencji*, Warsaw 2004, or C. Banasiński (ed.), *Polityka ochrony konsumentów i polityka konkurencji–razem czy osobno?*, Warsaw 2006.

4 Notable exception is work M. Kulesza, D. Sześciło, *Polityka administracyjna i zarządzanie publiczne*, Warsaw 2013.

5 Notable examples are J. Schwarze, *European Administrative Law*, Luxembourg 2006, C. Harlow, P. Leino, and G. della Cananea, P. Cane, *Research Handbook on EU Administrative Law*, Cheltenham 2017, or H.Ch. Hofmann, E.C. Ip, and P.L. Lindseth (eds.), *The Oxford Handbook of Comparative Administrative Law*, Oxford 2021.

© 2026 THE AUTHOR(S) | HTTPS://DOI.ORG/10.1163/9789004754638-007
This is an open access publication distributed under the terms of the CC 4.0 license BY-NC-ND.

priority-setting, and policy evaluation remain peripheral to mainstream legal scholarship.

Second, this academic gap mirrors the limited role that competition policy has come to play in practice within the Polish state apparatus. Neither public authorities – most notably the OCCP – nor market participants have framed competition protection as part of a broader economic governance strategy. Instead, competition law has been treated as a largely self-contained, technocratic domain, detached from national industrial policy, regulatory coordination, or long-term market structure planning. As a result, the OCCP has evolved into an authority preoccupied primarily with adjudication, procedural correctness, and case-by-case enforcement, rather than with formulating coherent strategic objectives or articulating a forward-looking competition policy. This may also reflect a lack of solid background and experience in competition enforcement among the OCCP's most recent presidents.

Yet in contemporary administrative systems – particularly those characterised by independent or semi-independent regulatory bodies – public authorities are not merely enforcers of legal norms. They are active creators of the economic order through strategic planning, policy coordination, and the deployment of non-legislative instruments, such as guidelines, notices, soft law, and priorities frameworks.[6] In competition law, such instruments serve not only to clarify the authority's enforcement intentions and methodologies but also to enhance transparency, predictability, and accountability.[7] Their importance has increased markedly in jurisdictions where competition authorities enjoy strong institutional independence, as they provide a normative basis for assessing and legitimising the authority's strategic choices.

The chapter analyses how the OCCP has understood and shaped competition policy and enforcement priorities from its inception to the present day. It enables us to assess not only the authority's effectiveness as an enforcer but also its legitimacy as a modern regulatory institution within the broader framework of Polish economic governance.

---

6 G. Peters, *Administracja publiczna w systemie politycznym*, Warsaw 1999, 406.

7 UNCTAD, Corporate Accountability in EU Competition Law, TD/B/COM.2/CLP/67, 11, A. Jasser, *Independence and Accountability*, JECLP 2015, no. 2, 71–72, J. Broulík, *Predictability: a mistreated virtue of competition law*, JAE 2024, no. 3, 376–377.

1 Competition Policy: Theoretical Perspectives

1.1 Polish Administrative Law

The concept of public policy – understood broadly as planning undertaken by public administration – has undergone a profound transformation in Polish administrative law and legal doctrine.[8] Under the communist system, the centrally planned economy made planning acts a core instrument of governance. The state, as the central organiser of economic life, relied on multi-level plans (national, sectoral, and local) that functioned not as guidelines but as normative acts assigning concrete tasks to subordinate units. Contemporary legal scholarship, shaped by the logic of the command economy, accepted the normative character of such planning acts while acknowledging their hybrid nature: they combined specific commands addressed to designated executors with general norms of conduct that outlined the state's overarching objectives.[9]

The systemic transformation of 1989 formally abolished this command model and introduced a market-based economic order. Yet planning did not disappear; it re-emerged in a qualitatively different form. Modern planning in public administration no longer prescribes production targets or binding economic indicators. Instead, it serves as a tool for strategic coordination, rationalisation, and foresight, guiding public intervention within a democratic, decentralised governance system. This renaissance of administrative planning is evident in the proliferation of national strategies, multi-annual programmes, development plans, and sectoral policies at local, regional, national, and supranational levels. Many of these instruments derive from Poland's membership of the EU, where policy coordination through strategic documents is an established feature of the European administrative space.[10]

In this sense, the growth of planning instruments in Poland can be seen as part of the Europeanisation of domestic governance structures. Obligations stemming from EU membership – whether directly through binding regula-

---

8 For overview, Z. Duniewska, M. Górski, B. Jaworska-Dębska, E. Olejniczak-Szałowska, M. Stahl, *Plany, strategie, programy i inne zbliżone formy prawne działania administracji*, [in:] *Podmioty administracji publicznej i prawne formy ich działania*, Toruń 2005, 141–175.

9 M. Stahl, *Akty współdziałania (koordynacji)* [in:] R. Hauser, Z. Niewiadomski, A. Wróbel (eds.), *Prawne formy działania administracji, System Prawa Administracyjnego*. Vol. 5, Warsaw 2013, 364.

10 K. Wlaźlak, *Inflacja prawa administracyjnego w zakresie planowania* [in:] D.R. Kijowski, P.J. Suwaj (eds.), *Kryzys prawa administracyjnego? Vol. II: Inflacja prawa administracyjnego*, Warsaw 2012, 118.

tions or indirectly through soft-law mechanisms such as the European Semester – have contributed to the growing importance of public policy documents. Even where incorporation of EU standards is formally voluntary, their political weight makes adoption practically unavoidable. The result is a dual influence: the historical legacy of centralised planning on the one hand, and the contemporary EU model of strategic coordination on the other.[11]

Competition policy fits directly within this broader framework of administrative planning. From the outset of Poland's economic transformation and the creation of the OCCP, competition policy was conceived as a core component of the state's economic governance.[12] It is difficult to determine the extent to which this reflected continuity with the socialist planning tradition or alignment with European practices, particularly the Commission's pragmatic, strategy-driven approach to market governance. Most likely, Polish competition policy emerged from a combination of both: a lingering belief in the need for state guidance of market development and a gradual adaptation to European regulatory norms.

Regardless of its historical origins, planning today plays an essential role in shaping the intentional, strategic activity of contemporary public administration. Modern administrative bodies do not merely apply statutory rules but actively shape social and economic relations through strategic documents. As observed, planning acts serve an integrative and rationalising function: they impose coherence on administrative action, orient it prospectively, and align diverse tasks within a unified framework of objectives and instruments.[13]

The legal nature of planning acts, however, remains contested. Polish legislation provides no unified definition or classification, resulting in a considerable diversity of forms, procedures, and legal effects.[14] Terms such as strategy, programme, plan, and concept are used inconsistently, and many documents lack clearly defined adoption procedures. Accordingly, their legal force varies: some bind administrative entities internally, while others operate only as expressions of political will or administrative preference.[15]

---

11 Ibidem, 119.

12 The very first Antimonopoly Act of 1990 provided for the creation of a competition policy (Article 19(7)), and the authority implemented its first competition development programme in its first year of operation – refer to section 6.2.

13 Z. Niewiadomski, *Prawne formy działania administracji,* [in:] Z. Niewiadomski (ed.), *Prawo administracyjne*, Warsaw 2009, 137.

14 I. Chojnacka, *Władztwo planistyczne gminy w orzecznictwie sądów administracyjnych i Trybunału Konstytucyjnego*, ST 2009, no. 1–2, 74.

15 M. Górski, J. Kierzkowska, *Strategie, plany i programy* [in:] R. Hauser, Z. Niewiadomski, A. Wróbel (eds.), *Prawo administracyjne materialne. System Prawa Administracyjnego.* Vol. 7, Warsaw 2012, 220.

Despite this doctrinal ambiguity, planning acts share a set of recognised characteristics. In Polish administrative law, they usually:

i. derive from explicit statutory authorisation;
ii. be adopted through a prescribed procedure;
iii. be prospective and goal-oriented;
iv. rationalise administrative objectives and coordinate implementation; and
v. bind administrative authorities internally, though not private parties, unless the law provides otherwise.

Their evaluation rests on political, planning, and legal criteria, with the first being dominant, as these acts function primarily as instruments of governance rather than adjudication.[16]

Viewed through this analytical lens, competition policy is a classic example of an administrative planning act. It is statutory in origin, prospective in orientation, and designed to structure future administrative activity. It provides a coherent internal framework for coordinating state interventions – competition enforcement, sectoral regulation, market liberalisation, and consumer protection – under a unified strategic vision. Although it has no direct normative effect on private entities, it binds public authorities internally and serves as an accountability instrument that guides their priorities and methods. Competition policy retains a predominantly political character, subject to political – not judicial – review.

In sum, competition policy in Poland should be understood as a hybrid planning instrument: legal in form, political in nature, and administrative in function. Its evolution illustrates both the strengths and the persistent weaknesses of the Polish model of public administration planning: the ambition to coordinate state intervention in the economy through strategic documents, and the recurrent difficulty in translating these documents into coherent, operational administrative practice.

1.2 Competition Law Doctrine

In competition law doctrine, competition policy is generally understood through its substantive aims and functional role rather than its formal legal structure. The simplest and most widely accepted definition treats competition policy as the set of laws and public measures designed to ensure that

---

16 J. Jeżewski, *Prawna determinacja aktów planowania przestrzennego w zakresie zadań ochrony środowiska (zagadnienia wstępne)* [in:] J. Supernat (ed.), *Między tradycją a przyszłością w nauce prawa administracyjnego*, Wrocław 2009, 257–258.

competition in the marketplace is not restricted in ways detrimental to society.[17]

From the government's perspective, competition policy is an integrated, cross-sectoral strategy that applies coherent competition principles across a broad spectrum of public policies and reflects a long-term political commitment to maintaining competitive markets.[18] For market participants, competition policy shapes the regulatory environment in which firms operate, defining permissible competitive behaviour and influencing rivalry between undertakings and their relations with consumers. In this sense, a country's competition policy may be understood as the sum of its competition laws, which prohibit anti-competitive conduct, and its public policies, which affect the structure and functioning of markets.[19]

Doctrinal analyses typically emphasise that competition policy is a mechanism for enhancing economic efficiency and fostering growth. It achieves these objectives through legislative, administrative, and regulatory instruments that constrain monopolistic structures and promote open, contestable markets – thereby increasing overall economic welfare. Functionally, competition policy is often divided into two broad dimensions:

i. regulation and deterrence of anti-competitive practices – including cartels, abuses of dominance, and anti-competitive mergers and
ii. structural reform of markets – eliminating regulatory barriers, expanding market access, and enhancing contestability.[20]

A continuing and essential component of competition policy is the systematic review and reform of existing regulations that distort or unnecessarily restrict competition and cannot be justified by legitimate public-interest objectives. The effectiveness of competition policy thus depends not only on the enforcement of antitrust norms but also on the state's capacity to identify, amend, or repeal regulatory barriers that hinder competition processes.[21]

From this broader perspective, competition policy extends well beyond law enforcement. It is a strategic framework for economic governance that integrates competition enforcement, regulatory reform, market monitoring, and

---

17 M. Motta, *Competition Policy: Theory and Practice*, Cambridge 2003, 1.

18 R. Deighton-Smith, *National Competition Policy: Key Lessons for Policymaking from its Implementation*, Australian Journal of Public Administration 2001, no. 60(3), 29.

19 G. Lang, *Competition Policy* [in:] D. Healey, W. Kovacic, P. Trevisán, R. Whish (eds.), *Competition Law Dictionary*, https://www.concurrences.com/en/dictionary/competition-policy-89181.

20 J. Teicher, *Competition policy* [in:] J.M. Shafritz (ed.), *International Encyclopedia of Public Policy and Administration*, Vol. 1: A-C, New York 1998, 468.

21 Ibidem, 469.

policy coordination. Properly implemented, competition policy serves as a tool for shaping a dynamic, efficient economic system, ensuring that markets remain open, innovative, and capable of delivering benefits to consumers and society at large.

2 Competition Policy in Poland: Legal Framework

All Polish competition statutes have provided for the development and adoption of a competition policy as a distinct instrument of public administration planning. From the outset of the post-1989 market transformation, competition policy was conceived simultaneously as a political act – expressing the government's economic strategy – and as a legal-administrative act intended to guide state activity in promoting and protecting competition. Its evolution mirrors the institutional development of the national competition authority.

The Act of 1990, Article 19(1)(6) and (7), assigned to the Antimonopoly Authority the tasks of preparing and reviewing draft legislation on monopolistic practices and the development of competition, as well as preparing government draft competition policies. These provisions captured the dual nature of competition policy: a governmental strategic instrument and an administrative planning document, with the NCA acting as its principal architect.

2.1 Political and Institutional Character

In its design, Poland's competition policy was intended to be a political act of the Council of Ministers, not a document adopted autonomously by the Antimonopoly Authority. This ensured coherence with the wider system of public policies and emphasised that competition policy was part of general economic governance, rather than a stand-alone initiative of the NCA. Such an approach reflected the interdependence of competition with other public policies, including industrial, consumer, innovation, trade, and regulatory policies.

Successive presidents of the competition authority sought to strengthen the OCCP's influence over policy formulation. Invoking its specialised expertise and enforcement experience, the authority advocated for a more prominent role in coordinating and shaping policy direction. On the 20th anniversary of the Polish NCA, President Małgorzata Krasnodębska-Tomkiel emphasised that although competition policy is a governmental responsibility, the OCCP is the actor 'best equipped to identify systemic threats to competition and propose remedial measures'.[22] Competition policy thus emerged from a dynamic interaction between political authority and administrative expertise.[23]

2.2 Legal Nature and Effects

The effects of competition policy are internal and pragmatic: it guides administrative discretion without being constrained by enforceable norms. Accordingly:

i. Judicial review of competition policy is excluded.
ii. Its implementation depends on political, not legal, responsibility.
iii. Accountability is exercised through governmental and parliamentary mechanisms rather than the courts.

Thus, while the policy provides strategic direction, it does not operate as a source of law in the strict sense.

2.3 The Role of the Polish NCA

Statutory provisions assigned the Polish NCA a coordinating and initiating role in developing government competition policy. It was authorised to:

i. draft the policy,
ii. submit it to the Council of Ministers for approval, and
iii. monitor and report on its implementation.

This role goes well beyond that of a technical secretariat. The OCCP is expected to act as:

i. an advocate for pro-competitive reforms,
ii. a promoter of regulatory coherence, and
iii. a guardian of competition within the broader administrative architecture.[24]

---

22 M. Krasnodebska-Tomkiel, *Perspektywy polityki konkurencji w Polsce–w 20. rocznicę powstania UOKiK* [in:] M. Krasnodebska-Tomkiel (ed.), *Zmiany w polityce konkurencji na przestrzeni ostatnich dwóch dekad*, Warsaw 2010, 515.

23 Unfortunately, President Małgorzata Krasnodębska-Tomkiel was dismissed for the very reason of adhering to competition policy and her mandate – refer to section 8.10.1.

24 J. Brol, V. M. du, J. Frąckowiak, W. J. Katner, A. Kidyba, E. Kiedrowicz, T. Komosa, C. Kosikowski, K. Kruczalak, E. Nowińska, W. Opalski, U. Promińska, W. Pyzioł, A. P. Skoczylas, *Komentarz do ustawy o przeciwdziałaniu praktykom monopolistycznym i ochronie interesów konsumentów* [in:] *Prawo handlowe*, Warsaw 2001, Art. 19.

Although the Council of Ministers formally adopted the policy, its substantive content was shaped predominantly by the OCCP's analytical perspective. As a consequence, Polish competition policy developed a horizontal, cross-sectoral profile, aimed at promoting competition across the entire economy rather than serving sector-specific objectives.

2.4 Evolution of the Statutory Framework

This model was preserved and refined in subsequent legislation. The Act of 2000, Articles 26(4) and (8), expanded the NCA's competence to include preparing government programmes in both competition and consumer policy, and introduced an obligation to submit periodic reports on their implementation.[25] This innovation strengthened administrative accountability and created a mechanism for evaluating progress towards strategic objectives.

Internally, the reporting obligation served as a tool of governmental oversight, providing information on the state of competition in Poland and facilitating coordination between the NCA and other ministries. Externally, it enhanced the transparency of public administration and provided stakeholders with insight into the direction of competition policy. It also reinforced the NCA's dual role as both an enforcement body and a policy coordinator.

Poland's EU accession did not alter this structure. The 2007 Act, Articles 31(4) and (9), reaffirmed these responsibilities, signalling the legislator's intent to maintain continuity while ensuring alignment with European regulatory standards.

2.5 Reporting Obligations

Competition and consumer policy programmes typically span multiple years. However, the statutory requirement to submit 'periodic reports' on their implementation remains ambiguous. The term is undefined. The conventional interpretation accepts a single report as sufficient.[26] Annual activity reports of the OCCP cannot fulfil this function, as they focus on enforcement activity rather than the broader evolution of the market competition.[27]

---

25 K. Jaroszyński [in:] T. Skoczny, (ed.), *Ustawa o ochronie konkurencji i konsumentów. Komentarz*, 2nd ed., Warsaw 2014.

26 C. Banasiński, E. Piontek [in:] C. Banasiński, E. Piontek, *Ustawa o ochronie konkurencji i konsumentów. Komentarz*, Warsaw 2009, Art. 31.

27 Opposite view by C. Banasiński [in:] A. Jurkowska-Gomułka, A. Piszcz (eds).

In the early 2000s, the OCCP submitted implementation reports irregularly, often as annexes to new policy programmes. Since 2014, no reports have been produced or published. This omission undermines transparency and weakens institutional accountability for the OCCP and the government in competition governance.

2.6 Substantive Scope of Competition Policy

Polish competition policy is horizontal, covering the entire national economy. It comprises three intertwined dimensions:

i. protection of competition – antitrust and merger enforcement by the OCCP;
ii. creation and strengthening of competition – liberalisation and removal of structural barriers, implemented largely by sectoral regulators; and
iii. support and promotion of competition – education, advocacy, and dissemination of pro-competitive principles by various public and quasi-public bodies.

Competition policy also sets substantive priorities, typically centred on transparency, limiting anticompetitive state interventions, promoting sectoral liberalisation, and strengthening institutional cooperation among sectoral regulators.[28]

2.7 Evaluation

Under Polish administrative law, competition policy meets the criteria of a planning act: it is based on statutory authorisation, adopted through a designated procedure, prospective, and intended to coordinate administrative action. However, its lack of normative force means it functions primarily as a political document, with practical relevance dependent on governmental commitment and the OCCP's interpretative initiative.

The absence of regular reporting and systematic public evaluation has eroded the role of competition policy as a mechanism for strategic guidance and accountability. As a consequence, Polish competition policy has ceased to function as an active planning instrument and has instead become a largely symbolic declaration of governmental intent. Its substantive impact should be shaped primarily by the OCCP's internal priorities rather than by any coherent, long-term governmental strategy. As subsequent sections demonstrate, even this symbolic dimension has effectively disappeared: since 2016, Poland

28 C. Banasiński, E. Piontek [in:] C. Banasiński, E. Piontek, Art. 31.

can no longer be said to have a competition policy or any meaningful prioritisation of enforcement.

3 Competition Policy versus Priorities of NCA

The absence of a meaningful, operational competition policy in Poland over the last decade has naturally shifted the centre of gravity from strategic policymaking to largely implicit prioritisation within the OCCP. This development, however, reveals an even deeper normative and administrative void in which the authority currently operates. The relationship between competition policy and OCCP prioritisation is determined by their nature and institutional origins. In the Polish system, competition policy is adopted by the government, addressed to the administration as a whole, and intended to be general, cross-cutting, and strategic. Historically, certain government policies contained loose references to enforcement directions that the OCCP was expected to follow, but these documents rarely exerted any practical influence.[29]

Following the implementation of the ECN+ Directive, the OCCP should have acquired clear competence to set its own enforcement priorities. These priorities should be specific, operational, and medium-term, serving as the bridge between high-level strategic objectives and day-to-day enforcement work. The ICN has succinctly described prioritisation as the process by which agencies translate strategic objectives into operational lines of action and allocate their limited resources to projects that best align with defined aims.[30] In this sense, whatever the government seeks to achieve through its competition policy, those aims must be aligned with and operationalised through the OCCP's enforcement priorities.

Competition policy has a broad scope and set of goals, but the importance of priority-setting for an organisation such as the OCCP is difficult to overstate. The authority is responsible for an increasing number of tasks – many of which, as earlier chapters have demonstrated, were introduced without any assessment of their administrative consequences. Priorities are therefore essential to ensure that the OCCP can distribute its limited resources sensibly across its statutory responsibilities. They also provide a framework for dec-

29 As will be shown in section 6.3, many periodic competition policies' formulated aims have already been achieved or are easily achievable, so their relevance for competition enforcement was rather limited.

30 ICN, *Competition Agency Practice Manual: Strategic Planning and Prioritisation*, 2010, 28.

iding which infringements merit investigation, which tools to employ, and which markets require closer scrutiny. Above all, priority-setting is inherently linked to the selection of enforcement instruments. Effective strategic planning involves not only determining which cases to pursue but also deciding how to pursue them, whether through investigations, guidelines, market studies, advocacy, amicus curiae submissions, or softer behavioural influence. When used skilfully, these instruments strengthen the authority's institutional capacity and foster the development of the analytical competencies required for systematic priority-setting.[31]

3.1 Doctrinal Understanding and Theoretical Significance of Priorities

Despite the centrality of prioritisation in contemporary European enforcement, Polish administrative law scholarship has barely addressed this institution. This neglect mirrors the general scarcity of normative material on priority setting in Polish law, which has traditionally focused on administrative policy but has not addressed the operational discretion of individual administrative authorities.[32] European competition law doctrine has produced extensive analyses of NCA priority regimes – chiefly in the context of the ECN+ Directive – which acknowledge the practical necessity for NCAs to move away from the strict legality principle towards controlled discretion in case selection.[33]

This development is driven by structural features of modern enforcement. NCAs face an ever-expanding universe of potential infringements, while public enforcement budgets remain finite. In addition, the complexity of markets, the rise of digital platforms, and the proliferation of vertical and conglomerate strategies require NCAs to invest heavily in expertise. Consequently, prioritisation has become indispensable at both the strategic and individual case management levels.

Across Europe, the expansion of competition rules and the broadening of NCA jurisdiction have made it impossible for agencies to investigate every potential infringement. As a result, many jurisdictions have moved away

31 M. Burke, *Prioritization in practice: insights from the Competition Commission South Africa,* JAE 2018, no. 6, 280.

32 It may come as a surprise that even the only comprehensive monograph devoted to discretion in Polish competition law does not mention priorities even once – C. Banasiński, *Dyskrecjonalność w prawie antymonopolowym,* Warsaw 2015.

33 The EU state of the art of doctrinal analysis of prioritisation is presented in the policy report by O. Brook, K. Cseres, *Priority Setting in EU and National Competition Law Enforcement,* SSRN, 2021.

from the strict legality principle – under which the authority must open proceedings whenever an infringement is alleged – towards a model based on discretionary prioritisation.[34] Broadly understood, prioritisation encompasses both defining strategic objectives and selecting cases. The ECN Recommendation reflects this dual meaning: NCAs should be able to plan their activities at a strategic level and assign different priorities to individual cases when exercising their enforcement powers.[35]

Prioritisation can operate explicitly, through formal guidelines or statutory authorisation, or implicitly, through institutional practice. Jurisdictions differ widely. At one end of the spectrum, the strict legality principle requires NCAs to investigate any complaint meeting basic formal criteria. At the other end, NCAs enjoy broad discretion to reject complaints and select enforcement targets. Merger control is a special case: filing thresholds limit discretion, yet call-in powers – now increasingly common – require NCAs to develop internal criteria to determine which unnotified transactions merit scrutiny.

Prioritisation in enforcement may occur at various stages of competition jurisdiction implementation. It may involve detecting infringements. There is a need to balance reactive policies with ex officio investigations. Another issue concerns the selection of enforcement targets. The following issues concern the proceedings themselves: (a) initiation of infringement proceedings – deciding not to investigate the case and (b) outcome of the case – deciding on the outcome of the case, especially on refraining from sanctioning anticompetitive conduct behaviour.[36]

3.2 Reasons and Risks of Prioritisation

NCAs prioritise for several reasons: resource scarcity, rising enforcement costs, and the need to prevent overenforcement or an excessive focus on particular sectors at the expense of others, or to bring forward developments that shape the market or the law in a given area. Prioritisation must respond to changes in market structure, economic context, and legislative expectations. It is also essential for balanced enforcement strategies that combine investigation, guidance, market analysis, and advocacy tools.

34 Ibidem.

35 ECN Recommendation on the Power to set Priorities.

36 N. Petit, *How much discretion do, and should, competition authorities enjoy in the course of their enforcement activities ? A multi-jurisdictional assessment*, Concurrences 2010, no. 1, 44.

However, prioritisation also entails risks. If poorly designed, it can lead to inconsistent treatment of undertakings, accusations of arbitrariness, or even corruption. It may also result in underenforcement, particularly if NCAs pursue 'quick wins' rather than economically significant cases – an issue evident in Poland's disproportionate focus on resale price maintenance investigations. A lack of transparency in priority-setting can further obscure enforcement patterns, especially in multi-mandate authorities where competition enforcement competes with consumer protection or regulatory functions for institutional attention.

Ultimately, prioritisation should reflect conscious planning rather than reactive behaviour. While NCAs should retain independence in setting enforcement priorities, their choices must remain anchored in the constitutional and statutory objectives of competition law and policy, as well as in the broader legal, political, and economic context. Priorities are therefore dynamic and jurisdiction-specific; they should evolve with markets.[37]

3.3 The Normative Deficit in the Polish System

Polish competition legislation has never explicitly regulated prioritisation. This omission is not exceptional in the Polish administrative landscape, which rarely provides legal foundations for priority-setting. Nonetheless, under European law, the situation is markedly different: the institution of priorities is ubiquitous, particularly in EU competition enforcement.[38]

The ECN+ Directive was intended to address this gap by requiring Member States to ensure that NCAs may reject complaints on priority grounds. Article 4(5) of the Directive is unambiguous. Yet the OCCP failed to implement this provision and did not even attempt to justify the omission in its narrative memorandum to the draft legislation. Only the Minister for EU Affairs identified this failure during public consultations, but the OCCP dismissed the need for judicial review of its complaint-handling and expressly opposed any mechanism that might 'burden the Office's staff'.[39]

---

37 H. Jennings, *Prioritisation in Antitrust Enforcement – A Finger in Many Pies*, Competition Law International 2015, no. 1, 31.

38 L. Idot, *Reform of Regulation 1/2003: Power to set enforcement priorities*, Concurrences 2015, no. 3, Art. N° 74117, W.P.J. Wils, *Discretion and prioritisation in public antitrust enforcement, in particular EU antitrust enforcement*, Concurrences 2011, no. 3, Art. No. 89797.

39 Table of comments submitted on the draft act amending the Act on Competition and Consumer Protection and certain other acts (UC69) as part of inter-ministerial consultations and opinions, 30.

Most strikingly, the OCCP argued that the government's adoption of competition policy– an entirely separate instrument – constituted sufficient transposition of Article 4(5).[40] This interpretation is plainly incorrect. The government's ability to adopt policy is not equivalent to granting an independent NCA statutory discretion to set priorities or reject complaints. Nor does it reflect the Directive's explicit requirement that NCAs must have such powers and be subject to judicial oversight when exercising them.

The OCCP's position thus reveals a fundamental misunderstanding of prioritisation as a governance instrument. By conflating priority-setting with the public interest clause, the authority reduces strategic planning to a case-by-case assessment of legal permissibility. The public interest clause, however, merely determines when intervention is legally justified; it does not mandate choosing among multiple interventions that all satisfy the public interest criterion. It is therefore conceptually incapable of supporting a coherent prioritisation framework.

Under the current legal framework, the OCCP maintains that Article 4(5) of the ECN+ Directive has been implemented by enabling the government to adopt competition policy. Neither the Competition Act nor any other Polish law authorises the Polish NCA to set its priorities in applying Articles 101 and 102 TFEU, or to reject formal complaints on the basis that they are not considered enforcement priorities. Currently, the only basis for rejecting a formal complaint is a lack of substantiation of a competition infringement and/or a lack of public interest.

3.4 Prioritisation in Practice: A System of Silence

Neither the Competition Act nor any subordinate legislation provides an explicit legal basis for prioritisation. Nonetheless, residual or implicit forms of prioritisation can be discerned in the OCCP's operations. Analysing this phenomenon is significantly hampered by the OCCP's failure to publicly articulate its enforcement priorities for more than a decade. There are no statutory or regulatory provisions specifying which circumstances may be considered when determining enforcement priorities. The OCCP necessarily engages in selective case initiation when instituting ex officio investigations. The Competition Policy of 2015, though still formally binding, also refers to priorities – though none appear to have been implemented. Finally, sporadic interviews and public remarks by the current president occasionally allude to certain pri-

40 Compliance table concerning the implementation of Directive (EU) 2019/1 of the European Parliament and of the Council, Parliamentary Print No. 2990, 31.01.2023, 14.

orities.[41] These, however, form only a scattered and incidental basis for analysis. It is therefore useful to examine these vestigial forms of prioritisation.

First, regarding the policy dimension of prioritisation, my research has revealed no strategic plans – long-, medium-, or short-term – whether for internal or external use. Neither the current nor the previous president of the OCCP has produced even a rudimentary strategic document, and at least none has ever been disclosed. One may attempt to infer their objectives from interviews or public statements, but such material is necessarily selective, anecdotal, and retrospective rather than prospective. Moreover, the OCCP does not publish presidential speeches on its website or in any other official form, which suggests a deliberate avoidance of statements that might generate expectations or create accountability. Neither of the two most recent presidents publishes programmatic or scholarly texts. The OCCP itself has ceased organising conferences or regular basis and has discontinued the earlier practice of publishing books or articles authored by its managers and staff. In the absence of programmatic documents or publicly declared ideas, it is impossible to infer any coherent or consistent enforcement priorities from the OCCP's public-facing activities – if indeed such priorities exist at all.

Second, prioritisation may also be understood as an instrument for selecting cases for intervention and/or as a basis for declining to pursue complaints. Before 2007, it was difficult to speak of prioritisation in this sense. Under the earlier Competition Acts, the legality principle applied: complainants could demand that proceedings be initiated, and the OCCP was obliged to investigate and issue a decision, which the complainant could then appeal. Since 2007, however, the OCCP has initiated proceedings exclusively ex officio. Any entity may file a complaint, but the complainant is entitled only to a formal response. The OCCP's decision not to proceed is not subject to review. As a result, the OCCP enjoys a form of investigative discretion analogous to that exercised by the European Commission, which 'enjoys a wide discretion

41 Example inteviews: *Nowe szaty UOKiK. Tomasz Chróstny zapowiada kolejne zdecydowane kroki,* https://www.money.pl/gospodarka/nowe-szaty-uokik-tomasz-chrostny-zapowiada-kolejne-zdecydowane-kroki-6596774892272512a.html; *Będą kary za drenowanie portfeli? Prezes UOKiK zapowiada walkę z nieuzasadnionymi podwyżkami,* https://www.forbes.pl/wiadomosci/specustwa-ws-koronawirusa-prezes-uokik-chce-walczyc-z-nieuzasadnionymi-podwyzkami/jr5sq56; *UOKiK bierze się za handlowców. Zaczniemy nakładać kary,* https://www.o2.pl/biznes/uokik-bierze-sie-za-handlowcow-zaczniemy-nakladac-kary-6867558994459264a; *Sztuczna inteligencja, piramidy finansowe, cyfrowi giganci. Prezes UOKiK o wyzwaniach na 2024 r.,* https://businessinsider.com.pl/wiadomosci/prezes-uokik-zdradza-plany-na-nowy-rok-lista-priorytetow-jest-dluga/eb7epwb; *Nowy Prezes i priorytety UOKiK,* https://codozasady.pl/p/nowy-prezes-i-priorytety-uokik.

in selecting the cases which it investigates and in which it continues proceedings up to the stage of a "final" decision'.[42]

The OCCP's case-selection practice is justified by reference to Article 1 of the Competition Act, which requires that intervention must serve the 'public interest'. This clause is treated as the principal criterion for case selection. Reliance on the public interest concept derives, in part, from the Supreme Court, which stated that 'A violation of the public interest allows the antitrust authority to make a specific selection of cases in which it will intervene. When considering whether there are grounds for initiating proceedings and then, after conducting them, issuing an appropriate decision, the antitrust authority must indicate what the public interest was in intervening in relation to the specific practice to which the proceedings related.'[43] This statement is frequently invoked by the OCCP when justifying decisions either to intervene or to decline intervention.

However, neither the Supreme Court's reasoning nor the OCCP's reliance on it withstands closer scrutiny. The public interest clause does not, in fact, provide any basis for prioritisation. It does not establish criteria for case selection; nor does it authorise the OCCP to create such criteria. The clause merely determines the legal permissibility of intervention. The absence of a public interest would preclude intervention, but its presence does not supply legal grounds for prioritising one case over another where the public interest requirement is equally satisfied. Nevertheless, the OCCP's administrative practice has evolved to treat the public interest as a proxy for prioritisation. This outcome is understandable on pragmatic grounds: it is the only justification available that has been externally endorsed by a judicial authority. Whether this can legitimately be described as 'prioritisation' is another matter. There is no evidence that the OCCP's case selection is grounded in any systematic, coherent, or repeated decision-making framework.

3.5 Absence of Priorities: Absence of Direction?

Following the adoption of the ECN+ Directive, the OCCP should now be formally empowered to set enforcement priorities. This marks a significant institutional development, as the capacity to define priorities is intended to be a statutory mandate rather than an informal managerial choice. Nonetheless, the OCCP's approach during the transposition of the Directive exposes deep

---

42 W. Wils, *Discretion and Prioritisation in Public Antitrust Enforcement, in Particular EU Antitrust Enforcement*, Concurrences 2011, no. 3, Art. No. 89797.

43 PSC judgment of 5.06.2008, III SK 40/07.

systemic weaknesses. Through a deliberate omission, the Competition Act neither defined nor regulated enforcement priorities, and therefore cannot perform a jurisdictional function. At best, it may serve as an informational tool to enhance transparency and public accountability. Paradoxically, although the ECN+ Directive expressly requires Member States to ensure that NCAs can set enforcement priorities, Poland remains at odds with these assumptions: the authority has neither operationalised this competence nor acknowledged its substantive importance for modern enforcement.

The OCCP equates priority-setting with applying the 'public interest' clause, treating it as the functional equivalent of discretionary case selection. This interpretation is conceptually and doctrinally flawed. The public interest requirement does not confer discretion; rather, it reflects the principle of legality: whenever the public interest is present, the OCCP must act. Substituting this clause for strategic enforcement planning reveals a fundamental misunderstanding of the purpose of enforcement priorities within a contemporary NCA governance architecture.

The failure of two consecutive OCCP presidents to formulate enforcement priorities or publish any structured action plan casts serious doubt on whether the authority still operates in a programme – or strategy-driven manner. If the current practice reflects a reversion to purely reactive enforcement, this is particularly striking given that the substantive framework of Polish competition law has remained unchanged for years, while the external competitive environment – digital platforms, algorithmic collusion, sustainability agreements, and geopolitical distortions – has transformed profoundly. These developments objectively require a defined strategic stance and a conscious allocation of resources.

Across Europe, the publication of enforcement priorities is standard administrative practice in many countries, including Belgium,[44] France,[45] Ger-

44 Priorities Paper 2025, https://www.belgiancompetition.be/sites/default/files/content/download/files/Priorities%20paper2025.pdf.

45 *2024–2025 Roadmap*, https://www.autoritedelaconcurrence.fr/sites/default/files/2024-02/feuille-de-route-2024-2025-EN.pdf .

many,[46] Lithuania,[47] Portugal,[48] and the UK.[49] Against this backdrop, Poland is now an outlier. It is one of the few major EU NCAs that publish no enforcement priorities, articulate no strategic plans, and do not acknowledge the institutional relevance of priority-setting. This stagnation is especially paradoxical given Poland's declared ambition to be a leading competition authority and its repeated self-promotion in rankings such as Global Competition Review's *Rating Enforcement.*[50]

4 Evolution of the Competition Policy in Poland

So far, this chapter has outlined the doctrinal understanding of competition policy and enforcement priorities, as well as the normative and administrative foundations of these instruments under Polish law. It is now necessary to consider the historical content of competition policy in Poland – and the factors that have contributed to its present atrophy. Although competition policy in Poland is currently in a profound decline, this has not always been the case. Tracing its evolution shows that, even with limited institutional and material resources, the OCCP could once function as an effective and forward-looking authority.

At the outset, however, it is important to highlight a significant research challenge concerning the earliest documents defining competition policy in Poland between 1990 and 2004. Despite formal inquiries submitted to both the OCCP and the Chancellery of the Prime Minister, it proved impossible to obtain the texts of these documents, as neither institution retains them. Archival research in libraries and the State Archives yielded only two relevant materials: (i) the government document Counteracting Monopolies and Strengthening Competition. Partial Strategy, adopted on 2 June 1999 and (ii)

46 *The competition policy agenda of the Federal Ministry for Economic Affairs and Climate Action up to 2025,* https://www.bundeswirtschaftsministerium.de/Redaktion/EN/Downloads/competition-policy-agenda-up-to-2025.pdf?__blob=publicationFile&v=1.

47 *The Competition Council Identifies Four Sectors To Prioritise This Year,* https://kt.gov.lt/en/news/the-competition-council-identifies-four-sectors-to-prioritise-this-year.

48 *Competition Policy Priorities For 2025,* https://www.concorrencia.pt/sites/default/files/documentos/documentacao-organizacao-adc/Competition%20Policy%20Priorities%20for%202025_EN.pdf.

49 *CMA draft Annual Plan launches the first phase of its new Strategy for 2026 to 2029,* https://www.gov.uk/government/news/cma-draft-annual-plan-launches-the-first-phase-of-its-new-strategy-for-2026-to-2029.

50 *UOKiK moves up in the ranking of competition authorities worldwide,* https://uokik.gov.pl/en/uokik-moves-up-in-the-ranking-of-competition-authorities-worldwide.

an internal OCCP document entitled Implementation of Tasks Included in the Document: 'Report on the State of Competition and Competition Policy for 2002–2003' in the First Half of 2002. For this reason, reconstructing the content of Poland's early competition policies required reliance on indirect sources – principally OCCP activity reports and sporadic public statements by successive OCCP Presidents.

Competition policies from later years (post-2004) remain available, though their publication raises further concerns. These documents have no official publisher and are merely uploaded by the OCCP to its website alongside miscellaneous informational materials. This means that, following the pattern set by earlier policies, they may simply disappear from public access at some point. It is difficult not to regard this as a *signum temporis* – a symptom of the diminishing importance that successive governments and, more recently, Presidents of the OCCP attach to competition policy as a tool of strategic governance in Poland.

4.1 Competition Policy in Poland: The Founding Years (1990–1997)

Competition policy has been an important government programme in Poland's economic development. From its inception, it encompassed the protection, creation, development, and promotion of competition, with distinct objectives and priorities for each dimension.[51] This observation is particularly apt for the first decade of Poland's economic transformation, culminating in its accession to the EU.

Anna Fornalczyk, the first President of the Antimonopoly Authority, recalled that during the Authority's inaugural year – aside from the challenges inherent in building a new institution – one of the key issues was how to implement its statutory mandate in practice. The overriding priority at that time was to create the structural and legal conditions necessary for the development of competition in the nascent market economy. This objective was pursued primarily through structural interventions, including the supervision of ownership transformations of state enterprises, merger control, and the division of dominant entities. This structural approach was underpinned by the conviction that preventing monopolistic practices through the demonopolisation of the economy would be more effective than a purely regulatory

51 M. Stefaniuk [in:] T. Skoczny (ed.), *Ustawa o ochronie konkurencji i konsumentów. Komentarz*. Warsaw 2009.

approach that aimed to sanction anti-competitive behaviour arising from entrenched monopolistic positions.[52]

This approach was explicitly articulated in the authority's first activity report in 1990, which emphasised that the Polish competition authority's principal aim was to demonopolise the economy. This was pursued through two statutory functions:

1) The structural function, which enabled the authority to influence:
   i. the division of large undertakings;
   ii. their transformation into commercial law companies;
   iii. the creation of new economic entities;
   iv. the elimination of intermediary structures within cooperatives; and
   v. the prevention of the emergence of new monopolies.

Effective performance of this function required continuous analysis of production concentration, levels of market monopolisation, and the actual effects of organisational changes initiated or implemented under antimonopoly decisions.

2) The regulatory function, aimed at counteracting monopolistic practices, including:
   i. imposing excessive prices by monopolists;
   ii. establishing onerous contractual terms by dominant firms; and
   iii. concluding agreements restricting competition.

A particularly acute challenge for the authority during the transition period was the prevalence of monopolistic practices imposed by state administrative bodies operating under obsolete regulations.[53]

The first competition policy can therefore be characterised as bottom-up: it was shaped by the Antimonopoly Authority itself, as a direct reflection of the Antimonopoly Act and the Authority's interpretation of what competition policy ought to be. However, the authority soon recognised that the programme of demonopolisation had to be integrated into the government's broader economic strategy. Consequently, at the end of 1990, it submitted to the government a document entitled *Government Programme for the Development of Competition.*[54] On this basis, in 1991, the Council of Ministers adopted the *Government Programme for the Development of Competition for 1991–1993* – Poland's first government competition policy.

---

52 A. Fornalczyk, *Początki polityki konkurencji w Polsce* [in:] M. Krasnodebska-Tomkiel (ed.), *Zmiany w polityce konkurencji na przestrzeni ostatnich dwóch dekad*, Warsaw 2010, 419–420.

53 Activity Report 1990, 2.

54 Activity Report 1990, 7.

This government programme required ministers and heads of central offices to incorporate competition-enhancing measures into their economic reform plans. It treated the protection and promotion of competition as central to the emerging market economy, thereby enforcing economic efficiency and safeguarding consumer interests. It further recognised the key role of antimonopoly policy, import liberalisation, and privatisation in achieving its objectives. During this period, the Office primarily implemented antimonopoly policy through structural measures to demonopolise the economy.[55]

A brief description of this programme appears in the Antimonopoly Authority's activity report. The report emphasised that the authority implemented the government programme by issuing decisions and actively participating in governmental decision-making processes – in particular, through the work of governmental committees, the Council of Ministers, teams preparing sectoral restructuring programmes, and bodies responsible for regulating natural monopolies. The implementation of the programme was shaped by the Office's two years of experience and the specific circumstances of Poland's economic transformation. The main factors influencing this process were: (1) a continuing economic recession, (2) stabilised yet still high inflation, (3) slowing privatisation, and (4) political instability marked by two changes of government. These circumstances fuelled pressures for protectionist measures: increases in customs and tax rates, direct state intervention through concessions and quotas, and support for large state-owned enterprises – treated as the price for maintaining social peace during reforms. Against this backdrop, an important additional task for the authority was to counter protectionist pressures driven by sectoral or regional interest groups.[56]

Between 1994 and 1997, work continued on preparing draft competition development programmes for the coming years. The OCCP produced several studies for this purpose, yet for unknown reasons, these drafts were never examined by the Council of Ministers. Despite these efforts, neither the draft documents nor the explanations for their rejection have been located or preserved, further illustrating the fragility of early competition policy documentation in Poland.[57]

---

55 *Polityka konkurencji*, https://web.archive.org/web/20010925123101/http://www.uokik.gov.pl/.

56 Activity Report 1992, 1–2.

57 *Polityka konkurencji* – see fn. 55.

4.2 Competition Policy in Poland: On the Road to the European Communities (1998–2003)

In 1998, the Council of Ministers adopted another policy document prepared by the OCCP: *Counteracting Monopolies and Strengthening Competition: A Partial Strategy*.[58] This document sets out the objectives, directions, and instruments of government action in areas relevant to the development of competition. A central element of the strategy was the identification of sectors in which:

a. the competitive mechanism functioned;
b. the competitive mechanism was limited; and
c. the competitive mechanism did not function at all.

The overarching aim of the policy was to create the conditions necessary for the emergence or development of competition in sectors where it was absent or impaired. This was to be achieved through structural and organisational transformations, ownership changes, legislative amendments, and the elimination or mitigation of restrictions affecting competition (such as quotas, customs duties, or state aid mechanisms). The strategy also emphasised the need to harmonise industrial and competition policy, to take into account EU requirements, and to strengthen consumers' position in the market. In addition to these general objectives, the strategy outlined more specific measures, including developing state aid regulations, enhancing the OCCP's powers and competences, and establishing regulatory agencies in sectors where competition could not be introduced for structural reasons.[59]

The OCCP asserted that it systematically submitted periodic reports on the implementation of this strategy, intended as an additional instrument of government competition policy. According to the OCCP's internal assessments of work undertaken in 1998–1999, significant progress had been made in establishing the legal foundations for demonopolisation and in liberalising economic activity across many sectors.[60] The OCCP claimed it actively participated in preparing restructuring programmes – for example, for the hard coal, fuel, and gas industries – and contributed to draft legislation, such as the Postal Law and the Telecommunications Law, both aimed at strengthening competition. Practical results of the policy's implementation included creating conditions for the demonopolisation of the long-distance telecommunications market, awarding licences to three independent operators, establishing the

---

58 Przegląd Rządowy 1998, no. 9, 147–156.

59 Ibidem.

60 *Polityka konkurencji* – see fn. 55.

legal basis for the marketisation of heat and electricity prices, and developing an outline policy for the creation and operation of special economic zones.[61]

There is, however, no publicly available information indicating whether the government adopted or implemented a competition policy during 2000–2001. Neither the OCCP nor the Chancellery of the Prime Minister could provide documentation or clarification during the preparation of this research. The absence of such evidence is itself informative, suggesting a period of institutional stagnation, discontinuity, or a loss of priority in governmental policymaking.

A competition policy was in force in 2002–2003, as confirmed by the introduction to the 2004–2005 Competition Policy. Based on the limited information available, it appears that the 2002–2003 policy was implemented during negotiations and preparations for Poland's accession to the EU. Its purposes included strengthening competitive mechanisms throughout the national economy and aligning regulatory and institutional arrangements with the requirements of the EU internal market. The policy emphasised the demonopolisation and liberalisation of sectors that had not previously been exposed to market competition, the enhancement of their competitive capacity, and the need to meet the challenges of operating within the Single Market.

Notably, the objectives formulated for 2002–2003 largely reproduced those set out in earlier policy documents. While this repetition may, to some extent, reflect continuity and stability in strategic aims, it may also indicate that progress – although visible at the legal and institutional level – was less advanced at the economic and structural level. The persistence of the same priorities over several consecutive years suggests that the transformation of sectoral structures, ownership patterns, and competitive dynamics was slower and more difficult than originally anticipated.

4.3 Competition Policy in Poland: Calm Administration in Lieu of Policy Leadership (2004–2014)

The period 2004–2014 was the only decade in which a coordinated, sustained, and consciously designed competition policy was pursued in Poland. Five policy documents were adopted during this time, although the last appears never to have been implemented in practice. The first two policies were two-year programmes; the next two covered three-year periods; and the final programme was intended to run for four years. The rationale for these extensions remains unclear, though it is plausible that either the OCCP or the govern-

61 Przegląd Rządowy – see fn. 58.

ment considered longer implementation periods more conducive to achieving more ambitious or complex objectives.

All programmes adopted during this period shared a broadly similar structure. Each began with an introductory section outlining the legal basis for competition protection in Poland and the EU, as well as the most important economic and legal developments relevant to the state of competition. The second part was divided into two sections: a horizontal section addressed to the OCCP, and a sectoral section addressed to sectoral regulators. This dual structure was mirrored in the drafting process: the OCCP prepared the horizontal part, while regulators contributed directly to the sectoral part. Another innovation was the inclusion of timetables for implementing individual tasks, specifying deadlines and responsible institutions. Three of the five policies were officially reported on, usually as an annexe to the subsequent programme.

4.3.1 Competition Policy 2004–2005

The first post-accession policy, adopted on 29 June 2004, identified the following horizontal priorities:

a) cooperation within European competition policy frameworks;
b) improving the effectiveness of competition policy; and
c) promoting the principles of competition.

The sectoral priorities were:

d) creating conditions for the development of competition in regulated infrastructure sectors;
e) supporting competition in sectors subject to specific regulations of particular economic or social importance; and
f) implementing competition principles in local markets.

The priorities were formulated in highly general terms. Only the specific actions assigned to each priority revealed the government's actual intentions.

Priority (a) centred on legal and organisational changes to the OCCP, many of which had already been implemented before the policy was adopted. Priority (b) envisaged greater use of economic analysis, enhanced training, the creation of a specialised anti-cartel unit, and the introduction of a leniency programme. Priority (c) focused on informational and educational activities. Sectoral priorities included strengthening competition in telecommunications, electronic media, energy, transport, postal services, and financial markets, as well as in professions of public trust and pharmaceuticals, and intensifying oversight of competition in local markets.

A report on implementation was published. Although most tasks were completed, some were not. The proposed specialist anti-cartel unit was abandoned in favour of flexible working groups for complex cases. This solution proved effective and inexpensive. The OCCP also highlighted improvements in its internal decision-making structure, particularly the systematic involvement of economists from the Market Analysis Department. Educational activities were also emphasised. Sectoral achievements were described largely in terms of legislative change, privatisation, and consolidation in the energy sector – although the OCCP did not consider consolidation inconsistent with increased competition, an assumption that is open to debate. Activities in local markets were strongly emphasised, with nearly 500 antimonopoly proceedings cited.

4.3.2 Competition Policy 2006–2007

Adopted on 24 April 2006, this policy set out a government vision for the development and promotion of competition through measures in three areas:

I. protection of competition;
II. creation and development of competition; and
III. supporting competition.

Priorities in area I focused on enhancing the OCCP's effectiveness, protecting competition in liberalised sectors and local markets, strengthening the Antimonopoly Court, and expanding international cooperation. Legislative changes were again envisaged. Area II focused on developing competition in electronic media, energy, transport, and postal services. Area III concerns promotional and educational initiatives.

Each priority was broken down into operational actions. Improving the detection of cartels included promoting the leniency programme, intensifying inspections and searches, and using economic analysis more frequently. Protecting competition in local markets again played a major role, with plans to strengthen regional offices announced. Sectoral priorities reflected EU-driven liberalisation obligations, including energy unbundling and the implementation of railway packages.

Although the 2006–2007 report is not publicly available, references in the 2008–2010 policy suggest an emphasis on institutional improvements, regulatory reforms in infrastructure sectors, the removal of restrictive regulations, and increased educational efforts.

4.3.3 Competition Policy 2008–2010

Adopted on 15 July 2008, this policy again grouped priorities into three areas, with slightly modified terminology. The substance remained largely unchanged:

a) increasing the effectiveness of competition protection,
b) combating practices that hinder liberalisation and demonopolisation, and
c) strengthening competition in local markets.

Sectoral priorities again focused on electronic communications, energy, transport, and postal services. Support priorities included education, public awareness, and participation in the ECN and OECD.

Planned measures included investment in equipment, the development of internal guidelines, training, inter-agency cooperation, further development of leniency, and – significantly – a planned increase in fines. Sectoral tasks stemmed from specific legal obligations, such as transposing EU directives and overseeing the termination of long-term energy contracts.

The implementation report relied heavily on quantitative indicators and concluded that all horizontal priorities were achieved and most sectoral priorities were largely fulfilled. However, it failed to address the crucial qualitative question: whether these measures improved competitive conditions in the economy.

4.3.4 Competition Policy 2011–2013

Adopted on 13 May 2011, this policy introduced a new structural framework (levels, areas, priorities, and actions), though it offered no substantive conceptual novelty. Horizontal priorities continued to emphasise detecting and eliminating anti-competitive agreements, with a new focus on combating bid rigging and certain vertical restraints. Enhanced transparency of the OCCP procedures was planned, along with strengthening merger control and preparing for euro-zone accession – an ultimately irrelevant objective.

Once more, infrastructure sectors, particularly rail transport, postal services, and electronic media, were the focus of sectoral priorities. Educational initiatives were also planned. A report on the implementation of this policy has not survived or was never prepared.

4.3.5 Competition Policy 2014–2018

Adopted in early 2014,[62] this was the first policy to integrate competition and consumer protection within a parallel planning framework. The introduction emphasises the need to combine competition policy and consumer issues, which is reflected in the idea of developing and implementing, in parallel, the Competition Policy for 2014–2018 and the Consumer Policy for 2014–2018, setting out the objectives to be pursued by all institutions responsible for these areas. Once again, the document's structure and nomenclature have been changed, this time for the better, by dividing it into two parts: horizontal and sectoral priorities.

Horizontal priorities envisaged significant legislative reforms:

a) introduction of leniency plus,
b) fines for natural persons,
c) a two-phase merger control system, and
d) development of private enforcement.

These reforms were implemented in 2015. Local market protection returned as a priority, and for the first time, optimisation of the public procurement system was highlighted. Sectoral priorities included competition in payment services. Educational and international cooperation activities remained standard features.

However, the policy never took practical effect. Neither the OCCP nor other competent authorities implemented it, and some regulators explicitly stated that it was never operationalised. This failure is closely linked to the dismissal of President Małgorzata Krasnodębska-Tomkiel, who had prepared the draft, and to the subsequent disengagement of her successor, Adam Jasser. The OCCP's 2014 activity report mentions only the new President's priorities and does not address the implementation of the newly adopted policy. This omission critically undermined the programme and set a precedent for its complete abandonment. It is difficult not to regard this as a cardinal sin, which weighed heavily on the fate of the competition policy prepared by the OCCP under the aegis of President Jasser, and which his successor treated in the same way.

4.4 Competition Policy in Poland: Systemic Atrophy after 2014

Although the government formally adopted the 2014–2018 policy, the OCCP prepared a new policy in 2015, which was approved shortly before the change

62 Neither the OCCP nor the Prime Minister's Chancellery could provide the exact date.

of government. The political impetus was clear: the outgoing government and the new OCCP President, Adam Jasser, sought to institutionalise their vision ahead of the November 2015 parliamentary elections. This document was distinctive in several respects.

First, a joint *Competition and Consumer Protection Policy* was adopted. Second, the document contained no temporal scope: it was intended to remain in force permanently, or at least until replaced by a subsequent governmental act. Third, it departed from the conservative substantive structure of previous policies and did not include a timetable or performance indicators for implementation. It was the intellectual project of the then-President and undoubtedly represented a comprehensive and original vision for shaping governmental competition policy. Fourth, because of this originality and the speed of the drafting process, the document was adopted extremely quickly, so other government bodies either refrained from commenting on the draft altogether or submitted only very limited remarks. Given the document's exceptional generality, the abandonment of meaningful consultation is unsurprising. One consequence of this truncated procedure was that sectoral priorities were reduced to a minimum.

The 2015 Policy was significantly shorter than earlier documents and relied on an even higher level of abstraction and generality. Its key message was the abandonment of divisions among the entities responsible for its implementation, in favour of creating a new foundation for a culture of competition centred on establishing a national network for competition and consumers. The starting assumption was that the tasks relating to the protection of competition and consumers are inherently complex and span the entire national economy. Accordingly, all entities engaged in or concerned with competition and consumer protection, irrespective of their legal or organisational status, should cooperate more effectively. The Policy assumed that combining competition and consumer protection objectives would create synergies and that the actions undertaken by the network should take both aspects into account.

According to the Policy, the network was to comprise: the OCCP; the Advisory Council to the President of the OCCP; external experts and academic circles; ministries; sectoral regulators; ombudsmen, particularly consumer ombudsmen; inspectorates and state control authorities; law enforcement agencies; other bodies operating within the sphere of local state and local government administration; undertakings and their representative associations; and non-governmental organisations, especially those representing consumer interests. The network was expected to operate through: the ongoing exchange of experience and opinions on developments in consumer product and service markets; the establishment of permanent operational contacts, joint training, and regular exchanges of information with judicial authorities on competition and consumer protection; the organisation of regular meetings with business and consumer organisations; and continuous market monitoring, including market research and the analysis and aggregation of signals from consumers, undertakings, and their representative organisations received by individual authorities.

The most evident weakness of the Policy was its ambiguity and lack of precision in defining its objectives. While the institutional component was an undeniable novelty, the substantive dimension was clearly underdeveloped. This represented a reversal of the logical order: the institutional framework and cooperation mechanisms should be designed and adjusted in light of clearly articulated policy goals. The establishment of a competition enforcement network, largely for its own sake, demonstrated that the Policy lacked sufficient reflection and a comprehensive approach to developing an effective competition policy.

However, the adoption of the Policy was not followed by any meaningful action by the OCCP or other entities ostensibly included in the network to give effect to its provisions. Some of those identified as members of the network were unaware of their designation and had not participated in the drafting process. As a result, the Policy has not been reflected in the programmes or strategic documents of sectoral regulators, state inspectorates, or law enforcement agencies. The OCCP's annual report for the first full year of the Policy's implementation (2016) contains no reference whatsoever to progress in establishing the network. The network thus remains a purely theoretical construct, and there are serious doubts about whether it will ever be implemented as envisaged by the Policy.

4.5 Competition Policy: An Imperfect Instrument of Government Planning

Competition policy is a potentially valuable tool for embedding the promotion of competition as a shared objective across public administration and among relevant stakeholders. As an instrument of governmental planning, it is not formally binding on administrative authorities; nevertheless, it provides indicators by which their performance may be assessed, thereby serving as an important mechanism of accountability. In Poland, competition policy is adopted by the Council of Ministers. Although not a programme of a single authority, and notwithstanding its potential applicability across the entire government administration, in practice, it provides guidelines for all market regulators and a substantial part of the government's economic administration.

On one view, this may appear to constrain the OCCP's independence and constitute an attempt to influence its operational choices. Yet, on another view, the OCCP plays a central role in preparing competition policy: it initiates the drafting process, collects comments, and ultimately presents the final text to the government. Between 1993 and 1997, the Polish NCA itself acknowledged that the government rejected the drafts it had prepared, although no reasons were ever publicly provided. Conversely, the adoption of the 2015 Policy illustrates how an effective OCCP President can persuade the same government to align its policies with his conceptual vision. Research into the legislative process in Poland further shows that the OCCP deliberately inserted legislative analyses and regulatory optimisation tasks into Competition Policy documents, using these directives as vehicles to promote its own legislative proposals.[63] Another example of this instrumental approach appears in the 2004 Policy, which 'planned' legislative changes that had already been implemented before its adoption. This suggests that the OCCP sometimes treated competition policies not as forward-looking plans but as a form of political validation and support for tasks already completed or underway. Sectoral regulators operated in much the same way: sectoral priorities typically reflected actions they were already taking or were required to take. In such circumstances, the documents resembled summaries of mandatory tasks rather than genuine planning instruments.

This may have been the fundamental weakness of these documents (except for the 2015 Policy): they were 'safe'. They identified actions that merely reiterated statutory obligations – which, by definition, had to be implemented – or listed extremely general objectives that would require long-term structural transformation. Certain objectives recurred across successive policies, suggesting either a lack of fresh ideas or a lack of consequences for failing to complete earlier tasks. These shortcomings were often disguised by increasingly elaborate terminology and overly complex structural formulations, intended to mask the superficiality or artificiality of certain priorities and to conceal the failure to engage a wider spectrum of public administration authorities in competition policy.

---

63 G. Kopińska, G. Makowski, P. Waglowski, M. M. Wiszowaty, *Tworzenie i konsultowanie rządowych projektów ustaw. Raport z badania nad sposobem prowadzenia konsultacji publicznych i tworzenia dokumentów towarzyszących rządowym projektom ustaw w 2012 roku*, Waraw 2014, 216.

Nevertheless, it would be wrong to deny that many of these policies succeeded in bringing a degree of structure and coherence to the government's economic administration and to the tasks it undertook. In numerous areas, there was meaningful consistency between the priorities and directives articulated in the policies and the activities of the OCCP and sectoral regulators. This enhanced the predictability of the OCCP's actions and strengthened institutional accountability. Furthermore, many of the priorities and measures in the policies provided stakeholders with clearer insight into the OCCP's institutional and organisational condition, which, when expressed positively, demonstrated the level of internal effort required to achieve more effective competition enforcement.

The analysis of these policies reveals four distinct periods: 1990–1997, 1998–2003, 2004–2014, and the period after 2015. Each reflects a different set of challenges, which are mirrored in the content and structure of the relevant policies.

The first period (1990–1997) was pioneering, occurring against the backdrop of major political change and frequent government turnover. Competition policy in this era necessarily focused on foundational matters: dismantling the centrally planned economy, eliminating monopolistic structures where feasible, establishing the basic institutional conditions for the subsequent application of competition rules, and educating about competition, its importance, and its meaning.

The second period (1998–2003) was dominated by legal approximation and institutional adaptation in preparation for EU accession. During these years, original policy thinking was conspicuous by its absence, and virtually all planning was subordinated to the accession process. Despite this lack of continuity and the apparent disarray in governmental and OCCP activity, Poland succeeded in laying solid legal and institutional foundations, which became unmistakably visible after 2004.

The third period (2004–2014) reflects the OCCP's intensive process of institutional learning and improvement. The internal organisation became consolidated, legal frameworks were Europeanised, and enforcement stabilised. Competition policies became more coherent, and the articulation of governmental and OCCP objectives became clearer. This period of increased maturity is best exemplified by the 2014 Policy, whose structure and language were finally transparent and which contained genuinely new ideas. These developments culminated in the 2014 amendment to the Competition Act. Ironically, however, the benefits of these improvements accrued primarily to the subsequent OCCP President, while the 2014 Policy itself was overtaken by political change rather than implemented.

The fourth period (post-2015) began with significant ambition but ended abruptly and in silence. The 2015 Policy broke sharply with earlier models, replacing priorities and concrete plans with general directives rooted in the concept of 'network governance'. Its intended role was to coordinate and restructure the management of competition and consumer protection in Poland. The idea of building a network was conceptually innovative and reflected broader trends in public administration that emphasise the advantages of network-based methods for performing public tasks. Yet this theoretical merit cannot obscure the substantial flaws in both the concept and its attempted implementation.

First, the assumption that combining competition and consumer protection policies would generate synergies was empirically unfounded. Since the merger of these areas within the OCCP, there has been little evidence of synergy and far more that competition enforcement has been crowded out by consumer protection. A network built around consumer protection priorities risked further marginalising competition policy.

Second, the network's proposed breadth raised serious questions about how much its members' interests converged and whether meaningful coordination across such a diverse set of entities was feasible. The immediate abolition of key elements of the network – such as the Advisory Council to the President of the OCCP – further undermined its coherence. Additionally, some assertions in the 2015 Policy were clearly exaggerated. The suggestion that agreements to establish the network had already been concluded in 2012–2013 appears more aspirational than factual.

Third, surveys of the administrative bodies listed as network members revealed that most were unaware of their purported membership and did not perceive themselves as belonging to any network structure. This highlights the significant disparity between the ambitious vision outlined in the 2015 Policy and the practical realities of public administration in Poland.

5 Competition Policy and Priorities of the Polish NCA: A No-Man's Land

An examination of the legal framework, doctrinal foundations, and, most importantly, the substantive content of successive competition policy documents reveals a complex and ultimately pessimistic picture of strategic planning and operational governance in Polish competition enforcement. Paradoxically, the two most mature and conceptually interesting policy documents – the 2014 and 2015 Policies – have not been implemented. The 2014 Policy exemplified a positive evolution of the traditional approach to competition policymaking and served as a well-designed development plan for the subsequent four-year period. The 2015 Policy marked a radical departure from previous practice: it offered an innovative and contemporary conceptualisation of public policy management, grounded in principles of network governance and administrative coordination.

Although the 2015 Policy remains formally in force, it has never been implemented in practice. Since its adoption, neither the Polish NCA nor any other public administration body has undertaken any steps to implement its provisions, monitor their implementation, or even simulate compliance. The document has thus been rendered obsolete by administrative inertia and political disinterest.

In the absence of an operative government competition policy, one might reasonably expect the OCCP to assume a compensatory role by articulating its own enforcement priorities or strategic objectives. This expectation has not been met. Neither the current President of the OCCP nor the immediate predecessor has formulated a coherent set of priorities, guiding principles, or medium- or long-term enforcement plans. As a result, it has become increasingly difficult to discern any deliberate or internally consistent strategic orientation in the authority's activities. The only element that appears to recur with any regularity across successive presidencies is a rhetorical fixation on increasingly intensive and deterrent fining, which serves as a convenient surrogate for strategic planning rather than as its outcome.

Although economic scholarship recognises that, in certain exceptional circumstances, the absence of a competition policy may be preferable to a partial or inconsistently implemented one, such reasoning does not apply in the Polish context.[64] Poland has a clear statutory basis for adopting a government competition policy and for a functioning competition authority whose decisions are subject to judicial review. What exists today is therefore not an absence of policy, but a fragmented, incidental, and largely reactive set of administrative practices that cannot plausibly be regarded as a coherent policy framework.

The OCCP does not fill this political void. As a matter of jurisdiction, the authority lacks explicit statutory authority to engage in discretionary case selection, although such selection is clearly exercised in practice. Despite lacking formal prioritisation instruments, the OCCP does not employ other available tools to plan its enforcement activities or to cultivate a broader culture of

64 A. Mattoo, *Can no competition policy be better than some competition policy?*, International Journal of Industrial Organization 19 (2001), 73.

competition. No enforcement priorities and no prospective documents on strategy or even tactics of action are publicly announced, undermining transparency, weakening accountability, and diminishing legal certainty for stakeholders.

This omission is particularly striking in light of the ECN+ Directive, which introduced a formal power for NCAs to set enforcement priorities – an institutional reform intended to establish a more coherent, standards-based model of competition enforcement across the EU. In principle, the ability to set priorities is intrinsically linked to the conferral of discretion. Poland illustrates the risks of a model in which discretion is minimal in law but extensive in practice. Increased discretion, coupled with statutory guarantees of independence, necessarily entails heightened institutional responsibility. Awareness of the risks inherent in prioritisation should therefore form part of any considered approach to strategic case selection – yet no such awareness is evident in current OCCP practice.

The failure to adopt or implement a competition policy – whether governmental or internal to the OCCP – cannot be regarded as a positive development when compared with the more structured and transparent approach of the first two decades of the authority's existence. The absence of such a framework has eroded continuity, predictability, and transparency in enforcement activity. It also evidences the broader decline of a culture of competition in Poland and the instrumental treatment of institutional mechanisms designed to ensure that the OCCP functions as an independent and effective NCA.

During the 2023 implementation of the ECN+ Directive, one of the primary arguments for introducing enhanced guarantees of independence for the President of the OCCP was the need to facilitate longer-term planning of competition and consumer protection policy. Yet several years later, no government competition policy has been adopted, nor has the President of the OCCP – the primary beneficiary of these enhanced guarantees – taken steps to formulate such a policy or to articulate even a minimal set of enforcement priorities.

Membership of the EU ensures a basic level of policy coherence through the direct and indirect application of EU competition policy. The OCCP, whether voluntarily or out of necessity, participates in implementing EU competition rules and remains embedded in the broader European enforcement architecture, albeit often passively. The authority has not entered a distinctive national path of development nor made visible attempts to align itself with global trends in competition enforcement and policy coordination; however, these efforts appear largely symbolic and are motivated primarily by reputational considerations, such as securing favourable assessments in international rankings (e.g. Global Competition Review[65]), rather than by an internally generated strategic vision.

In summary, what currently exists in Poland is a situation characterised by formal continuity but substantive stagnation: a competition policy that remains legally valid yet practically inert, and a competition authority engaged in day-to-day enforcement without guidance from any strategic framework or articulated policy direction.

65 Commenting on the GCR rating, the current President of the OCCP confirmed his strong belief in his excellent execution of competition policy, stating that 'the highest rating we have received so far is also an incentive and encouragement for us to continue working hard to promote fair competition'. *UOKiK moves up in the ranking of competition authorities worldwide*, https://uokik.gov.pl/en/uokik-moves-up-in-the-ranking-of-competition-authorities-worldwide.

CHAPTER 7

Anticompetitive Practices

From the very beginning of Polish competition enforcement, counteracting anticompetitive practices by undertakings has constituted one of its core tasks. Since the first modern competition statute entered into force in 2000, the core provision on anticompetitive practices has remained unchanged. To a large extent, the case law developed under the 1990 Act remains relevant, as the provisions in force between 1990 and 2000 did not differ materially from the current legal framework.[1] While perceptions of cartels and other anticompetitive conduct evolved throughout the twentieth century, the need to combat such practices is no longer questioned in Poland. Polish legislation governing anticompetitive behaviour has been drafted in close alignment with European competition law and is therefore largely harmonised with EU rules. Nevertheless, certain particularities of Polish substantive law and administrative enforcement practice remain visible.

Anticompetitive practices may take the form of anticompetitive agreements or the abuse of a dominant position. These two categories are treated separately under the law because they present distinct analytical problems and require different legal and economic frameworks. This book, therefore, follows the same distinction and addresses them separately.

1 Extraterritoriality Principle

Competition law is an inherently elastic instrument for countering anticompetitive practices. One manifestation of this elasticity is its extraterritorial application. Extraterritoriality is understood here in a legislative or normative sense, namely as the competence to apply domestic law to persons or conduct occurring outside national borders.[2] The OCCP itself emphasises that a defin-

1 From the outset, the 1990 Act distinguished two principal categories of anticompetitive conduct, providing open catalogues of prohibited agreements and abuses of a dominant position. The principal legislative change introduced by the 2000 Act concerned bid rigging. Initially, the prohibition applied only to agreements between undertakings participating in a tender. Since 2004, however, bid rigging has been expressly extended to cover agreements not only among bidders but also between bidders and the tender organiser.

2 M. Martyniszyn, *Ekstraterytorialne stosowanie prawa konkurencji: ku efektywnemu ograniczaniu luk*, PPP 2025, no. 5, 106.

© 2026 THE AUTHOR(S) | HTTPS://DOI.ORG/10.1163/9789004754638-008
This is an open access publication distributed under the terms of the CC 4.0 license BY-NC-ND.

ing feature of competition law, as expressed in Article 1 of the Competition Act, is its extraterritorial reach, which extends to conduct by foreign undertakings, provided that its effects are felt in Polish territory.[3]

This approach has been consistently upheld by the courts, which hold that the Competition Act applies to practices carried out by both Polish and foreign undertakings if those practices cause or may cause effects within Poland, even where the conduct itself takes place abroad.[4] Conversely, the Act does not apply to anticompetitive practices whose effects materialise exclusively outside Polish territory, even if the undertakings concerned are based in Poland.[5] The Competition Act is neutral regarding the nationality or seat of undertakings and contains no subjective limitations on its scope. Accordingly, any undertaking, including a foreign one, may benefit from the Act's protection if competition-restricting practices produce effects in Poland.[6]

Applicability, however, does not equate to enforceability. For a long time, the practical effectiveness of the Competition Act in extraterritorial cases was significantly limited. Prior to the implementation of the ECN+ Directive, the OCCP lacked legal instruments to compel foreign undertakings to comply with cease-and-desist orders. Since 2023, the OCCP may request mutual assistance from other EU NCAs to enforce its decisions under Articles 101 or 102 TFEU. Outside this framework – particularly in relation to merger control or non-EU undertakings – the OCCP remains without effective enforcement tools.[7] The position of foreign undertakings changes once an OCCP decision is appealed, as such proceedings are civil in nature and the enforcement of judgments may rely on international instruments such as the Lugano Convention, which provides broader enforcement possibilities.[8]

2 The Notion of Undertaking

Competition law primarily regulates the conduct of undertakings. As a result, restrictions on competition arising solely from consumer behaviour fall outside its scope. More broadly, natural persons who do not engage in commercial activity are not considered undertakings, which may be relevant to new

3 OCCP decision DOK 4/2020.

4 CCCP judgment of 28.09.2022, XVII AmA 70/20.

5 R. Molski, *Eksterytorialne stosowanie prawa ochrony konkurencji*, RPEiS 2002, no. 3, 14.

6 CCCP judgment of 18.12.2002, XVII Ama 19/01.

7 Which is typical for most NCAs – M. Martyniszyn, *'Competitive Harm Crossing Borders: Regulatory Gaps And A Way Forward'*, JCLE 2021, No. 3, 686.

8 C. Banasiński, E. Piontek, Art. 1.

parental liability regulations. A distinctive feature of the Polish Competition Act is its exceptionally broad definition of an undertaking, which aims to capture all actual market participants regardless of their legal form or function, including whether they pursue profit or provide public services.[9]

Case law confirms that this definition encompasses entities such as cemeteries,[10] housing cooperatives,[11] public and private universities,[12] private secondary schools,[13] collective rights management organisations (including ZPAF[14] and ZAIKS[15]), and even churches.[16] The Act thus captures entities that would not typically be regarded as undertakings under other branches of law.

Local government authorities provide a particularly illustrative example. Although they are public authorities, they may be treated as undertakings when acting as economic operators rather than exercising public authority. The decisive criterion is the nature of the activity performed.[17]

In several respects, Polish competition law adopts a broader notion of an undertaking than EU competition law. This is evident, for example, in relation to public health insurance institutions.[18] While their status under EU competition law depends on additional functional criteria,[19] the Polish Competition Act has been applied to both healthcare chambers[20] and the National Health Fund.[21]

2.1 Extended Liability: Parent Undertaking

The implementation of the ECN+ Directive significantly broadened the scope of liability under Polish competition law. Liability now extends beyond undertakings directly involved in competition infringements to parent undertakings

9 PSC judgment of 7.04.2004, III SK 22/04.
10 CCCP judgment of 12.12.2006, XVII Ama 105/04.
11 CCCP judgment of 24.10.2001, XVII Ama 107/00.
12 PSC judgment of 7.04.2004, III SK 22/04.
13 PSC judgment of 9.03.2006, I CSK 135/05.
14 OCCP decision RWA 10/2007.
15 OCCP decision RWA 21/2004.
16 OCCP decision RLU 26/2004.
17 CCCP judgment of 3.08.2005, XVII Ama 36/04.
18 G. Materna, *Publiczne instytucje ubezpieczenia zdrowotnego w świetle prawa antymonopolowego*, PiP 2005, no. 6, 65.
19 Judgments of the CJEU of 16.03.2004 – *AOK Bundesverband* (Cases C-264/01, C-306/01, C-354/01 and C-355/01), and Court of First Instance of 4.03.2003 - *FENIN* (Case T-319/99).
20 CCCP judgment of 5.02.2003, XVII Ama 18/02.
21 OCCP decision RLU 28/2007.

that exercise decisive influence over infringing subsidiaries. This development formalised the 'single economic unit' concept in Polish law by introducing Articles 6b and 9a of the Competition Act.[22]

Where an infringement of Article 6(1) or Article 9(1) of the Competition Act, or of Articles 101 or 102 TFEU, is established, it is deemed to have been committed not only by the direct infringer but also by the undertaking exercising decisive influence over it. Procedurally, this allows the OCCP to initiate a single set of antimonopoly proceedings against both entities, provided that doing so contributes to the effective enforcement of competition rules.

This expansion of liability is reinforced by changes to the fining regime. When calculating fines, the OCCP must now take into account the combined turnover of both the infringing undertaking and the undertaking exercising decisive influence over it. Moreover, the OCCP may impose joint and several liability for fines on both entities. These changes are likely to lead to a substantial increase in the level of fines imposed in practice.

3 Anticompetitive Agreements

Article 6 of the Competition Act establishes a general prohibition on agreements whose object or effect is to eliminate, restrict, or distort competition on the relevant market. Three cumulative elements must be established to prove an infringement:

i. the existence of an agreement;
ii. an anticompetitive object or effect;
iii. an elimination, restriction, or distortion of competition.

Although Article 6 does not expressly state this, it is generally assumed that anticompetitive agreements can be concluded only between independent undertakings, and that such independence must be assessed on a case-by-case basis.[23] Accordingly, the OCCP takes the view that the Competition Act does not exclude agreements whose object or effect is to eliminate, restrict, or otherwise distort competition, merely because they are concluded within a capital group. In such cases, the OCCP examines the actual degree of autonomy of the undertakings in shaping their market conduct, in particular the extent to which a formally dependent undertaking enjoys freedom of action

22 In the past, the OCCP attempted to establish liability based on a parental relationship between undertakings, but the legality of such a practice awaits judicial review – OCCP decision DOK-6/2020.

23 K. Kohutek [in:] M. Sieradzka, K. Kohutek, *Ustawa o ochronie konkurencji i konsumentów. Komentarz*, Warsaw 2024, Art. 6.

vis-à-vis the controlling undertaking. Where such autonomy exists, the OCCP considers that the undertakings can coordinate their behaviour through an agreement in a manner relevant for competition law.[24] Consequently, in the OCCP's approach, the fact that undertakings belong to the same capital group does not automatically preclude the application of Article 6. If the internal arrangements leave sufficient scope for independent decision-making, the agreement may be classified as anticompetitive and subject to scrutiny under competition law.[25]

3.1 The Notion of an 'Agreement'

Polish law follows EU competition law in adopting a broad understanding of the notion of an agreement.[26] Article 4(5) defines agreements to include contracts, concerted practices, and decisions of associations of undertakings. Accordingly, anticompetitive coordination may take the form of formal or informal agreements, concerted practices that reduce strategic uncertainty without a formal contract, or binding acts of associations.

Based on this definition and extensive case law, three basic forms of anticompetitive coordination can be distinguished.

First, agreements sensu stricto. These may take the form of contracts or informal arrangements that restrict competition. The courts have repeatedly stressed that the Competition Act adopts a flexible, substance-oriented approach: it is sufficient to establish that a concurrence of wills between undertakings occurred, irrespective of form, legal enforceability, or terminology used.[27] Agreements may be concluded orally or in writing, explicitly or implicitly. Their legal classification under civil law is immaterial. What matters is mutual consent to coordinate market behaviour to the detriment of competition and other market participants. The concurrence of wills may be direct or indirect and may occur through intermediaries.[28]

Second, concerted practices. These constitute coordination without a formal agreement, where undertakings knowingly substitute practical cooperation for the risks of competition. Polish courts have held that repeated parallel conduct – such as simultaneous price changes by competitors producing the same products – may give rise to a presumption of a concerted practice

---

24 OCCP decision DOK-34/2007.

25 PSC judgment of 16.01.2003, I CKN 1200/00.

26 K. Kwok, *The Concept of 'Agreement' under Article 101 TFEU: A Question of EU Treaty Interpretation*, European Law Review 2019, no. 44, 196.

27 CCCP judgment of 12.06.2007, XVII Ama 64/06.

28 CCCP judgment of 15.03.1995, XVII Amr 66/94.

where it cannot be explained by normal market conditions.[29] The distinction between concerted practices and lawful parallel behaviour remains crucial. Parallel behaviour arising from rational market adaptation is lawful, whereas concerted practices involve conscious coordination aimed at reducing strategic uncertainty.[30] Exchange of information between competitors may facilitate collusion and, in certain circumstances, may itself constitute an anticompetitive agreement, even without a broader cartel arrangement.[31] However, Polish doctrine and case law emphasise the need for a careful, economically grounded assessment in order to avoid over-enforcement.[32]

Third, decisions of associations of undertakings. Historically, associations have often served as platforms for representing collective interests and lobbying. However, they may also facilitate collusion or impose anticompetitive constraints on members. Polish case law has repeatedly confirmed that associations of undertakings may themselves be liable for competition infringements. A notable example concerns professional associations, such as bar associations, which were found to restrict competition by adopting internal resolutions or codes of conduct that limited price competition or access to the profession. Membership in an association does not shield undertakings from liability; on the contrary, it may facilitate coordination.[33]

These categories are not mutually exclusive and may overlap. Once anticompetitive coordination is established, the precise form of cooperation plays only a subsidiary role in the application of Article 6.

3.2 Object or Effect of the Agreement

The Competition Act clearly separates the concepts of object and effect. Either is sufficient to establish an infringement. Consequently, an agreement may be prohibited even if it fails to produce anticompetitive effects, provided that its object is anticompetitive. Conversely, an agreement without an anticompetitive intent may still be unlawful if it produces restrictive effects.[34]

The OCCP frequently examines both the object and the effects of agreements. The anticompetitive object may be explicit or inferred from the agreement's content, its economic context, and the parties' behaviour. Certain cat-

29 PSC judgment of 24.04.1996, I CRN 49/96.

30 CCCP judgment of 11.06.1997, XVII Ama 17/97.

31 OCCP decision DOK-7/2009.

32 S. Jóźwiak, *Wymiana informacji między konkurentami jako praktyka ograniczająca konkurencję — kierunki rozwoju analizy prawno-ekonomicznej*, Warsaw 2011, 26.

33 CCCP judgment of 14.03.1997, XVII Ama 11/97.

34 CCCP judgment of 1.03.1993, XVII Amr 37/92.

egories of agreements – so-called hardcore restrictions – are presumed to be anticompetitive by object, thereby eliminating the need for detailed effects analysis. Decisions based solely on anticompetitive effects are rare. As a rule, the OCCP relies on the anticompetitive object of an agreement, that is, on restrictions whose very nature reveals a sufficient degree of harm to competition. This approach reflects the authority's selection strategy policy, which focuses on cases involving clear forms of coordination such as market allocation, price fixing, bid rigging, and, more recently, no-poach arrangements. By contrast, cases resting exclusively on an effects-based analysis are significantly more demanding, as they require extensive economic assessment, substantial evidentiary effort, and prolonged proceedings, and are therefore pursued only exceptionally.

3.3 Elimination, Restriction, or Distortion of Competition

Elimination of competition occurs when effective rivalry between actual or potential competitors is entirely excluded, even though undertakings would otherwise be willing to compete. Restriction of competition refers to situations in which rivalry remains possible but is significantly limited, for example, with respect to certain products, geographic areas, customers, or contractual conditions. Other distortions of competition include any deviations from the normal functioning of market mechanisms that alter the outcome of free rivalry.[35]

Anticompetitive agreements typically constrain the market independence of undertakings that are not parties to the agreement. However, not every limitation constitutes an infringement: normal legal, economic, or social constraints that affect all market participants equally fall outside the scope of Article 6.

3.4 Exemplification of Prohibited Agreements

The Act provides a non-exhaustive list of prohibited practices, which illustrates the breadth of anticompetitive coordination covered by Article 6.

i. Price fixing. Fixing prices or other trading conditions, directly or indirectly, is one of the most serious infringements, as it undermines the core mechanism of competition. Case law confirms that price fixing may concern the entire price or individual price components and may occur in both horizontal and vertical relationships. Resale price maintenance has been a particularly frequent enforcement focus. Not all competitors need

35 CCCP judgment of 21.05.1992, XVII Amr 13/92.

to be involved in price fixing – it suffices for two parties to collude to constitute such behaviour an infringement of the Competition Act.[36] The OCCP has fined, inter alia, clothing and sports distributors and retailers equipment,[37] producers of windows and doors,[38] and manufacturers of wood-based panels.[39] In the Kronopol case, minimum resale prices were enforced through deterrence measures, including financial sanctions against noncompliant distributors.[40] Similar practices were identified in cases involving Akuna Polska, where distributors were forced to set fixed retail prices and restricted in their trading choices with partners.[41] Certain sectors, such as taxi services[42] and construction, appear particularly prone to price-fixing practices.

ii. Limiting or controlling production, sales, technical development, or investment. Such agreements aim to restrict supply, typically leading to higher prices. They may include specialisation agreements, production quotas, or investment restraints. Crisis cartels, concluded during economic downturns, are explicitly prohibited. A notable example involved companies providing outdoor advertising services agreeing to reduce billboard availability and set minimum rental prices to 'optimise' the billboard network.[43] Another case concerned agreements between ironworks and contractors that limited access to scrap metal.[44] Particularly illustrative is the case in which two national fuel producers agreed at the same time to cease production of a declining petrol type; while the business rationale was understandable, the coordinated nature of the decision rendered it unlawful.[45]

iii. Market sharing. Market division may be geographic, product-based, customer-based or even employee-based. Polish enforcement practice includes cases involving exclusive rights to sell specific products, such as kosher vodka,[46] as well as anticompetitive conduct by pharmacists'

36 CCCP judgment of 1.03.1993, XVII Amr 37/92.

37 OCCP decision RKT-16/2011.

38 OCCP decision RLU-9/2011.

39 OCCP decision DOK-3/2017.

40 OCCP decision DOK-8/2012.

41 OCCP decision DOK-7/2012.

42 For example, taxi companies operating on the same local market, which were fined in 2011 (OCCP decision RBG-9/2011) and subsequently in 2012 (OCCP decision RBG-29/2012).

43 OCCP decision RPZ-21/2002.

44 CCCP judgment of 8.06.1996, XVII Amr 15/96.

45 OCCP decision DOK 99/2007.

46 CCCP judgment of 8.11.1993, XVII Amr 27/93.

associations discouraging the establishment of new pharmacies.[47] Market-sharing agreements have also been identified in insurance markets,[48] animal feed production,[49] and passenger transport. In one notable case, a complainant undertaking itself was found to be party to a market-sharing arrangement and avoided a fine only because it unknowingly disclosed the infringement to the OCCP.[50] Another notable case concerned Merida, which prohibited its distributors from selling bicycles online or via auction platforms, allowing only passive online presentation and in-store sales collection.[51]

iv. Discriminatory trading conditions. Applying dissimilar conditions to equivalent transactions may distort competition by placing certain trading partners at a disadvantage. This form of discrimination often arises in vertical relationships. In the Philips Poland case, preferential rebates granted to one distributor without objective justification were found to infringe competition law.[52]

v. Tying and bundling. Making the conclusion of an agreement conditional upon acceptance of unrelated obligations may facilitate market entry or leverage market power. While more common in abuse-of-dominance cases, tying may also result from anticompetitive agreements.

vi. Exclusionary agreements and collective boycotts. These practices aim to restrict access to the market or eliminate non-participating undertakings. They may take the form of exclusive dealing or coordinated refusals to supply. Exclusive dealing should be assessed with caution since it is not illegal but it may be treated as such in given circumstances. Therefore the OCCP should limit its intervention to these agreements which pose a threat to the public interest and are not covered by the block exemption.[53] A prominent example involved exclusive broadcasting rights granted by the Polish Football Association, which foreclosed access for competing broadcasters.[54] Another case concerned public hospitals restricting access to specialised medical tests to exclude private providers from publicly funded healthcare markets.[55]

---

47 CCCP judgment of 6.07.1994, XVII Amr 8/94.
48 OCCP decision RBG-28/2011.
49 OCCP decision RBG-7/2020.
50 OCCP decision RPZ-11/2018.
51 OCCP decision RKT 1/2023.
52 OCCP decision DOK 87/2006.
53 CCCP judgment of 27.10.1992, XVII Amr 21/92.
54 OCCP decision DOK 49/2006.
55 OCCP decision RLU-31/2012 and RBG 13/2006.

vii. Bid rigging and collusive tendering. Collusion in public or private tenders undermines competitive procurement. Polish case law includes examples of both horizontal and vertical bid rigging. In one case, a consortium comprising the two largest waste-collection undertakings was found to be a sham arrangement designed to preserve market shares rather than address genuine technical constraints.[56]

4 Relativisation of the Prohibition of Anticompetitive Practices

The prohibition on anticompetitive agreements is not absolute. The Competition Act provides de minimis, individual, and block exemptions, which rationalise enforcement and allow the OCCP to focus on the most serious infringements. Under the de minimis rule, agreements are exempt if competitors' combined market share does not exceed 5% or if non-competitors' individual market shares do not exceed 10%. Hardcore restrictions are excluded from this exemption. Individual exemptions apply where agreements generate efficiencies that outweigh their restrictive effects and satisfy four cumulative conditions.[57] The burden of proof rests entirely with the undertaking invoking the exemption, and the standard is high.[58] Finally, block exemptions adopted by the Council of Ministers provide safe harbours for specific categories of agree-

---

56 OCCP decision RLU-38/2012. This was the OCCP's first decision in which cooperation between undertakings within a consortium – cooperation that, in principle, is lawful – was called into question. The OCCP ultimately decided not to impose a fine on the undertakings concerned. Instead, the decision was explicitly preventive and aimed at signalling the limits of permissible cooperation in tender procedures. Its primary purpose was to identify and warn undertakings whose conduct, although formally framed as consortium cooperation, could be regarded as anticompetitive in bidding processes.

57 Those four premises are:

i. contribution to the improvement of production or distribution of goods, or to technical or economic progress;
ii. allowing the buyer or user a fair share of the benefits resulting therefrom;
iii. not imposing upon the undertakings concerned such impediments as are not indispensable to the attainment of these objectives;
iv. not affording these undertakings the possibility of eliminating competition in the relevant market in respect of a substantial part of the goods in question.

58 CCCP judgment of 23.04.1992, XVII Amr 5/92.

ments, including vertical agreements[59] and technology transfer agreements.[60] These instruments further align Polish competition law with EU practice while preserving national enforcement autonomy.

4.1 Enforcement Trends

4.1.1 The First Years: High Intensity, Limited Cartel Focus

Polish competition enforcement was exceptionally active in its early years. This is reflected in the enforcement ratio, the number of proceedings initiated, and the volume of decisions issued. However, this intensity did not translate into robust cartel enforcement. From today's perspective, cartel prosecution was not a central focus of the OCCP during its formative period. This was largely due to societal transformation and the need to educate the public (including businesses) about the importance of competition law and policy. [61] As a result, enforcement efforts in the 1990s were primarily directed at unilateral conduct by former state monopolies and other dominant undertakings, with a strong emphasis on advocacy.

This does not mean, however, that cartel enforcement was entirely absent. Contrary to the widespread narrative that serious cartel enforcement began only after Poland's accession to the EU, enforcement activity against competitor agreements already existed in the early 1990s.[62] OCCP report from 1992 indicate that numerous proceedings concerned horizontal agreements. The authority explicitly identified the growing number of complaints and notifications relating to emerging cartels as a phenomenon likely to intensify as market relations develop in a transitioning economy.[63] Thus, while cartel enforcement was institutionally weak, it was not conceptually absent.

---

59 Regulation of the Council of Ministers of 22.05.2023 on the exemption of certain types of vertical agreements from the prohibition of competition restricting agreements of certain vertical agreements, JoL 2023, item 1033.

60 Regulation of the Council of Ministers of 17.04.2015 on the exemption from the prohibition on competition-restricting agreements of certain categories of agreements concerning the transfer of technologies, JoL 2015, item 585.

61 M. Martyniszyn, M. Bernatt, 32–35

62 J. Pecotić Kaufman, *Intensity of Cartel Enforcement in Central and Eastern Europe: A Comparative Analysis*, 12–13, http://dx.doi.org/10.2139/ssrn.5809203.

63 Activity Report 1992, 5.

4.1.2 Professional Associations and the Limits of Competition Law

One of the most distinctive lines of Polish case law concerns professional associations (liberal professions). These organisations typically have a dual legal character. On the one hand, they are professional associations engaged in economic activity. On the other hand, they perform delegated public functions and operate as decentralised elements of public administration. Membership is usually mandatory, and access to the profession depends on the association's administrative decisions.

Despite this hybrid status, professional associations are treated as undertakings or associations of undertakings under the Competition Act. The OCCP has imposed fines on organisations representing pharmacists,[64] medical doctors,[65] architects,[66] advocates,[67] notaries,[68] tax advisers,[69] and farmers.[70] In most cases, the infringement involved adopting binding ethical codes or internal regulations that restricted competition, often under the threat of disciplinary sanctions, including exclusion from the profession.

Typical examples include restrictions on opening new professional offices,[71] prohibitions on price competition,[72] or bans on participation in tenders where price constituted the sole selection criterion.[73] Particularly illustrative were cases involving notaries, architects, and pharmacists, where ethical rules effectively limited market entry or price competition.

The most controversial intervention in this area concerned the Supreme Medical Council's position on homoeopathy. The OCCP found that a resolution discouraging doctors from prescribing homoeopathic products restricted competition in the market for prescription homoeopathic medicines.[74] The courts overturned this decision, emphasising that competition law cannot compel professionals to provide services that lack scientific validity. The CCCP judgment clearly delineated the boundary between competition enforcement and legitimate regulatory objectives rooted in the public interest and profes-

---

64 Antimonopoly Authority decision of 17.08.1993, DO-II-500-8-93/1285.
65 OCCP decision RPZ 10/2005.
66 OCCP decision DOK-106/06.
67 CCCP judgment of 14.05.1997, XVII Ama 11/97.
68 CCCP judgment of 14.05.2003, XVII Ama 55/02.
69 OCCP decision RKT-31/2006.
70 OCCP decision RPZ 24/2007.
71 CCCP judgment of 06.06.2017, XVII AmA 6/17.
72 CCCP judgment of 18.9.2007, XVII Ama 125/06.
73 CCCP judgment of 16.1.2007, XVII Ama 18/06.
74 OCCP decision DOK-6/2011.

sional standards.[75] This case illustrates the structural limitations of competition law when applied to regulated professions.

4.1.3 Resale Price Maintenance: The Holy Grail of (Not Only) Polish Antitrust

Resale Price Maintenance is one of the most intensely debated issues in antitrust law[76] and one of the most common and widespread categories of agreements investigated by NCAs.[77] During the European Commission's discussions on revising the Vertical Block Exemption Regulation, NCAs stated that they had no substantial experience or empirical evidence of instances in which resale price maintenance had led to, or could have led to, efficiency gains. They therefore agreed that RPM should remain classified as a hardcore restriction under the VBER. More specifically, some NCAs argued that resale price maintenance is typically not indispensable for achieving the efficiency gains that could otherwise justify an exemption.[78] Poland and the OCCP in particular are no exception in this respect. There is a significant body of critical doctrinal literature that questions the automatic treatment of RPM as a hardcore restriction and points to the excessively narrow space left for its economic justification.[79] The OCCP, however, has shown no willingness to

75 CCCP judgment of 30.12.2014, XVII AmA 163/11, and Court of Appeals judgment of 01.04.2016, VI ACa 75/15.

76 For an overview of discussions, see B. Jedlicková, *Resale price maintenance and vertical territorial restrictions: theory and practice in EU competition law and US antitrust law*, Cheltenham 2016 or Ł. Grzejdziak, *Ustalenie cen odsprzedaży towarów w prawie europejskim i amerykańskim. Studium prawnoporównawcze*, Łódź 2020.

77 As evidenced by the OECD – Roundtable on Resale Price Maintenance, DAF/COMP (2008)37, https://www.oecd.org/content/dam/oecd/en/publications/reports/2009/09/resale-price-maintenance_bd8c934a/126ecbc8-en.pdf. For a recent case overview, see D. Fritz, S. Saljanin, Ch. Wey, EU *Resale Price Maintenance: An overview of EU and national case law*, e-Competitions 2025, Art. N° 121710.

78 *Summary of the contributions of the National Competition Authorities to the evaluation of the Vertical Block Exemption Regulation, 5*, https://competition-policy.ec.europa.eu/system/files/2021-06/VBER_IA_summary_contributions_from_NCAs.pdf.

79 J. Fidala, *Narzucanie minimalnych i sztywnych cen odsprzedaży z punktu widzenia celu oraz skutków rynkowych*, iKAR 2012, no. 3, D. Aziewicz, *Resale Price Maintenance in Poland–Further Steps to its Liberalization or Stuck in a Status Quo?*, YEARS 2016, no. 9(13); B. Turno, A. Zawłocka-Turno, *Standard prawny oceny wertykalnych porozumień cenowych polegających na ustalaniu sztywnych (lub minimalnych) cen odsprzedaży na gruncie ustawy o ochronie konkurencji i konsumentów*, iKAR 2016, no. 1.

revise its enforcement approach, particularly because RPM cases account for a substantial share of its interventions and enforcement decisions.[80]

An analysis of the OCCP's enforcement practice shows a consistently high number of vertical cases, predominantly involving resale price maintenance. In 2024, the authority concluded proceedings against Empire Brands, imposing a fine of approximately PLN 350,000 for fixing resale prices for pet food sold via online stores and shopping platforms, in breach of both Polish and EU competition law.[81] A similar infringement was found in the Spokey case, which was fined PLN 500,000 for fixing minimum resale prices and for monitoring distributors' price compliance.[82] In another decision, the OCCP found that Fellowes, an authorised distributor of office equipment, had agreed with its distributors not to sell below specified resale prices. Fellowes monitored compliance, retaliated against non-compliant distributors, and was informed by distributors of deviations from the arrangements; a fine of PLN 434,000 was imposed.[83] Comparable conduct was identified in the Solgar case, where the undertaking was fined approximately PLN 1.2 million and two managers, who were personally responsible for the infringement, were fined PLN 280,000.[84] Last but not least, the publisher and distributors of the *Harry Potter* book series were fined for engaging in price fixing. The publisher received information from distributors about instances in which *Harry Potter* books were sold at prices below the agreed-upon prices. In addition, wholesalers required booksellers – both in writing and orally – to adhere to the agreed resale prices.[85]

In several cases, RPM was accompanied by additional restrictive practices. One such example is the Dahua case, concluded in 2023. Dahua Technology Poland, one of the largest suppliers of electronic monitoring equipment, entered into anticompetitive arrangements with its distributors, including both price-fixing and market sharing. The OCCP imposed fines on six undertakings and seven managers directly involved in the collusion, totalling nearly PLN 37 million.[86]

---

80 For an overview of Polish cases, see G. Materna, *Wertykalne porozumienia cenowe – ewolucja orzecznictwa sądowego i praktyki decyzyjnej Prezesa UOKiK*, Glosa 2017, no 2; or M. Modzelewska de Raad, *Poland: Enforcement of vertical restraints in Poland – Practitioner's insight*, Concurrences 2019, no. 2, Art. N° 89871.

81 OCCP decision RKR 6/2024.

82 OCCP decision RŁO 1/2021.

83 OCCP decision RKR 1/2021.

84 OCCP decision DOK 4/2021.

85 OCCP decision RKT-17/2005.

86 OCCP decision DOK 5/2023.

A particularly significant cluster of RPM cases emerged in the automotive sector. Between 2013 and 2021, KIA Poland and eleven authorised dealers colluded on resale prices and divided the market, effectively preventing consumers from obtaining competing offers. The OCCP imposed total fines exceeding PLN 405 million, including more than PLN 331 million on KIA Poland alone, as well as sanctions on five managers.[87] Similar conduct was identified in the Iveco Poland case, in which the importer and ten distributors coordinated customer allocation and pricing. Fines exceeded PLN 238 million for undertakings and PLN 2.5 million for managers.[88] In a further decision concerning DAF truck dealers, the OCCP found market sharing, price fixing, and bid rigging that lasted at least seven years and imposed fines totalling PLN 122 million on five undertakings and eight managers, with partial leniency and settlement reductions granted in one instance.[89]

Vertical restraints, and RPM in particular, constitute the most numerous and economically significant category of infringements pursued by the OCCP. Classified as hardcore restrictions, they are relatively straightforward to establish and are treated with particular severity, as reflected in the high fines imposed on both undertakings and individual managers. This strict enforcement approach is generally upheld by the courts. Given the quantitative importance of RPM cases in Polish competition enforcement, there is little indication that a more nuanced or effects-based approach to RPM will emerge in the foreseeable future.

4.1.4 Sports Associations and Wage Coordination

A new line of jurisprudence has emerged concerning sports associations. To some extent, it reflects the reinvigorated enforcement trends observed at the EU level. The first significant case concerned the Polish Automobile and Motorcycle Federation (PZM) and Ekstraliga Żużlowa (Speedway Extra League – SEL). Under its agreement with PZM, SEL manages speedway competitions at the highest league level in Poland, while PZM organises competitions in the first and second speedway leagues.

The OCCP found PZM responsible for adopting regulations governing speedway competitions that set maximum remuneration rates payable by clubs to athletes, with SEL participating in the development of these rules. As a result, neither Extra League clubs nor clubs in other speedway leagues could

87 OCCP decisions DOK 3/2024, DOK 4/2024, DOK 5/2024.
88 OCCP decision DOK 2/2024.
89 OCCP decisions DOK 6/2021, DOK 8/2021.

offer remuneration exceeding the predetermined caps. These limits were introduced in 2013 and remained in force throughout the 2014 season.

The conduct of PZM and SEL also affected competition beyond Poland. Polish speedway competitions are regarded as among the strongest in the world, attracting numerous foreign athletes, while Polish riders regularly compete abroad. Consequently, remuneration levels in Polish leagues may serve as benchmarks in other jurisdictions. For this reason, the OCCP concluded that the agreement also infringed Article 101 TFEU. Financial penalties totalling PLN 5.2 million were imposed on PZM and SEL.[90]

The second notable case concerned the Polish Basketball League and its leading clubs. It involved an agreement to coordinate conduct towards professional players during the COVID-19 pandemic, specifically to suppress players' remuneration in the 2019/2020 season. Following the league's premature termination, the clubs agreed with the Polish Basketball League not to pay players their full contractual salaries. These arrangements failed to account for each player's individual financial circumstances. Under the unlawful agreement, player contracts were to be terminated without payment of remuneration for the remainder of the season. The OCCP imposed fines totalling PLN 946,440.50 on 17 entities for their participation in the infringement.[91]

Both cases may be viewed as part of a broader global trend towards heightened scrutiny of employer coordination in labour markets, including wage-fixing and no-poach agreements, as examined in the following subsection.

4.1.5 Labour Markets: A New Enforcement Frontier

The sports-related cases paved the way for the OCCP to adopt a broader focus on labour markets. Competition enforcement in labour markets has become an emerging trend among national competition authorities. It primarily concerns antitrust enforcement, although merger control may also be affected. Several NCAs have issued guidelines or policy notes on this topic, including

90 OCCP decision DOK 1/2022.
91 OCCP decision DOK 1/2023.

those from Slovakia,[92] the UK,[93] the US,[94] the OECD,[95] and the EU.[96] The OCCP followed this trend by issuing guidelines on anticompetitive labour-market practices in 2024.[97]

These guidelines explain the role of competition law in labour markets, emphasising that restrictions on competition in this area harm both employees' welfare and overall economic growth. They aim to clarify the application of competition law to labour market practices, with a particular focus on no-poaching agreements, wage-fixing arrangements, and non-compete clauses.

The most recent cases concern the practices of the two largest retail chains in Poland – Biedronka[98] and Dino[99] – and their relations with transport companies that serve them. The OCCP conducted searches and initiated investigations into a possible anticompetitive agreement among transport companies. In particular, the authority is examining whether the undertakings entered into unlawful arrangements that prevented them from competing for employees. The investigation focuses on the so-called 'grace period' or 'blockage' system, i.e. informal agreements between employers that may have hindered drivers from changing jobs and restricted the recruitment of workers previously employed by competitors. As a result, drivers' employment mobility may have been significantly limited. The OCCP is also assessing whether Bie-

92 *Competition in the Labour Market,* https://www.antimon.gov.sk/data/files/2943_competition_labour_market.pdf?csrt=4468750418287948916.

93 *Employers advice on how to avoid anti-competitive behaviour,* https://www.gov.uk/government/publications/avoid-breaking-competition-law-advice-for-employers/employers-advice-on-how-to-avoid-anticompetitive-behavior.

94 *Antitrust Guidelines for Business Activities Affecting Workers,* https://www.ftc.gov/system/files/ftc_gov/pdf/p251201antitrustguidelinesbusinessactivitiesaffectingworkers2025.pdf.

95 *OECD Study on Competition in Labour Markets,* https://www.oecd.org/content/dam/oecd/en/publications/reports/2020/03/competition-issues-in-labour-markets_02ec78ba/66980788-en.pdf.

96 A. Aresu, D. Erharter, B. Renner-Loquenz, *Antitrust in labour markets,* EU Competition Policy Brief 2024, no. 2.

97 *Collusion and Abuses on the Labour Market. Competition Law vs Employee Matters,* https://uokik.gov.pl/en/Download/725.

98 *Collusion in the labour market? President of UOKiK presses charges against Biedronka and transport companies,* https://uokik.gov.pl/en/collusion-in-the-labour-market-president-of-uokik-presses-charges-against-biedronka-and-transport-companies.

99 *Another collusion on the labour market? President of UOKiK launches a preliminary investigation,* https://uokik.gov.pl/en/another-collusion-on-the-labour-market-president-of-uokik-launches-a-preliminary-investigation.

dronka and Dino imposed, enforced, or coordinated the use of such prohibited practices. Both proceedings are pending at the explanatory stage.

Cases concerning sports associations and retail chains have been accompanied by media communications from the OCCP suggesting that the authority is acting to protect employees, particularly.[100] However, a closer examination of the OCCP's decisions does not support this narrative. Any protection of employees' interests appears incidental, stemming from the authority's primary objective of safeguarding market efficiency. In this context, the OCCP's portrayal of its intervention as employee-centred enforcement seems unconvincing.[101]

4.1.6 Bid Rigging: Local, Persistent, and Predominant

Bid rigging is a significant component of Polish cartel enforcement and reflects a broader pattern across Central and Eastern Europe. Comparative studies show that enforcement against bid rigging is particularly pronounced in Bulgaria, Latvia, Czechia, Poland, and Slovakia, where between 80% and 86% of all cartel infringement decisions concern collusive tendering. This demonstrates that competition authorities in these jurisdictions focus heavily on bid rigging, which is central to their cartel enforcement.[102]

A distinctive feature of OCCP enforcement in this area is its strong local focus. Bid-rigging cases typically involve local markets and relatively small-scale tenders. To strengthen enforcement performance, the current OCCP President established a separate department at headquarters dedicated exclusively to bid-rigging. However, apart from this organisational change, no further structural or methodological improvements were introduced.[103] As a result, the reform proved ineffective. The specialised unit's enforcement output was no better than that of regional offices, which handle a much broader range of competition matters. In 2025, the dedicated department was abolished, and bid-rigging cases were redistributed to other units and regional branches of the OCCP.

---

100 *Zmowa na rynku pracy? Prezes UOKiK stawia zarzuty Biedronce i firmom transportowym*, https://uokik.gov.pl/zmowa-na-rynku-pracy-prezes-uokik-stawia-zarzuty-biedronce-i-firmom-transportowym.

101 T. Sztyma, *Antykonkurencyjne porozumienia na rynku pracy – zarys tematyki*, PiZS 2025, no. 4, 37.

102 J. Pecotić Kaufman, *Intensity Of Cartel Enforcement In Central And Eastern Europe: A Comparative Analysis*, http://dx.doi.org/10.2139/ssrn.5809203, 17.

103 Refer to section 4.7.3.

The local character of bid-rigging enforcement is further illustrated by the sectors involved in recent OCCP decisions. These include municipal waste disposal,[104] transport of children to schools,[105] bread supply,[106] delivery of vegetables to military units,[107] road maintenance,[108] supply of railway sleepers,[109] towing and parking services,[110] delivery of software and computer equipment,[111] supply of heat energy,[112] provision of chemical products to mines,[113] supply of vegetables and preserves,[114] as well as the construction of water and sewage infrastructure.[115]

Bid rigging constitutes not only a competition law infringement but also a criminal offence under Polish law. However, it is uncommon for competition proceedings and criminal investigations to run in parallel. Some OCCP decisions indicate that bid-rigging detection has been enabled through cooperation with other public authorities, law enforcement bodies, or contracting authorities themselves.

4.1.7 From Market Study to Infringement Decision

Market studies played an important role in the initial phase of competition enforcement in Poland. As discussed earlier in Chapter 3, their significance diminished considerably over the following two decades. Nevertheless, despite their limited use in recent years, there are still examples demonstrating the potential value of market studies for effective enforcement.

A notable example is the OCCP's market study into the distribution of hard coal to households, conducted in 2022–2023.[116] The study aimed to gather comprehensive information on the hard coal market and assess the state of competition, with particular focus on thermal coal consumed by individual customers. A sharp price increase and a coal shortage in Poland prompted

---

104 OCCP decision RPZ 12/2022.
105 OCCP decision RKR-3/2022.
106 OCCP decision RWR-8/2016.
107 OCCP decision RPZ-12/2009.
108 OCCP decision RŁO-60/2013.
109 OCCP decision DOK-2/2020.
110 OCCP decision RKT-4/2017.
111 OCCP decision RWR-1/2019.
112 OCCP decision DOK-5/2020.
113 OCCP decision RKT-46/2013.
114 OCCP decision RGD-11/2019.
115 OCCP decision RKR-1/2019.
116 *Kto prowadzi składy węgla w Polsce?*, https://archiwum.uokik.gov.pl/aktualnosci.php?news_id=19157.

this inquiry. The study acknowledged that thermal coal in Poland is not a homogeneous product and can be classified by various criteria, including type, class, and sorting. It revealed that the household thermal coal retail market is highly fragmented. Importantly, the OCCP analysed contractual arrangements between producers and importers on the one hand, and distributors on the other. This analysis identified resale price maintenance practices. In particular, the OCCP found that Atex, an undertaking engaged in the import, distribution, and wholesale and retail sale of hard coal, imposed resale prices on its distributors. As a result, distributors cooperating with Atex could not sell coal to consumers at prices below the company's set prices. In December 2022, the OCCP initiated infringement proceedings against Atex, and in 2024, imposed a fine of nearly PLN 2.5 million.[117]

It is regrettable that the OCCP does not conduct market studies on a broader or more regular basis. There is no publicly available explanation for this policy choice, despite the clear enforcement benefits illustrated by the coal market case. It appears that market studies have increasingly been replaced by dawn raids, which – despite being an extraordinary and intrusive investigative tool – have become a routine instrument in the OCCP's practice and, troublingly, even a proxy for measuring enforcement success.[118]

5 Abuse of a Dominant Position

The Competition Act prohibits the abuse of a dominant position. Dominance itself is not unlawful; on the contrary, it may reflect the success of an undertaking's business strategy. What is prohibited is the excessive exercise of market power that restricts competition. A dominant undertaking may freely increase its market share across various markets, provided that the means used to achieve this objective are not contrary to the Competition Act.[119]

The Act defines a dominant position as one that enables an undertaking to prevent effective competition in the relevant market and to act, to a significant extent, independently of its competitors, contracting parties, and consumers. A rebuttable presumption of dominance arises where an undertaking's market share exceeds 40%. This presumption is purely formal and may be overturned.[120] Dominance may also be established only for certain periods;

117 OCCP decision DOK 1/2024.

118 Refer to section 7.8.1.

119 CCCP judgment of 12.02.1993, XVII Amr 33/92.

120 CCCP order of 3.10.1994, XVII Amr 5/93.

temporary fluctuations in market shares or market power resulting from changing strategies or exogenous shocks are insufficient to establish dominance.[121] Polish law recognises both unilateral and collective dominance, and both forms are covered by the Competition Act.

Abuse of dominance may consist of an act or an omission.[122] Its essence lies in depriving other market participants of their economic independence, forcing them to operate under less favourable conditions or eliminating them from the market altogether.[123] Abuse may also take the form of exploitative conduct towards other undertakings or consumers. In interpreting the notion of 'abuse', emphasis is placed on the existence of a real threat that poses a serious and potential risk of harm, sufficient to compel the weaker party to accept contractual terms that would not be accepted under normal competitive conditions. It is irrelevant whether the threat ultimately materialised.[124]

5.1 Exemplification of Prohibited Conduct

While the Competition Act does not define the term 'abuse of dominance', it provides a non-exhaustive list of examples. Dominant conduct often fulfils more than one of the listed categories. These include:

i. Direct or indirect imposition of unfair prices or other trading conditions, including excessive or predatory pricing, delayed payment terms, or other unfair conditions. This category encompasses strategies that manipulate prices to the detriment of contractors or consumers, particularly when prices bear no reasonable relation to the economic value of the goods or services offered.[125] Price differentiation, in itself, is not unlawful and may reflect competitive dynamics.[126] To establish abuse, prices are typically compared with production costs and, where appropriate, with prices in neighbouring competitive markets.[127] Proof is often complex. For example, pricing below a competitor's costs does not, in itself, establish predatory pricing and may reflect economies of scale or efficiency gains.[128] A notable case concerned the National Health Fund, which was fined for setting prices for dental services below the cost of

121 CCCP judgment of 26.04.1995, XVII Amr 73/94.
122 CCCP judgment of 15.05.1996, XVII Amr 21/96.
123 CCCP judgment of 10.05.1993, XVII Amr 6/93.
124 CCCP judgment of 1.03.1995, XVII Amr 59/94.
125 CCCP judgment of 26.02.1993, XVII Amr 35/93.
126 CCCP judgment of 15.09.1992, XVII Amr 18/92.
127 CCCP judgment of 25.06.1992, XVII Amr 10/92.
128 CCCP judgment of 12.10.1994, XVII Amr 30/94.

provision. Expert evidence showed that the prices did not cover dentists' costs, leading the Fund to discontinue the practice.[129]

ii. Limiting production, sale, or technological development to the detriment of contractors or consumers, including unjustified refusals to deal or to grant access to essential infrastructure. While refusals to contract may be objectively justified – for example, because of non-payment[130] or prior unfair competition[131] – dominant undertakings may not refuse to provide services without objective justification if they can do so. This was illustrated by the case against PGNiG, which refused to transmit gas imported by an independent trader despite having the technical capacity to do so, thereby protecting its monopoly position.[132]

iii. Applying dissimilar conditions to equivalent transactions, thereby placing certain contractors at a competitive disadvantage. This discriminatory practice must be assessed with caution, as dominant undertakings are not obliged to offer identical terms to all contractors. However, any differences must be objectively justified. Courts have condemned unjustified selective fees,[133] particularly in situations of supply shortages,[134] where fair allocation among contractors is required.[135] Rebate schemes are frequently scrutinised, including cases involving municipalities that privileged municipal undertakings over private ones.[136] A clear example of lawful differentiated contractual conditions is the Wrigley case. The OCCP analysed whether the use of different pricing and discounts was discriminatory. It concluded that there was no violation because the differences were justified by sales through separate distribution channels. This decision shows that varied pricing or rebates are not inherently abusive or anti-competitive if they are based on legitimate business reasons and objective criteria, rather than exclusionary intent.[137]

iv. Tying or bundling, i.e. making the conclusion of a contract conditional upon acceptance of an additional, unrelated obligation. This practice aims at foreclosing markets for competing products or services. The assessment focuses on whether the additional obligation has a sub-

129 OCCP Decision DOK 28/2007.
130 CCCP judgment of 8.11.1995, XVII Amr 38/95.
131 CCCP judgment of 3.08.1994, XVII Amr 18/94.
132 OCCP decision DOK 91/2005.
133 CCCP judgment of 13.11.1996, XVII Amr 41/96.
134 Ibidem.
135 CCCP judgment of 22.10.1997, XVII Ama 23/97.
136 OCCP decision RWR-10/2011.
137 OCCP decision DOK-8/2010.

stantial or customary link to the main contract. Examples include municipalities conditioning access to utilities on unrelated charges[138] or licensors obliging licensees to bear costs unrelated to the licensed activity.[139]

v. Preventing the emergence or development of competition, particularly through structural strategies such as cross-subsidisation.[140] Typical cases include forcing the use of selected suppliers without technical justification, or compelling contractors to purchase materials exclusively from the dominant undertaking, under threat of being refused access to essential infrastructure.[141]

vi. Imposing onerous contractual terms that yield unjustified profits is a classic exploitative abuse. Such terms deviate from those typical of comparable contracts and enable the dominant undertaking to extract additional profits solely by virtue of its market power.[142] These practices are particularly common among natural monopolies, including municipal utilities that impose unfair pricing structures on consumers.[143]

vii. Market partitioning according to territorial, product, or subjective criteria. Mere price differentiation across local markets is not sufficient to establish abuse if objectively justified.[144] However, where differentiation aims to exclude competitors or distort competition, it constitutes abuse.[145] Examples include municipalities favouring their own market operators through differentiated fees,[146] or monopolistic funeral service providers discriminating against competitors.[147]

The prohibition of abuse of dominance is absolute. Unlike anticompetitive agreements, the Competition Act provides no exemptions.

---

138 OCCP decision RKR 10/2011 or RŁO 14/2011.

139 PSC judgment of 20.06.2006, III SK 8/06.

140 CCCP judgment of 23.03.1994, XVII Amr 59/93.

141 CCCP judgments of 27.10.1992, XVII Amr 22/92 or 27.10.1992, XVII Amr 20/92.

142 CCCP judgment of 24.01.1991, XV Amr 2/90.

143 OCCP decision RKR 18/2011.

144 CCCP judgment of 12.10.1994, XVII Amr 30/94.

145 CCCP judgment of 28.05.1997, XVII Ama 13/97.

146 CCCP judgment of 11.05.1994, XVII Amr 64/93.

147 CCCP judgment of 11.05.1994, XVII Amr 61/93.

5.2 Enforcement Trends

5.2.1 From Systemic Transition to Enforcement Activism: The Formative Years of Abuse Control

The OCCP was established when the economy was almost entirely state-owned, with many undertakings operating under monopoly conditions. It is therefore unsurprising that preventing unilateral anticompetitive conduct quickly became a central focus of enforcement activity. This orientation was evident in the authority's first activity report, which identified abuses of a dominant position as the most frequent form of competition infringement. [148] The very first decision issued by the competition authority illustrates this approach: it ordered a price reduction for Fiat 125p vehicles sold by FSO in Warsaw, which, at the time, was the sole manufacturer and dominant supplier of medium-sized passenger cars in Poland. That decision was subsequently annulled by the court.[149]

The competition authority emphasised the distinctive nature of natural monopolies in Poland, which, during the early transition period, retained the characteristics of administrative monopolies. Prices for electricity, heat, and liquid fuels were set by the Minister of Finance, while modern legal and institutional frameworks for regulating these sectors were largely absent.[150] In response, the authority undertook initiatives to embed regulatory solutions in legislation, thereby laying the foundations for sector-specific regulatory agencies and for the training and organisation of expert bodies that would eventually staff them.[151] A second form of intervention, which may now seem striking, involved the direct participation of representatives of the antimonopoly authority on the supervisory boards of single-shareholder state-owned enterprises, such as Polskie Sieci Energetyczne, Telekomunikacja Polska, and major combined heat-and-power plants. The permanent presence of competition authority representatives on these boards was intended to facilitate oversight of monopolists' activities and to allow some influence over their strategic programmes.[152] While this approach may have been defensible as a short-term, transitional solution, in the longer run, such direct involvement in the governance of undertakings proved problematic and ultimately contributed to

148 Activity report 1990, 3.

149 Ibidem.

150 Activity report 1992, 6.

151 Ibidem.

152 Ibidem.

the premature termination of the first President's mandate, as discussed in Chapter 3.

A further distinctive feature of the first decade of the OCCP's operation was the predominance of antimonopoly proceedings initiated at the request of undertakings, which were binding on the authority. Between 1990 and 2000, such proceedings accounted for approximately 70–80% of all cases, depending on the year. This was reflected in the authority's reports, which frequently framed cases as disputes between individual undertakings, for example, 'Chio Lilly Chips' v. 'E. Wedel', 'Zajazd Galicja' v. Euro American Konsorcjum 'Autotak', or 'Technogaz' v. Linde Gaz Polska.[153] Superficially, this resembled the adversarial model typical of common-law jurisdictions. In reality, however, the system remained inquisitorial and administrative, with the OCCP responsible for initiating, conducting, and concluding proceedings.

5.2.2 From Market Leaders to Market Constraints: Regulating Legacy Dominance

In the early 1990s, the Polish economy was characterised by numerous incumbent market leaders. Many of these undertakings subsequently lost their dominant positions due to market liberalisation, structural transformation, and technological progress. A particularly illustrative example is Ruch. Until 1992, Ruch was an almost complete monopolist in the distribution of press and publications. For decades, Ruch functioned in public perception as a synonym for press distribution outlets in Poland.

In 1992, the competition authority issued two decisions finding that Ruch had abused its dominant position. The first concerned its contractual relations with retailers. Until March 1990, Ruch applied a uniform agency and commission agreement to its retail network. Subsequently, a variety of contractual models were introduced across Ruch's different branches, including lease, rental, agency, and franchising agreements. The granting of greater formal independence to Ruch's branches resulted in the mass termination of existing contracts and their replacement with new agreements that were significantly less favourable to retailers. The second decision addressed Ruch's conduct vis-à-vis a press publisher. Despite its monopoly position in domestic press distribution, Ruch refused to distribute the publisher's magazine, invoking alleged transport capacity constraints. In both cases, the authority found that Ruch's conduct constituted an abuse of a dominant position, ordered the cessation of

153 Activity Report 1995, 19–20.

the practices, and imposed financial penalties.[154] In 2025, Ruch ultimately ceased all operations.

Another prominent group of cases concerned Telekomunikacja Polska (TP), which for many years held a monopoly in the market for traditional fixed-line telephony. TP was the addressee of numerous decisions issued by the OCCP. Over time, the authority found that TP had committed a range of competition infringements, including:

i. unlawful demands, consisting of threats to disconnect one of the mobile operators from international traffic unless it accepted settlement rules imposed by TP;
ii. the imposition of unreasonably short deadlines and onerous negotiation conditions that effectively prevented mobile operators from responding to TP's demands in a timely manner;
iii. refusal to conclude an agreement with a local operator specifying the terms of interconnection between their networks;
iv. refusal to grant a local operator a share of revenues generated through inter-network cooperation;
v. unfair setting and application of excessive fees for the lease of telecommunications lines, thereby conditioning access to different levels of the telecommunications services market;
vi. unfair pricing of universal telecommunications services with the aim of eliminating competing operators and cross-subsidising or favouring selected groups of subscribers at the expense of others, including those awaiting access to public network services; and
vii. termination, without legal basis, of an inter-operator agreement with a mobile operator and the imposition of unequal settlement terms unrelated to the actual costs of interconnection, to the detriment of the development of mobile telephony services.[155]

Although traditional fixed-line telephony no longer plays a central role in the Polish telecommunications market, and TP – now part of the Orange group – operates as one of four major mobile network operators, the company's historical significance in the development of Polish competition law should not be underestimated.

Possession of a monopoly position could also lead to structural remedies, including decisions ordering the breakup of undertakings. Such measures were relatively common in the early 1990s. A notable example is the 1993 decision requiring PGNiG, the Polish incumbent gas monopolist, to be split

154 Activity report 1992, 5.

155 Activity report 1997, 18.

into separate entities in two stages: first, separating construction, production, and design activities, and second, isolating geophysical and drilling operations.[156] This decision was never implemented and was withdrawn by the authority a few years later.

5.2.3 Natural and Local Monopolies as the Backbone of Early Abuse Enforcement

The majority of decisions issued by the OCCP concerned local monopolies, many of which were also natural monopolies. Although the number of such cases fluctuated over time, regional offices consistently played a central role in investigating and prosecuting these infringements. As early as 1992, the authority reported that numerous complaints – primarily from housing cooperatives and municipal associations – concerned the financing of energy and gas networks and equipment, as well as the conditions under which energy suppliers assumed such infrastructure investments. The core dispute typically centred on the allocation of costs for the construction, maintenance, and operation of energy networks, and the extent to which these costs could be shifted to end users.[157]

A representative example is the case brought by a housing cooperative against a local heat energy company. The complaint concerned the imposition of onerous contractual terms, in particular the company's refusal to contribute to financing heating infrastructure built at the cooperative's expense, which subsequently became the heat supplier's property and generated unjustified benefits for it. In addition, the cooperative allegedly abused its dominant position by selling heat energy at discriminatory prices in favour of selected economic entities. The OCCP confirmed the validity of these allegations.[158] In subsequent years, the authority issued numerous similar decisions. For instance, in its decision of 13 October 2000, the OCCP penalised a local heat supplier for passing on to consumers the risk of heat losses occurring between the measurement point (located before the heat exchanger) and the delivery point (after the exchanger), thereby charging for heat energy that had not actually been consumed.[159] Another form of abuse was addressed in a decision dated 28 September 2006, in which the OCCP found that a heat supplier had abused its dominant position by refusing to issue technical conditions for

156 Activity report 1993, 5.
157 Activity report 1992, 6.
158 Activity report 1995, 22.
159 OCCP decision RGD 27/2000.

connecting heat-generating equipment to its network and by denying consent to route a heat pipeline through its property to enable such connection.[160]

An analysis of the OCCP's decisional practice shows that undertakings in the district heating sector frequently engaged in unilateral conduct that restricted competition, primarily by exploiting the lack of effective competition in local heating markets. The limited substitutability between district heating and alternative heat sources is a key factor explaining why abuses of dominance in these markets pose a particularly serious threat to consumers. Importantly, such practices adversely affect both industrial customers and individual household consumers to a comparable extent.[161]

Another notable area of enforcement concerned local funeral services markets. In one case, a funeral home was found to have engaged in exclusionary practices to eliminate competitors. The undertaking offered free storage of corpses in the only available cold storage facility in the city – rented from a provincial hospital – on condition that it was entrusted with organising the entire funeral, while charging storage fees to customers who chose competing funeral service providers. The OCCP ordered the discontinuation of this practice.[162] Similar abuses were identified in the closely related market for cemetery services. In this context, the most frequent addressees of OCCP decisions were organisational units of the Catholic Church, which administer the majority of cemeteries in Poland. It is now well established that, when performing such activities, parishes qualify as undertakings within the meaning of the Competition Act.[163] For example, the OCCP found that a rectoral church had abused its dominant position by restricting funeral service providers' access to essential cemetery services, including grave digging, construction, and reconstruction, and by reserving the provision of a full range of funeral services to the cemetery administrator from the moment the deceased's body was delivered to the cemetery chapel.[164]

Abuses of dominance in local markets were also frequently committed by local government entities. Under the Competition Act, municipalities and provinces may be regarded as undertakings when they engage in economic activities.[165] Accordingly, the OCCP ordered a municipality to cease abusing its dominant position in the local market for the provision of bus-stop infra-

160 OCCP decision RKT-69/2006.

161 I. Szwedziak-Bork, *Nadużywanie pozycji dominującej przez przedsiębiorstwa ciepłownicze na lokalnych rynkach ciepła*, iKAR 2016, no. 4, 45.

162 Activity report 1994, 9.

163 CCCP judgment of 12.01.2006, XVII Ama 105/04.

164 OCCP decision RLU-26/2004.

165 CCCP judgment of 03.12.2003, XVII Ama 139/02.

structure by imposing onerous, non-uniform contractual terms that created differentiated conditions of competition and varying fees for individual carriers to maintain bus stops.[166] In another case, the OCCP found that a municipality had abused its dominant position by requiring undertakings that collect municipal waste to use only two designated waste disposal facilities under a municipal waste management plan adopted by the local council.[167]

Although the fight against local monopolies was a central pillar of Polish competition enforcement for many years, this area has seen a marked decline in importance. Over the past decade, the number of decisions addressing abuses in local markets has steadily declined, and under the OCCP's current leadership, enforcement in this field has been virtually abandoned. This development appears to reflect a deliberate policy choice, as the current president does not regard restrictions in local markets as a priority for competition enforcement. The marginalisation of this area is further evidenced by the declining role of regional offices, as discussed in Chapter 4. It is difficult to identify a coherent justification for this policy shift, particularly given that the reduced focus on local markets has not been accompanied by a corresponding intensification of enforcement at the national level. Such an approach risks squandering the OCCP's institutional legacy and accumulated expertise over several decades.

5.2.4 Selective Enforcement and the Retreat from State-Related Dominance Control

In recent years, allegations have been made that the OCCP has shown leniency towards state-owned undertakings.[168] Proponents of this view argue that during the period of political and economic transformation, Polish competition law was vigorously enforced against agreements that restrict competition and against abuses of dominant positions by state-owned undertakings. By contrast, since 2015 – when the OCCP issued its last decision finding an abuse of a dominant position by a state-owned undertaking – the application of competition law to such entities has been significantly reduced.[169]

166 OCCP Decision RKT 68/2006.

167 OCCP Decision RKT 54/2007.

168 J. Menkes, 68–69, or M. Bernatt, M.K. Sznajder, *Praworządność w prawie gospodarczym–o rozszerzeniu stosowania testu LM w wyroku Sądu w sprawie T-791/19, Sped-Pro przeciwko Komisji Europejskiej i płynących z tego konsekwencjach dla stosowania prawa konkurencji w Polsce*, EPS 2022, no. 12, 7.

169 M. Bernatt, M.K. Sznajder.

This line of reasoning is persuasive and largely accurate. Compared with the period before 2016, the OCCP has become statistically less interventionist in several large state-owned companies. This observation rarely supports the most far-reaching critiques. In some cases, the decline in enforcement reflects structural changes in the market position of the undertakings concerned rather than selective under-enforcement. A frequently cited example is PKP Cargo, which for many years served as an incumbent champion in the rail freight sector – the second-largest rail cargo market in Europe.[170] However, after more than two decades of formal independence alongside persistent political control, the company lost a substantial share of its market and now retains only a fraction of its former market share.[171] As a result, PKP Cargo ceased to be a frequent addressee of decisions concerning unilateral conduct, largely due to market developments rather than regulatory forbearance.

A more problematic example is provided by PKN Orlen, the incumbent champion in the production and distribution of fuels and petrochemical products. As discussed in greater detail in the following chapter, Orlen's pricing policy has raised serious concerns under competition law. The most striking episode was a sharp decline in retail fuel prices in the period immediately preceding the parliamentary elections on 15 October 2023, followed by a gradual but steady increase thereafter. Orlen, particularly after its merger with Lotos S.A., was accused of 'artificially' lowering prices, setting them independently of objective cost drivers such as global crude oil prices, excise duties, fuel charges, VAT, and the PLN/USD exchange rate.[172] Such abrupt price reductions should be interpreted as part of a legally questionable strategy pursued by vertically integrated oil companies, with independent petrol station operators as the primary victims.

Despite substantial grounds for regulatory involvement, the OCCP refrained from intervening. Available external academic analyses indicate that 'the price reductions were inconsistent with Orlen's historical pricing policy and could not be justified by external economic factors. Comparisons with crude oil prices in Europe, retail fuel prices in other EU Member States, and exchange rate movements leave little doubt that the pricing strategy was designed to

---

170 *Nadmiar etatów i problemy z zarządzaniem. Czy PKP Cargo da się uratować?*, https://klubjagiellonski.pl/2024/07/30/nadmiar-etatow-i-problemy-z-zarzadzaniem-czy-pkp-cargo-da-sie-uratowac/.

171 *Niepewna kontynuacja działalności PKP Cargo*, https://www.parkiet.com/transport/art42781421-niepewna-kontynuacja-dzialalnosci-pkp-cargo.

172 K.K. Kowalczyk, *Jak statystycy złapali Orlen na „ustawianiu" inflacji*, https://www.rp.pl/opinie-ekonomiczne/art39497451-krzysztof-a-kowalczyk-jak-statystycy-zlapali-orlen-na-ustawianiu-inflacji.

generate positive public sentiment ahead of the elections, thereby benefitting the ruling political camp. In this sense, Orlen's conduct cannot be plausibly explained by a concern for the public interest but appears to have been motivated by particular interests. Moreover, credible evidence suggests that this pricing policy posed risks to national fuel security, ultimately necessitating the release of compulsory fuel reserves.'[173]

A further illustration of the current leadership's cautious and selective enforcement posture may be found in the OCCP's handling of matters involving the Polish Football Federation (PZPN), an entity that, at the relevant time, appeared to benefit from a particularly favourable political and regulatory environment.[174] Unlike other sports associations, where OCCP interventions were decisive and well-founded, the authority's actions vis-à-vis the PZPN remained largely superficial. The OCCP initiated proceedings concerning the Federation's practice of charging betting companies a fixed fee amounting to 0.5% of their total gross revenue for access to sports competition results. This fee was calculated based on the bookmaker's overall revenue, regardless of whether it came from competitions organised by the PZPN and the Polish league or from other sporting events. The OCCP itself acknowledged that this practice could constitute an abuse of a dominant position.

Nevertheless, the authority discontinued the proceedings after the method of calculating the fee and its amount were modified during the investigation. The current President of the OCCP publicly presented this outcome as a personal success.[175] This approach is difficult to grasp. It allowed the PZPN to avoid antitrust liability, and, more importantly, the OCCP refrained from formally establishing that an abuse of dominance had occurred. Instead, the authority merely closed the investigation and issued a public statement. In substantive terms, the OCCP's intervention did not alter the competitive situation, as the agreement had been revised before and independently of the authority's actions.[176]

---

173 M. Kamiński, A. Szafrański, *Prawna, polityczna czy żadna? Odpowiedzialność w spółce z udziałem Skarbu Państwa w sektorze energetycznym – rozważania na przykładzie cen paliw ciekłych na polskim rynku w latach 2022–23*, Warsaw 2025, 134.

174 *PiS chciał przepchnąć setki milionów dla PZPN,* https://www.sport.pl/pilka/7,65037,30760001,jadczak-ujawnil-gigantyczny-skandal-wokol-pzpn-pis-chcial-im.html.

175 *PZPN i Ekstraklasa zmieniają praktyki,* https://archiwum.uokik.gov.pl/aktualnosci.php?news_id=20283.

176 *UOKiK kończy wieloletnie postępowanie w sprawie opłat za wyniki i… przypisuje sobie zasługi za wypracowanie nowego modelu rozliczeń,* https://igamingpolska.pl/uokik-konczy-wieloletnie-postepowanie-w-sprawie-oplat-za-wyniki-i-przypisuje-sobie-zaslugi-za-wypracowanie-nowego-modelu-rozliczen/.

Equally problematic were the explanatory proceedings initiated in case of Nielsen Audience Measurement. These proceedings followed an intervention by a former prominent member of the ruling party, who had been appointed head of public television. After the change of government and the takeover of public media, audience figures declined markedly. According to the new public media management, these results were allegedly inaccurate and attributable to Nielsen's supposed abuse of a dominant position.[177] On this basis, the OCCP launched explanatory proceedings 'to preliminarily determine whether AC Nielsen's rules for continuous television audience measurement may constitute a violation of the Competition Act'.[178]

From the outset, the allegation appeared unfounded and revealed a fundamental misunderstanding of the OCCP's institutional role. The authority is not a media regulator tasked with assessing audience-measurement methodologies or the credibility of viewership data, but a competition authority responsible for safeguarding competitive market structures. Unsurprisingly, after three years of investigation, the proceedings concluded with a finding that no infringement of competition law had occurred.[179] The OCCP also initiated similar explanatory proceedings concerning an alleged anticompetitive agreement in the radio audience research market.[180] Despite conducting dawn raids, no evidence of any competition-law violation was identified.[181]

Together, these cases challenge the primary goals of competition enforcement. They neither clearly identified competitive harms nor engaged with market dynamics in a way typical of antitrust analysis. Instead, they seem to reflect a broad and somewhat unclear understanding of the OCCP's role, applying competition-law tools to areas more related to media policy and public debate. While this does not necessarily indicate political misuse, it raises valid concerns about the limits of competition enforcement and the potential issues of using competition-law procedures in situations where the competitive impact is minimal or indirect.

---

177 *Instytut krytykowany przez szefa TVP trafił pod lupę UOKiK,* https://businessinsider.com.pl/biznes/media/uokik-sprawdza-instytut-nielsena/njyns07.

178 *Badania oglądalności pod lupą UOKiK. Jacek Kurski zlecił urzędową kontrolę Nielsena,* https://www.money.pl/gospodarka/wiadomosci/artykul/jacek-kurski-tvp-badania-telemetryczne,127,0,2232703.html.

179 *Nielsen nie narusza ustawy o ochronie konkurencji i konsumentów, prowadząc własne badania,* https://www.wirtualnemedia.pl/nielsen-nie-narusza-ustawy-o-ochronie-konkurencji-i-konsumentow-prowadzac-wlasne-badania,7170535549724801a.

180 *Rynek reklamy radiowej i badanie słuchalności stacji radiowych – postępowanie wyjaśniające,* https://archiwum.uokik.gov.pl/aktualnosci.php?news_id=18229.

181 *Rynek radiowy – zakończenie postępowania wyjaśniającego,* https://uokik.gov.pl/rynek-radiowy-zakonczenie-postepowania-wyjasniajacego.

5.2.5 Allegro: One and Only?

Digital markets have become a central focus of contemporary antitrust enforcement worldwide.[182] Until recently, however, the OCCP had achieved little in this area. This changed in 2022, following the conclusion of the Allegro abuse-of-dominance proceedings. Allegro is the leading Polish online trading platform, providing marketplace services to independent sellers while also operating its own official store and selling goods directly to consumers, thereby competing with those sellers.

The OCCP found that Allegro had abused its dominant position by systematically favouring its own retail offers and official store. The infringement, inter alia, consisted of the undue use of control over the platform's search and display mechanisms. Allegro granted its retail activities access to a range of sales and promotional tools on the allegro.pl platform that were unavailable to independent sellers. These included, among others, discount coupons, the so-called 'black bar', the 'third dot' feature, recommendation carousels, the ability to modify offer descriptions and parameters, the ability to adjust prices of published offers, search phrase suggestions, cross-recommendations, dedicated return forms, and the official store logo. Independent sellers were excluded from using these features.

Preferential access to these tools significantly enhanced the effectiveness of Allegro's sales activities across various stages of the purchasing process, including generating consumer interest and influencing the final purchasing decision. Allegro's offers benefited from superior visibility and positioning relative to those of independent sellers, whose products were consequently displayed less prominently and were therefore less likely to be selected by consumers. For this conduct, the OCCP imposed a fine exceeding PLN 206 million for abuse of a dominant position.[183]

The Allegro decision marks the OCCP's first major enforcement action in a large digital market case. This underscores a broader concern: until 2022, the authority's presence in digital markets had been largely symbolic. Following the Allegro decision, the OCCP declared that 'Like other leading antitrust authorities, we put e-commerce and digital markets high on our enforcement agenda.'[184] On 27 May 2025, the OCCP initiated explanatory proceedings against Allegro regarding a closely related practice: the alleged preferential

182 *Enforcing competition law in digital markets and ecosystems: Policy challenges and options*, https://unctad.org/system/files/official-document/ciclpd74_en.pdf.

183 OCCP Decision DOK-3/2022.

184 OECD Annual Report on Competition Policy Developments in Poland 2022, 10.

treatment of its own delivery solutions. At the time of writing, these proceedings have not resulted in formal charges.[185]

In general, OCCP's enforcement in e-commerce primarily targets practices that harm collective consumer interests rather than abuses of dominant market positions. This trend indicates a preference for cases that are easier to handle in terms of procedure and evidence. More complex cases involving market dominance, which require detailed economic analysis and market definition, are less common. Additionally, consumer protection enforcement tends to attract more media attention and public scrutiny, likely influencing OCCP's enforcement decisions.

6 Decisions of the OCCP

A separate chapter of the Competition Act sets out the procedure for issuing decisions in cases involving anticompetitive practices. Upon completion of antimonopoly proceedings instituted under Articles 6–9 of the Competition Act or Articles 101 and 102 TFEU, the President of the OCCP issues administrative decisions. The Act provides for several types of decisions, the most important of which are as follows:

i. Infringement decision with an order to cease the practice – issued where the conduct of an undertaking infringes Articles 6 or 9 of the Competition Act or Articles 101 or 102 TFEU.
ii. Infringement decision with a declaration of discontinuance – issued where the undertaking has ceased the infringing conduct before the decision is adopted. The burden of proving that the practice has been discontinued rests with the undertaking concerned.
iii. Commitment decision – issued where, in the course of proceedings, it has been rendered plausible – on the basis of the circumstances of the case, information contained in the notification, or information forming the basis for instituting proceedings ex officio – that the prohibitions laid down in Articles 6 or 9 of the Competition Act or Articles 101 or 102 TFEU may have been infringed, and the undertaking concerned agrees to undertake or discontinue specific actions aimed at preventing such infringements. In such a decision, the OCCP makes the proposed commitments binding.

185 *Allegro faworyzuje własne metody dostawy kosztem InPostu? Sprawie przygląda się UOKiK*, https://www.cashless.pl/17108-allegro-inpost.

Although the OCCP is formally open to conclude proceedings with commitment decisions, its practical use remains limited. To raise awareness among undertakings and facilitate the use of this instrument, the OCCP issued *Clarifications on the issuance of commitment decisions in cases of competition-restricting practices and practices that infringe collective consumer interests.* Nevertheless, since 2015, fewer than ten commitment decisions have been adopted.

Commitment decisions play a marginal role in Polish antitrust enforcement. The OCCP has consistently treated them as an exceptional tool, applying them only where competition concerns can be effectively remedied without a finding of full infringement and where commitments are clear, verifiable, and capable of restoring competitive conditions. The very limited number of such decisions adopted since 2015 confirms the authority's reluctance to rely on commitments as a routine enforcement mechanism.

This cautious approach is illustrated by the Benefit Systems and PGNiG cases. In Benefit Systems, the OCCP accepted commitments only after the undertaking proposed targeted measures to address suspected exclusionary practices in both the sports-benefit and fitness-club markets, including guaranteed access for at least one competing operator and safeguards against discriminatory treatment of clubs.[186] In the PGNiG case, commitments were accepted only after the monopolist undertook to amend contractual clauses that hindered customer switching, and only after strict reporting obligations were imposed. In both cases, commitments were used to dismantle clearly identified competitive obstacles rather than to avoid substantive assessment.[187] It is noteworthy that both cases concerned non-compete clauses. This cautious enforcement pattern may indicate that the OCCP is keen to improve its enforcement statistics while remaining insufficiently confident in the robustness of its legal position to subject these cases to full judicial review through infringement decisions and fines.

The Mennica Polska decision further demonstrates the OCCP's restrained use of commitments. There, commitments were accepted only as a complement to a formal infringement finding and the imposition of a fine, not as a substitute for enforcement.[188] Taken together, these cases show that commitment decisions in Poland function as a narrowly applied corrective instrument, used selectively where they can credibly restore competition without undermining the deterrent effect of antitrust enforcement.

---

186 OCCP Decision DOK 5/2021.

187 OCCP Decision DOK 1/2012.

188 OCCP Decision No. RWR 29/2012.

TABLE 7.1 OCCP anticompetitive practice decisions by year, practice, and decision type (Source: OCCP activity reports)

Year	Type of practice	Competition law breach	Competition law compliance	Interim	Discontinuance	Practice stopped	Commitments	Procedural fine
2024	Horizontals	5	0	0	0	0	0	6
	Verticals	4	0	0	0	0	2	0
	Unilateral conduct	2	0	0	0	0	0	0
2023	Horizontals	7	0	0	0	0	0	8
	Verticals	2	0	0	0	0	0	0
	Unilateral conduct	0	0	0	0	0	0	0
2022	Horizontals	6	0	0	0	0	0	0
	Verticals	1	0	0	0	0	0	2
	Unilateral conduct	1	0	0	0	0	0	0
2021	Horizontals	7	0	0	0	0	0	0
	Verticals	5	0	0	0	0	0	3
	Unilateral conduct	1	0	0	0	0	0	0

TABLE 7.1 OCCP anticompetitive practice decisions by year, practice, and decision type (*cont.*)

Year	Type of practice	Competition law breach	Competition law compliance	Interim	Discontinuance	Practice stopped	Commitments	Procedural fine
2020	Horizontals	12	0	0	0	0	0	0
	Verticals	2	0	0	0	0	0	0
	Unilateral conduct	1	0	0	0	0	0	0
2019	Horizontals	11	0	0	0	0	0	0
	Verticals	1	0	0	0	0	0	0
	Unilateral conduct	0	0	0	0	0	0	0
2018	Horizontals	3	0	0	0	0	0	0
	Verticals	0	0	0	0	0	0	0
	Unilateral conduct	0	0	0	4	0	1	0
2017	Horizontals	7	0	0	0	0	0	0
	Verticals	5	0	0	0	0	1	0
	Unilateral conduct	6	0	0	0	0	0	0

TABLE 7.1 OCCP anticompetitive practice decisions by year, practice, and decision type (*cont.*)

Year	Type of practice	Competition law breach	Competition law compliance	Interim	Discontinuance	Practice stopped	Commitments	Procedural fine
2016	Horizontals	0	2	0	0	7	0	1
	Verticals	0	0	0	1	3	0	0
	Unilateral conduct	3	2	0	0	5	4	1

6.1 Enforcement Ratio

The table 7.1 present the number of OCCP decisions issued in antitrust cases in 2016 and 2024.

6.2 Assessment of Enforcement Trends (2016–2024)

An analysis of enforcement activity between 2016 and 2024 shows that the OCCP's antitrust enforcement has been overwhelmingly focused on anticompetitive agreements, with horizontal agreements constituting the dominant category in both quantitative and substantive terms. Although formally classified as 'horizontal agreements', most of these cases in practice concern bid rigging in public procurement.

This pattern has been particularly pronounced in recent years. In 2023, all substantive infringement decisions concerned anticompetitive agreements: six involved bid rigging, two involved resale price maintenance, and only one concerned a horizontal agreement outside the public procurement context. A similar pattern is evident in 2022, with seven of eight decisions addressing anticompetitive agreements and only one concerning abuse of a dominant position.

The growing use of procedural sanctions – particularly in horizontal cases – suggests a greater focus on enforcing procedural obligations rather than a qualitative shift in substantive enforcement priorities. This development reflects a pragmatic, at times opportunistic, enforcement strategy rather than a recalibration of competition policy objectives.

Enforcement against vertical restraints remains moderate. While infringement decisions do occur, their number is noticeable, and commitment decisions are used selectively. Abuse of dominance cases show the most restrained enforcement profile, with meaningful activity largely confined to the earlier years of the period analysed. In later years, such cases become sporadic or disappear altogether, suggesting a strategic retreat from complex investigations of dominance.

Across all categories, the near absence of compliance findings and interim measures indicates a preference for final, deterrence-oriented decisions rather than declaratory or precautionary interventions.

7 General Enforcement Issues

Finally, three cross-cutting issues merit attention when assessing competition enforcement. First, they reveal how the last two OCCP presidents have defined and measured 'effective' enforcement, with a strong emphasis on procedural activity rather than substantive outcomes. Second, they illustrate the consequences of this approach for the structure and credibility of antitrust enforcement, including a shift toward more easily demonstrable enforcement outcomes. Third, they demonstrate that the limited effectiveness of competition law enforcement in Poland cannot be attributed solely to the OCCP's enforcement policy but also reflects systemic weaknesses in the judicial review of competition cases by civil courts.

7.1 Dawn Raids as a Proxy for Enforcement Success

Dawn raids constitute an intrusive procedural and investigative tool that may be indispensable for uncovering secret concerted practices. Originally used in criminal investigations, this instrument was later transplanted into competition enforcement as an exceptional measure. Its extraordinary nature is underscored by the requirement of prior judicial authorisation and the police's involvement during the search. A dawn raid does not presuppose the existence of an infringement; rather, it serves to verify substantiated suspicions. When this legal context is ignored – particularly in brief or sensationalist press communications – the instrument may be misconstrued as evidence of wrongdoing. One would therefore expect the leadership of an independent competition authority to demonstrate a nuanced understanding of both the legal constraints and the enforcement implications of dawn raids.

The OCCP has openly acknowledged that 'since around 2017, UOKiK has been implementing a more active policy of conducting dawn raids'.[189] In subsequent years, the authority has repeatedly framed maintaining a 'steady number of investigations and dawn raids' as an enforcement objective success.[190] In 2023, the OCCP emphasised that a 'large and stable number of dawn raids remains one of UOKiK's priorities', noting that court authorisations were obtained in nine cases, with searches at 44 undertakings and inspections at a further six entities. The authority further highlighted that – 'it had surpassed its previous record for the number of locations searched

189 OECD Annual Report on Competition Policy Developments in Poland 2021, 4.
190 OECD Annual Report on Competition Policy Developments in Poland 2022, 6.

simultaneously'.[191] In 2024, the OCCP confirmed the continuation of this policy, emphasising both the volume of dawn raids and their increased 'effectiveness', as measured by the number of undertakings targeted in each inspection.[192]

The explicit presentation of dawn raids as a standing enforcement priority is both striking and troubling. It is striking because it amounts to an open admission that procedural activity is being prioritised over substantive adjudication. The OCCP ignores that this mechanism should be used only on an exceptional basis, not as a routine means of evidence gathering; however, there is a growing impression that it has effectively become a standard investigative practice. Empirically, the persistently high number of searches is not matched by a corresponding rise in substantive infringement decisions. It is troubling because elevating the volume of dawn raids to a benchmark of success risks conflating investigative intensity with effective competition enforcement. Such an approach facilitates easily communicable enforcement 'achievements', which may be publicly portrayed as robust cartel enforcement, despite their limited connection to final decisions or tangible deterrent effects. Under the current leadership, the routine publicisation of dawn raids has thus become an enforcement narrative in its own right – something that was exceptional rather than standard practice in earlier periods.

The OCCP's growing reliance on searches raises broader questions about the judiciary's role in approving such invasive actions on a widespread basis. Judicial oversight of search warrants appears largely superficial. CCCP seldom conducts a thorough review of whether the OCCP has provided sufficient concrete and credible reasons to suspect a competition law infringement, nor does it carefully evaluate whether a search is necessary and proportionate. Additionally, the opportunity to effectively challenge a search authorisation is largely illusory, further undermining judicial oversight. This situation risks reducing judicial approval to a mere procedural step and calls into question the overall effectiveness of judicial control.

7.2 From Substantive to Procedural Enforcement

An analysis of the intervention ratio in recent years shows a marked rise in fines for procedural infringements. Over the past three years, this trend has become particularly pronounced, with the number of procedural fines in 2023 nearly matching the number of sanctions for substantive competition law infringements. This development is difficult to interpret as a positive sign of

191 OECD Annual Report on Competition Policy Developments in Poland 2023, 4–5.

192 OECD Annual Report on Competition Policy Developments in Poland 2024, 4.

effective competition enforcement. A growing focus on procedural violations risks diverting the OCCP's limited resources from substantive antitrust analysis to ancillary compliance issues.

To some extent, this increase is a predictable consequence of the authority's declared priority of maintaining a high level of investigative activity, particularly through dawn raids. The OCCP itself has explicitly linked procedural enforcement to its search policy, noting that, due to its intensive use of dawn raids, it issued several decisions for failure to cooperate during inspections, resulting in significant aggregate fines.[193] In a subsequent report, the authority similarly highlighted sanctions imposed for refusing to provide information or for submitting false or misleading information responses.[194] Procedural enforcement has thus become an integral by-product of an investigative strategy centred on frequent and expansive searches.

The rise in procedural infringements may also reflect a declining willingness among undertakings to cooperate with the authority. This erosion of institutional authority is notable, though it cannot be entirely dissociated from the OCCP's own enforcement posture. In one illustrative case, an undertaking subjected to a prolonged dawn raid failed to provide access to electronic data and was fined PLN 350,000, while its chairperson was fined PLN 50,000.[195] Such relatively modest personal sanctions are unlikely to produce meaningful deterrence, either general or individual, and may instead signal that obstructing investigations entails limited risk.

The Dell case offers a revealing example of the OCCP's current enforcement approach. Dell was investigated by the authority for potentially anticompetitive arrangements with distributors and authorised resellers. The proceedings culminated in a commitment decision, in which Dell agreed to modify its sales model – an outcome that is relatively rare given the OCCP's traditionally restrictive stance on commitments.[196] However, in parallel, the authority imposed a substantial procedural fine of EUR 1.4 million for repeatedly providing false and misleading information during the investigation.[197] Dell did not appeal either decision. Although the OCCP formally treated the two decisions as separate, their timing and outcome strongly suggest interdependence. The case exemplifies a broader tendency to prioritise procedurally straightforward sanctions over complex substantive adjudication, enabling the authority to

193 OECD Annual Report on Competition Policy Developments in Poland 2023, 4–5.
194 OECD Annual Report on Competition Policy Developments in Poland 2024, 4.
195 OCCP decision RŁO-7/2024.
196 OCCP decision DOK-6/2024.
197 OCCP decision DOK-7/2024.

project an image of robust enforcement while avoiding more demanding economic and legal analysis.[198]

Taken together, these developments indicate that the OCCP's growing reliance on procedural infringements reflects an opportunistic enforcement strategy. Procedural cases are formalistic, require limited economic assessment, and are comparatively easy to investigate and adjudicate. They therefore offer quick and visible 'successes' that can be readily communicated to the public, even if their contribution to effective competition protection remains questionable.

7.3 Inefficiency of Judicial Review

The retention of civil courts' jurisdiction over appeals against OCCP decisions is traditionally justified on the basis of their supposed effectiveness. In particular, adjudication on the merits and the formal power to amend the authority's decisions are presented as advantages over administrative courts, which are limited to reviewing legality and may only uphold or annul a decision, remitting the case to the authority for reconsideration.[199] While these arguments are theoretically appealing, practice has largely discredited them. Empirical analysis of civil court case law shows that, notwithstanding their broader formal powers, civil courts tend in practice to act like administrative courts, refraining from substantive adjudication and avoiding decisive rulings on the merits.[200]

Two emblematic cases illustrate the dysfunction of this model. The first concerns the cement cartel – the largest cartel uncovered by the OCCP. The infringement decision, adopted in 2009, imposed fines on seven undertakings.[201] As of the end of 2025, the case remains before the Supreme Court after multiple rounds of judicial review. While the decision has become final and binding for some parties – either because they did not appeal or ultimately paid the imposed fines – the proceedings against most cartel participants have continued for over sixteen years. There is still no certainty that the

198 *Poles overpaid for Dell computers. There is a penalty from the OCCP*, https://www.rp.pl/biznes/art41288831-polacy-przeplacali-za-komputery-della-jest-kara-uokik; *Dell fined by the OCCP. It must pay PLN 6 million*, https://businessinsider.com.pl/biznes/dell-ukarany-przez-uokik-musi-zaplacic-6-mln-zl/3v1v18x; *Huge fine for Dell. It must pay millions of zlotys and change its sales model*, https://next.gazeta.pl/next/7,151243,31383472,ogromna-kara-dla-firmy-dell-musi-zaplacic-6-mln-zl-i-zmienic.html.

199 M. Bernatt, *Sprawiedliwość*, 280.

200 M. Szydło, *Sądowa kontrola decyzji Prezesa UOKiK w świetle prawa unijnego i prawa polskiego*, EPS 2015, no. 7, 16.

201 OCCP decision DOK 7/2009.

Supreme Court will resolve the matter definitively. Ironically, this prolonged and ineffective judicial process coincided with the OCCP's 2025 announcement of a possible resurgence of cartel behaviour in the cement sector, prompting renewed investigative proceedings and dawn raids.[202] Both the outcome of the original case and the new investigation are uncertain.

An even more striking example is the interchange fee case involving 20 banks. The case concerns a long-standing agreement on interchange fees, set independently of actual costs and determined through coordinated action to maintain supra-competitive profits for Visa and MasterCard transactions.[203] After nearly twenty years of litigation and repeated transfers between courts, the case has once again returned to the court of first instance – the CCCP. Any ruling at this stage will almost certainly be appealed, making a final resolution unlikely in the near future. In the meantime, the real value of the contested amount – approximately PLN 141 million – has eroded dramatically due to inflation, falling to roughly two-thirds of its original value. This case offers a stark illustration of the limited effectiveness of civil courts in delivering timely, deterrent, and economically meaningful outcomes in competition law enforcement.

8 Conclusions

Anticompetitive practices – whether unilateral or multilateral – lie at the core of competition enforcement. In this respect, the OCCP has played an important role, and Poland's economic transformation owes much to early and intensive competition enforcement, particularly in dismantling monopolistic structures at both national and local levels. These achievements, however, are largely confined to the first two decades of the authority's operation. Since then, the intensity of substantive market interventions has gradually declined. While part of this trend may be explained by increased compliance awareness among undertakings and improvements in competitive market structures, the sharp reduction in enforcement activity over the past decade correlates closely with the policy choices of the last two OCCP Presidents.

At present, enforcement against anticompetitive agreements dominates the OCCP's activity. Cases concerning vertical restraints – especially resale

202 *A come-back of a concrete cartel? The President of UOKiK initiates preliminary investigation and orders searches*, https://uokik.gov.pl/en/a-come-back-of-a-concrete-cartel-the-president-of-uokik-initiates-preliminary-investigation-and-orders-searches.

203 OCCP decision DAR-15/2006.

price maintenance – as well as bid rigging account for the bulk of decisions. There is a conspicuous lack of robust enforcement against classic, economy-wide cartels. RPM enforcement appears concentrated in selected markets, often through a series of decisions targeting the same or closely related sectors. Bid rigging, once a strong pillar of enforcement, has recently become less effective, exacerbated by misguided organisational reforms and the marginalisation of regional offices, which historically played a crucial role in detecting local collusion.

Some efforts to expand enforcement into new areas are nevertheless evident. The emerging case law on sports associations is particularly noteworthy, though it is undermined by a difficult-to-justify selective approach to intervention, raising concerns about transparency and accountability. Labour market issues have also gained prominence, but largely through guidelines, advocacy, and soft law. While this may suggest a shift towards broader social objectives, such as employee protection, closer scrutiny indicates that the OCCP continues to pursue traditional competition policy goals, with any social benefits remaining incidental rather than deliberate.

The most troubling development is the steady erosion of enforcement against unilateral conduct. Once the cornerstone of Polish competition law enforcement, abuse-of-dominance cases have become marginal. Over the past decade, such cases have appeared only sporadically, with meaningful activity largely confined to the earlier years, particularly 2016–2017. Since then, enforcement has dwindled markedly, signalling a strategic reallocation of resources away from complex dominance cases towards more straightforward agreement-based infringements.

This retreat from unilateral enforcement of conduct is closely linked to the deliberate weakening of regional offices under the current leadership. As a result, local monopolies – formerly a defining feature of OCCP case law – have virtually disappeared from enforcement practice. Former state monopolies likewise generate far fewer cases than before. Alarmingly, this decline coincides with signs of selective enforcement and potential governmental influence, despite the implementation of the ECN+ Directive. This demonstrates that enhanced formal guarantees of independence have not translated into stronger or more consistent enforcement outcomes.

Finally, the growing emphasis on procedural enforcement, at the expense of substantive adjudication, raises serious concerns. The OCCP increasingly highlights the number of dawn raids as evidence of effective enforcement, treating procedural activity as a proxy for success. This narrative obscures the underlying decline in substantive decisions and reflects an opportunistic enforcement strategy. Structural constraints – most notably the protracted and ineffective system of judicial review before civil courts – undermine deterrence and further weaken enforcement outcomes. Together, these factors cast doubt on the current effectiveness and long-term credibility of Polish competition enforcement.

CHAPTER 8

Merger Control

1 Merger Control in Poland: Evolutionary Snapshot

Merger control played a central role in the early years of the Polish NCA. Poland entered the 1990s with a highly monopolised economy, whose structure was fundamentally ill-suited to fostering effective competition. This posed the authority with a combination of legal, political, and cultural challenges. From the outset, the OCCP's objectives were shaped by the imperative to demonopolise the economy and prevent the replacement of state monopolies with private ones.[1] The merger control regulations in force at that time were rudimentary. Article 11(1) of the Antimonopoly Act of 1990 provided that any intention to merge or transform economic entities was subject to notification to the Antimonopoly Authority.

This regulatory design reflected the broader interventionist character of merger control during the early transition period. Enforcement was not limited to assessing concentrations; it also included deconcentration measures, including decisions ordering the division of undertakings. Such decisions were not uncommon: 12 were issued in 1991, 4 in 1992, and 5 in 1993.[2]

Systemic change in merger control occurred in 1995, when specific notification criteria were introduced. This reform symbolically concluded the turbulent infancy period, during which authority focused mainly on transforming former state undertakings, and marked a shift towards a more targeted system of supervision. Turnover-based criteria were introduced. A distinctive feature of the system was a four-stage mechanism for acquiring additional blocks of shares or holdings, under which a concentration had to be notified each time a new threshold was exceeded. Unsurprisingly, the number of notifications skyrocketed, reaching more than 1,000.[3] The Act of 2000 subsequently limited the gradual notification system, reducing the number of notifications.

The latest development in this evolution is the current Competition Act, which will be discussed in detail.

1 Refer to Section 6.4.1.
2 Activity report 1995, 27.
3 Refer to the table in Section 8.3.

© 2026 THE AUTHOR(S) | HTTPS://DOI.ORG/10.1163/9789004754638-009
This is an open access publication distributed under the terms of the CC 4.0 license BY-NC-ND.

2 The Notion of 'Concentration'

The first fundamental element of merger control is the definition of concentration. Unlike the EUMR, the Competition Act does not provide a general definition of concentration. Instead, it lists the types of transactions that constitute concentrations. This legislative approach is imperfect because it fails to account for the diversity and complexity of business concentration structures encountered in practice. In some cases, transactions may combine several listed forms. In contrast, in some cases, the distinction between categories – most notably between the creation of a joint venture and the acquisition of joint control – may be difficult to draw. An incorrect qualification of the transaction may result in the notification being returned.

The most significant consequence of the absence of a general definition is that, unlike under the EUMR, Polish law does not require a concentration to result in a lasting change of control. Any transaction within the statutory catalogue is treated as a concentration. As a result, even temporary or transitional changes of control may trigger a notification obligation. This feature of the Polish regime leads to the notification of short-lived or incidental situations, thereby undermining the strategic rationale for merger control. In combination with the OCCP's understaffed merger department, it does not constitute a sound enforcement strategy.

Pursuant to Article 13(2) of the Competition Act, the following transactions constitute concentrations:

i. the merger of two or more independent undertakings;
ii. the acquisition, whether by purchase of shares, securities, or assets, or by any other means, of direct or indirect control over one or more undertakings;
iii. the creation of a joint undertaking by undertakings;
iv. the acquisition by an undertaking of all or part of another undertaking's assets, provided that those assets generated turnover in Poland exceeding EUR 10 million in at least one of the two financial years preceding the notification.

This catalogue is exhaustive. Consequently, certain transactions that were subject to notification before 2007 no longer fall within the merger control regime. These include quasi-concentrations that do not result in the acquisition of control and interlocking directorates, in which a person holding a management or supervisory position in one undertaking assumes a comparable position in another, without an acquisition of control.

2.1 Merger

A merger is a classic form of concentration, encompassing both incorporations and amalgamations. It must involve independent undertakings but does not necessarily result in the liquidation of the legal entities participating in the transaction. It is one of the few forms of concentration in which two parties formally appear in the proceedings.

2.2 Acquisition

The acquisition of control is by far the most frequently notified form of concentration. The Competition Act broadly defines control as the ability to exercise decisive influence over another undertaking, taking into account all legal and factual circumstances. This definition reflects EU competition law concepts but is applied more expansively in practice.

Control may be acquired directly or indirectly, including through subsidiaries or contractual arrangements. This distinction is essential for determining which entity is obliged to notify the concentration. As a rule, notification must be made by the undertaking that ultimately exercises control, even if the transaction is formally carried out by a subsidiary or special-purpose vehicle.[4]

Control may be sole or joint. Joint control arises in a variety of situations, including equal shareholdings, unanimity requirements, or veto rights that extend beyond protecting minority financial interests. The existence of joint control must be assessed based on the legal arrangements and factual circumstances. Family or personal ties between shareholders are insufficient on their own.

The Polish system requires notification not only of the acquisition of control, but also of changes in the quality of control. Transitions from sole to joint control, from joint to sole control, and changes in the composition of controlling undertakings are all notifiable. Both the positive and negative (blocking) controls may trigger notification obligations.[5] However, the OCCP's lack of clear guidance on the boundary between negative control and legitimate minority protections creates significant legal uncertainty. In the case of a change from sole to joint control, the obligation to notify rests exclusively with the undertaking that actively acquires joint control, and not with the undertaking whose position changes from sole to joint control. This allocation of the notification duty departs from the approach under the EUMR, under

4 Refer to Section 9.6.

5 OCCP Merger guidelines, 18.

which all undertakings that acquire joint control are, as a rule, jointly responsible for notification. In contrast to EUMR, the acquisition of joint control under Polish law does not constitute the creation of a joint venture. In the Polish system, it constitutes a distinct form of concentration and does not require establishing joint control over a newly created undertaking. This conceptual separation further differentiates the Polish merger control framework from that of the EUMR.

Polish law, unlike the EUMR, also treats incidental and temporary acquisitions of control as notifiable. This includes situations arising unintentionally, such as temporary voting majorities at shareholders' meetings. These scenarios illustrate the formalistic nature of the Polish regime and its limited sensitivity to economic reality.

2.3 Joint Venture

The creation of a joint venture is the second most common form of concentration and the most problematic from an interpretative perspective. The Polish approach is exceptionally broad. Both concentrative and cooperative joint ventures are notifiable, and there is no requirement that they perform all functions of an autonomous economic entity.

Notification is required regardless of the distribution of shares or voting rights. A joint venture may be created through the establishment of a new entity, the accession of partners to an existing entity, or the transformation of an existing company. The third scenario often overlaps with the acquisition of joint control and is particularly controversial, as it may fall outside notification thresholds depending on turnover calculations.

The OCCP has also taken the position that substantial changes or extensions of the activities of an existing joint venture may constitute a new concentration requiring notification. The decisive factor is whether the target undertaking's scope of activities changes as a result of the transaction. Where an undertaking already carries out a given activity and the transaction merely results in a shift from sole to joint control, the concentration is classified as an acquisition of joint control. By contrast, where the undertaking begins a new activity or its existing activity is materially altered as a result of the transaction, the operation is treated as the creation of a joint venture.[6] This interpretation, set out in soft-law guidance, has been applied in practice, leading to re-notifications. It has been criticised for introducing legal uncertainty and for extending merger control beyond its traditional scope.

6 OCCP Merger guidelines, 20.

2.4 Acquisition of Assets

The acquisition of assets is the fourth and most controversial category of transactions classified as concentrations under Polish merger control. For a transaction to qualify as a concentration, the acquired assets must constitute organised property capable of participating independently in economic activity and generating turnover. In other words, the assets must form an economic unit rather than a mere collection of individual items.

The Competition Act adopts a functional approach, linking the notification obligation to the ability to attribute turnover to the acquired assets. The decisive criterion is whether the assets generated turnover in the territory of the Republic of Poland exceeding EUR 10 million in at least one of the two financial years preceding notification.

The OCCP has consistently interpreted the term 'assets' broadly. In its decisional practice, it has recognised as notifiable concentrations the acquisition of production plants, distribution infrastructure, trademark rights, press titles, and even leases of part or all of another undertaking's assets. In some cases, the authority has accepted that the transfer of intangible assets alone – such as intellectual property rights – may constitute a concentration, provided that those rights enable the acquiring undertaking to continue or take over the economic activity previously carried out by the seller.

2.5 Staggered Transactions

The concept of staggered transactions represents a relatively recent and significant extension of Polish merger control.[7] Introduced by the 2014 amendment to the Competition Act, it was intended to address situations in which undertakings divide a single economic transaction into several formally separate steps to avoid merger scrutiny. Under the current rules, transactions between the same persons or undertakings within two years that involve the acquisition of undertakings or assets belonging to the same capital group are treated as a single concentration and must be notified jointly.

Before this amendment, the legal status of staggered transactions was highly contested. The OCCP had taken the position in several decisions that such transactions were notifiable, arguing that their economic unity should prevail over their formal separation.[8] However, the CCCP rejected this approach,

---

7 N. Levy, *European Merger Control: A Guide to the Merger Regulation*, Newark 2007, 5.

8 Decisions of the OCCP of 11.02.2004, RPZ-2/2004 and of 11.02.2004, RWR-7/2004.

emphasising the absence of a clear statutory basis for aggregating separate transactions.[9]

The Act does not clearly specify whether the obligation arises upon the conclusion of the first agreement, the last transaction, or when the economic effects of the transaction materialise. The Dino case illustrates these ambiguities. Over several months, the undertaking entered into a series of agreements with one of its franchisees, gradually transforming their relationship. Initially, a franchising agreement was concluded. This was followed by the acquisition of real estate used by the franchisee, which was then leased back to the franchisee. Finally, Dino sought to acquire the franchisee's equipment and other operational assets. Only the final stage was notified to the OCCP. According to the authority, these steps constituted a single staggered concentration that should have been notified earlier. The OCCP argued that, taken together, the transactions resulted in the acquisition of decisive influence over the franchisee, whose economic independence had been effectively eliminated. On this basis, the authority imposed a fine for late notification. While the fine itself was relatively modest and the decision was not appealed, the case highlights the far-reaching implications of the staggered-transactions concept.[10]

Although the concept of staggered transactions aims to enhance the effectiveness of merger control, its current formulation and application lack precision. The OCCP's decisional practice does not yet provide clear guidance on how to assess complex, multi-stage transactions, nor does it adequately address the treatment of completed transaction stages. As a result, the staggered-transactions regime remains an area of considerable uncertainty, reinforcing the impression that Polish merger control relies heavily on *ex post* discretion rather than *ex ante* predictability. The issue is exacerbated by a jurisdictional gap in Polish law regarding interconnected transactions. Recital 20 of the EUMR states that formally separate transactions that are closely linked by conditions or economic dependence should be treated as a single concentration to prevent circumvention of the merger rules. Poland's merger control regime lacks a comparable concept, so such interconnected transactions fall within the OCCP's authority. This contrasts sharply with the European Commission's approach, which actively initiates infringement pro-

9 Judgments of the CCCP of 21.03.2005, XVII Ama 29/04 and of 5.10. 2005, XVII Ama 38/04 and judgment of the CA of 28.04.2008, VI ACa 1288/07.

10 OCCP decision DKK-270/2019.

ceedings and asserts jurisdiction over economically integrated concentrations, even when they are structured as multiple formal steps.[11]

3 Turnover Thresholds

Determining which transactions are subject to notification requires specifying objective criteria that trigger merger control. In contemporary merger control systems, turnover is the most commonly used jurisdictional criterion. It is objective, relatively easy for undertakings to assess ex ante, and provides a clear, administrable threshold. The underlying assumption is that turnover reflects a degree of market presence and economic significance. Depending on the jurisdiction, total (worldwide) turnover, domestic turnover, or both may be considered.[12] As a rule, the turnover of the entire capital group of the acquiring undertaking and that of the target undertaking are aggregated for jurisdictional assessment.

The principal disadvantage of the turnover criterion is its purely formal character. It disregards the transaction's substantive characteristics and the actual competitive situation in the relevant market. This weakness is often mitigated by introducing de minimis exemptions, typically based on the target undertaking's turnover, which exclude transactions that lack material competitive relevance from notification obligations.

By contrast, the market share criterion is inherently subjective and significantly more difficult for undertakings to apply. It requires prior market definition and competitive assessment, which are often complex and contentious. It allows authorities to capture transactions of limited economic scale but high competitive significance, particularly in local or highly concentrated markets. This solution existed under the Competition Act 2000. Pursuant to Article 13a of that Act, the de minimis exemption did not apply to concentrations that created or strengthened a dominant position in the relevant market. The abandonment of this criterion in favour of purely turnover-based thresholds simplified notification obligations but reduced the system's sensitivity to structurally harmful local transactions.

---

11 Refer to L. Villani, *"After Thunder Comes Rain": The ECJ Finally Rules on the Boundaries of the EUMR Standstill Obligation*, Market and Competition Law Review, 2019 No. 1, and D. Tayar, É. Lejeune, *Scope and implications of the standstill obligation in European merger control*, Concurrences 2021, no. 3, Art. N° 101232.

12 *Setting Notification Thresholds for Merger Review*, https://www.internationalcompetitionnetwork.org/wp-content/uploads/2018/05/MWG_SettingMergerNotificationThresholds.pdf.

3.1 Turnover Value

The Polish merger control system is based solely on objective turnover thresholds. Pursuant to Article 13(1) of the Competition Act, a concentration is subject to notification if, in the financial year preceding notification:

i. the combined worldwide turnover of the undertakings participating in the concentration exceeds EUR 1,000,000,000, or
ii. the combined turnover of those undertakings in the territory of Poland exceeds EUR 50,000,000.

The worldwide turnover threshold appears particularly problematic, as it may trigger notification obligations even where none of the undertakings concerned conducts meaningful economic activity in Poland. This undermines the effects-based rationale of merger control and has been a persistent source of criticism in doctrine.[13]

Turnover thresholds were designed to provide objective, measurable jurisdictional criteria and thereby ensure legal certainty for undertakings, yet in the digital economy, they have become increasingly ill-suited to capturing transactions with potentially significant competitive effects. Merger control systems based exclusively on turnover are largely blind to acquisitions of start-ups, data-driven businesses, or firms whose competitive value lies primarily in intangible assets rather than current revenues, enabling large digital platforms to complete hundreds of acquisitions without scrutiny by NCAs.[14] A related and equally problematic category concerns so-called acquihires, namely transactions that primarily aim to acquire teams of employees rather than revenue-generating businesses, even though they may nevertheless affect innovation and labour markets.[15] Despite the urgency of these challenges, the OCCP has shown no discernible willingness to address them.

3.2 No Adaptation of Thresholds

The nominal values of the turnover thresholds have remained unchanged since 2007. Over nearly two decades, this legislative inertia has led to a substantial *de facto* expansion of the notification obligation due to inflation. To

13 M. Błachucki, *System*, 158–159.

14 R. Podszun, *Thresholds of Merger Notification: The Challenge of Digital Markets, the Turnover Lottery, and the Question of Re-interpreting Rules*, [in:] P.L. Parcu, M.A. Rossi, M. Botta (eds.), *Research Handbook in Competition & Technology*, Cheltenham 2024.

15 R. Patel, R. Phillips, *Are employee acquisitions a gap in European merger control?*, CPI 2024, no. 1.

TABLE 8.1 Values of original and adapted thresholds (Source: Author's estimations)

Value in 2007	Value in 2024
1,000,000,000	3,255,223,546,91
50,000,000	162,761,177,35
10,000,000	32,552,235,47

illustrate this effect, the impact of cumulative inflation was calculated using the compound interest method (Table 8.1).[16]

This comparison shows that, in real terms, the statutory thresholds have lost a significant share of their original value. To preserve their original economic significance, the relevant amounts would need to be increased by approximately threefold. The failure of both the legislator and the OCCP to initiate such an adjustment has led to a gradual but systematic expansion of merger control obligations, contrary to the declared objective of reducing administrative burdens. As a result, Poland stands out as a jurisdiction in which static nominal thresholds, combined with broad extraterritorial reach, continue to expand merger control jurisdiction without a corresponding reassessment of its economic justification.

4 The (Slightly) Decreasing Extraterritoriality Principle

The territorial scope of the OCCP's jurisdiction is set out in Article 1 of the Competition Act. The principle of extraterritoriality is particularly relevant in antitrust enforcement, but it also plays a significant role in merger control. The Act provides that it governs the prevention of anticompetitive concentrations of undertakings and applies to those concentrations that have, or may have, effects within the territory of the Republic of Poland. While this provision introduces an effects-based jurisdictional standard, it does not itself define the criteria for establishing such effects. Instead, it serves as a general guideline, further specified in Articles 13 and 14 of the Competition Act, which regulate the notification obligation.

16 Wskaźniki cen towarów i usług konsumpcyjnych, https://stat.gov.pl/obszary-tematyczne/ceny-handel/wskazniki-cen/wskazniki-cen-towarow-i-uslug-konsumpcyjnych-pot-inflacja-/.

Those provisions rely exclusively on formal turnover thresholds, calculated from worldwide and domestic turnover. Notably, the notification obligation may arise even where only the worldwide turnover threshold is met, regardless of whether the transaction has any discernible competitive effects in Poland. This regulatory design creates an internal inconsistency. While Article 1 suggests an effects-based limitation of jurisdiction, Articles 13 and 14 establish a purely formal system of merger notification, detached from any substantive assessment of effects. It may therefore reasonably be concluded that the legislator – indeed, the OCCP itself, which was instrumental in drafting these provisions – constructed a mutually contradictory framework.

The OCCP has long been aware of this inconsistency and has sought to mitigate its consequences through interpretative guidance. In particular, the authority has stated that 'extraterritorial concentrations, i.e., those between undertakings established outside the territory of the Republic of Poland, are also subject to control, provided that they have at least a potential impact on the territory of the Republic of Poland'.[17] As the Act does not specify the criteria for assessing such an impact, the OCCP assumed that the condition of effect is satisfied if at least one participant in the concentration (or its capital group) has turnover in Poland. This interpretation was criticised for being inconsistent with Article 1 of the Act and for extending merger control to transactions that, by their nature, could not affect competition in the Polish market.[18]

This approach remained in force for nearly a decade. In October 2024, however, it was partially revised. The amendment concerned the establishment of joint ventures outside Poland. It clarified that where such a joint venture does not operate in Poland, the transaction is not subject to notification.[19] Merely six months later, the OCCP modified this interpretation once again, stating that where the markets in which the newly created undertaking will operate – or in which vertical links will arise – do not cover the territory of Poland or any part thereof, and where the undertaking does not plan to expand its activities into Poland within the following three years, the statutory condition of an effect on the territory of the Republic of Poland should be regarded as not fulfilled.[20]

---

17 Merger Guidelines, 2015, 12

18 A. Stawicki, E. Stawicki (eds.), *Ustawa o ochronie konkurencji i konsumentów. Komentarz*, 2016, LEX.el, Art. 1.

19 *Kontrola koncentracji – aktualizacja wyjaśnień Prezesa UOKiK*, https://uokik.gov.pl/kontrola-koncentracji-aktualizacja-wyjasnien-prezesa-uokik.

20 Merger Guidelines, 2025, 13

The OCCP President expressly acknowledged that this interpretative shift was not dictated by the wording of the statute but was motivated by a desire to reduce the number of notifiable concentrations and to 'help businesses conduct transactions more efficiently by reducing "bureaucratic burdens"'.[21] This admission raises serious legal concerns. The OCCP's jurisdiction to review concentrations is a matter of statutory law and cannot be altered by administrative interpretation or soft law. The president's explicit recognition of this tension calls into question the legal awareness underpinning these actions.

Beyond the legality issue, the way these changes were introduced is also problematic. The revisions have been fragmentary, frequent, and reactive, suggesting the absence of a coherent and well-considered policy. Moreover, none of these interpretative changes were preceded by stakeholder consultations; instead, they appear to reflect the President of the OCCP's unilateral initiatives.

The notification of extraterritorial concentrations remains problematic for the Polish merger control system, with a noticeable number of such cases reported each year. This situation is primarily due to the unchanged worldwide turnover threshold and the imprecise formulation of notification requirements. The legally questionable attempts to address these statutory deficiencies through repeated amendments to soft-law instruments demonstrate a lack of systemic reflection on merger control within the OCCP. They reveal an institutional reluctance to engage in structured dialogue with stakeholders, further undermining legal certainty and the predictability of merger control enforcement in Poland.

5 Exemptions

Notification criteria in merger control use formal jurisdictional rules as proxies for actual competitive importance. These criteria are abstract, so exemptions are necessary to reduce rigidity. Exemptions exclude minor or unlikely-to-raise-concerns transactions from initial review. Article 14 of the Competition Act lists several situations where notification isn't required. If the controlled entity's turnover in Poland didn't exceed EUR 10 million in the last two years, no notification is required. Similarly, if no undertaking involved generated over EUR 10 million, or the combined turnover of acquired parts did not exceed EUR 10 million, notification can be waived. Technical or temporary

21 *Kontrola koncentracji – ułatwienia dla przedsiębiorców*, https://uokik.gov.pl/kontrola-koncentracji-ulatwienia-dla-przedsiebiorcow.

transactions, such as short-term share acquisitions for resale or debt security, are exempt. Transactions from insolvency proceedings are exempt unless controlled by a competitor or a group of that competitor. Transactions within the same capital group are also exempt. These exemptions are absolute; if met, no review is needed regardless of potential competition effects. The OCCP doesn't issue formal clearance, but if a notification is submitted despite an exemption, it is returned and confirmed not under review.

5.1 De Minimis Turnover

From a practical perspective, the de minimis turnover exemption is of paramount importance. It constitutes the most frequently applied basis for excluding transactions from notification. Following the 2014 amendment, it is now clear that all types of concentrations – acquisitions of control, mergers, joint ventures, and asset acquisitions – are exempt where the target undertaking or acquired assets generate turnover in Poland not exceeding EUR 10 million. Although it initially improved the system by excluding transactions lacking a genuine domestic nexus, its effectiveness has been substantially eroded by inflation and the lack of periodic adjustments. As a result, an increasing number of transactions fall within the notification obligation, placing additional strain on an already understaffed merger control department and contributing to the systematic lengthening of merger review timelines.[22]

5.2 Capital Group Exemption and the State Treasury

Another essential exemption concerns intra-group concentrations. Transactions carried out entirely within a single capital group are excluded from notification. However, there is one notable exception. According to the established interpretation of the OCCP, undertakings directly controlled by the State Treasury do not form a single capital group.[23] As a result, concentrations between state-controlled undertakings are subject to merger control, whereas concentrations within capital groups headed by individual state-owned undertakings are exempt.

This interpretation is legally and economically contentious, though historically understandable. Polish merger control was introduced during a period of systemic transformation, when the vast majority of undertakings were

22 Refer to Section 4.7.5.

23 *Zamiar koncentracji dokonywanej z udziałem spółek Skarbu Państwa,* https://archiwum.uokik.gov.pl/interpretacja_przepisow.php#faq2524.

state-owned. At the time, treating all such undertakings as part of a single capital group would have excluded most concentrations from scrutiny and undermined the process of demonopolisation. Consequently, the OCCP adopted a formalistic approach based on the legal autonomy of state-owned enterprises.

These historical justifications have largely lost their relevance. State-controlled undertakings are today subject to intensive governmental supervision, including coordinated ownership policies, personnel decisions, and strategic direction. This is evidenced by the Polish government's intensive policy of renationalising many industries, including banking and energy, undertaken between 2015 and 2023.[24] The continued refusal to recognise the State Treasury as forming a capital group, therefore, appears opportunistic and serves primarily to preserve the OCCP's jurisdiction. The paradox is reinforced by the European Commission's similarly formalistic stance in the PKN Orlen/Lotos case, implicitly accepting that Polish state-controlled undertakings do not constitute a single economic unit.[25] This convergence of positions suggests that considerations extending beyond purely legal analysis may have influenced enforcement policy.

5.3 Family Does Not Form a Capital Group

The OCCP also assumes that family ties, in themselves, do not give rise to a capital group. According to the Merger Guidelines, kinship between shareholders is insufficient to establish joint control unless accompanied by an agreement – written or oral – demonstrating coordinated exercise of decisive influence.[26] Consequently, undertakings controlled by members of the same family are treated as independent for merger control purposes, even where ownership structures are identical. Despite the OCCP's apparent confidence, an unresolved conceptual question remains: should a marriage be treated as a single economic unit for merger control purposes? Where spouses have lived and worked together for many years, pooling resources and coordinating their economic activities, there may be plausible grounds for such an interpretation.

OCCP's approach is consistently applied across competition law enforcement. In antitrust cases, the authority has recognised, for example, that

---

24 A. Svetlicini, *State-Controlled Entities in the EU Merger Control: the Case of PKN Orlen and Lotos Group*, YARS 2020, no. 13, 195–198.

25 COMP/M. 9014 PKN Orlen/Grupa Lotos.

26 OCCP Merger Guidelines, 18.

spouses participating in public tenders may be treated as independent undertakings capable of engaging in bid-rigging arrangements.[27] While this interpretation undoubtedly promotes formal legal certainty, it risks underestimating the economic reality of family-controlled business structures. In particular, it may create unnecessary legal complications in cases of family succession or inheritance. Under the Competition Act, such events are currently treated, on general grounds, as forms of concentration, notwithstanding their distinctive social and economic context. There are legitimate reasons to consider whether these situations should be addressed through a dedicated, carefully tailored regulatory framework rather than being subsumed under standard merger control rules.

6 Peculiarities of Polish Merger Notification

When analysing the Polish notification obligation, several solutions emerge that are rare – if not exceptional – in comparative terms. These peculiarities do not merely reflect stylistic legislative choices; they generate tangible jurisdictional distortions, inflate transaction costs in an essentially arbitrary manner, and – paradoxically – may exclude genuinely domestic and potentially harmful concentrations from control while capturing foreign-to-foreign transactions with no meaningful Polish nexus.

6.1 Extraterritorial Joint Ventures

A Polish saying holds that 'misfortunes come in pairs'. The merger control regime offers an apt illustration: two structurally questionable features coincide and reinforce one another. The first is reliance on the worldwide turnover threshold as an autonomous trigger for notification, without a genuinely operational 'local nexus' filter. The second is an extraordinarily broad understanding of the 'creation of a joint venture', which, in Polish practice, may encompass virtually any form of cooperation structured through a jointly used undertaking, regardless of whether the arrangement is concentrative, cooperative, temporary, or durable. The combined effect is predictable: each year the OCCP reviews notifications concerning joint ventures established in remote jurisdictions – China, Japan, India, or various Mashriq states – where neither the transaction nor the resulting entity bears any realistic connection to the Polish market. At the same time, purely domestic transactions can

27 OCCP decisions RKR 35/2014 or RWR 24/2010.

remain outside OCCP jurisdiction where they fail to satisfy the national turnover thresholds, even if they are significant for local competition.

The authority has attempted to moderate this jurisdictional overreach through interpretative 'corrections' in soft law, as discussed earlier. Yet these adjustments are legally fragile, inherently partial, and – because they operate downstream from the statutory thresholds – cannot cure the underlying inconsistency. They function less as a systemic solution and more as a tactical attempt to obscure the problem's visibility.

The Nord Stream 2 (NS2) case illustrates the pathology at its most pronounced. The case is also exceptional because it involved the highest penalty ever imposed by the OCCP for a competition infringement.[28] In 2020, the OCCP imposed fines totalling more than PLN 29 billion on Gazprom and more than PLN 234 million on five other undertakings involved in the project.[29] The transaction was initially intended to be structured through shareholdings in Nord Stream 2 AG, a Swiss company wholly owned by Gazprom. Uniper, Engie, OMV, Shell, and Wintershall were expected to acquire 10% stakes each, with Gazprom retaining 50%, and to finance construction proportionally. The equity participation model ultimately did not materialise, and Gazprom remained the sole shareholder. Nevertheless, the OCCP treated the subsequent 2017 financing agreements as substantively equivalent to the planned concentration and inferred that the lenders' role remained indispensable and structurally comparable to equity participation. The authority further reasoned that pledges over shares created a 'quasi-shareholding' position, in the sense that default could convert lenders into shareholders and thus grant them a governance-relevant stake. The authority concluded that the agreements confirmed a stable alignment of economic interests and organisational commitment, sufficient, in its view, to constitute the creation of a joint undertaking (or at least a single continuing concentration spanning the original equity plan and the subsequent financing model).

The courts rejected this approach. The first-instance court annulled the decision,[30] and the Court of Appeal upheld that outcome.[31] The Court of Appeal accepted that a joint venture may, in principle, be formed through an existing entity – particularly one that previously had no meaningful commercial activity or underwent a radical shift in profile. However, it insisted on a strict conceptual minimum: there must be (i) an undertaking, (ii) a joint

28 OCCP Decision No. DKK-65/2013.

29 The aggregate fine amounted to approximately EUR 6,827,692,100.

30 Judgment of the CCCP of 21.11.2022, XVII AmA 11/21.

31 Judgment of the Court of Appeals of 16.10.2023, VII AGa 1/23.

company, and (iii) establishment by undertakings. On that basis, it emphasised that a joint venture cannot be reduced to a 'joint endeavour', the pursuit of a common interest, or coordinated financing. In the court's view, the legal hallmark of creating a joint venture is the acquisition of an equity stake in an undertaking. Debt financing, including loans to an existing undertaking, does not constitute the creation of a joint venture. The court also treated the contractual rights contained in the financing documentation as narrower than shareholder rights and insufficient to amount to decisive influence over NS2's commercial conduct. Since, on that reasoning, the OCCP lacked jurisdiction to review the transaction, the court did not proceed to the merits of the OCCP's competitive assessment.

The NS2 case can be read in two ways. It may be invoked to justify retaining oversight of foreign-to-foreign transactions, as some exceptional projects can have substantial effects in Poland. Yet the general policy implication points in the opposite direction: outside truly atypical scenarios, the probability that extraterritorial joint ventures with no operational Polish nexus will materially restrict competition in Poland is low. A rational jurisdictional design, therefore, requires optimisation – capturing genuinely relevant foreign-to-foreign transactions while minimising unnecessary compliance and delay costs.[32]

6.2 Joint Venture or Takeover?

Even within the internal taxonomy of notifiable transactions, the Polish rules create structural ambiguity in distinguishing between the creation of a joint venture and the acquisition of joint control. Unlike EU merger law, the Competition Act does not differentiate between concentrative and cooperative joint ventures, nor does it require that the joint venture be 'full-function' in the sense of performing, on a lasting basis, all the functions of an autonomous economic entity. The consequence is that joint ventures of a purely cooperative or transitory nature – arrangements that would typically fall outside merger control in EU practice and instead be assessed under antitrust rules – remain notifiable in Poland.[33] It is difficult to identify a coherent legislative rationale for such an expansive approach, particularly because it requires notification of arrangements that are temporary, reversible, or operationally limited.

---

32 M. Błachucki, *Establishment of Nord Stream 2 under Polish Merger Control Rules*, ECLR 2024, no. 8, 346.

33 R. Stankiewicz, *Joint ventures w prawie antymonopolowym*, PPH 2007, no. 8, p.16.

To clarify the concept, the OCCP explains that notification of the creation of a joint undertaking covers not only the establishment of a new entity but also scenarios in which one participant incorporates a company and others subsequently acquire or subscribe for shares, as well as situations in which the founders use an existing undertaking (for example, a company operating within the capital group of one founder).[34] The stated purpose of this explanation is to distinguish 'creation of a joint venture' from 'acquisition of joint control'. The distinction matters because the turnover calculation differs: for joint ventures, the turnover of the founders' capital groups is taken into account, whereas for acquisitions, the turnover of the acquiring group and the target is decisive.

However, the formal criteria are often insufficient to resolve borderline cases. The parties' expressed intention – reflected in the transaction documentation – plays a significant role, as do the arrangement's economic rationale and the sequencing of steps. Timing can be particularly informative: where an existing entity is 'repurposed' for joint activity, the transaction can be framed either as the establishment of a joint venture or as the acquisition of joint control. These interpretative variables create significant legal uncertainty, largely because the OCCP has tended to adopt an expansive approach in its decisional practice, thereby expanding the notification perimeter. While anti-circumvention instincts are understandable, using non-binding guidelines to effectively increase notification obligations risks shifting core jurisdictional questions from statute to administrative interpretation – precisely the opposite of what merger control requires for legal certainty.

6.3 Acquisition of Lease Agreements

A further peculiarity concerns the Polish treatment of asset acquisitions. The OCCP interprets 'acquisition' broadly to include transactions that, in economic substance, grant rights amounting to the ability to dispose of part of another undertaking's assets. This includes not only sale agreements but also other contracts that confer extensive, long-term control over assets, enabling the acquirer to operate them as if it were the owner. This approach is particularly relevant in sectors where operational control is frequently decoupled from ownership – such as petrol station networks, retail chains, and wholesale facilities – where premises are commonly leased rather than owned.[35] The

34 Merger Guidelines, 20.

35 Interpretacja przepisów, https://archiwum.uokik.gov.pl/interpretacja_przepisow.php#faq2523.

inconsistency in terminology is notable. Property may be acquired only if it already exists, whereas a right – such as a lease or rental – arises only upon the conclusion of the contract, making it conceptually difficult to characterise this as an acquisition. Neither the Competition Act nor the OCCP's decisional practice addresses this distinction, leaving the issue unresolved.

From a market-effects perspective, a long-term lease can be functionally equivalent to a sale when it grants the lessee extensive rights: broad use rights, the freedom to invest without prior consent, and the ability to sublease or transfer use to third parties. The courts have recognised this functional equivalence. The tricky question, therefore, is not whether leases can be caught in principle, but when a set of leased assets constitutes an organised part of an undertaking capable of generating turnover.[36]

The FDW/FDB case illustrates the boundary problem. The OCCP fined an egg producer (FDW) for acquiring part of the assets of another egg farm (FDB) via a lease covering four poultry farms, two hatcheries, and associated infrastructure and equipment. The OCCP treated hens as non-essential assets for turnover attribution because of their limited life cycle and replaceability, while treating the infrastructure as the decisive productive asset. FDW was fined PLN 339,000 and paid the fine.[37] The decision demonstrates a willingness to look beyond formal asset lists to functional economic capacity, and it shows that the OCCP can, at least in some cases, analyse production realities with sophistication.

6.4 Managerial Acquisitions

Although personal unions that did not entail a change of control ceased to be notifiable after 2007, the Competition Act still provides that control may be acquired where members of the management board or supervisory board of one undertaking constitute more than half of the members of the management board of another undertaking. On this basis, the OCCP has developed a line of case law holding that specific managerial configurations constitute concentrations.

The concept of personal unions refers to a situation in which a natural person holds a position within the structures of at least two companies. It covers both situations in which the majority of the members of the body (management board, supervisory board, or board of directors) of a given company are persons holding positions in the bodies of another company, and any

36 Judgment of the CCCP of 7.03.2016, XVII AmA 14/15.

37 OCCP Decision No. DKK-145/2017.

other situations in which the members of the body of a given company hold positions in the bodies of another company.[38]

The TERG/Electro.pl case is illustrative. A natural person who chaired TERG's supervisory board was appointed president of Electro.pl's sole management board. The OCCP treated this as TERG's acquisition of control over Electro.pl and held that notification should have been made before the shareholders' resolution appointing the board member.[39] In Sadrob/Exdrob, a change in board composition shifted a previously non-majority personal union into a majority one, leading the OCCP to conclude that Sadrob gained control of Exdrob.[40] In PŻM/FRS, both undertakings were controlled by the State Treasury. The same natural person first served as head of PŻM and was then appointed president of FRS, leading the OCCP to conclude that PŻM controlled FRS and to impose a PLN 45,000 fine.[41]

These cases are analytically interesting because personal unions can indeed affect competitive dynamics, particularly among competitors. However, they also reveal the system's rigidity. In PŻM/FRS, the 'concentration' was effectively the product of government decisions rather than market autonomy, underscoring the artificiality of treating state-controlled undertakings as independent units. Moreover, the moderate level of some fines suggests a fiscal rather than a deterrent logic, reinforcing the impression that formal jurisdictional triggers sometimes dominate substantive competition objectives.

6.5 Security on Shares

The OCCP has also considered whether pledges over shares can trigger a notification obligation. As a rule, a pledge is a security instrument rather than a governance transaction. However, it may become merger-relevant if it grants – formally or in practice – rights that confer decisive influence. The Act provides an exemption for temporary acquisitions or subscriptions of shares made to secure debts, provided that the acquirer does not exercise any rights attached to the shares other than the right to sell.[42] The policy rationale is straightforward: enabling rapid security without waiting for merger clearance, while excluding governance influence that could distort competition.[43]

38 A. Bielecki, *Przeciwdziałanie antykonkurencyjnym uniom personalnym w organach spółek kapitałowych w prawie polskim, unijnym i amerykańskim*, Warsaw 2025, 48.

39 OCCP Decision No. DKK-132/2013.

40 OCCP Decisions No. DKK-88/08 and DKK-89/2008.

41 OCCP Decision No. DKK-265/2019.

42 T. Skoczny [in:] T. Skoczny (ed.), 630.

43 C. Banasiński, E. Piontek (eds.), Art. 14.

In practice, the exemption is narrowly construed. Rights such as voting, appointing and dismissing board members, or influencing asset disposal go beyond the 'right to sell' and can therefore remove the transaction from the exemption.[44] The OCCP's case law is limited – nine decisions in total, mostly concerning banks and energy companies – but it consistently holds that a pledge becomes notifiable when additional contractual rights attach to it and, crucially, when the pledgee intends to exercise them.[45]

The AmeriGas/GDS case remains the most instructive. AmeriGas obtained control of its distributor through a registered pledge, along with additional governance-like rights that gave it influence over key management decisions. AmeriGas exercised those rights, including blocking the sale of a separate part of GDS's assets, some of which were subsequently acquired by AmeriGas. The OCCP imposed a PLN 730,000 fine,[46] which the court upheld.[47] The case emphasises the Polish system's breadth, including its willingness to treat even temporary or contingent governance configurations as notifiable – an approach that differs from EU practice and increases compliance sensitivity around security structures.[48]

6.6 Merger Despite Lack of Agreement

Finally, Polish practice recognises that a concentration may occur even without a written agreement. In the Sezam-Śrem/Klementynka case, the OCCP found that Sezam-Śrem took control of part of Klementynka's assets in a food wholesaling context, despite the absence of a written acquisition contract. The authority relied on the factual circumstances and the economic reality of the transaction: the transfer of key supplier and customer relationships, key employees, goods for distribution, and trade secrets (including prices, customer lists, and payment terms). The former owner became the manager of the acquired operations and informed counterparties that only the legal form was changing, while the business continued. On this basis, the OCCP held that the takeover of key organised assets was sufficient to constitute a concentration.[49]

---

44 A. Wierciński [in:] A. Stawicki, E. Stawicki (eds.), 435.

45 OCCP Decisions RLU-43/2005, RLU-44/2005 or RLU-45/2005.

46 OCCP Decision DKK-161/2020.

47 Judgment of the CCCP of 16.02.2022, XVII AmA 2/21.

48 M. Błachucki, *Ustanowienie zastawu na akcjach lub udziałach a obowiązek zgłoszenia zamiaru koncentracji Prezesowi UOKiK*, PPH 2022, no. 11, 41 .

49 OCCP Decision No. DKK-86/2017 of 05.06.2017.

The CCCP largely accepted the interpretative direction but overturned the decision on formalistic grounds, requiring the OCCP to attribute turnover to individual components of the acquired assets.[50] That approach is difficult to reconcile with the economic logic of asset acquisitions and with accounting reality: organised assets generate turnover as a functional whole, not as an arithmetical sum of isolated components. Nevertheless, the case remains valuable because it confirms two points. First, concentrations can take the form of *de facto* arrangements or coordinated conduct rather than formally documented transfers. Second, employees, management, and intangible operational assets may – under certain conditions – form part of the 'property' capable of constituting an organised segment of an undertaking.[51]

7 Merger Tests

In addition to the notification obligation, a key issue in any merger control system is how notified transactions are assessed. A merger test is a set of criteria used to evaluate a notified transaction. The merger test constitutes the core of the merger control system. It consists of a set of legal premises that enable the competition authority to distinguish between pro-competitive and anticompetitive concentrations. The premises of the test are specific economic categories to which legally relevant effects are attributed. This does not exclude the existence of subsidiary merger control tests based on other, non-economic values. Within the group of economically oriented tests, a distinction is traditionally drawn between the dominance test and the significant impediment to effective competition (SIEC) test.

Until 2007, Polish law applied the dominance test. As part of the legislative approximation to EU law, the Competition Act was amended to align the merger test with that applied under the EUMR.

7.1 SIEC: The Basic Economic Test

The SIEC test is grounded in economic theory and enables the antimonopoly authority to predict the competitive consequences of a notified concentra-

50 Judgment of the CCCP of 22.10.2019, XVII AmA 49/17.

51 M. Błachucki, *Pojęcie koncentracji polegającej na nabyciu części mienia innego przedsiębiorcy oraz obliczanie obrotu na potrzeby notyfikacji Prezesowi UOKiK takiej transakcji*, PUG 2022, no. 11, 56.

tion.[52] Pursuant to Article 18 of the Competition Act, the OCCP shall issue a decision consenting to the implementation of a concentration that does not result in a significant impediment to competition in the market, in particular through the creation or strengthening of a dominant position.

An analysis of this provision leads to the conclusion that Polish law has adopted the significant impediment to competition test. The introduction of the SIEC test constituted a significant shift in merger analysis. It is no longer necessary to demonstrate dominance to prohibit a concentration. Instead, the entire market environment is assessed, including the effects on competitors, trading partners, and consumers. A good illustration is the *Empik/Merlin* prohibition. Despite the combined market share remaining below 30%, the OCCP took into account the extreme fragmentation of the remaining market and Empik's enhanced buyer power following the transaction, and, on that basis, prohibited the concentration.[53]

7.2 Public Interest Test: A Subsidiary Test

The public interest test supplements the SIEC test. Pursuant to Article 20(2)(2) of the Competition Act, the OCCP issues a decision consenting to the implementation of a concentration that significantly impedes competition – particularly through the creation or strengthening of a dominant position – where refraining from prohibiting the concentration is justified, in particular because of its positive impact on the national economy.

This test is complementary and may be applied only where the SIEC analysis shows that the concentration would significantly restrict competition. It is exceptional in character, as it can be used solely to authorise anticompetitive concentrations. It cannot serve as a basis for political intervention to block non-problematic transactions. In this sense, the test may facilitate the creation of national champions but cannot be used to pursue broader protectionist objectives.

An essential function of the public interest test is to grant the OCCP a degree of administrative discretion, enabling it to balance competition with other public values. However, neither the Competition Act nor its legislative materials provide guidance on how this balancing should be conducted. This raises concerns about whether the application of the public interest test is

52 M. Błachucki, *Ewolucja regulacji testów oceny koncentracji w polskim prawie antymonopolowym*, [in:] H. Gronkiewicz-Waltz, K. Jaroszyński (eds.), *Europeizacja publicznego prawa gospodarczego*, Warsaw 2011, 38.

53 OCCP Decision DKK-12/2011.

compatible with the independence requirements set out in the ECN+ Directive.

The use of this test inevitably introduces political considerations into merger control, as determinations concerning national security, economic security, or employment are inherently political. Paradoxically, the OCCP's past practice does not support the view that formal guarantees of independence prevent politicisation. Most public-interest decisions were adopted during periods when such guarantees existed, whereas the most prominent rejection of political arguments – concerning a concentration involving State Treasury-controlled undertakings – occurred when the authority lacked those guarantees.

The public interest test is rarely applied. No case has relied on it in the past fifteen years, and historically, the number of such decisions has not exceeded nine.[54] When used, the burden of proof rests entirely with the notifying undertakings, and the standard of evidence is exceptionally high.[55]

7.3 Merger Tests: Resisting Change

An analysis of the existing merger assessment standards may suggest that the Competition Act adopts a pluralist approach to objectives and departs from a purely economic approach to concentration assessment. However, this impression is neither confirmed by the wording of the Act itself nor, even more clearly, by the OCCP's decisional practice. In reality, the economic SIEC test is the basic, almost exclusively applied standard in Polish merger control. The public interest test, although formally present in the statutory framework, does not function as a genuine subsidiary test but rather as a marginal and largely dormant instrument.

Over the past decade, the OCCP has neither applied the public interest test in any merger case nor seriously considered its application. This state of affairs does not appear to reflect a deliberate and principled commitment by the OCCP to a purely economic model of merger control. Instead, it should be understood as an expression of institutional inertia in Polish merger control and a broader lack of reflection on the evolving socio-economic context and on international debates concerning the objectives of competition law and merger control. In this sense, the Polish merger control regime appears

54 Detailed list of OCCP decisions, see M. Błachucki, *Public interest considerations in merger control assessment*, ECLR 2014, no. 8, 386.

55 M. Błachucki, R. Stankiewicz, *Decyzja zezwalająca na dokonanie koncentracji z naruszeniem testu istotnego ograniczenia konkurencji (art. 20 ust. 2 ustawy antymonopolowej)*, PUG 2010, no. 6, 5.

static and resistant to change, despite the growing discussion – both at the EU level and globally – on the role of non-economic values in competition enforcement.

The need to take a position on the objectives of merger control became particularly evident in 2019, when PKN Orlen notified its intention to acquire control of Polska Press. PKN Orlen, a fuel company controlled by the State Treasury, has in recent years served as an essential instrument of state capitalism and a vehicle for the re-nationalisation of previously privatised undertakings. Through the notified transaction, Orlen acquired a publishing group that owned almost all regional daily newspapers in Poland, as well as numerous online news portals. During the proceedings, competitors, social organisations, and the Ombudsman raised serious concerns, primarily relating to the threat to media pluralism and the risk that regional press outlets could become dependent on the central government.

The OCCP rejected these arguments, concluding that the concentration would not create a significant impediment to competition and that considerations of media pluralism fell outside the scope of the SIEC test.[56] For the first time in the history of Polish merger control, the Ombudsman appealed a merger decision, arguing that the OCCP had failed to assess the concentration's impact on freedom of the press and had improperly allowed a State-controlled undertaking to acquire a major private media group. The court fully endorsed the OCCP's position, holding that assessing media pluralism does not fall within the competition authority's statutory competence in merger proceedings. According to the court, taking such considerations into account would constitute action without legal basis. It would undermine legal certainty by preventing undertakings from conducting a predictable self-assessment of the notifiability and permissibility of concentrations.[57]

The position adopted by both the OCCP and the CCCP should not have come as a surprise, but it did.[58] For more than two decades, the OCCP has consistently maintained – in its decisional practice and official statements – that it has no competence in relation to media pluralism, whether in merger control or in cases concerning anticompetitive practices.[59] Under the Polish

56 OCCP Decision DKK 34/2021.

57 Jugdment of the CCCP of 7.06.2022, XVII Ama 43/21.

58 C. Banasiński, M. Rojszczak, *The role of competition authorities in protecting freedom of speech: the PKN Orlen/Polska Press case*, ECJ 2022, no. 2, or K. Majcher, *Media Pluralism and Independence: Legal Assessments of the Agora/Eurozet and PKN Orlen/Polska Press Transactions (Poland)*, JECLP 2022, no. 6.

59 B. Cebula, *Impact of Concentration on Pluralism in Media* [in:] C. Banasiński (ed.), *Consumer Protection and Competition Policy?*, Warsaw 2006, 190.

constitutional framework, the protection of freedom of speech and pluralism in broadcasting is entrusted to the NBC. However, this body's competences do not extend to the press or online media, and in practice it is widely regarded as highly politicised and institutionally weak. Moreover, Polish press law has remained essentially unchanged since the communist era, and, apart from abolishing censorship, successive governments have failed to develop a coherent regulatory framework for the media market. In this context, expecting the OCCP to serve as a de facto media regulator was unrealistic and legally unfounded.

The Polska Press case highlights the need for a broader debate on the objectives of merger control in Poland. It may be worth considering expanding the scope of the public interest test and transferring the competence to apply it to a political authority, following the German model.[60] Such a solution would create a clearer separation between competition enforcement and political decision-making while preserving legal certainty for undertakings. However, it is difficult to expect such a debate to take place in a system where, for more than a decade, no coherent competition policy has been articulated and where the OCCP itself operates without clearly defined enforcement priorities.

Finally, any attempts to 'discover' non-economic values within the SIEC test or to introduce non-statutory considerations into merger assessment would be clearly *contra legem*. Such practices would inevitably lead to a profound erosion of legal certainty for market participants. They would further politicise the OCCP's decision-making, undermining both the legitimacy and predictability of Polish merger control.

8 Decisions in Merger Cases

8.1 Substantive Decisions

Following merger control proceedings, OCCP may issue four types of decisions: (i) Clearance – if the concentration doesn't significantly impede competition, unconditional approval; (ii) conditional clearance – if restrictions can be removed; (iii) extraordinary clearance – if anticompetitive but justified by public interest; and (iv) prohibition – if it would significantly impede competition with no remedies.

60 OECD, Efficiencies in Merger Control–Note by Germany, DAF/COMP/WP3/WD(2025)17, 6–7.

Merger decisions expire two years after issuance. During this period, the parties may proceed with and complete the transaction. If the transaction is not completed within this time, the parties must re-notify the concentration. The 'validity' period may be extended by one year upon request. The OCCP is generally receptive to such applications; over the last decade, seven extension requests have been granted.

8.2 Formal Conclusion of Proceedings

Merger proceedings may also be concluded on formal grounds, without a substantive assessment of the transaction. First, the OCCP may return the notification form where a formal obstacle prevents adjudication on the merits. This occurs most commonly when the notification is incomplete and not corrected in a timely manner; when the transaction is exempt under Article 14 of the Competition Act; when the notification is premature or speculative; when the wrong entity submitted the notification; or when the form lacks essential information.[61] Returned notifications constitute a relatively small proportion of cases, generally not exceeding 5% of all filings. Second, proceedings may be discontinued if they become groundless, for example, due to the parties' withdrawal of the notification or the referral of the case to the European Commission. Discontinuances are very rare in Polish merger control practice.

8.3 Merger Intervention Ratio

The Table 8.2 below illustrates the OCCP's intervention ratio in merger cases and covers only decisions concluded on substantive grounds.[62]

The Table 8.2 shows that, over the period covered, the authority has intervened in only a small share of merger cases. The vast majority of concluded proceedings result in unconditional clearances, typically well above 95% in recent years. Remedies are imposed infrequently, usually in the low single digits annually, while prohibitions are sporadic, with several years recording none. Overall, the intervention ratio (remedies plus prohibitions relative to concluded cases) is consistently very low, indicating a predominantly clearance-oriented enforcement practice, with targeted intervention reserved for exceptional cases.

---

61 M. Błachucki, *System*, 311–312.

62 Decisions on discontinuance of proceedings or return of the notification forms are omitted.

TABLE 8.2 Merger intervention ratio (Source: OCCP activity reports)

Year	Concluded	Clearance	Remedies	Prohibitions
2024	312	309	3	0
2023	310	307	3	0
2022	327	326	1	0
2021	300	295	4	1
2020	266	261	5	0
2019	267	260	5	2
2018	229	228	1	0
2017	206	205	1	0
2016	215	196	2	0
2015	228	218	1	0
2014	190	169	4	0
2013	177	156	2	0
2012	155	136	1	0
2011	187	166	3	2
2010	188	147	2	0
2009	123	97	1	3
2008	177	153	2	0
2007	263	203	2	0
2006	265	215	1	1
2005	329	265	0	2
2004	218	175	1	2
2003	151	149	2	0
2002	169	168	1	0
2001	542	n/a	n/a	n/a
2000	1107	911	0	0
1999	1079	917	0	0
1998	1511	1510	0	1
1997	1227	1225	0	2
1996	378	377	0	1
1995	333	333	0	0
1994	405	404	0	1
1993	537	513	13	7
1992	740	718	9	9
1991	974	895	63	4
1990	192	167	17	8

9 Remedies in Merger Cases

After conducting evidentiary proceedings, the OCCP may conclude that the concentration under examination is likely to result in a significant restriction of competition in the relevant market. Such a finding does not automatically lead to a prohibition decision. Remedies may modify the transaction to eliminate or prevent the identified anticompetitive effects. Pursuant to Article 19(2) of the Competition Act, the OCCP may impose obligations on undertakings intending to carry out a concentration or accept commitments proposed by them. Historically, Polish merger control did not provide undertakings with any formal mechanism to propose remedies on their own initiative, as the relevant provisions referred exclusively to conditions imposed by the OCCP. This changed in 2015, when a procedural substitute for a genuine system of conditional clearance was introduced, enabling parties to submit commitments during merger proceedings.[63]

Polish merger control procedure is structured as a two-phase process. Where potential competition concerns are identified, the notifying party is formally informed of the authority's preliminary assessment. At this stage, the party may respond, including by submitting proposed remedies to eliminate the identified competition concerns. Both the notifying party and the OCCP may therefore propose remedies. The submission of remedy proposals initiates a negotiation process.

The OCCP enjoys broad discretionary powers when deciding on remedies in merger cases. Remedies may be structural, behavioural, or hybrid. OCCP decisions demonstrate a clear preference for structural remedies. This preference is justified by the authority on the basis that mergers typically produce lasting structural changes in the market, and that preventing their negative effects therefore requires structural intervention. Structural remedies are also easier to implement and monitor, as they generally do not require long-term supervision mechanisms. These remedies involve a permanent modification of the transaction's structure or of the undertakings participating in it and are generally considered more effective and easier to enforce. Structural remedies imposed by the OCCP have included, inter alia:

i. the obligation to dispose of part of the assets of the acquired undertaking, such as chlorine electrolysis installations;[64]

---

63 J. Łukawski, *Decyzje wyrażające warunkową zgodę na dokonanie koncentracji w świetle prawa unijnego i najnowszych zmian polskiego prawa antymonopolowego*, EPS 2015, no. 7, 30–31

64 OCCP Decision DOK-116/2006.

ii. the permanent and irreversible divestiture of rights to specific retail outlets;[65]
iii. the sale of shares acquired as a result of the transaction to an independent investor;[66]
iv. the permanent and irreversible disposal of rights to a specified group of pharmacies.[67]

When the concentration produces vertical or conglomerate effects, behavioural remedies may be applied. These remedies require the undertaking to behave in a specified manner after the transaction, for example, by maintaining access conditions, licensing arrangements, or supply obligations. Behavioural remedies are more difficult to monitor and enforce, particularly in Poland, where the Competition Act does not provide a clear legal basis for appointing trustees to supervise compliance. For this reason, the OCCP has never appointed trustees, as it lacks statutory authority to do so. The primary instrument for monitoring compliance with remedies is the reporting obligation imposed on undertakings. These obligations require periodic reports on the implementation of remedies. Since most remedies are structural, these reports are quite straightforward.

Behavioural remedies have been applied in several cases. For example, in the Wienerberger/Terreal Holding concentration, clearance was granted on the condition that the acquiring undertaking continue to license the Creaton brand to Creaton Polska free of charge, covering production, distribution and advertising of roofing products.[68] In the Air Liquide/Betamed case, involving healthcare services funded by the National Health Fund, the remedies ensured continuity of patient care and maintained competitive conditions in tenders organised by the Fund.[69] In another case concerning the acquisition of ACP Europe & Eurocylinder by Air Products & Chemicals, the OCCP imposed obligations on contract extensions, non-discriminatory supply, and price ceilings for Polish wholesale customers of liquid CO_2.[70]

Vertical mergers pose competition risks, such as market foreclosure. Remedies focus on keeping distribution open, often through behavioural measures that require competitors to have access to or supply. An example is the Carey Agri/Polmos Białystok merger, which involved a major distributor and a fla-

65 OCCP Decision DKK-76/2008
66 OCCP Decision DOK-71/2007
67 OCCP Decision DKK-206/2023.
68 OCCP Decision DKK-227/2023.
69 OCCP Decision DKK-191/2021.
70 OCCP Decision DKK-51/2019.

voured vodka producer.[71] One of the imposed conditions required the merged entity to maintain the distribution of competing producers' alcohol products at a specified level, thereby safeguarding the openness of the wholesale distribution channel.

When imposing structural remedies, the OCCP evaluates whether the divested business segment can operate independently and provide genuine competitive pressure. Standalone business units are preferred because they require fewer carve-out measures and can be transferred more swiftly. However, in some cases, the authority permits the divestiture of non-standalone asset packages, provided the separation is practical and timely. These packages often include intellectual property rights and key personnel. A notable example is the Agros Nova/Kotlin merger in the jam market, where remedies included divesting a production line, along with brand rights, contracts, and critical human resources, to maintain the divested business's viability as a viable competitor.[72]

9.1 Referrals and Remedies

The OCCP and the European Commission cooperate in allocating merger cases. Although the Commission is not always willing to refer cases even where the conditions of Article 9 EUMR are formally met,[73] cooperation has generally been effective, albeit sporadic. Most referrals occur under Article 4(4) of the EUMR, though successful Article 9 referrals have also occurred.[74] Given the criteria under Article 9, it is unsurprising that many referred cases result in conditional clearances.[75] Earlier concerns that the Sped-Pro judgment would undermine merger referrals have proved unfounded.[76]

A recent example concerns the acquisition of TIM S.A. by FEGA & Schmitt Elektrogroßhandel, both active in the wholesale electrical goods market.[77] The agreed remedy required the divestiture of one TIM store, including the transfer of the lease, employee contracts, business records, and customer base.

---

71 OCCP Decision DOK-123/2005.

72 OCCP Decision DKK-9/2009.

73 Case M.8665–Discovery/Scripps.

74 For instance Cases COMP/M.4522 Carrefour/Ahold Polska, COMP/M.6822–Groupe Auchan/Real/Real Hypermarket Romania, or recently M.9952 – PKN ORLEN/ PGNiG.

75 The only exception would be Case M.8611–Smithfield / Pini Polonia.

76 M. Malaga, *Does the 'more appropriate' authority need to be independent? Rule of law implications for case referrals with respect of concentrations*, YARS 2022, no. 1, 134.

77 Case M.11095 – WÜRTH/TIM.

The buyer was required to be independent of both parties and capable of continuing wholesale operations.[78]

9.2 Merger Remedies and the Phantom of Effectiveness

A distinctive feature of Polish merger control is the public disclosure of remedies. Since 2015, disclosure of remedy implementation deadlines may be withheld, but only upon the notifying party's request. All other elements of remedies remain public. This differs from EU practice and has been criticised in legal doctrine.[79] The likely explanation is that OCCP remedies are generally straightforward and implemented over extended periods, limiting the practical impact of disclosure.

Compared with remedies accepted by the European Commission, OCCP remedies are strikingly concise and general. They typically rely on basic reporting obligations and lack detailed enforcement mechanisms. This may explain both the authority's preference for structural remedies and the limited effectiveness of remedy enforcement. While some increase in remedy complexity is evident, it has not been accompanied by improved legal certainty. [80] Particular criticism concerns the vague definition of acceptable purchasers in divestment remedies.[81]

A fundamental weakness of the Polish system is the absence of any systematic ex post evaluation of remedies, which was carried out in the early days of the authority.[82] There is no publicly available information indicating that the OCCP has assessed whether the remedies it imposed have restored or preserved effective competition over the past two decades. As a rule, merger cases are considered closed once the final report on remedy implementation is submitted. Several cases are known in which divested assets failed to become a viable competitive force and were closed shortly thereafter by the purchaser.[83] These failures have not prompted any visible reflection or policy adjustments by the authority.

Specific remedies raise doubts because of their largely symbolic nature. They are presented as practical solutions to identified competition problems, yet in practice, they amount to little more than a regulatory placebo.

78 OCCP Decision DKK-24/2024.

79 J. Łukawski, *Decyzje*, 30.

80 J. Łukawski, *O potrzebie wyjaśnień Prezesa UOKiK w sprawie zgody warunkowej na dokonanie koncentracji przez przedsiębiorców*, iKAR 2020, no. 5, 27.

81 T. Skoczny, *Zgody szczególne w prawie kontroli koncentracji*, Warsaw 2014, 698.

82 Activity Report 1992, 29–34.

83 OCCP Decisions DOK-86/2007, DKK-40/2014, or DKK-180/2016.

This is particularly evident where undertakings accept commitments that merely mirror their anticipated regulatory obligations,[84] or where a state-owned undertaking is, in practice, required to divest assets to another state-controlled entity.[85] In such cases, the remedy's formal structure conceals the absence of any genuine competition effect.

Another problem is that the remedies agreed by the OCCP do not ensure that the independent buyer will be a genuine competitor. A particularly problematic example concerns mergers between pharmacy chains. In many cases, divested pharmacies are sold to natural persons who then rejoin the same chain as franchisees. Given the structure of franchise agreements in the pharmacy sector – where the franchisor exercises almost complete control over pricing, supply, branding, and commercial strategy – the franchisee lacks genuine economic independence.[86] Remedies of this kind do not create an effective competitor and merely preserve the appearance of compliance. Such 'alibi remedies' undermine the OCCP's credibility over the long term and weaken its legitimacy as a technocratic and independent authority.

The next source of controversy is the OCCP's reliance on rigid and mechanical remedial solutions. This is particularly visible in retail mergers, where competitive assessment is often based on quantitative indicators such as sales volume or retail floor space. In two cases spanning more than a decade – JMD/Plus Discount[87] and Carrefour/Tesco (Wrocław)[88] – the OCCP accepted remedies requiring reductions in sales area in certain stores. This reliance on sales area as a proxy for competitive pressure reveals an inability or unwillingness to develop a more refined qualitative analysis of retail markets and reflects an overreliance on simplistic metrics.

Academics criticised the OCCP for its categorical refusal to modify conditional decisions.[89] Under previous OCCP leadership, requests to amend remedies – most often to extend implementation deadlines – were consistently rejected. The authority argued that prolonging a situation in which competition was restricted could not be justified on public-interest grounds and was detrimental to both consumers and undertakings. This approach changed radically after 2020.

---

84 OCCP Decision DKK-156/2017.

85 OCCP Decision DKK-82/2022.

86 M. Błachucki, *Franczyza i inne relacje umowne a wywieranie decydującego wpływu na innego przedsiębiorcę*, PS 2024, no. 7–8, 172.

87 OCCP Decision DKK-76/2008.

88 OCCP Decision DKK-277/2021.

89 J. Łukawski, *O potrzebie*, 27; M. Błachucki, *System*, 395

Between 2020 and 2025, the OCCP issued eight decisions modifying conditional clearances, all of which concerned extensions of remedy implementation deadlines. This liberal approach has produced unsettling results. It has created a justified expectation among stakeholders that obtaining an extension has become almost automatic. The Air Products case illustrates this tendency particularly well. The initial implementation period for the structural remedy spanned three years.[90] It was prolonged by six months,[91] then another six months.[92] Despite rather superficial efforts to implement the imposed remedies, the undertaking obtained two extensions of the deadline. The structural remedy took four years to be implemented. The OCCP's decisions contained only general justifications and failed to provide convincing reasons for the repeated delays.

The Vectra case provides an even more troubling example. In 2020, Vectra received a conditional clearance with a straightforward structural remedy involving asset divestiture.[93] One year later, the OCCP granted an extension of the implementation deadline.[94] Nearly another year later, a second extension was granted.[95] Despite the extended deadlines, the undertaking failed to implement the remedies. Although infringement proceedings were initiated for non-compliance, they were ultimately discontinued in 2024, allegedly because the ECN+ Directive was implemented, which removed the possibility of sanctioning delayed implementation of remedies.[96]

This sequence of events provides a vivid illustration not merely of failed remedy implementation but of failed enforcement. While there were legitimate reasons to reconsider the OCCP's previously rigid approach to modifying remedies, the current policy has shifted to the opposite extreme. The effectiveness of merger remedies in Poland increasingly resembles a phantom. Remedies exist in form and are presented as decisive interventions, yet their capacity to restore or protect effective competition is doubtful. Without meaningful enforcement, credible sanctions, and systematic evaluation, merger remedies risk becoming purely symbolic in Polish merger control rather than an effective competition-law instrument.

90 OCCP Decision DKK-51/2019.
91 OCCP Decision DKK-122/2021.
92 OCCP Decision DKK-238/2022.
93 OCCP Decision DKK-25/2020.
94 OCCP Decision DKK-205/2021.
95 OCCP Decision DKK-55/2022.
96 Refer to Chapter 11.

10 Prohibitions: The Black Swans of Merger Control

The Competition Act provides for two situations in which the OCCP may prohibit a concentration. First, pursuant to Article 20(1), the authority shall prohibit a concentration that would create or strengthen a significant impediment to competition in the market, in particular by creating or strengthening a dominant position. Secondly, pursuant to Article 95(2), the OCCP may present to the undertaking or undertakings participating in the concentration the conditions referred to in Article 19(2), setting a deadline for responding to the proposal; failure to respond or a negative response results in the issuance of a prohibition decision under Article 20(1).

Prohibitions in merger cases are exceptionally rare. Their relatively higher incidence in the early 1990s coincided with the systemic transformation of the Polish economy, during which the competition authority faced newly liberalised markets and profound structural distortions that required decisive intervention. After this initial adjustment period, prohibitions declined sharply and remained largely absent for many years. The near absence of prohibitions after 2014 may be explained by the OCCP's practice of communicating competition concerns at an advanced stage of proceedings. This often led undertakings to withdraw notifications to avoid a formal prohibition decision, thereby reducing the number of prohibitions recorded in official statistics.

Against this background, the re-emergence of prohibitions over the past six years is both notable and surprising. Given the consistently low overall intervention ratio in Polish merger control, this renewed use of prohibitions raises questions about the economic justification and internal consistency of some of these decisions. These doubts were echoed by the courts, which quashed all prohibition decisions that were appealed in recent years.

Several prohibition cases merit closer examination.

10.1 A Prohibition Too Far: The Energy Merger Case and Its Aftermath

One of the most significant prohibitions in the OCCP's history concerned PGE's planned acquisition of Energa.[97] The OCCP concluded that the transaction would significantly restrict competition in the broadly defined electricity market. Although the transaction was primarily vertical – linking electricity generation, wholesale and retail supply, and distribution – the authority emphasised that the concentration would fully internalise surplus electricity flows and weaken competitive constraints on the merged entity.

97 OCCP Decision DKK-1/2011

The case was embedded in a clear political context. First, the transaction formed part of the Energa privatisation conducted by the Ministry of the Treasury, with budgetary considerations central. Second, during the OCCP proceedings, the government adopted a revised Energy Policy through 2030, which explicitly identified the takeover of Energa by PGE as a means of achieving strategic objectives, including energy security, diversification of the fuel mix, development of renewable energy sources, and construction of nuclear power plants. Third, the OCCP had previously authorised anti-competitive consolidations in the energy sector on the basis of the public interest grounds test.[98] In this case, however, the authority rejected the government's position and openly questioned the assumptions underlying the Energy Policy itself.

The resulting prohibition was regarded in doctrine as well-reasoned and justified,[99] although alternative solutions were also proposed.[100] The CCCP upheld the decision,[101] which, at the time, was widely regarded as confirming not only the soundness of the legal reasoning but also the OCCP's legitimacy and integrity. This period is often described as the high point of the authority's de facto independence, despite the absence of formal guarantees.

The aftermath, however, was paradoxical. A few months later, Prime Minister Donald Tusk dismissed the OCCP President, Małgorzata Krasnodębska-Tomkiel. No official reasons were provided, but commentators immediately linked the dismissal to the prohibition decision and the authority's opposition to government plans for energy sector consolidation.[102] It was a true paradox – liberal Prime Minister Donald Tusk dismissed a technocratic President of the OCCP for defending the free market.[103] The episode has since been interpreted as a turning point in the erosion of the *de facto* independence and institutional standing of competition policy in Poland, irrespective of subsequent formal safeguards.

98 OCCP Decisions No DKK–163/2006, DOK–29/2007, DKK-32/2007.

99 Sz. Gołębiowski, *Kontrola koncentracji w sektorze elektroenergetycznym*, Warsaw 2013, 123.

100 T. Skoczny, *Consolidation of the Polish Electricity Sector. The Merger Law Perspective*, YARS 2011, no. 1, 198.

101 CCCP judgment of 14.05.2012, XVII AmA 41/11.

102 For example W. Surmacz, *Dymisja prezesa UOKiK, czyli czas „trzaskania statystyk"*, https://www.forbes.pl/wiadomosci/dymisja-prezesa-uokik-czyli-czas-trzaskania-statystyk/yool3w2, P. Musiałek, *Prezes UOKiK odwołana za twardą politykę antymonopolową*, https://biznesalert.pl/musialek-prezes-uokik-odwolana-za-twarda-polityke-antymonopolowa/ or *Przeciw arbitralnym decyzjom polityków*, https://for.org.pl/2014/02/11/komunikat-for-w-zwiazku-z-odwolaniem-prezesa-uokik/.

103 M. Martyniszyn, M. Bernatt, 12

10.2 Empik/Merlin: Bankruptcy as Collateral Damage?

Merger assessment is fundamentally predictive. No matter how advanced the analytical tools are, it is impossible to predict exactly how markets will develop. Outcomes after a decision are usually influenced by multiple factors, not just the competition authority's intervention. The Polish Empik/Merlin case exemplifies this, as it ended with the target company exiting the market and filing for bankruptcy. Although this result isn't solely due to the merger prohibition, it highlights the inherent uncertainty of forward-looking merger reviews and the difficulty of separating regulatory effects from broader market forces.[104]

The case, initiated in 2010, concerned Empik's proposed acquisition of Merlin. Empik operated a nationwide chain of media stores and held a strong position in e-commerce. Meanwhile, Merlin was the oldest Polish online retailer of books, music, and other media products. The OCCP prohibited the transaction, concluding that it would restrict competition in domestic markets for online retail sales of non-specialist books and music and adversely affect upstream purchasing markets.[105]

The decision was distinctive for at least two reasons. First, the OCCP conducted its largest market survey to date, gathering opinions from over 1,000 undertakings, which played a decisive role in the assessment. Second, the authority treated online and traditional retail as separate relevant markets. From today's perspective, this assessment appears highly questionable. Even at the time, critics argued that prohibiting the consolidation of market leaders would not resolve structural fragmentation in Polish e-commerce and that the absence of strong, recognisable domestic platforms would shape consumer behaviour to the detriment of local competitors.[106]

The prohibition proved disastrous for Merlin, which rapidly declined from a market leader to a marginal entity and eventually entered repeated bankruptcy proceedings.[107] Empik/Merlin illustrates a broader dilemma in merger

---

104 The bankruptcy of iRobot at the end of 2025 revived the same debate on the European Commission's opposition to Amazon's planned acquisition of that company: D. Moss, *The Demise of iRobot: How Antitrust Enforcers Missed the Elephant in the Room*, https://www.progressivepolicy.org/the-demise-of-irobot-how-antitrust-enforcers-missed-the-elephant-in-the-room/.

105 OCCP decision DKK-12/2011.

106 I. Szwedziak-Bork, *Decyzje koncentracyjne w sprawach Empik/Merlin oraz Czerwona Torebka/Merlin, czyli dlaczego wszyscy chcieli złowić Merlina*, iKAR 2013, no. 5, 128.

107 *Merlin.pl broni się przed upadłością*, https://crn.pl/aktualnosci/merlin-pl-broni-sie-przed-upadloscia/.

control: even decisions grounded in careful economic analysis may yield outcomes detrimental to competition in dynamic, fast-evolving markets. This risk is inherent in competition intervention and increases with the degree of regulatory involvement. Deterministic narratives that attribute such outcomes solely to competition authority decisions oversimplify complex economic processes.

10.3 Nord Stream 2 and Decisional Overreach

The NS2 case was discussed earlier in this chapter.[108] What is particularly noteworthy from the perspective of merger prohibitions is that the prohibition and dissolution order was issued not in standard merger control proceedings initiated by notification, but as a result of infringement proceedings initiated *ex officio*. This was the first such case under the current Competition Act.

The OCCP intervened to prevent the creation of NS2. The authority concluded that Gazprom would fully exploit it. Given the significant excess capacity of gas transmission infrastructure, Gazprom would redirect gas flows to pipelines with lower usage costs. As a consequence, the concentration would result in preferential treatment of NS2 and a reduction in the utilisation of alternative pipelines for transporting gas from Russia to the European Economic Area. In particular, Gazprom could reduce or cease gas transit through the Yamal pipeline crossing Polish territory. Since Gazprom's share of gas supplies to Poland already exceeded 40%, the authority argued that the merger would further strengthen Gazprom's position vis-à-vis Polish buyers. The OCCP also claimed that reduced transit through Poland could lead to higher gas prices and hinder competition in downstream markets. Ultimately, NS2 was said to have significantly strengthened Gazprom's negotiating position on the Polish market.[109]

As indicated earlier, the courts quashed the OCCP's decision for lack of jurisdiction over the transaction.[110] As a result, Polish courts did not examine the substantive merits of the decision. This is regrettable, as the case illustrates the inherent limitations of economic analysis in merger control. Such analysis relies on economic models and forecasts, which can quickly become obsolete. Indeed, the fundamental assumptions underlying the OCCP's assessment of

---

108 Refer to Section 6.1.

109 OCCP decision DKK-178/2020.

110 Judgments of the CCCP of 21.10.2022, XVII AmA 11/21, and Court of Appeal of 16.10.2023, VII AGa 1/23.

NS2 were rendered entirely irrelevant by subsequent geopolitical developments following Russia's aggression against Ukraine.

Some commentators have suggested that the fines imposed may have been politically motivated. First, the proceedings coincided with broader political opposition to NS2 at both national and EU levels.[111] Secondly, the OCCP initiated its investigation shortly after Gazprom avoided an EU fine in proceedings concerning alleged abuse of dominance in Central and Eastern Europe.[112] The OCCP's communication strategy reinforces these suspicions. Press releases announcing the proceedings bore explicit political overtones, such as 'OCCP against NS2',[113] or highlighted the nationality of consortium members.[114] While this does not conclusively prove politicisation, such rhetoric sits uneasily with the principles of independence and technocratic enforcement expected of a competition authority.

The NS2 case should therefore not be treated as a benchmark for merger control enforcement, but rather as an illustration of decisional overreach and extravagant fining under the OCCP's current leadership. The stark contrast between the authority's public narrative and the judicial outcome ultimately undermined the credibility of the enforcement action.[115]

10.4 Radio Prohibition: An Epic Defeat on the Merits

The final case concerns the prohibition of Agora's acquisition of Eurozet, a media-sector transaction. The OCCP concluded that the merger would significantly impede competition in the radio advertising market and in the broadcasting of radio programmes. According to the authority, the transaction would create a duopoly and marginalise the remaining radio groups and stations. The two leading groups – Eurozet and RMF FM – would jointly hold approximately 70% of the national market. In several local markets, Agora would have controlled more than 40% of radio frequencies. On the national

111 A. Stawicki, A. Bryńska, *The Polish NCA Imposes Record Fines on Gazprom for Nord Stream 2 Gun-Jumping*, JECLP 2021, no. 12, no. 2, 115.

112 M. Martyniszyn, *On extraterritoriality and the Gazprom case*, ECLR 2015, no. 7, 291.

113 *UOKiK przeciw Nord Stream 2*, https://archiwum.uokik.gov.pl/aktualnosci.php?news_id=14322. Needless to say, Nord Stream 2 was not the party to the infringement proceedings.

114 *Nord Stream 2 – Prezes UOKiK może nałożyć 50 mln euro kary na Gazprom*, https://archiwum.uokik.gov.pl/aktualnosci.php?news_id=16454.

115 M. Błachucki, *Establishment of Nord Stream 2 under Polish Merger Control Rules*, ECLR 2024, no. 8, 346.

advertising market, the merged entity would have faced only one equally strong competitor.[116]

The OCCP's reasoning was rejected in full by the courts.[117] This was a precedent-setting case: for the first time in Polish merger control, a prohibition decision was overturned on appeal and replaced with an unconditional clearance.[118] The CCCP not only reviewed the legality of the OCCP's decision but also conducted its own evidentiary proceedings, including witness hearings, and carried out an independent economic and market analysis. This was highly unusual, as Polish common courts have traditionally avoided substantive economic assessments.[119]

The OCCP's theory of harm – based on the risk of a duopoly and coordinated effects – was found insufficiently substantiated. The courts emphasised that the theory had no basis in national or EU case law and was not supported by compelling evidence. The rejection of the theory, together with the court's willingness to rule on the merits, marked a significant departure from judicial deference to administrative economic assessments.

Additional doubts surrounded the OCCP's approach. The identified competition concerns were essentially local, which would usually justify remedies rather than an outright prohibition. The authority failed to provide a convincing explanation for why remedies were not considered. This omission further undermined the decision's credibility.[120]

The case also raised suspicions that competition law was being used instrumentally to pursue broader political objectives, particularly regarding media ownership and pluralism.[121] Although such objectives may be legitimate public policy concerns, they fall outside the remit of merger control. The OCCP's failure to clearly separate competition analysis from political considerations contributed to the collapse of the decision on appeal.

Given that mergers are lawful transactions and that prohibitions should remain exceptional, the accumulation of procedural, evidentiary, and substantive deficiencies in the Agora/Eurozet case fully justifies its characterisation as an epic defeat for the OCCP on the merits.

---

116 OCCP decision Decision DKK-1/2021.

117 Judgments of the OCCP of 12.05.2022, XVII AmA 61/21, and of Court of Appeals of 27.02.2023, VII Aga 1023/22.

118 A. Celejewska-Rajchert, F. Drgas, *Sądowa kontrola decyzji Prezesa UOKiK w sprawach koncentracji–wybrane aspekty w oparciu o najnowsze orzecznictwo (sprawy* Agora/*Eurozet oraz Orlen/Polska Press*), iKAR 2023, no. 4, p.114.

119 M. Kozak, *Glosa do wyroku Sądu Ochrony Konkurencji i Konsumentów z 12 maja 2022 r. w sprawie XVII AmA 61/21*, iKAR 2022, no. 4, 122.

120 M. Kozak, *Glosa*, 123.

121 M. Bernatt, M. K. Sznajder, 8.

11 Prospects for Polish Merger Control

Any meaningful changes to the Polish merger control system are likely to result from external influences rather than domestic initiative. The current leadership of the OCCP does not regard merger control as a relevant or priority area of competition enforcement and has allowed institutional inertia to persist. As a result, endogenous reform should not be expected.

The most immediate and inevitable change will follow from the implementation of the EMFA.[122] From a systemic perspective, EFMA will not alter the core legal framework of merger control in Poland but will introduce a duty of cooperation with the broadcasting regulator in cases involving media concentrations. This, however, raises two unresolved structural issues. First, the Polish broadcasting regulator's jurisdiction is limited to radio and television services, whereas EMFA applies to the entire media sector. This creates an institutional mismatch. Either the regulator will be required to issue opinions beyond its statutory competence, or its jurisdiction will need to be extended. The latter option appears highly unlikely, as the regulator's competences are anchored in the Constitution and there is little political appetite for constitutional amendments. As a result, EMFA is likely to be implemented only partially, leaving press and electronic media mergers effectively outside any coherent pluralism assessment framework.

At the EU level, the Commission has been actively encouraging NCAs to advocate for the introduction of call-in powers. In Poland, however, there is no public debate on this issue, and even the President of the OCCP has not raised it. From a political perspective, this is unsurprising. It is doubtful that the current government would seek to strengthen the position and powers of a political appointee from the previous administration. From a competition policy perspective, such a reform would also be undesirable without robust accountability mechanisms and transparent, competitive procedures for appointing OCCP leadership. Enhancing the authority's powers without first securing institutional safeguards would merely increase the risk of another politically dependent leadership appointment.

A more theoretically appealing development within EU merger control is the increased reliance on antitrust provisions to scrutinise transactions below notification thresholds. Formally, there are no legal barriers to such an approach in Poland. In practice, however, the prospects of a 'Polish Tower-

122 For the overview, M.L. Stasi, *Media mergers between competition law and the European Media Freedom Act,* [in:] P.L. Parcu, M.A. Rossi, and M. Botta (eds.), *Research Handbook On Competition And Technology,* Cheltenham 2025.

cast' scenario are minimal.[123] First, the absence of a coherent and deliberate competition policy paradoxically creates a de facto safe harbour for minor, non-notifiable mergers. Secondly, such an approach would require a fundamentally different enforcement methodology, including systematic inspections of internal documents and a serious examination of the strategic motives behind acquisitions – tools the OCCP has never used in merger cases. Thirdly, given the authority's traditional focus on RPM and its recent interest in labour markets and digital services, it is doubtful that the OCCP would allocate its increasingly limited enforcement resources to complex below-threshold merger cases.

In sum, Polish merger control is likely to remain characterised by inertia, selective external adaptation, and a lack of strategic vision. Without institutional reform and a genuine reorientation of competition policy priorities, merger control will remain marginal within Polish competition enforcement.

12 Conclusions: Merger Control in Poland – Marginalisation within an Overextended NCA

At the beginning of the OCCP's operation, merger control was an essential and visible element of competition enforcement and highly valued by several early presidents of the authority. Over the last decade, however, it has been marginalised, systematically underdeveloped, and under-resourced within the Polish competition law system. This marginalisation is most clearly reflected in the resources the OCCP devotes to this area.

Merger control – one of the most consequential instruments of competition policy – is staffed at a strikingly low level. With only 17 employees, the Merger Control Department is not merely underrepresented; it is effectively peripheral within the organisation. Its staffing is almost identical to that of the President's Office and materially smaller than that of units responsible for communications and international cooperation. In practical terms, the OCCP devotes more personnel to shaping external narratives, managing its external presence, and directly supporting the president than to reviewing mergers that could permanently alter market structures and materially affect the functioning of the Polish economy and the prosperity of businesses and consumers in Poland. Such a distribution of resources cannot credibly be reconciled with any claim that merger control is a strategic priority. This imbalance is struc-

123 On Towerast implications refer to M. Kyle, O. Shah, V. Man, *Hot tub time machine? What role for Towercast in EU merger control*, JECLP 2024, no. 6.

tural rather than incidental. Merger control requires advanced legal, economic, and analytical capacity, yet it is resourced at a level comparable to internal coordination units rather than core enforcement departments. As a result, merger control plays an operationally insignificant role relative to its importance in protecting competition, innovation, and consumer welfare.

This marginalisation is equally evident in the legal framework. Merger control has long been treated as a secondary, structurally sidelined component of Polish competition enforcement, as evidenced by the near-total absence of statutory reform over the past decade. The only legislative changes introduced in 2023 weakened the merger sanctioning system and widened the jurisdictional gap in this area, an issue analysed in the chapter on sanctions. Other changes – some of them substantively desirable, particularly regarding extraterritorial mergers – have been implemented exclusively through soft law instruments that effectively modify statutory rules. This approach is unacceptable. It constitutes a legal ersatz for serious legislative reform, reflecting that the current OCCP leadership is neither prepared nor willing to articulate and pursue a coherent reform agenda.

The chapter demonstrated that multiple elements of the Polish merger control system require statutory amendment. Foremost, there must be a fundamental reassessment of merger jurisdiction. The OCCP should focus its limited resources on transactions genuinely connected to the Polish market. This necessarily entails a reduction in the number of notifiable extraterritorial mergers. The most practical and principled way to achieve this would be to abolish the global turnover threshold, which represents an unreflective and poorly adapted transposition of the EU model. Other thresholds also require reassessment. While I see no justification for introducing call-in powers – at least in the absence of meaningful transparency and accountability safeguards – abolishing the global threshold would require reconsidering the national de minimis exemption and supplementing the notification obligation with a market-share criterion, as existed under the Competition Act of 2000.

The scope of notifiable transactions requires revision. Introducing the durability of the change of control should be a defining criterion. The current system, which captures temporary, incidental, or purely factual changes in control, is impractical and legally unsound. Legal certainty demands abandoning the imposition of competition liability for acts beyond the undertaking's control or for conduct whose sanctioning serves neither individual nor general prevention. The definition of a joint venture also requires reconsideration. This concerns not only the distinction between joint ventures and joint control and the related turnover calculation rules, but also the broader question of which joint ventures should fall within the scope of merger control and which should instead be assessed under antitrust rules. Clear statutory rules must be adopted to ensure that joint ventures cleared in merger proceedings remain subject to subsequent antitrust scrutiny where appropriate. Comparable solutions exist in other systems, notably in Germany.

Further clarification is also required on staggered and interrelated transactions. The relevant provisions should expressly apply not only to acquisitions involving the same target capital group but also to transactions carried out by undertakings belonging to the same capital group on the acquiring side. Limiting the rule to direct active participants creates an unjustified enforcement gap.

Reform of merger control must also translate into a substantive shift in enforcement policy. Greater analytical effort should be devoted to complex or potentially anticompetitive concentrations, while simpler transactions should be processed more swiftly. This requires rebuilding institutional memory, improving IT support for case handlers, and reforming the design and enforcement of merger remedies. The current practice of routinely extending remedy deadlines must end, and effective monitoring mechanisms – such as the use of trustees – should be introduced.

Finally, these changes necessitate a reform of the OCCP's approach to merger guidelines. Recent amendments were chaotic and adopted without consultation. The OCCP should move away from issuing fragmented, ad hoc guidance and instead commit to periodic updates of comprehensive general guidelines. This would enhance transparency and accountability. Guidelines must not serve as a vehicle for quasi-legislative activity. They should clarify statutory provisions, not replace them. Moreover, Polish merger guidelines should be grounded in domestic enforcement experience rather than mechanically replicating foreign models.

Merger control in Poland has become a casualty of the existing institutional model. It has gradually been displaced from the enforcement priorities of successive OCCP Presidents, a process that has clearly accelerated over the last decade. Systemic dysfunctions are deepening. Their visibility is obscured by stable caseload numbers and a constant intervention ratio, but this stability reflects inertia rather than effective policy. Mandatory ex ante merger control allows such passivity to persist, yet this state of affairs is neither socially desirable nor normatively defensible. Only a broader revival of competition policy could reverse this trend. Given the current OCCP leadership's track record, however, the prospects for such a revival must be assessed as limited.

CHAPTER 9

Antimonopoly Proceedings

1 Introduction

Antimonopoly proceedings provide the procedural framework for examining two fundamental categories of competition cases: those concerning practices that restrict competition and those relating to merger control. In the most general terms, these proceedings define the procedural path the OCCP must follow to issue an administrative decision that, first, ensures the legality and substantive correctness of that decision and, second, guarantees effective protection of the rights and interests of the entities affected by it.[1]

Ordinary administrative cases are examined under the procedural rules set out in the APC and are then subject to judicial review by administrative courts. Antimonopoly proceedings, by contrast, are primarily governed by the Competition Act and are supplemented by references to all major procedural codes – administrative, civil, and criminal – while judicial review of OCCP decisions is, as a rule, entrusted to the civil courts, in particular the CCCP. This specific regulatory architecture raises a number of fundamental questions, ranging from the legal nature of antimonopoly proceedings to more detailed issues concerning the operation of particular procedural institutions.

Under the Competition Act, antimonopoly proceedings may take the form of cases concerning practices that restrict competition or of merger control cases. Formal antimonopoly proceedings may, in both categories, be preceded by explanatory proceedings. Although there are differences in the regulation of these individual forms of proceedings, they are not decisive for the overall assessment of the procedural model. For this reason, the analysis below focuses on the general structure of antimonopoly proceedings, with specific deviations and exceptions discussed where necessary.

The importance of the Competition Act's procedural provisions cannot be overstated. Compared with earlier statutes, these provisions are more developed and account for almost two-thirds of the Act. Compared with other administrative procedures, antimonopoly proceedings are relatively modern and, in several respects, have set trends subsequently followed by Polish administrative legislation more broadly. Many of these modern solutions are the result of a direct reception of European Union law and global antitrust

1 S. Kasznica, 107.

© 2026 THE AUTHOR(S) | HTTPS://DOI.ORG/10.1163/9789004754638-010
This is an open access publication distributed under the terms of the CC 4.0 license BY-NC-ND.

standards. This influence has intensified significantly following the implementation of the ECN+ Directive.

The full impact of the ECN+ Directive's implementation on antimonopoly proceedings remains to be established in practice. Article 3 of the Directive affirms that the general principles of EU law and the Charter of Fundamental Rights of the European Union apply fully to both EU and national competition proceedings. This provision has effectively dispelled earlier doubts about whether Member States' procedural autonomy could limit the application of these standards in purely national competition cases. In this sense, the Directive has, indirectly and without explicit harmonising intent, led to a partial harmonisation of national competition procedures, irrespective of whether EU competition law is directly applicable in a given case.[2]

2 Explanatory Proceedings

The Competition Act provides for two types of proceedings before the OCCP: explanatory proceedings and formal antimonopoly proceedings. These proceedings are legally independent, although explanatory proceedings may precede the initiation of formal antimonopoly proceedings. Both types are initiated exclusively ex officio – except in merger control, where initiation requires a notification by the parties – by an order of the OCCP. A complainant has no legally enforceable right to demand the initiation of proceedings, and in this respect, the OCCP retains full discretion.[3]

Explanatory proceedings are instituted where circumstances indicate a potential infringement of the Competition Act, whether in relation to a particular sector of the economy, the protection of collective consumer interests, or in other situations expressly provided for by law. Their objectives include determining whether an infringement has occurred that may justify initiating antimonopoly or consumer protection proceedings; conducting market inquiries, including assessments of market structure and concentration; verifying notification obligations in merger cases; and identifying initial violations affecting legally protected consumer interests.

Explanatory proceedings are used to verify initial signals, complaints, or information gathered by the OCCP regarding possible infringements and to conduct sectoral market inquiries. Their function is limited to gathering infor-

---

2 K. Kowalik-Bańczyk, *Dyrektywa ECN+ – sposób na podwyższenie ochrony prawnej przedsiębiorców w postępowaniach antymonopolowych?*, EPS 2019, no. 10, 10.

3 HAC order of 12.12.2012, II GSK 1912/12.

mation necessary to define the scope and subject matter of potential formal proceedings[4] and to carry out a preliminary assessment of market behaviour.[5]

The regulation of explanatory proceedings is notably sparse, with only two statutory provisions governing them. Given their formally ancillary status, the OCCP has not considered it necessary to provide a more comprehensive procedural framework. A defining feature of explanatory proceedings is the absence of parties. As a consequence, no entity other than the authority itself has access to the case file, nor does anyone have the right to challenge the outcome of these proceedings.[6] Even undertakings that were the subject of explanatory proceedings are not informed of their substantive conclusions; at most, they may ascertain that the proceedings have been closed, without any indication of reasons or findings.

Statutory time limits provide that explanatory proceedings should not exceed four months, or five months in particularly complex cases – limits that were extended in 2015 from the previous periods of 30 and 60 days. These time limits are just instructive.[7] They are much longer, in practice. The average duration of these proceedings in 2023 and 2024 was around two years.[8] The proceedings are concluded by an order devoid of reasoning and not subject to appeal, and their outcome cannot be reviewed by either the CCCP or administrative courts.[9] Findings from the explanatory proceedings may provide grounds for instituting antimonopoly proceedings. The result of the explanatory proceedings is neither conclusive nor binding, and no rights or obligations may be affected by the outcome of this procedure. The conclusion of the explanatory proceedings is a purely procedural act with no substantive relevance.[10] Even though explanatory proceedings do not determine rights or obligations and are purely procedural, their initiation suspends limitation periods and may therefore affect the duration of an undertaking's potential liability.

Although formally understated, explanatory proceedings play a crucial role in competition enforcement. They precede the vast majority of antitrust cases and often involve collecting most of the evidence later relied upon in formal proceedings, including inspections and searches that significantly interfere

4 PSC judgment of 3.10.2013, III SK 67/12.
5 Judgment of the CCCP of 13.03.2023, XVII AmA 45/21.
6 G. Materna, *Ograniczenie prawa wglądu do materiału dowodowego w postępowaniach przed Prezesem UOKiK*, PPH 2008, no. 4, 28.
7 CA judgment of 5.10.2005, VI ACa 1146/04.
8 OCCP estimation in response to PI request.
9 Order of the VAC of 19.08.2013, IV SAB/Wa 123/13.
10 CA judgment of 8.11.2018, VII AGa 1429/18.

with economic activity.[11] The implementation of the ECN+ Directive has further enhanced their importance by interrupting limitation periods. Given their practical significance and the breadth of discretion enjoyed by the OCCP, the current lack of procedural safeguards and accountability mechanisms is hard to justify.

Explanatory proceedings are both surprisingly powerful and opaque. The combination of broad investigative powers, the absence of parties, limited access to files, and the suspension of limitation periods makes them a highly intrusive mechanism. A major structural deficiency is the asymmetry in access to the investigation file. Undertakings have insight only into the material formally incorporated into the evidentiary record at the stage of antimonopoly proceedings. They have no means of verifying what information was gathered during the investigative phase but was ultimately excluded from the case file. As a result, undertakings cannot assess whether potentially exculpatory evidence was omitted, whether deliberately or inadvertently. This lack of transparency weakens procedural safeguards and undermines the parties' ability to exercise their rights of defence effectively. This raises concerns about procedural fairness.

3 (No) Pre-notification in Polish Merger Control

In many mature merger control systems, proceedings are preceded by a pre-notification phase, during which notifying parties may discuss matters with the competition authority before formally submitting a notification. In some jurisdictions – most notably before the European Commission – pre-notification is effectively mandatory, forming an integral part of the notification process and significantly reducing the risk of incomplete filings or procedural delays. By contrast, Polish merger control does not provide for a pre-notification phase.

In exceptional circumstances, the President of the OCCP may allow the notifying party to present its position orally at a meeting with authorised representatives of the Office, including before proceedings are initiated. While this mechanism may superficially resemble a pre-notification process, it does not serve the same function. Such meetings are extremely rare and typically occur only at the insistence of foreign undertakings familiar with more inter-

11 A. Nowakowska, *Perspektywa prawnoporównawcza ochrony praw przedsiębiorcy w postępowaniu wyjaśniającym poprzedzającym postępowanie antymonopolowe*, PPP 2025, no. 7–8, 150.

active merger control systems. The OCCP's established practice – grounded in its merger guidelines – does not contemplate a genuine pre-notification phase, nor does it encourage early engagement aimed at procedural efficiency or substantive clarity.[12]

The absence of a pre-notification phase has several practical consequences. First, it increases the risk of incomplete or deficient notifications, which in turn prolongs proceedings through requests for supplementary information. Second, it limits the OCCP's ability to identify substantive or jurisdictional issues early, thereby reducing procedural predictability for undertakings. Third, the lack of structured early dialogue fosters a more formalistic and less cooperative model of merger control, contrary to best practices promoted by the European Commission and many EU Member States. Consequently, the Polish system operates with lower administrative efficiency and reduced legal certainty for market participants, while the OCCP forgoes an important tool for managing its caseload and improving the quality of substantive assessment. As a result, transaction costs are being effectively increased for all.

OCCP's reluctance to institutionalise pre-notification dialogue contrasts with the European Commission's practice. This divergence fosters a more formalistic and rigid enforcement model, undermining predictability for undertakings and straining the authority's resources. From a regional perspective, the Polish approach appears increasingly difficult to justify, particularly as neighbouring jurisdictions continue to modernise their procedural frameworks in line with EU best practices.

4 Initiation of Antimonopoly Proceedings

The Competition Act provides that antimonopoly proceedings may be initiated either ex officio or upon a motion. As a general rule, proceedings to sanction infringements of the Competition Act are brought ex officio. This category includes proceedings concerning anticompetitive practices and other infringement proceedings. Proceedings in which an undertaking seeks authorisation for a transaction – most notably merger control proceedings – are brought upon a motion submitted by the notifying party. Transactions subject to mandatory notification must be suspended until a decision is issued. Where a concentration is implemented without prior clearance and the undertaking subsequently notifies the OCCP, the notification is returned as inadmissible, and the authority initiates proceedings ex officio to impose a fine for failure to

12 M. Błachucki, *System*, 171.

notify. As a result, initiation of proceedings upon a motion plays only a limited role in practice and is largely confined to merger control.

4.1 Antitrust Investigations

All antitrust cases are instituted ex officio. As noted earlier, until 2007, it was possible to initiate antimonopoly proceedings upon a motion submitted by an undertaking harmed by an infringement of the Competition Act. This possibility was eliminated by the adoption of the current Act, significantly strengthening the OCCP's discretion in case selection.[13]

The initiation of antimonopoly proceedings requires the OCCP to issue a formal order. This formalisation of the initiation is relatively unusual in Polish administrative law and arguably elevates the procedural significance of this stage. The initiation order must clearly specify the conduct challenged by the authority and is binding on the OCCP at subsequent stages of the proceedings. The factual description of the conduct defines the subject matter of the proceedings, while the legal basis consists of allegations of infringement of specific provisions of competition law.[14] Although the possibility of amending the initiation order has sparked controversy, case law permits limited modifications, provided that they do not alter the core of the alleged infringement.[15]

Although no person may effectively demand initiation of antimonopoly proceedings in antitrust cases, the Competition Act provides a formal mechanism to notify the OCCP of a suspected infringement. Pursuant to Article 86 of the Act, any person may submit a written notification expressing a suspicion that anticompetitive practices have been applied. This notification mechanism was introduced in 2007 as a substitute for the abolished right to trigger proceedings.

Such notifications typically include an identification of the allegedly infringing undertaking, a description of the factual background, an indication of the allegedly infringed provisions of national or EU competition law, a prima facie substantiation of a breach of Articles 101 or 102 TFEU, and the identifying details of the notifying party. Supporting evidence may also be attached. The OCCP is obliged to verify the notification and inform the notifying party of the outcome of that verification within statutory time limits. However, the author-

13 Refer to Section 2.4.

14 PSC judgment of 6.02.2018, III SK 8/17.

15 G. Materna, *Ograniczenia dopuszczalności zmiany przez Prezesa Urzędu Ochrony Konkurencji i Konsumentów zakresu analizy sprawy po wszczęciu właściwego postępowania administracyjnego*, Glosa 2018, no. 4, 92.

TABLE 9.1 Number of notifications and proceedings (Source: OCCP activity reports)

Year	Notifications	Explanatory proceedings	Antimonopoly proceedings
2024	386	15	11
2023	304	32	3
2022	274	24	11
2021	655	38	12
2020	686	64	7
2019	485	56	14
2018	568	64	12
2017	592	87	9
2016	N/A	96	21
2015	570	177	34
2014	469	177	35
2013	469	354 (177)	87 (35)
2012	438	290 (176)	112 (54)
2011	409	177	18
2010	369	161	20
2009	413	193	27
2008	292	187	29
2007	231	171	37

Note: In 2012 and 2013, the OCCP provided information on how many proceedings were initiated solely on the basis of notifications – refer to the number in brackets.

ity's response does not constitute an administrative decision and is not subject to judicial review.[16]

Empirical data on notifications, explanatory proceedings and formal antimonopoly proceedings reveal two deeply troubling trends as evidenced by the Table 9.1. First, there is a clear and sustained decline in the number of explanatory and antimonopoly proceedings initiated by the OCCP. No convincing explanation has been offered for this contraction in enforcement, which inevitably results in a declining intervention rate. Secondly, the data show the extremely limited impact of formal notifications. Although the OCCP has introduced a whistleblower programme allowing the submission of unstruc-

16 HAC order of 12.07.2011, II GSK 1035/11.

tured signals, the number of initiated proceedings remains only a fraction of the number of incoming notifications.

What is particularly striking is that this pattern persists despite the formally binding principle of legality, which would imply an obligation to prosecute competition infringements. In practice, however, the President of the OCCP retains unfettered discretion to initiate proceedings and personally authorises each case. The examination of formal notifications is not subject to any meaningful judicial oversight: the CCCP reviews only appeals against administrative decisions, while administrative courts merely verify whether the OCCP responded at all. These statistics therefore provide a vivid illustration of the highly centralised and discretionary – indeed, Caesarist – model of competition enforcement currently prevailing in Poland.

4.2 Merger Investigations

Merger control proceedings are brought exclusively on a motion by the undertaking concerned. By contrast, proceedings concerning merger infringements – such as failure to notify or gun-jumping – are initiated ex officio. In such cases, the decision to act rests with the President of the OCCP, and the internal evaluation committees do not participate. With respect to merger infringements, the principle of legality is applied relatively strictly. Unlike in antitrust matters, there is no formal complaint mechanism in merger control, although occasional informal signals are received. These merger-infringement cases remain marginal and supplementary, serving as an *ultima ratio* for enforcing compliance with notification obligations.

Merger proceedings are initiated upon submission of a notification, subject to detailed formal requirements set out in the implementing regulations.[17] The notification is subject to a statutory fee amounting to PLN 15,000.[18] Procedural improvements are evident in the current notification form (WID), which introduces a simplified structure and reduces information burdens, particularly when no affected markets are identified. Although Poland maintains a single unified notification form, the scope of information obligations that can be waived has expanded, increasing procedural flexibility. The detailed merger statistics were provided in the previous chapter.

17 Regulation of the Council of Ministers of 23.12.2014 on the notification of the intention of concentration of undertakings, JoL 2018 item 367.

18 Around EUR 3 800.

5 Time Limits

Time limits play a crucial systemic and organisational role in antimonopoly proceedings. They not only discipline the authority's conduct and ensure procedural efficiency but also protect undertakings against prolonged legal uncertainty. In competition law, where proceedings may have significant reputational and economic impact, the duration of enforcement action is itself an element of proportionality and fairness.

The Competition Act distinguishes between two categories of time limits. The first concerns the statutory duration of proceedings, which sets the time the OCCP should take to conclude a case once it has been initiated. The second concerns limitation periods, which define the temporal scope of the authority's competence to initiate proceedings. These two sets of rules pursue different objectives and operate under different legal logics.

5.1 Statutory and Actual Duration of Proceedings

The statutory duration of proceedings depends on the type of case. In antitrust cases, the Competition Act sets a five-month time limit for issuing a decision. In merger control, the time limits are considerably shorter: one month for Phase I proceedings and four months for Phase II proceedings. This differentiation reflects the legislator's assumption that antitrust cases are typically more complex and require extensive factual and economic analysis, whereas most mergers should be capable of swift clearance.

A fundamental difference exists, however, in the legal nature of these time limits. In antitrust proceedings, the five-month limit is merely instructive. Its expiry does not deprive the OCCP of the competence to adjudicate the case, and any procedural acts undertaken after the time limit has expired remain legally valid.[19] The only procedural consequence of non-compliance is informing the parties of the delay, providing reasons, and setting a new deadline. The Competition Act does not regulate the length or number of such extended deadlines, leaving the OCCP with very broad discretion in practice.

The time limits applicable in merger control proceedings are substantive. If the OCCP fails to issue a decision within the statutory period, a legal fiction of clearance arises.[20] This solution reflects the strong need for legal certainty in merger control, where transactions are often subject to strict commercial

19 The judgment of the HAC of 24.02.1987, IV SA 915/86.

20 The resolution of the Supreme Court of 26.11.1993, III CZP 63/93. See also the comment of T. Woś to this resolution, PiP 1995, no. 1.

timelines and financing arrangements. It also serves as an important structural safeguard against administrative inertia.

The introduction of a two-phase merger control system in 2015 was intended to align Polish law more closely with EU standards and to ensure that straightforward cases are resolved quickly. In practice, the distinction between Phase I and Phase II has become blurred. The OCCP initiates Phase II proceedings relatively easily, relying on broadly framed statutory criteria such as 'complexity' or the need for market inquiry. The decision to open Phase II is made by an administrative order that is not subject to appeal, and its justification is often cursory.

Moreover, in both phases, the effectiveness of statutory time limits is significantly weakened by the extensive use of stop-the-clock provisions. Any request by the OCCP for additional information or clarification suspends the running of the time limit. Given the absence of a genuine pre-notification phase in Polish merger control, such requests are made in the vast majority of cases. As a result, the formal time limits provide only a rough framework and do not reflect the actual duration of proceedings.

Empirical data confirm earlier concerns (Table 9.2). While Phase I merger proceedings remain relatively stable in duration, Phase II proceedings often extend well beyond one year and, in some cases, approach two years. This is difficult to justify substantively and is counterproductive for both administrative efficiency and market certainty. Long-running merger investigations often require repeated evidentiary exercises to update outdated data, thereby further prolonging proceedings and increasing administrative costs.

Furthermore, to determine the average time taken to examine cases, it is also worth noting the average duration of explanatory proceedings, which

TABLE 9.2 Average actual duration of merger proceedings (Source: OCCP activity reports)

Year	Phase I		Phase II	
	Days	Decisions	Days	Decisions
2024	42	309	373	3
2023	41	299	379	11
2022	38	317	283	10
2021	33	287	255	13
2020	33	234	203	9

TABLE 9.3 Average actual duration of proceedings in antitrust cases concluded in a given year (Source: OCCP decision registry)

Year	Days	Decisions
2024	706	13
2023	676	9
2022	614	8
2021	755	13
2020	874	15

almost always precede the initiation of antimonopoly proceedings. According to OCCP, it's two years.[21]

Antitrust proceedings present an even more troubling picture. Despite a decline in the number of cases initiated, the average duration of antitrust cases remains very long, often approaching two years (Table 9.3). When combined with the periods of explanatory proceedings, this totals almost four years. This suggests that delays are not primarily driven by caseload pressure but rather by structural inefficiencies in internal decision-making, excessive centralisation of authority, and a lack of effective procedural discipline.

5.2 Limitation Periods

Limitation periods define the temporal boundaries of the OCCP's enforcement powers and are therefore a key element of legal certainty. They balance the public interest in effective competition enforcement against the need to protect undertakings from indefinite exposure to liability.

Under Article 76 of the Competition Act, the general limitation period for instituting proceedings is five years from the end of the year in which the infringement occurred, or, in the case of fines, from the end of the year in which the decision imposing the fine became final. This general framework applies across different categories of infringements, though its practical significance varies.

Historically, Polish competition law provided for an exceptionally short limitation period in antitrust cases. Before 2015, proceedings could not be initiated if more than one year had elapsed since the infringement ceased. This approach was criticised as inadequate, particularly for secret cartels and

21 Source: OCCP PI request.

other complex infringements that are difficult to detect.[22] The 2014 amendment extended this period to five years, bringing Polish law closer to European standards.

The implementation of the ECN+ Directive further strengthened the OCCP's enforcement capacity by introducing mechanisms that suspend the running of limitation periods. Under the new rules, the limitation period is suspended as soon as at least one undertaking participating in the infringement is notified of investigative measures. The suspension continues until the explanatory proceedings are concluded in respect of all undertakings involved. In practice, this may substantially extend the authority's temporal jurisdiction, particularly given the OCCP's broad discretion in conducting explanatory proceedings.

While these changes undoubtedly enhance enforcement effectiveness, they also raise concerns about legal certainty. The combination of extended limitation periods and lengthy explanatory proceedings means that undertakings may remain exposed to potential liability for extended periods, even before formal proceedings have been initiated. This is particularly problematic given the lack of transparency and judicial oversight of explanatory proceedings.

Limitation periods apply only to the initiation of proceedings. Once proceedings are validly brought within the statutory period, the OCCP retains full competence to adjudicate the case, regardless of how long the proceedings ultimately take. Therefore, the limitation regime does little to constrain the overall duration of competition enforcement.

6 Party to the Proceedings

The definition and regulation of a party's legal status in antimonopoly proceedings have evolved significantly over time. The Competition Act adopts different concepts of party status depending on the type of proceedings atissue, reflecting the substantive and procedural diversity of competition enforcement.

Until 2007, it was legally possible to initiate antimonopoly proceedings on the motion of an undertaking that had suffered harm from a competition infringement. This mechanism was subsequently abolished, marking a decisive shift towards a fully ex officio enforcement model. Under the current

22 T. Skoczny, *Konsekwencje przyszłego systemu stosowania art. 81 i 82 TWE dla prawa i orzecznictwa w zakresie ochrony konkurencji w Polsce (part II)*, Prawo Unii Europejskiej 2001, no. 9–10, 4.

framework, Article 88 of the Competition Act provides that, in cases concerning anticompetitive practices, a party to the proceedings is any person against whom proceedings are brought relating to the application of provisions prohibiting restrictive practices.

Initially, party status was limited to undertakings alleged to be parties to an anticompetitive agreement or to have abused a dominant position. The scope of party status was later expanded in line with the progressive broadening of substantive liability under competition law. Following the 2014 amendment, managers who intentionally contributed to competition infringements committed by undertakings became parties to the proceedings. A further extension followed the implementation of the ECN+ Directive, which introduced liability – and, consequently, party status – for undertakings that exercise decisive influence over an infringing undertaking. As a result, the notion of a party has expanded alongside the development of attribution rules and personal liability mechanisms in Polish competition law.

Article 88 provides an autonomous, exhaustive regulation of party status in antitrust cases. Consequently, no other entities may acquire party status or challenge antitrust decisions. This restrictive approach is particularly significant in the context of vertical agreements, where the number of potentially infringing parties may be considerable. In such cases, the selection of undertakings against which proceedings are initiated is not left to the OCCP's unfettered discretion. Rather, the authority must determine, having regard to the circumstances of the case and the objectives of competition enforcement, the scope of the parties necessary to ensure the effective restoration of undistorted competition. The guiding principle should be to encompass the widest possible range of relevant participants, while maintaining procedural efficiency and proportionality.[23] However, in the other judgment, the Supreme Court acknowledged that conducting antimonopoly proceedings solely against the organiser of a vertical agreement does not constitute a defect in the decision that would justify its annulment.[24]

In merger control proceedings, party status is governed by Article 94 of the Competition Act. A party is any person required to notify the intended concentration. The Act provides an exhaustive list of such entities, including merging undertakings acting jointly, the undertaking acquiring control, undertakings jointly creating a joint venture, and undertakings acquiring part of another undertaking's assets. Thus, the concept of party status in merger pro-

23 PSC judgment of 4.10.2017, III SK 47/16.

24 PSC judgment of 15.02.2019, I NSK 11/18.

ceedings is narrower than the broader notion of 'participants' sometimes used in comparative merger control discourse.[25]

In contrast to the EUMR, Polish merger proceedings recognise only the notifying undertakings as parties.[26] Competitors, suppliers, customers, and consumers do not enjoy party status, nor are they entitled to access the case file or to challenge the authority's decision.[27] Their involvement is limited to submitting information in the course of market inquiries, without procedural guarantees comparable to those afforded to parties.

7 Public Interest Intervenients

Polish administrative law provides for the participation of certain entities acting in the public interest in administrative proceedings. These entities are granted the rights of a party, although their procedural position remains distinct from that of parties proper. This framework applies, with minor modifications, to antimonopoly proceedings. Three categories of public-interest interveners may be identified: the Public Prosecutor, the Ombudsman, and social organisations.

Under Article 182 of the APC, the Public Prosecutor may request the initiation of administrative proceedings where necessary to eliminate a situation contrary to binding law. This competence extends to antimonopoly proceedings. Although the prosecutor does not acquire party status, he or she is vested with procedural rights equivalent to those of a party. The Ombudsman occupies a similar position, whose intervention is limited to cases involving alleged infringements of civil rights or liberties.[28]

Both the Public Prosecutor and the Ombudsman act exclusively in the public interest and do not have an individual legal interest in the outcome of

25 Under the EUMR, there is no such distinction, but there is a uniform concept of 'undertakings concerned' – see Point C.II of the Commission Consolidated Jurisdictional Notice under Council Regulation (EC) No 139/2004 on the control of concentrations between undertakings, OJ UEC 95, 16.4.2008.

26 E. Modzelewska-Wąchal, *Ustawa o ochronie konkurencji i konsumentów. Komentarz*, Warsaw 2002, 309.

27 Antimonopoly Court order of 11.03.1991, XVII Amr 5/91.

28 Art. 14 of the Act of 15.07.1987 on the Commissioner of Civil Rights Protection, JoL 2001, no. 14, item 147.

proceedings.[29] Their rights are procedural and do not extend to acts such as entering into commitments or requesting a settlement decision.[30]

A third category of public interest participants is social organisations. Such an organisation may request the initiation of proceedings or admission to pending proceedings if this is justified by its statutory objectives and the social interest. However, this competence applies only to proceedings that may be initiated exclusively ex officio.[31] The admissibility of social organisations in antimonopoly proceedings is highly controversial, particularly given the enumerative definition of parties and the need to protect business secrets.[32] Allowing social organisations to participate as quasi-parties would undermine the objective of limiting the number of participants and of safeguarding confidential information.[33]

Social organisations may, however, participate in proceedings by submitting opinions on the case. This involvement does not confer the rights of a party and remains purely consultative, akin to the role of amicus curiae.

Public interest interventions in antimonopoly proceedings are exceedingly rare. Under the current Competition Act, no social organisation has ever been admitted as a participant with party rights. There has been only one recorded intervention by the Public Prosecutor, who challenged a decision in a case concerning an anticompetitive agreement.[34] The Ombudsman intervened in a single merger case; however, the OCCP denied most of the procedural rights normally guaranteed under the APC.[35] This practice sets a troubling precedent, undermining both the credibility and the legitimacy of competition enforcement in Poland.

8 Interim Decisions

The institution of interim decisions was introduced into Polish competition law by the 2000 Act, drawing on interim measures under Article 8 of Regula-

29 B. Adamiak, J. Borkowski, *Polskie postępowanie administracyjne i sądowoadministracyjne*, Warsaw 1997, 106.

30 W. Dawidowicz, *Zarys procesu administracyjnego*, Warsaw 1989, 34.

31 B. Adamiak, J. Borkowski, 108.

32 This tendency to limit the number of participants in the proceedings before the OCCP is criticized J. Olszewski, *Nowa ustawa o ochronie konkurencji i konsumentów*. Part I, MoP 2001, no. 14, 725.

33 HAC order of 7.12.1983, II SA 1605/83.

34 OCCP decision DOK-97/2007.

35 Refer to Section 4.3.

tion 1/2003. This mechanism has been retained in Article 89 of the 2007 Competition Act. Where, in the course of antimonopoly proceedings, it is established that the continued application of a contested practice may cause serious and irreparable harm to competition, the OCCP may, before the conclusion of the proceedings, issue an interim decision ordering the undertaking concerned to cease specific conduct. Importantly, the lodging of an appeal does not suspend the execution of such a decision.

According to the OCCP, the purpose of interim measures is to prevent irreversible damage to market structures during the pendency of proceedings and to preserve the effectiveness of subsequent enforcement. By temporarily restraining allegedly anticompetitive behaviour, the authority gains the time needed to conduct a full substantive assessment. The adoption of an interim decision thus presupposes a high probability of harm and the risk of irreversible effects, marking a significant departure from the traditional framework of administrative procedure.[36]

The first interim decisions issued by the OCCP concerned TP, the former incumbent telecommunications operator, and ordered it to refrain from implementing a drastic increase in charges for international voice calls routed through alternative operators. Without such intervention, alternative operators would likely have been forced out of the market, producing irreversible competitive harm.[37]

Despite the authority's initial emphasis on interim measures, their practical use has declined sharply. Between 2015 and 2025, no interim decisions were issued. This stands in stark contrast to the OCCP's earlier declarations regarding the importance of this instrument. Contrary to the official narrative, interim decisions have proven to be procedurally burdensome and resource-intensive. Their adoption requires an evidentiary and analytical effort comparable to that needed for a final decision and often generates extensive judicial disputes. These praxeological considerations appear to be the primary reason for the OCCP's de facto abandonment of interim measures in recent years.

36 M. Bychowska, M. Krasnodębska-Tomkiel, 27.

37 OCCP decisions DOK-127/05 and DOK-19/06.

9 Evidence Proceedings

9.1 General Characteristics and Applicable Law

The distinctiveness of antimonopoly proceedings is particularly evident in the regulation of evidence. Pursuant to Article 84 of the Competition Act, matters concerning evidence are governed by Articles 227–315 of the CPC, while investigative measures involving inspections and searches are, by analogy, additionally subject to provisions of the Code of Criminal Procedure. As a result, Polish antimonopoly proceedings are characterised by a highly formalised evidentiary model, reflecting the extensive investigatory powers vested in the OCCP, including quasi-police powers.

9.2 Means of Evidence

Antimonopoly proceedings typically rely on the following categories of evidence: documents, witness testimony, expert opinions (including those from scientific or research institutes), interrogations of the parties, and other evidence. The first three categories are partially regulated under the Competition Act, while the remaining categories are governed by the CPC.

The regulation of documentary evidence is particularly strict. As a rule, only original documents or certified copies may be used as evidence. Certification may be carried out by a public authority, a notary, an advocate, a legal adviser, or an authorised employee of the undertaking. This level of formality is increasingly difficult to reconcile with the realities of modern competition infringements, especially cartel cases, where agreements are rarely documented in formally executed instruments and evidence is predominantly digital or indirect.[38]

Witness testimony plays a secondary role and is used sparingly in antimonopoly proceedings. When relying on this evidence, the party must precisely identify the facts each witness must establish. Expert evidence, by contrast, should play a central role in competition cases, given their economic complexity. An expert provides not facts, but a specialist interpretation, and the subject of an expert opinion must be factual, not legal. Despite this, the OCCP makes limited use of expert opinions. No public data is available on this point. Upon request, the OCCP confirmed that no experts were appointed in any

---

38 R. Janusz, M. Sachajko, T. Skoczny, *Nowa ustawa o ochronie konkurencji i konsumentów*, KPP 2001, no. 3, 204.

proceedings concerning anti-competitive practices or merger control conducted in 2023 and 2024.

Because the catalogue of evidence is not exhaustive, the CPC allows the OCCP a broad margin of discretion to admit other forms of evidence, such as audio or video recordings, technical drawings, plans, billing data, or electronic records. Interrogation of the parties is auxiliary evidence and is used only when other evidence is unavailable or insufficient to clarify relevant factual circumstances. Where the party is a legal person, the interrogation concerns individuals authorised to represent it.

9.3 Collecting Evidence: Investigatory Instruments

Evidence in antimonopoly proceedings may be obtained by three principal methods: requests for information (RFI), inspections, and searches.

9.3.1 Request for Information (RFI)

The RFI is a fundamental investigative tool used by competition authorities, including the OCCP. Its regulatory framework has been significantly strengthened following the implementation of the ECN+ Directive. Under the previous legal regime, RFIs could also be addressed to natural persons on a voluntary basis. Since 2023, cooperation by natural persons has been mandatory, and refusal to cooperate may now result in sanctions.

The OCCP has indicated that this competence will be used, in particular, to approach natural persons who engaged in anticompetitive practices while conducting business activity (i.e., while having the status of an undertaking) and subsequently ceased such activity. In practice, it was not uncommon for entrepreneurs operating as natural persons, seeking to avoid liability before the OCCP, to temporarily suspend their business activities.[39] Natural persons have a specific right to refuse to provide information where an answer could lead to criminal liability for themselves or for their spouse, ascendants, descendants, siblings, relatives in the same line or degree, as well as persons in a relationship of adoption, guardianship or custody, or a person in a cohabiting relationship. However, liability under the Competition Act is not regarded as criminal in nature.

This limited right to refuse cooperation has been criticised as overly narrow, with some commentators arguing that it should encompass the full priv-

39 Narrative memorandum for the draft act amending the Act on Competition and Consumer Protection and certain other acts, Parliamentary Print No. 2990, 25.

ilege against self-incrimination as recognised in criminal proceedings.[40] Such far-reaching conclusions are difficult to accept, as they disregard both the Competition Act's legal character and the nature of the obligations it imposes. Accordingly, in antimonopoly proceedings, the right to remain silent is reduced to the principle that an undertaking or a natural person cannot be compelled by the authority – through an RFI under threat of sanctions – to admit to a competition law infringement. It is therefore impermissible for the OCCP to direct questions to undertakings against whom proceedings are pending that suggest an answer, concern manifestly unlawful conduct, or require opinions, assessments, or legal qualifications of specific events from the perspective of competition law. This principle, however, does not restrict the NCA's powers to request information about facts or existing documents.[41]

Pursuant to Article 50(1) of the Competition Act, any undertaking or natural person must cooperate when approached by the Polish NCA with an RFI. The RFI must specify: (1) the scope of the requested information; (2) the purpose of the request; (3) the time limit for submitting a response; and (4) the penalties for failing to provide the information or for providing false or misleading information. Non-cooperation may result in a financial fine of up to 3% of the turnover achieved in the financial year preceding the year in which the fine is imposed.

The primary addressees of RFIs are undertakings, irrespective of their procedural status. The obligation to respond applies not only to undertakings that are parties to antimonopoly proceedings, but also to any entity that is an undertaking (or an association thereof) capable of providing the requested information.[42] In merger control proceedings, RFIs are frequently directed to competitors or contractual partners of the notifying parties.

Article 50(1) does not delineate the scope of the OCCP's powers by enumerating specific circumstances in which they may be exercised.[43] Consequently, the RFI is a universal instrument that may be used in both explanatory and antitrust or merger proceedings. The formal requirements applicable to RFIs under Polish law broadly correspond to those set out in Article 11(1) and (2) of the EUMR. However, a significant difference remains: RFIs issued by the Polish NCA are binding administrative decisions, whereas under the EUMR, the European Commission may choose between issuing a simple request and

40 P. Korycińska-Rządca, *Uprawnienia dochodzeniowe Prezesa Urzędu Ochrony Konkurencji i Konsumentów a Dyrektywa Parlamentu Europejskiego i Rady (UE) 2019/1 – wybrane zagadnienia*, Białostockie Studia Prawnicze 2023, no. 4, 189.

41 CCCP judgment of 21.06.2023, XVII AmA 82/21.

42 CA judgment of 17.05.2016, VI ACa 630/15.

43 CA judgment of 1.03.2012, VI ACa 1033/11.

adopting a formal decision. This divergence arguably reflects a structural characteristic of Polish competition law practice, shaped by a historically low level of voluntary cooperation by undertakings with the national authority.

Disputes concerning the scope of the requested information cannot be effectively resolved during the pendency of antimonopoly proceedings in Poland. Only after an undertaking or a natural person has been fined for failing to provide the requested information may the grounds and scope of the RFI be judicially reviewed.[44] The provisions of the Competition Act grant the OCCP wide discretion in assessing the relevance of the requested information to the case. Notably, Polish courts have not adopted heightened standards of specificity and justification for RFIs comparable to those developed under EU law.[45]

Undertakings are obliged to provide information not only concerning their own activities but also regarding their entire capital group, where so requested by the OCCP.[46] This obligation extends to documents held by other entities within the same group, regardless of their place of incorporation or establishment. As a result, RFIs may have extraterritorial effects. Extensive RFIs may pose particular challenges for multinational enterprises, especially in foreign-to-foreign transactions reviewed by the Polish NCA, where the relevance of the requested documentation to the national jurisdiction may be tenuous.[47]

9.3.2 Inspection and Search

A distinct method of evidence gathering involves inspections and searches at an undertaking's premises. The essence of an inspection lies in conducting specific evidentiary activities with the consent and cooperation of the undertaking concerned. During an inspection, the inspector may request that specific documents or data carriers be made available or handed over, but the scope of the inspector's powers does not extend to unilateral access to such materials without the undertaking's cooperation. By contrast, a search may be conducted without the undertaking's consent, and even in its absence, provided that prior authorisation is obtained from the CCCP. In this respect, a search closely resembles a search conducted by law enforcement authorities

---

44 M. Błachucki, *System,* 235.

45 CCCP judgment of 28.06.2024, XVII AmA 80/20.

46 Z. Sengören Özcan, A. Ak, *On Whose Door to Knock? Information Requests of the Turkish Competition Authority Extending to Foreign Parent Companies,* JECLP 2024, no. 1, 41–47.

47 M. Blachucki, *Requests for information and access to files in Polish merger procedure in light of recent Nord stream 2 developments* [*Poland*], JECLP 2025, no. 5, 304.

in criminal proceedings.[48] In antitrust cases, such measures are of fundamental importance and are frequently employed. By contrast, in merger control proceedings, they have historically played a marginal role. This is because, in merger cases, undertakings are generally interested in securing a swift resolution and therefore tend to provide the requested information promptly. Moreover, unlike cartel arrangements, mergers constitute lawful transactions, and there is typically no need to resort to coercive investigative measures to prevent the destruction or concealment of evidence.

Characteristic features of these investigatory powers include the absence of an obligation to notify the undertaking in advance of a planned inspection, the possibility of conducting a search in the absence of the undertaking or its authorised representative, the lack of statutory time limits for inspections, and the possibility of conducting an inspection concurrently with an inspection by another authority, which is generally prohibited.

During antimonopoly proceedings, an inspection may be conducted by an authorised employee of the OCCP or the Trade Inspection Authority at any undertaking, within the scope of the proceedings. Inspectors are entitled, in particular, to:

i. enter land and buildings, premises or other rooms, as well as means of transport, belonging to the inspected entity;
ii. request access to files, books, all types of documents and information carriers related to the subject matter of the inspection, including copies and extracts thereof, and to take notes from such materials;
iii. take notes from correspondence and other materials;
iv. require the inspected party to prepare copies or printouts of materials, correspondence, and information stored on data carriers, devices or IT systems;
v. request oral explanations relating to the subject matter of the inspection; and
vi. seal premises, rooms, or objects to the extent necessary to conduct the inspection (competence introduced by the 2023 amendment).

An inspection may be conducted in the presence of officials of other EU national competition authorities, experts, or police officers. This reflects the increasing importance of cross-border cooperation within the ECN, particularly in complex cartel investigations with a transnational dimension.[49]

---

48 A. Jabłonowska, *Zmiany w przepisach dotyczących kontroli oraz przeszukania w toku postępowania przed Prezesem Urzędu Ochrony Konkurencji i Konsumentów*, PUG 2015, no. 3, 2.

49 OCCP may assist the European Commission under the FSR regime. In fact, the first search in such a case took place in Poland and led to the first judicial review –

The undertaking subject to inspection is obliged to cooperate fully. In particular, it must:

i. provide the requested information;
ii. allow access to land, buildings, premises, rooms, and means of transport;
iii. make available and hand over materials or other items that may constitute evidence in the case; and
iv. allow access to IT data carriers, devices, or systems, including correspondence sent by electronic means.

Inspectors may use recording devices to capture images or sound during the inspection or any individual activities conducted during it, provided that the inspected party is informed in advance. The inspected party is likewise entitled to record the course of the inspection. These recordings may later serve as evidence in proceedings concerning the legality of the inspection or the inspectors' conduct.[50]

During inspections, issues concerning legal professional privilege frequently arise. If the inspected party declares that certain documents or correspondence disclosed during the inspection – including those stored on IT data carriers or systems – constitute written communications between the undertaking and an independent advocate, legal adviser, or EU lawyer, produced for the purpose of exercising the undertaking's right to defence in connection with the proceedings conducted by the OCCP, the inspector is obliged to leave such documents at the place of inspection. The same applies to documents prepared solely to obtain legal advice from such legal professionals. The burden of proving that the documents meet the conditions for legal privilege rests with the inspected party. Following their submission, the CCCP must, within one month, issue a decision to either return the documents to the undertaking or release them, in whole or in part, to the OCCP for the proceedings.

There is an interesting recent development. The regulation of legal professional privilege (LPP) introduced into the Competition Act was framed in reference to EU law. The established position under EU law is that LPP applies exclusively to communications with external, independent lawyers. The European Commission has explicitly stated that 'in 2023, Poland introduced legislation that specifically precludes the recognition of in-house LPP in competi-

---

P.D. Camesasca, K.E. Sideri, *European Commission's inspection powers under the EU FSR outside the European Union: Case T-284/24 R Nuctech*, JECLP 2025, no. 1.

50 CCCP judgment of 22.11.2022, XVII Amz 92/22.

tion law investigations. According to national competition authorities, the practice in several Member States is based on the Akzo caselaw.'[51]

Nevertheless, in 2025, Polish courts delivered a series of judgments extending LPP protection to Polish in-house lawyers, provided they are members of the professional corporation of legal advisers.[52] The position adopted by the Polish courts is surprising and difficult to regard as anything other than judicial voluntarism aimed at correcting the statutory provisions.

In merger control proceedings, the OCCP is limited to conducting inspections. Before 2015, the authority was also authorised to conduct searches in merger cases; however, this competence was abandoned during the legislative amendment process without explicit justification. The European Commission retains the power to conduct searches in merger proceedings (Art. 13 EUMR), and when such dawn raids are carried out in Poland, the Commission is assisted by the OCCP.[53] Inspections in merger cases remain exceptionally rare, having been conducted only twice in the OCCP's history.

In other categories of cases, the OCCP may conduct searches. These may be carried out in matters concerning:

i. practices that restrict competition in the course of explanatory proceedings and antimonopoly proceedings and
ii. the preliminary determination of potential infringements of Articles 5–7 of the Digital Markets Act during explanatory proceedings.

Searches are conducted to locate and secure information from files, books, correspondence, documents, IT data carriers, devices, systems, and other items that may constitute evidence. A search may be carried out only where there are reasonable grounds to believe that such information or items are located at the premises or among the belongings of the undertaking concerned. The OCCP may rely on information obtained from complaints submitted by other undertakings or from leniency applications to justify such measures.

A search requires prior authorisation by the CCCP, granted upon application by the OCCP. The court must issue its decision within 72 hours of receipt of the application. The undertaking subject to the search may lodge an appeal against the decision authorising the search within seven days of its delivery. The appeal is lodged with the court of the second instance through the CCCP

---

51 *Legal professional privilege in competition law investigations: has the status of in-house lawyers changed?*, Competition Policy Brief No 1/2025, 2.

52 For example, CCCP order of 28.04.2025, XVII Amz 14/25, which was upheld, in the part concerning the justification of legal professional privilege, by the order of the Court of Appeal of 2.09.2025, VII AGz 473/25.

53 One key restriction is that the EUMR does not cover searches at private premises.

and does not suspend the execution of the search. The introduction of this appellate remedy constitutes a significant procedural safeguard and follows the Constitutional Tribunal's 2019 judgment,[54] which held that the exclusion of judicial review of search authorisations was unconstitutional. Nevertheless, as indicated in Chapter 7, the CCCP authorises a dozen or more searches per year, which may be regarded as a very lenient form of judicial oversight.[55]

Search activities may be extensive. Inspectors may examine all rooms at the search location to verify whether evidence of a potential infringement is present. For electronic data, inspectors prepare forensic copies on available IT media. Initially, following the judgment of 7 March 2017, the selection of seized electronic documents was conducted on-site at the premises under inspection.[56] Following the implementation of the ECN+ Directive, the selection of relevant documents is now carried out at the OCCP headquarters. As a result, the OCCP may sift through the data on site or at the OCCP's premises, but may retain only data relevant to the proceedings (within the temporal and material scope of the search, without LPP).

9.4 Burden and Quality of Proof

The Competition Act does not comprehensively regulate the allocation and standard of the burden of proof in antimonopoly proceedings. Although the Act introduces certain legal presumptions – most notably the presumption of a dominant position where an undertaking's market share equals or exceeds 40% – it lacks general provisions governing evidentiary burdens. The CCCP's jurisprudence consistently holds that, before imposing an antimonopoly fine, the OCCP must establish that the undertaking has infringed the Competition Act. The undertaking is not required to demonstrate the absence of an infringement and may remain silent throughout the entirety of the proceedings.[57]

According to the CCCP, the burden of proof rests entirely with the authority initiating the antimonopoly proceedings, namely the OCCP. Consequently, the OCCP may not shift the burden of proof to the party under investigation or require it to produce exculpatory evidence.[58] This principle reflects the

54 Constitutional Tribunal judgment of 16.01.2019, P 19/17.
55 Refer to Section 7.8.1.
56 CCCP judgment of 7.03.2017, XVII Amz 15/17.
57 CCCP judgment of 21.12.1994, XVII Amr 47/94.
58 CCCP judgment of 10.09.1992, XVII Amr 15/92.

inquisitorial nature of administrative antimonopoly proceedings and aligns with the presumption of legality of economic conduct.

Nevertheless, although undertakings are not obliged to actively participate in antimonopoly proceedings, passivity is rarely advantageous. Parties are entitled to submit evidence and to request that the authority take specific evidentiary measures. A lack of cooperation exposes the undertaking to the risk that the authority will base its decision exclusively on selected incriminating evidence.[59] Administrative courts have emphasised that the authority conducting administrative proceedings is not obliged to seek exculpatory evidence on behalf of a passive party, particularly where that party deliberately refrains from cooperating.[60]

A distinguishing feature of antitrust cases is that the OCCP often lacks direct evidence of anticompetitive conduct, particularly in cartel cases. It is undisputed that, in the absence of direct evidence, the existence of an anticompetitive agreement may be established through indirect evidence, including economic analysis and factual presumptions.[61] When relying on such presumptions, the antimonopoly authority must not only demonstrate parallel conduct among the alleged participants but also convincingly exclude alternative, rational economic explanations for such behaviour.[62] This requires a comprehensive analysis of all relevant market conditions to assess whether the conduct in question was economically rational or the result of prior unlawful conduct coordination.[63]

9.5 Forms of Evidence Proceedings

A fundamental distinction between administrative and civil proceedings concerns how evidentiary activities are conducted. In civil proceedings, the general rule is to hold evidentiary hearings, whereas in administrative proceedings – including antimonopoly proceedings – evidentiary activities are predominantly conducted in camera. In practice, virtually all evidentiary measures in antitrust cases are carried out as part of office (cabinet) proceedings.

In camera proceedings constitute the basic form of evidentiary proceedings in administrative adjudication. Unlike hearings, such proceedings are entirely document-based. Nevertheless, the OCCP may conduct all evidentiary activ-

59 HAC judgment of 20.05.1998, I SA/Ka 1605/96.
60 HAC judgment of 10.07.1996, SA/Ka 1171/95.
61 CCCP judgment of 11.121996, XVII Ama 62/96.
62 CCCP judgment of 1.03.1993, XVII Amr 37/93.
63 PSC judgment of 6.03.1997, I CKN 44/97.

ities within this framework, including the examination of witnesses and experts. The procedural course of cabinet proceedings is not comprehensively regulated by procedural law. While certain provisions govern specific procedural acts, the overall conduct of the proceedings remains largely at the discretion of the authority.

Despite their informal character, all fundamental principles of evidentiary proceedings apply. In particular, the party must actively participate in the evidentiary process and be summoned to appear for evidentiary acts, such as taking witness testimony or expert opinions. The non-public nature of in camera proceedings does not affect either the rules governing the assessment of evidence or the application of the principle of objective truth.

In addition to in-camera proceedings, the OCCP may hold a hearing. Unlike in general administrative proceedings, the obligation to hold a hearing in antitrust proceedings – particularly in merger control – is discretionary, and the mandatory hearing provisions of the APC do not apply. Article 60(3) of the Competition Act provides that the OCCP may summon parties and witnesses to a hearing and consult experts; however, the wording of this provision makes clear that a hearing is optional. Hearings are public unless they involve information constituting business secrets or other legally protected secrets. Hearings are held only sporadically in antitrust cases and have been virtually absent in merger proceedings.

A proposal was put forward to introduce mandatory hearings in merger cases.[64] Such proposals overlook the considerable administrative burden of organising hearings and the strict statutory time limits applicable to merger control proceedings. Mandatory hearings would likely generate additional procedural complications without offering a meaningful solution. Organising meetings with the parties is procedurally straightforward and does not entail significant formal constraints. The difficulty, however, lies in the absence of clear, consistent rules governing the OCCP's organisation of such status meetings. Given the prevailing Caesarist model of competition enforcement, it appears unlikely that the current OCCP would be willing to meaningfully limit its discretion in this regard.

64 D. Aziewicz, *Czy warto rozprawiać o koncentracjach? Rozważania o możliwości i zasadności oraz sposobie wprowadzenia rozprawy do postępowania antymonopolowego w sprawach koncentracji jako elementu obligatoryjnego*, iKAR 2020, no. 4, 16.

10 Access to Files

The right of access to the case file is a fundamental procedural right in antimonopoly proceedings. Given the inquisitorial nature of these proceedings and the rarity of public hearings, access to the files is indispensable for the effective exercise of the rights of defence. A failure to ensure such access constitutes a serious procedural violation and may result in the annulment of the proceedings.[65]

Polish law does not provide a statutory definition of case files. They are understood to include all materials documenting the course of the antimonopoly proceedings.[66] This includes all evidence produced and any other materials collected by the authority during the proceedings. Case files constitute the factual basis for establishing the relevant circumstances of the case.

Traditionally, case files have been maintained in paper form, under internal archiving regulations. However, as of 1 January 2026, electronic communication will become mandatory, meaning correspondence will be conducted almost exclusively electronically. This development will necessitate significant organisational adjustments within the OCCP, with the practical implications yet to be assessed.

The right of access to files is regulated in Articles 72 and 73 of the APC and encompasses:

i. the right to examine the files, exercised at the authority's premises in the presence of the case handler;[67]
ii. the right to make notes and copies, interpreted broadly to include reproduction by any available technical means, provided that it does not affect the physical integrity of the documents; and
iii. the right to obtain certified copies confirming the conformity of the copy with the original contained in the files.

This right applies fully to parties and public-interest interveners, although, in practice, it is exercised predominantly by parties to the proceedings. Experts may also be granted access to files as necessary to prepare expert opinions. The list of persons entitled to access files is exhaustive. However, certain infor-

65 G. Rząsa, *Nieważność postępowania sądowoadministracyjnego jako podstawa skargi kasacyjnej*, Warsaw 2011, 310.

66 M. Błachucki, *Dostęp do akt sprawy administracyjnej na podstawie Kodeksu postępowania administracyjnego a dostęp do informacji publicznej znajdującej się w aktach sprawy administracyjnej*, [in:] E. Pierzchała, M. Woźniak (eds.), *Dostęp do informacji publicznej w Polsce i w Europie – wybrane zagadnienia prawne*, Opole 2010, 139.

67 Z. Janowicz, *Kodeks postępowania administracyjnego. Komentarz*, Warsaw 1995, 185.

mation in case files may be accessed under the Public Information Act. It should be stressed that the Act does not provide access to all files but only to those materials that contain public information.[68]

The party may access the files at any time during the antimonopoly proceedings or after they conclude. The only condition is prior consultation with the case handler regarding the technical requirements for presenting the files to the party. The OCCP prepared detailed technical rules governing the exercise of the right of access to files.[69] If the files are transferred to the court, the court must provide the party with access to them.

Special rules apply to documents submitted by leniency applicants. These documents are not accessible until the conclusion of the evidentiary proceedings. Even thereafter, access may be restricted to protect business secrets. Amendments introduced in 2023 further strengthened the protection of leniency materials, reflecting developments in EU case law, including the *Pfleiderer* judgment (C-360/09).[70]

11 Transparency of Antimonopoly Proceedings

Access to case files is a key, though not the only, mechanism for ensuring the transparency of antimonopoly proceedings. Equally important are the rules governing the flow of information between the antimonopoly authority and the party to the proceedings. Transparency in this respect is particularly relevant in two situations. First, when the authority informs the undertaking of which specific conduct has led to the initiation of antimonopoly proceedings. Second, when the authority communicates the competition concerns identified during merger control proceedings. In both instances, accurate and sufficiently detailed information is indispensable to enable the undertaking to understand the scope of the allegations, present its position effectively, and submit relevant evidence. Notably, in this respect, the Polish Competition Act differs significantly from EU competition law.

First, Polish law does not provide for the OCCP to issue a formal Statement of Objections (SO) at the stage of initiating proceedings. This procedural instrument, which plays a central role in EU antitrust enforcement, has no direct equivalent under Polish law. Nevertheless, this does not leave the undertaking uninformed about the conduct that triggered the initiation of pro-

68 M. Błachucki, *Dostęp do akt sprawy*, 135.
69 *Udostępnienie akt sprawy*, https://uokik.gov.pl/bip/udostepnienie-akt-sprawy.
70 ECLI:EU:C:2011:389.

ceedings. The order initiating antimonopoly proceedings performs a function broadly analogous to that of the SO. It sets out the legal basis for the proceedings and describes the alleged anticompetitive conduct at the centre of the investigation.

Compared with an SO, the order initiating proceedings is typically more concise and synthetic. However, it fulfils the same essential function of delimiting the scope of the proceedings. The order must clearly indicate to the undertaking which specific conduct the OCCP is challenging and is binding on the authority at subsequent stages of the proceedings. The description of the conduct determines the essential subject matter of the case, while the legal basis invoked by the authority constitutes the allegation of an infringement of the legal order. Any subsequent modification to the factual or legal basis of the allegations would require initiating new proceedings.[71]

A paradoxical effect of implementing the ECN+ Directive is evident in procedural transparency. Article 74 of the Competition Act provides that, when issuing a decision concluding the proceedings, the OCCP may take into account only those allegations in respect of which the parties have had an opportunity to express their views. This provision reflects the general principle of active party participation in administrative proceedings. Prior to the 2023 amendment, the OCCP relied on Article 74 as the basis for developing a practice of providing parties with a detailed and updated justification of allegations at later stages of the proceedings.

Following the 2023 amendment, the obligation to justify allegations has been formalised and incorporated into Articles 49(3) and 49(4) of the Competition Act. Under the current legal framework, the OCCP must present such justification at the outset of the proceedings. On the one hand, this development should be assessed positively, as it strengthens legal certainty and formalises the party's right to be informed of the allegations. However, this approach may reduce transparency at later stages of the proceedings. Because the justification is provided at an early stage and is necessarily based on evidence collected to that point, the OCCP is no longer under a clear obligation to communicate subsequently obtained evidence or new facts to the party. As a result, the undertaking may not be fully informed of the evidentiary basis on which the final decision will be adopted.

The situation differs in merger control proceedings, where transparency has evolved more significantly. Before the 2015 amendment, notifying parties frequently complained that they were either not informed at all about the competition concerns identified by the OCCP or were informed only at a

71 PSC judgment of 6.02.2018, III SK 8/17.

very late stage of the proceedings, leaving no realistic opportunity to submit additional evidence or propose remedies. Under the amended legal framework, when the OCCP identifies competition concerns arising from a concentration, it is obliged to provide the undertaking with a written communication explaining the nature of those concerns.

The undertaking is given two weeks to respond to this communication. Only after the authority has examined the response may discussions about potential remedies begin.[72] As explained in the explanatory memorandum accompanying the amendment, the communication of competition concerns is intended to precede any discussion of remedies. Although both the OCCP and the undertaking are formally entitled to propose remedies under Polish law, in practice, the OCCP typically initiates such proposals. The introduction of the obligation to communicate competition concerns at an earlier stage is therefore expected to enhance the undertaking's role in shaping remedial outcomes. The presentation of the concerns does not predetermine the OCCP's decision, and the negotiations have a genuine substantive dimension. Although reservations were not used frequently, they either led to a reconciliation of positions and an agreement or persuaded the undertaking that the planned concentration would significantly restrict competition on the market, resulting in the withdrawal of the application for authorisation of the concentration.[73]

In addition to formal communications, the OCCP may organise informal meetings with the parties to discuss the status of the case. The parties may also request such meetings. Although informal, these exchanges may help clarify the authority's concerns, address factual or legal issues, and expedite proceedings. Informal meetings are typically held where complex issues arise that require clarification beyond written submissions.

Finally, transparency is supported by the party being informed of the case handler's identity and being able to contact them at any time. However, such contacts may take place only informally, for example, by telephone or email. All formal communications between the OCCP and the party must be in writing and form part of the case file. To regulate contacts between undertakings and OCCP case handlers and to enhance the transparency of antimonopoly proceedings, the authority issued guidelines.[74] However, these guidelines are

72 J. Łukawski, *Decyzje*, 30.

73 A. Sadkowska, *Znaczenie zastrzeżeń wobec zgłoszonej koncentracji w postępowaniach przed Prezesem UOKiK i ich podobieństwo do Statement of Objection*, iKAR 2019, no. 2, 29.

74 Wyjaśnienia w sprawie reguł kontaktów z przedsiębiorcami w związku z kompetencjami orzeczniczymi Prezesa UOKiK (2015).

dialectical: while declaring the objective of transparency, they in fact lead to a high degree of formalisation in contacts and may even hinder them. As a result, their practical significance is doubtful.

12 Protection of Business Secrets

In antimonopoly proceedings, business secrets are frequently processed and therefore require adequate protection. The Competition Act refers to the definition of a 'business secret' set out in Article 11(4) of the Act on Combating Unfair Competition. Under this definition, a business secret comprises technical, technological, organisational, or other information of economic value that is not publicly available and in respect of which the undertaking has taken the necessary steps to preserve its confidentiality. The definition refers to acting with 'due diligence' but does not specify the measures required to protect trade secrets. While the Directive speaks of 'reasonable measures in the circumstances', the Polish legislator adopted the concept of due diligence, to be interpreted in accordance with Article 355 §§ 1 and 2 of the Civil Code. This concept applies not only to undertakings but also to other persons, such as information managers. An 'authorised person' includes both the undertaking owning the information and other persons entitled to use or dispose of it, for example, a licensee.[75]

In the OCCP practice, information typically regarded as constituting business secrets includes, inter alia, data on market shares, production and sales volumes, sources of supply and distribution, tax declarations, financial statements, discount policies, and pricing formulas. Restrictions on access to such information may apply not only to third parties but also to parties to the same proceedings, and, in certain circumstances, even to a party and its parent company.[76]

The determination of whether specific information constitutes a business secret is based on cooperation between the undertaking and the antimonopoly authority. Access to business secrets may be restricted either upon a reasoned request by the undertaking or *ex officio* by the OCCP. Any restriction of access is effected by an order that may be appealed. Undertakings are

---

75 M. Sieradzka, *Ochrona tajemnicy przedsiębiorstwa w postępowaniu przed Prezesem UOKiK – zagadnienia wybrane*, PPP 2019, no. 7–8, 20.

76 G. Materna, *Ograniczenie prawa*, 31.

expected to indicate explicitly whether the information they submit contains business secrets.[77]

A request to restrict access to business secrets must be substantiated and accompanied by a non-confidential version of the document concerned. The OCCP assesses such requests when the material is incorporated into the case file.[78] The authority has issued guidelines governing the procedure for submitting and assessing requests for confidentiality.[79]

The OCCP may also restrict access ex officio where the undertaking has failed to submit a request, but the authority determines that the information is confidential. Moreover, employees of the OCCP are subject to a statutory obligation to protect business secrets and other legally protected information acquired in the course of proceedings.

Judicial practice has clarified that restrictions on access to files do not automatically infringe the rights of defence or undermine the effectiveness of judicial review. A violation arises only where the restricted information was relied upon by the authority in its decision and was relevant to its merits. Where unjustified restrictions are shown to have affected the decision-making process, they may constitute grounds for annulment on procedural grounds. The court emphasised that merely being denied access to certain documents in the case file does not automatically constitute a violation of the right to a defence. Instead, the crucial factors are the scope, character, and impact of the restricted information on the decision-making process.[80] Unjustified restrictions on access to the case file may provide grounds for challenging a decision. If a party can demonstrate the significance of the restricted information to the decision-making process, it may effectively challenge the decision on procedural grounds.[81]

13 Exchange of Information and Evidence

When conducting antimonopoly proceedings, the OCCP may encounter difficulties in obtaining or sharing information and evidence with other national authorities and foreign competition authorities. This raises two interrelated issues: first, whether such exchange of information and evidence is permis-

77 P. Korycińska-Rządca, *Ochrona*, 150.

78 PSC resolution of 8.04.2010, III SZP 1/10.

79 Informacja o sposobie składania wniosku o ograniczenie prawa wglądu (2017).

80 Orders of CCCP of 4.11.2022, XVII Amz 341/21, 342/21, 342/21, 343/21, 344/21.

81 M. Blachucki, *Requests*, 308.

sible and, if so, to what extent; and secondly, whether undertakings may authorise the OCCP to disclose confidential information to foreign NCAs, and whether the OCCP is legally empowered to do so.

The Competition Act significantly restricts the use of information obtained during antimonopoly proceedings. As a general rule, such information may not be used in proceedings under separate legal provisions, except in limited cases. These include criminal proceedings; other proceedings conducted by the OCCP; cooperation with the European Commission and EU NCAs under Regulation 1/2003, the DMA, and the FSR; cooperation with sectoral regulators; and private enforcement proceedings, to the extent permitted by law.

Regarding cooperation with the European Commission, the exchange of information is, in principle, not subject to significant restrictions. Although the EUMR is not explicitly referenced, the Commission may require the OCCP to transfer evidence relevant to merger proceedings. Cooperation with EU NCAs is limited to the framework of Regulation 1/2003 and the DMA. A comparison of the regulation of information exchanges in antitrust and merger cases shows that antitrust provisions are fairly well developed, providing a basis for day-to-day administrative cooperation, whereas the merger provisions are still in their infancy period.[82]

Under the current legal framework, the OCCP may disclose only publicly available information in merger control cooperation with foreign NCAs. There is no explicit legal basis for transferring confidential information from case files, even with the undertaking's consent.

As a result, the only legally secure method for transferring confidential information in merger cases is for the undertaking itself to submit the relevant information directly to the foreign authority. *De lege ferenda,* it would be advisable to amend the Competition Act to establish a clear and transparent legal basis for the OCCP's transfer of confidential information to other competition authorities. Such a framework should be based on the explicit and voluntary consent of the undertaking, exclude any implied consent, and limit the scope of the transferred information strictly to what is necessary for the proceedings.

82 M. Błachucki, S. Jóźwiak, *Exchange of Information and Evidence between Competition Authorities and Entrepreneurs' Rights*, YARS 2012, no. 5(6), 165.

14 Suspension of Antimonopoly Proceedings

Antimonopoly proceedings should, as a rule, be conducted smoothly and continuously to ensure their timely and effective conclusion. However, obstacles may arise during the proceedings. Where such obstacles are temporary and removable, the appropriate procedural response is to suspend the proceedings.

The legal basis for suspending antimonopoly proceedings is found in both the APC and the Competition Act. The APC sets out the grounds for mandatory suspension (Article 97 § 1) and optional suspension (Article 99 § 1). Suspension is a procedural decision subject to appeal. The legal effect of suspension is to interrupt procedural time limits under the APC.

The Competition Act introduces an additional, autonomous ground for suspension in Article 87(3). Under this provision, if another EU NCA is conducting proceedings in the same case under Articles 101 or 102 TFEU and the OCCP has initiated antimonopoly proceedings in that case, the OCCP may, by decision, suspend its proceedings until the competent EU NCA has adopted a decision. This provision reflects the decentralised enforcement system for EU competition law and helps prevent duplication of proceedings concerning the same factual and legal circumstances. The decision to suspend proceedings in this situation is discretionary and lies entirely with the OCCP.

The most controversial issue regarding suspension concerns the OCCP's practice of allowing the suspension of proceedings in merger control cases.[83] An analysis of the nature of concentration proceedings raises serious doubts about the admissibility of this practice. A distinctive feature of merger control is the existence of strict statutory deadlines for concluding proceedings, which are substantive rather than procedural. Article 103 of the APC provides for the suspension of procedural deadlines upon the suspension of proceedings; however, this provision does not apply to substantive deadlines and is limited to selected time limits specified in the APC itself.

As a consequence, when proceedings governed by substantive-law deadlines are suspended, those deadlines continue to run. If such a deadline falls during the suspension, the OCCP loses its competence to decide the case, rendering the proceedings legally ineffective. In merger control cases, this may have particularly serious consequences for the public interest, including the tacit authorisation of potentially anticompetitive concentrations. In this context, the negative condition for suspending proceedings at a party's request – namely, the threat to the public interest – assumes decisive import-

---

83 OCCP orders in cases DKK1-422/22/15, DKK1-421/43/15 or DKK-2.421.60.2018.

ance. Accordingly, the suspension of merger control proceedings must be regarded as legally inadmissible.[84]

Proceedings may be suspended either ex officio (mandatory suspension) or at a party's request (optional suspension). Decisions refusing to suspend proceedings, as well as decisions resuming suspended proceedings, are not subject to judicial review.[85] Decisions suspending proceedings or refusing to resume suspended proceedings may be appealed to the CCCP.[86]

15 Discontinuation of Antimonopoly Proceedings

Antimonopoly proceedings are, in principle, intended to culminate in a substantive decision that definitively determines the legal position of the party concerned. The discontinuation of proceedings, therefore, constitutes an exception to the normal course of proceedings and results in a non-substantive termination of the case.[87]

The institution of discontinuation is primarily regulated in Article 105 of the APC, which requires the authority to discontinue proceedings that have become irrelevant for any reason. Discontinuation is justified by the existence of permanent and insurmountable obstacles to the continuation of the proceedings.[88] Its legal effect is the termination of the proceedings, the annulment of procedural actions taken therein, and a determination that the proceedings will not be continued.[89]

The Competition Act introduces a specific and autonomous regime governing the discontinuation of antimonopoly proceedings. This regime is characterised by two distinctive features. First, it sets out circumstances in which the OCCP is obliged to discontinue proceedings. Second, it provides that discontinuation takes the form of a ruling, which, as a rule, is not subject to appeal.

The Act distinguishes between mandatory and optional discontinuation. Pursuant to Article 75(1), the OCCP is obliged to discontinue proceedings in the following situations: (1) withdrawal of a merger notification; (2) a decision

84 M. Błachucki, *Zawieszenie postępowania antymonopolowego i kontrola sądowa czynności Prezesa UOKiK w tym zakresie*, AUWrP 2022, no 334, 768.

85 OCCP orders in cases DKK1-421/43/15 or DOK3-421-11/06.

86 OCCP orders in cases DKK1-421-18/07 or DKK-2.421.60.2018.

87 G. Łaszczyca, A. Matan, *Umorzenie ogólnego postępowania administracyjnego*, Kraków 2002, 15.

88 Judgment of the HAC of 10.03.2000, III SA 474/99.

89 W. Chróścielewski, *Glosa do wyroku NSA z dnia 20 września 1999 r., II SAB/Ka 13/99*, OSP 2000, no. 7–8.

not to impose a fine in infringement proceedings; and (3) the assumption of the case by the European Commission. Optional discontinuation may occur where a competent EU NCA has adopted a decision in the same case.

The OCCP most frequently discontinues proceedings on the grounds of irrelevance pursuant to Article 105 of the APC. The most questionable aspect of this practice is the discontinuation of proceedings when the OCCP concludes that the undertakings' conduct complies with competition law. In such circumstances, the OCCP incorrectly assumes the proceedings are irrelevant.[90] Where all constitutive elements of an administrative case are present, the authority should issue a substantive decision confirming the legality of the conduct in question. Discontinuing such cases amounts to avoiding adjudication and undermines legal certainty. A change in this administrative practice is therefore fully justified from a dogmatic perspective and would contribute positively to the stability and predictability of economic relations.[91]

Antimonopoly proceedings may conclude in two distinct legal forms. Discontinuation under Article 75 of the Competition Act takes the form of a ruling, whereas discontinuation under Article 105 of the APC takes the form of a decision. There is no convincing substantive or formal justification for this dualism. Moreover, it gives rise to a corresponding dualism in judicial jurisdiction. Discontinuation decisions adopted under Article 75 of the Competition Act are subject to review by administrative courts, whereas appeals against discontinuation decisions adopted under Article 105(1) of the APC fall within the jurisdiction of the CCCP.[92]

16 Costs of Antimonopoly Proceedings

The costs of antimonopoly proceedings include expenses incurred by the OCCP and other participants. The general principle governing the allocation of costs is that liability depends on the outcome of the case. An undertaking found to have infringed competition law is obliged to bear the costs of the proceedings.

This principle is subject to certain exceptions. In particularly justified cases, the OCCP may order the losing party to reimburse only part of the

---

90 C. Banasiński, M. Bychowska, *Kompetencje decyzyjne Komisji Europejskiej i Prezesa UOKiK wynikające z rozporządzenia Rady UE nr 1/2003 w świetle zasady równoległego stosowania wspólnotowego i krajowego prawa antymonopolowego*, PPH 2009, no. 3, 7.

91 M. Błachucki, *Kontrola czynności prezesa UOKiK w przedmiocie umorzenia postępowania* [in:] G. Łaszyca (ed.), *Stosowanie prawa administracyjnego*, Warsaw 2024, 153.

92 Judgment of the CCCP of 9.08.2010, XVII Am A 83/09.

costs or may refrain from charging costs altogether. Irrespective of the outcome of the proceedings, the OCCP may impose on a party the obligation to reimburse specific expenses resulting from unreliable or manifestly unfair conduct. This includes, in particular, costs arising from the refusal to provide explanations, the submission of false or misleading explanations, the concealment of evidence, or the delayed presentation of evidence. Most often, these expenses relate to the delivery of official correspondence and are rarely more than 100 EUR.

In merger control proceedings, undertakings are also obliged to bear the costs of expert opinions commissioned by the OCCP. Despite this statutory framework, the OCCP has rarely ruled on or awarded costs in merger cases because the amounts are negligible.

The OCCP decides on the allocation of costs by order, which may be included in the decision terminating the proceedings. Such an order is subject to appeal. A ruling of the CCCP dismissing or upholding a complaint against a decision on costs that was not included in the decision concluding the proceedings may be appealed to the court of the second instance.[93]

17 Legal Remedies and Change of Final Decisions

The Competition Act guarantees that a party may challenge decisions issued by the OCCP. An appeal is the primary legal remedy available to a party seeking to contest decisions of the authority. Likewise, an order issued by the OCCP may, in principle, be challenged by way of an objection. However, the objection is available only where the Competition Act or the APC expressly provides for it. The majority of procedural orders may be contested by objection. The time limit for appealing is one month; before 2014, it was two weeks, which was regarded as too short.[94] A related amendment introduced a three-month deadline for forwarding the appeal, together with the case file, to the CCCP. This is an important procedural improvement, as in certain cartel cases, the OCCP previously required at least six months to transmit the files. The appeal is lodged with the court through the OCCP.

At this juncture, it is necessary to clarify when OCCP decisions are regarded as final and when they become enforceable. A foundational principle of Polish administrative law is that only final and legally binding decisions constitute the source of rights and obligations for their addressees and may be enforced.

93 PSC resolution of 6.08.2015, III SZP 3/15.

94 B. Turno, *Termin na wniesienie odwołania od decyzji Prezesa UOKiK*, PPH 2008, no. 6, 26.

Article 16 of the APC makes a normative distinction between (i) final decisions (i.e. decisions that cannot be challenged by appeal to a higher administrative authority or subjected to reconsideration) and (ii) legally binding decisions (i.e. final decisions that can no longer be challenged before an administrative court and are therefore binding in the strict sense). This raises a structural difficulty with OCCP decisions, which are subject to a so-called 'appeal' not before an administrative court, but before a common (civil) court.

This difficulty stems from the historically ill-considered transfer of jurisdiction in competition matters – administrative in nature – to a civil rather than an administrative court. Despite more than three decades, the APC has not been fully adapted to this procedural architecture, resulting in several doctrinally complex and practically problematic consequences. Several such consequences may be identified.

First, OCCP decisions are, as a rule, final under Article 16 APC, as they are not subject to review by an administrative appeal authority and are not reconsidered by the OCCP itself. Secondly, as final decisions, they are in principle enforceable, albeit only to the extent that they do not impose administrative fines. Thirdly, lodging an appeal does not automatically suspend enforceability, as neither the APC nor the CPC provides for such an effect. Suspension may be granted only by the CCCP upon a reasoned request by a party. Fourthly, with regard to administrative fines, OCCP decisions may be enforced and subjected to administrative execution within 14 days of the decision becoming enforceable, that is, either upon expiry of the time limit for appealing to the CCCP or upon the civil court judgment becoming final.[95]

These consequences show that the procedural model for judicial review of OCCP decisions remains internally inconsistent and, substantively, difficult to justify. In particular, the simultaneous classification of OCCP decisions as 'final' (in an administrative-law sense) while still subject to review by a civil court creates an analytically unstable framework for determining enforceability and interim protection.

When discussing legal remedies, the issue of amending final OCCP decisions may also arise. A cardinal principle of administrative procedure is the stability of administrative decisions. The APC provides that final decisions may not be amended except in extraordinary circumstances. These extraordinary procedures are regulated in Articles 145–156 of the APC and include, inter alia, the resumption (reopening) of proceedings, revocation, amend-

95 M. Błachucki, *Pojęcie 'decyzji ostatecznej' organu regulacyjnego i antymonopolowego, Glosa do wyroku Naczelnego Sądu Administracyjnego z dnia 14 października 2022 r. (sygn. akt I GSK 2933/18)*, ZNSA 2024, no. 1, 165.

ment, and declarations of invalidity in respect of final decisions issued by public authorities. Importantly, this principle of stability is further strengthened in the context of OCCP decisions.

First, final OCCP decisions may not be amended by any other public authority; only the OCCP itself may do so. Secondly, a party cannot compel the OCCP to initiate extraordinary proceedings under Articles 145–156 APC to amend a final decision. This rule is expressly set out in Article 82 of the Competition Act and is confirmed in judicial practice.[96] The sole exception concerns merger control: a party may apply for an extension of the validity of a merger clearance decision. Such decisions are valid for two years and may be extended by one year at the party's request, provided that market conditions have not changed since the decision was adopted.

Accordingly, final OCCP decisions may be amended only ex officio and by the OCCP itself. The legal grounds for such intervention are set out in Articles 145–156 of the APC and include reopening antimonopoly proceedings, revoking, amending, or declaring a final decision invalid. The initiation and outcome of such extraordinary procedures remain within the OCCP's discretion. If a decision is amended, the party may challenge it by appeal to the CCCP.[97] It should be noted, however, that the OCCP uses these competences only exceptionally, with the notable practical exception of merger decisions.

18 Mutual Assistance within Poland and the EU

Cooperation between public administrative bodies constitutes a distinct category of legal relationships within administrative governance, whether in the domestic sphere or in transnational administrative cooperation. The APC elevates cooperation among public administrative bodies to a general principle of Polish administrative procedure (Article 7b). Furthermore, the APC contains Section VIIIa on European Administrative Cooperation, comprising seven provisions (Articles 260a–260f APC), intended to regulate such cooperation as comprehensively as possible.

The APC is, however, subsidiary in this domain. It cannot serve as an autonomous legal basis for cooperation. Accordingly, where EU law sets out cooperation obligations and prescribes their modalities, or where specific national provisions do so, the provisions of the APC do not apply. This is particularly relevant in competition matters, where sector-specific EU instru-

96 CCCP judgment of 25.06.2001, XVII Ama 31/01.

97 HAC order of 11.02.2009, II GSK 749/08.

ments and the Competition Act provide the primary legal bases for cooperation.

Cooperation is also regulated in the Competition Act. Article 72 provides that public administration bodies are obliged to make available to the OCCP any files and information in their possession that are relevant to proceedings pending before the OCCP. This provision establishes a general obligation of domestic administrative cooperation with the OCCP and, importantly, provides a clear legal basis for the transfer of requested information. The role of the cooperating bodies is limited to providing information; they do not become participants in the antimonopoly proceedings. Consequently, they exercise no control over the manner in which the information is used, the scope of its deployment, or the course of the proceedings.

A significant limitation of this cooperation regime is that failure to cooperate is not subject to sanctions. As a result, the effectiveness of cooperation varies considerably in practice, as does the quality and completeness of the information provided. Moreover, the OCCP has limited instruments to verify the accuracy of the information obtained or to compel supplementation beyond issuing further requests.

Within the framework of domestic cooperation, the OCCP may also seek legal assistance from Polish courts. Pursuant to Article 61 of the Competition Act, the OCCP may request that the competent district court hear witnesses or obtain expert opinions, where justified by the nature of the evidence or by serious inconvenience or significant costs associated with obtaining the evidence directly.

It is, in certain respects, paradoxical that cooperation between the OCCP and EU NCAs is substantially more developed than cooperation with domestic authorities and courts. This asymmetry is largely explained by the ECN's institutional evolution, which has progressively deepened operational cooperation in competition enforcement. There are no fully comparable, detailed rules governing mutual assistance in merger control cases, which remain more structurally segmented nationally, notwithstanding parallel reviews and practical coordination.

Cooperation within the ECN acquired a qualitatively new dimension following the implementation of the ECN+ Directive. The most significant novelty introduced by the Directive is the formal mechanisms of cross-border legal assistance among ECN members.[98] These reforms concern, in particular, four areas: (i) the harmonisation of rules on inspections and searches; (ii) the

98 M. Botta, *The Draft Directive on the Powers of National Competition Authorities. The glass half empty and half full*, ECLR 2017, no. 10(38), 471.

introduction of mutual assistance instruments; (iii) the obligation to serve documents on behalf of other NCAs; and (iv) the establishment of the principle of recognition of foreign decisions and their enforcement.

In 2023, the Polish legislator introduced a new Section VIIa into the Competition Act, entitled 'Mutual assistance in matters of notification or enforcement of fines or periodic penalty payments in cases concerning infringements of Articles 101 and 102 TFEU.' Articles 113m–113u fully implement Articles 25–28 of the ECN+ Directive. The national provisions largely reproduce the wording and structure of the Directive, with only limited modifications.

According to information from the OCCP, these provisions had not been applied in practice by the OCCP from their entry into force until the end of 2025. This does not imply a lack of cooperation with other EU NCAs. On the contrary, cooperation continues routinely and without material obstacles. The new provisions are intended for exceptional situations, namely when ordinary procedural tools prove insufficient and formal assistance from another NCA is necessary.

19 Conclusions

Antimonopoly procedure historically derives from the general administrative procedure. With the adoption of successive competition statutes and their subsequent amendments, further divergences from the general model have been introduced. Although this trend has not been uniform over time, in recent years, antimonopoly proceedings have again moved away from the classic model of jurisdictional administrative proceedings under the APC, with a substantial likelihood of further emancipation. These differences are already visible at the level of general principles and are then developed in detail through specific provisions. Nevertheless, despite increasing autonomisation, antimonopoly proceedings remain, in essence, administrative proceedings – albeit of a special type.

A further important finding is that antimonopoly proceedings have become increasingly immune to subsequent amendments to the APC. The sources of this 'immunity' are twofold. First, antimonopoly procedure often constitutes a more modern and detailed regulatory framework than the general administrative procedure. Second, it is increasingly enriched with procedural institutions unknown to the APC, thereby reducing the functional relevance of general rules.

Antimonopoly proceedings increasingly incorporate institutions typical of adversarial judicial proceedings. The principal driver of this development appears to be an uncritical imitation of foreign procedural models. Such transplantation of foreign structures may, in the long term, threaten the internal coherence of antimonopoly proceedings. The implementation of the ECN+ Directive presented an opportunity for more systematic reform. However, the 2023 amendment must be assessed critically. Certain provisions were transposed almost literally without adequate systemic reflection, while others introduced original solutions promoted by the OCCP that have produced consequences of even greater concern.

The institution most clearly modelled on criminal procedure is the explanatory proceedings framework. This is an unusual institution, largely unknown in general administrative practice, yet undeniably useful in OCCP practice, with its practical significance continuing to grow. Unfortunately, procedural guarantees – above all, accountability constraints on the OCCP – have not expanded proportionately. The wide scope of largely uncontrolled discretion aligns closely with a Caesarist model of competition enforcement in Poland.

A significant part of the 'criminalisation' of procedure is traceable to explanatory proceedings, most notably in relation to dawn raids. It is therefore important to emphasise the enhanced legal protection for searched undertakings in relation to the conduct of searches. Although the implementation of the ECN+ Directive did not introduce express rules on LPP, the CCCP, in a move that surprised both the OCCP and the European Commission, developed protection for in-house lawyers who are legal advisers. The post-Directive expansion of RFI regulations remains controversial. Case law also confirms that information may be requested from undertakings not only about their own operations but also about their corporate groups, including foreign entities. In this respect, Polish regulation and jurisprudence broadly reflect the acquis communautaire.

The procedural provisions on access to files, restrictions on access, and the scope of information communicated to parties are extensive. These regulations could serve as a model for the outdated APC and many special administrative procedures. Paradoxically, however, implementation of the ECN+ Directive has resulted in a regression in certain procedural rights. The replacement of the previously developed, informal 'statement of objections' practice at the end of the evidentiary phase with a formalised and justified order served at the outset – intended to satisfy Directive requirements – has significantly weakened the ongoing flow of information and, thereby, the procedural position of parties. Adapting the Polish procedure to the ECN+ framework did not necessitate abandoning the earlier transparency-enhancing mechanisms, yet this was the choice made under the current OCCP leadership.

Not all newly introduced institutions have proven successful. Interim decisions are a particularly clear example: the OCCP has largely ceased using them. While this is partly attributable to the decline in initiated proceedings, the decisive factor appears to be the instrument's legal construction. An interim decision is a full administrative decision that must meet all standards of legality and reasoning and is subject to legal remedies. In practice, particularly in a system where a case is often handled by a single case handler, the cost-benefit balance does not favour deploying interim measures.

The peculiarity of antimonopoly proceedings is particularly evident in the areas of challenging, amending, and enforcing OCCP decisions. These rules are difficult to justify. A rather unusual form of legal 'chaos' has emerged regarding when an OCCP decision should be considered final, what that means, and to what extent it is enforceable. The differentiated rules for enforcing administrative fines, as opposed to other obligations, exacerbate the problem. This disorder is further intensified by inadequate CPC provisions and a flawed interim protection regime that is not automatic but depends on a party's request. It is also unclear why final OCCP decisions cannot be amended upon a party's request. This solution was introduced by the first Antimonopoly Act of 1990 and has been repeated largely by legislative inertia in successive statutes. It restricts the rights of addressees and raises doubts about proportionality and substantive justification.

Against the background of Polish procedural law, antimonopoly proceedings stand out – this time positively – for the breadth of domestic and international cooperation mechanisms. The OCCP may obtain information from all public administration bodies, a feature not universal across special administrative procedures. The Competition Act sets clear limits on when, what, and to whom the OCCP may disclose information. The provisions on European cooperation are even more extensive, reflecting the continuing institutional maturation of the ECN. Nonetheless, most cooperation remains informal, though this may evolve over time.

The underdevelopment of international cooperation rules in merger cases is noteworthy, but appears to reflect a broader structural issue linked to the decentralised design of EU merger control and the varying national implementation frameworks. Finally, the use of waivers requires clearer regulation. Waivers are not well developed in Polish administrative procedure, and their use in antimonopoly proceedings, without an explicit statutory basis, entails a non-trivial legal risk. A structured waiver framework – common in practice in many EU jurisdictions participating in parallel merger reviews – would enhance legal certainty and facilitate efficient cross-border coordination, provided it is designed with robust safeguards and explicit, voluntary consent requirements.

CHAPTER 10

Sanctions for the Competition Law Infringements

1 Introduction

An efficient competition policy requires an adequate system of sanctions. Competition law imposes additional transaction costs on undertakings, which, in some cases, lead to the prohibition of certain commercial arrangements. Those competition limitations on the freedom of enterprise may provide some incentive for companies to attempt to escape scrutiny from competition authorities. Therefore, the sanctions for competition law violations should deter such violations and outweigh the profits from any potential deviation. This chapter analyses the sanctions imposed for competition infringements in Poland. The regulation of sanctions has evolved since the first Act of 1987. The latest chord in this story is the changes resulting from the implementation of the ECN+ Directive. This is the second most significant amendment to the Competition Act concerning sanctions, after the 2015 amendment. The Directive, in the part concerning penalties, is clearly focused on the principles of corporate liability, regardless of the legal and organisational form in which they operate, in order to maximise compliance. It should come as no surprise that the scope of antitrust liability, both subjective and objective, under the Competition Act expanded in 2023. In addition, soft-law regulations on leniency have been codified as statutory law, which can be seen as strengthening legal certainty and predictability. The 2023 amendments also codified some of the conclusions drawn from case law. A brief analysis of auxiliary civil and criminal sanctions is provided in the final section of the chapter.

2 The Liability under the Competition Act

An analysis of the provisions of the Competition Act leads to the conclusion that the legal liability associated with compliance is administrative and legal in nature. This liability is enforced against obligated entities, i.e. undertakings and selected natural persons, in the event of a breach of administrative legal obligations under the Competition Act. The OCCP is the only public authority competent to impose fines and structural sanctions for infringements of the Competition Act. During the court proceedings, the CCCP also enjoys this

© 2026 THE AUTHOR(S) | HTTPS://DOI.ORG/10.1163/9789004754638-011
This is an open access publication distributed under the terms of the CC 4.0 license BY-NC-ND.

competence.[1] Furthermore, liability for infringing competition law is objective, irrespective of the person's guilt or awareness.[2] Subjective elements of competition act infringement are essential only when determining the actual amount of the fine.[3]

Financial penalties are an important component of administrative liability for breaches of competition law. The Constitutional Tribunal's case law makes clear that administrative financial penalties may be imposed for violations of statutory obligations.[4] As the Tribunal pointed out, the essence of administrative fines is to motivate entities to fulfil their obligations to the state in a timely and proper manner.[5] Administrative sanctions are primarily preventive in nature,[6] and the essence of administrative fines is to compel compliance with orders and prohibitions.[7] The fundamentally preventive nature of administrative sanctions does not preclude their instrumental repressive character. With regard to financial penalties, it can be extremely difficult, if not impossible, to distinguish between prevention and repression.

A characteristic feature of administrative law is that a single legal act often includes a variety of legal sanctions. Therefore, it is justified to identify the legal sanction with the entirety of legal guarantees securing the implementation of the law. The consequence is that the Competition Act determines the direct civil-law consequences of competition infringements. These civil sanctions differ from those under antitrust and merger provisions (see the end of the chapter for more on this).

Administrative liability is distinct in nature from other criminal or civil liabilities. Therefore, a violation of competition law may result in indirect civil liability, including compensation, imposed under the Damages Directive and the Private Enforcement Act (discussed in the next chapter). Criminal liability, on the other hand, is regulated separately and is not imposed for infringement of the Competition Act. The Criminal Code autonomously and exclusively penalises one type of behaviour, i.e. bid rigging, which is subject to criminal sanctions (discussed at the end of the chapter).

---

1 T. Ławicki, *Glosa do wyroku SN z dnia 22 lutego 1994 r., I CRN 238/93*, PiP 1995, no. 7, 102.

2 M. Krasnodębska-Tomkiel, *Changes in Competition Policy over the Last Two Decades*, Warsaw 2010, 518.

3 Judgment of the PSC of 21.04.2011, III SK 45/10.

4 Judgment of CT of 15.01.2007, P 19/06.

5 Judgment of CT of 1.03.1994, U 7/93.

6 Judgment of CT of 24.01.2006, SK 52/04.

7 Judgment of CT of 15.01.2007, P 19/06.

3 Antitrust Sanctions

Sanctioning is an indispensable part of competition enforcement. Cartels and abuse of dominance are illegal, and hence the reaction from the state should be swift and adequate. The administrative character of infringed norms determines that this reaction is pecuniary and structural when necessary. The OCCP may impose two types of sanctions on undertakings: financial and structural. Financial sanctions are more common and may be imposed on a wider range of entities. They consist in the obligation to pay a specified amount of money as a negative consequence of violating the provisions of the Competition Act. Structural sanctions, on the other hand, should be understood as the authoritative intervention of the OCCP undertaken in order to shape a competitive market structure that has been disrupted as a result of an administrative offence committed by an undertaking, regulated accordingly in national or EU competition law, e.g. through the division of the assets or the forced sale of assets. The differences among the sanctions stem from their different objectives. The primary purpose of financial sanctions is retribution and retaliation for a violation of a legal norm, which may, to a limited extent, involve redressing the damage by refunding monopoly profits. Structural sanctions are primarily corrective. Their purpose is to restore competition in the market and offset the negative effects of market distortion caused by an entrepreneur's unlawful acquisition of significant market power. The enforcement of structural sanctions is undoubtedly a hardship for the undertaking, but despite his subjective sense of being punished, retribution is secondary.

The Competition Act provides for sanctions that may be imposed both on undertakings and natural persons. Undertakings are the primary target of sanctions provided in the Act, since they aim at counteracting anticompetitive behaviour of undertakings. However, the OCCP followed the footsteps of many other NCAs and decided to advocate for and enforce antitrust liability against natural persons, mainly managers.

3.1 Sanctions for Undertakings

Basic sanctions for infringing the competition act are financial sanctions. The basic norm is provided for in Article 106 of the Competition Act. This provision establishes closed lists of substantive and procedural infringements for which fines are levied and sets the maximum fine amount.

In principle, the imposition of all fines rests with the OCCP's administrative discretion. In practice, this discretion is limited, and the Polish NCA rarely refrains from imposing a fine when it identifies an infringement of the Competition Act. Historically, this was different: in the early years, the authority levied few, or only small, fines, assuming that undertakings must learn the rules first.[8] Sanctions may be imposed for violations of substantive and procedural rules. In the first case, the sanctions are more severe because the potential effects of such violations could be more harmful to the public interest. The latter group provides for sanctions for procedural infringements, the gravity of which is adjusted to the nature of those infringements. Fines for infringement of substantive and procedural provisions are independent of each other. Should an undertaking infringe substantive and procedural provisions, the amount of the fine for a procedural infringement is not correlated with the amount of the fine for substantive infringements. While the grounds for imposing financial penalties for procedural and substantive violations and for determining their amount differ, the general principles for determining the penalty's amount in terms of achieving its objectives and proportionality are common.[9]

The OCCP can impose a fine of up to 10% of the turnover from the previous accounting year if a company, even unintentionally, violates: 1. the general ban on anti-competitive practices outlined in Articles 6 and 9; 2. Article 101 or 102 of the TFEU. These fines are essential measures to penalise serious infringements of competition law.

The second group of competition infringements penalised under Article 106 are procedural delicts. Sanctions for procedural infringements were substantially revised in 2023. First, the maximum fine amount was changed from a fixed amount to a percentage. As a result, basic procedural infringements are subject to fines of up to 3% of the turnover earned in the accounting year preceding the year in which the fine is imposed, if the undertaking, even if unintentionally:

i. provided false data in the application for extension of validity of a merger decision as referred to in Article 23;
ii. failed to provide information requested by the OCCP pursuant to Articles 12(3), 19(3) or 50, or provided false or misleading information;
iii. prevents or hinders the commencement or conduct of an inspection or dawn raid performed within proceedings pursuant to Article 105a, subject to Article 105d(2);
iv. does not implement final decisions.

8 M. Martyniszyn, M. Bernatt, 32.
9 PSC judgment of 27.10.2015, III SK 3/15.

Procedural fines are intended to ensure the appropriate course of proceedings. They are levied for behaviour that contravenes a procedural obligation, regardless of whether that duty was subsequently fulfilled.

Another important change concerns the fine for delay in implementing the final decision or judgment. The change was fundamental. Before 2023, the fine was levied whenever a delay occurred, regardless of whether the decision or judgment was ultimately executed, and it was retaliatory and punitive. After the implementation of the ECN+ Directive, the fine is executive and coercive, aimed at compelling the undertaking or a natural person to fulfil obligations arising from a final decision or judgment. As an execution measure, the fine is independent of other fines and may be imposed several times (the *ne bis in idem* principle does not apply). This fine is imposed at an amount not exceeding 5% of the undertaking's average daily turnover achieved in the financial year preceding the year in which the penalty is imposed, for each day of delay (Article 107).

For procedural and substantive infringements, the upper limit of financial penalties is set as a percentage of the undertaking's annual turnover. This approach appears to serve the purpose of proportionally reflecting the severity of the offence and applying sanctions in line with the entrepreneur's actual impact on the market.[10]

3.2 Extended Liability: Associations

The Competition Act has long permitted the imposition of fines on associations of undertakings, and this option has been used in practice on numerous occasions (Table 10.1). Between 2010 and 2020, the OCCP issued 63 decisions on practices employed by associations of undertakings.[11] Until the implementation of the ECN+ Directive, there were no detailed regulations governing the imposition of financial penalties on business associations, and, moreover, these penalties were low because they were calculated based on the turnover generated mainly from the contributions of businesses affiliated with these associations.[12]

New provisions concerning associations of undertakings are set out in Article 106(1a–1f) and establish an upper limit on the fine imposed when an asso-

10 M. Modzelewska de Raad, *System kar pieniężnych w polskiej ustawie o ochronie konkurencji i konsumentów – potrzeba i kierunek dalszych zmian*, iKAR 2015, no.2, 93–105.

11 J. Affre, M. Restel, *Nowy model wymierzania kar pieniężnych za naruszenia konkurencji przez związki przedsiębiorców – rodzaje ryzyka i konsekwencje*, iKAR 2023, no. 12, 74.

12 M. Król-Bogomilska, *Zmiany dotyczące kar pieniężnych w polskim prawie antymonopolowym po wdrożeniu dyrektywy ECN+*, EPS 2024, no. 9, 19–32.

ciation of undertakings commits an infringement related to its members' activities. Such a penalty may not exceed 10% of the total turnover of the association's members operating in the market affected by the infringement, as calculated for the financial year preceding the year in which the fine was imposed. Upper limits and rules for imposing fines on individual members of an association of undertakings in the event of the association's insolvency have also been specified, including the application of the principle of joint and several liability. A member of the association may be released from this liability if it can prove that it did not implement the decision of the association of entrepreneurs causing the infringement of the Competition Act, was not aware of the existence of such a decision, or actively distanced itself from it before the proceedings were initiated.

TABLE 10.1 Total amount of antitrust fines (2014–2024) (Source: OCCP decision registry)

Year	Total amount of fines for practices restricting competition (million PLN) (before judicial review)
2024	650.1
2023	45
2022	241
2021	127,3
2020	187.2
2019	5.2
2018	1.1
2017	136.9
2016	3.8
2015	14.2
2014	7

The regulation of the liability of business associations has been the subject of much controversy. The imprecise nature of the key concept of 'violations related to the activities of members of an association of undertakings' has been pointed out.[13] By the end of 2025, the OCCP had neither initiated any

13 J. Affre, M. Restel, *Nowy model wymierzania kar pieniężnych za naruszenia konkurencji przez związki przedsiębiorców–rodzaje ryzyka i konsekwencje*, iKAR 2023, no. 12, 81.

proceedings nor imposed any penalties on associations of undertakings under the new rules (Table 10.2).

TABLE 10.2 Highest antitrust fines (2014–2024) (Source: OCCP decision registry)

Year	Highest fines (million PLN)	Party/practice	Decision number
2024	406	Kia – vertical restrictions, price fixing, market sharing	DOK-5/2024
2024	238	Iveco – vertical restrictions, price fixing, market sharing	DOK-2/2024
2023	36.3	Dahua Technology – vertical restrictions price fixing, market sharing	DOK-5/2023
2023	2.4	Merida – vertical restrictions, market sharing	RKT-1/2023
2022	206	Allegro – abuse of a dominant position of digital marketplace	DOK-3/2022
2022	7.2	Kärcher – vertical restrictions, price fixing, market sharing	RKR-2/2022
2021	118.1	DAF – vertical restrictions, market sharing	DOK – 8/2021
2020	120	Veolia – power heating cartel	DOK-5/2020
2020	32.6	Benefit Systems – fitness clubs cartel	DOK-6/2020
2019	1.9	Airbus – tender collusion – market for fox vaccines	RPZ-5/2019
2018	0.93	Infomex – tender collusion – server hosting and colocation	RKR-3/2018
2017	60.7; 39.3; 19.8	Kronospan Szczecinek, Kronospan Mielec, Pfleiderer Wieruszów – wood-based panel cartel	DOK-3/2017

3.3 Fines for Managers

The competition law was once applied primarily to undertakings that could be held liable for infringing the Act. Liability of natural persons has therefore been exceptional and limited to certain formal infringements, such as failure to comply with a final decision of the OCCP or a court judgment, or failure to notify of a merger. In such situations, the person managing the undertaking or a member of its management body may have been fined up to 195,000 PLN (circa 48,000 EUR). It is important to note that, in the history of the OCCP, such a fine has never been imposed.

Despite this low rate of intervention against natural persons, the OCCP has decided to introduce liability for natural persons for infringements of substantive antitrust rules under the Competition Act. As explained in the narrative memorandum accompanying the 2014 amendment, this change aimed to increase the effectiveness of anticartel enforcement by providing a direct incentive for natural persons to cooperate and expose their employers (undertakings), thereby boosting deterrence. The memorandum cited Germany and the Netherlands as examples that particularly influenced Polish regulation.[14] Five years after the statutory changes, the OCCP published *Guidelines on the method for imposing fines on managers under Articles 106a and 111 of the Competition and Consumer Protection Act (30 July 2020)*.

Under Article 4(3a) of the Competition Act, one group of natural persons that may be held liable for competition infringements is the group of managing persons. This group comprises anyone managing the undertaking, including those performing management functions or serving on a management body. Unfortunately, the term 'person performing a managing function' is vague, which may cause many problems in interpreting this provision. In practice, this will be any person who is a member of the undertaking's management body, a person in a managerial position, or any other person who manages the undertaking or their undertaking and has real influence on the undertaking's market behaviour or their undertaking's market behaviour.[15] Managing persons may be prosecuted only for a limited number of infringements. Namely, infringements regulated in Art 6.1.1–6 of the Competition Act[16] or Art 101.1.a–e of TfUE. A managing person may be held liable only if the undertaking has been found in breach of these provisions. However, additional requirements must be met. Should the undertaking be found liable for infringement of Art 6.1.1–6 of the Competition Act or Art 101.1.a–e of the TfUE, the managing person will also be liable if the infringement occurred during the period when they performed their managing functions and intentionally led the undertaking to infringe the said antitrust provisions. Summing up, to hold a natural person liable for antitrust infringements, the OCCP will be

14 This explanation is quite surprising because despite some apparent similarities the regulation of natural persons liability for infringement of antitrust rules differs in those jurisdictions from the one in Poland and above all has a quasi-criminal character.

15 M. Kulesza, *Zakres podmiotowy pojęcia osoby zarządzającej w znowelizowanej ustawie o ochronie konkurencji i konsumentów*, iKAR 2015, no. 4, 109.

16 It covers all expressly forbidden antitrust infringements except bid rigging. This is because bid rigging constitutes a criminal offence for natural persons under the Criminal Code. Such an exclusion prevents the risk of double jeopardy (criminal and administrative) for the same behaviour.

obliged to prove that they had a managing position which allowed them to intentionally or negligently exercise a direct influence on the undertaking's involvement in the anticompetitive agreement.

The 2023 Amendment introduced Article 6b(4), significantly broadening the scope of penalties for managers who deliberately allow an undertaking to use certain agreements that restrict competition. This change was introduced by the provision in the newly added Article 6b, which allows the penalisation of an 'undertaking exercising decisive influence' over an undertaking that has violated the prohibition on agreements under Article 6(1) of the Competition Act or Article 101 TFEU. Article 6b(4) provides that in the case of such infringements, 'Article 6a shall apply to the managers of the undertaking exercising decisive influence.' This provision significantly broadens the scope of application of the mechanism for punishing managers who deliberately allow an undertaking to infringe the prohibition on certain agreements that restrict competition. This amendment introduces the basis for imposing financial penalties not only on the person managing the entity that committed the infringement, but also on the person managing the entity 'exercising decisive influence' over the entrepreneur who committed the infringement.[17]

The managing person's position in proceedings before the OCCP is linked to the undertaking. They share the same procedural rights in antimonopoly proceedings. The OCCP institutes the same proceedings against the undertaking and the managing person for the same anticompetitive behaviour. However, the managing person may also become a party to the antimonopoly proceedings after proceedings against the undertaking have been instituted, provided that new facts are discovered indicating possible involvement of this person in infringing antitrust provisions. The managing person may be found in breach of antitrust rules only if the undertaking has been fined for the same anticompetitive behaviour. The maximum fine for the managing person is 2 million PLN (circa 460 thousand EUR). The managing person has the right to appeal in parallel with the undertaking. Should the court set aside the fine in relation to the undertaking, it will have the same exonerating effect on the managing person. A natural person may also file a leniency application and be granted full or partial immunity from a fine. In fact, the possibility of receiving leniency applications from natural persons has been one of the decisive arguments in favour of establishing natural persons' antitrust liability rules, as such applications could further destabilise cartels and other prohibited agreements.

17 M. Król-Bogomilska, *Zmiany dotyczące*, 21.

The introduction of natural persons' liability for competition infringements has sparked the most controversy. Many commentators have pointed out that such liability is penal in nature and should be enforced within the criminal justice system.[18] However, under the Competition Act, the enforcement of all competition rules is purely administrative. The basic difference between administrative and criminal procedure in Poland is that the former does not recognise the presumption of innocence of the party to the proceedings, and that legal professional privilege is rather limited in administrative proceedings.[19]

Below are two illustrative examples of fines imposed on managers. I have extracted the amount of the fine, the individual's position, and the actions taken as the justification for the fine (Tables 10.3 and 10.4).

Despite some controversy over the imposition of fines on natural persons, penalties on managers in Poland remain relatively moderate. The highest fines issued so far amount to only 10% and 15% of the statutory maximum, and in most cases, they represent only a few per cent of the cap. In practice, such sanctions are likely to be absorbed by employers or covered by insurance policies. As a result, their deterrent effect appears limited.

The Veolia case is particularly noteworthy for involving a leniency application. Contrary to the drafters' expectations for the 2015 amendment, the application was submitted jointly by the undertaking, rather than independently by the manager against the employer. This undermines the assumption that the threat of personal liability would erode loyalty and incentivise managers to report antitrust violations by their companies. Neither this case nor subsequent ones suggest that individual liability has meaningfully encouraged managers to turn against their employers.

Although the OCCP actively promotes its enforcement campaign targeting managerial involvement in antitrust infringements, the practical outcomes to date remain modest. The limited severity of fines and the absence of cases demonstrating the intended behavioural effects indicate that the policy has yet to achieve its anticipated deterrent impact.

---

18 R. Stankiewicz, M. Pawełczyk, *Opinia prawna sporządzona na zlecenie Ośrodka Badań, Studiów i Legislacji Krajowej rady Radców Prawnych w przedmiocie zmian do ustawy o zmianie ustawy o ochronie konkurencji i konsumentów oraz zmianie niektórych innych ustaw*, http://legislacja.rcl.gov.pl/lista/2/projekt/85314/katalog/85321.

19 M. Błachucki, *Procedural safeguards at the evidence stage of administrative proceedings in the light of the legal standards of the European Convention of Human Rights* [in:] C. Nowak (ed.), *Evidence in EU fraud cases*, Warsaw 2013, p 81.

TABLE 10.3 Dahua and distributors

Decision No. DOK-5/2023

A practice restricting competition on the domestic market for the distribution of electronic products used in monitoring systems, access control devices, and security-related accessories. The infringement consisted of concluding an agreement that involved:

1. Fixing prices for Dahua-brand products; and
2. Dividing markets for Dahua-brand products by allocating specific customers and sales transactions to designated distributors.

Person / Position	Fine	Role and conduct identified by the OCCP
Sales Department Manager → Country Leader → Country Manager (Dahua)	PLN 245,000	– Responsible for supervising the sales department, maintaining contacts with key distributors, achieving sales targets, and organising product training. – Participated in price-fixing practices and was aware of the distribution-sharing arrangements between Dahua and its distributors. – Evidence indicated that he was aware of the illegality of the conduct.
Commercial and Operations Director (Dahua)	PLN 75,000	– Supervised sales, technical, and marketing teams; part of top management though not a formal management board member. – Participated in Dahua partner meetings where Dahua representatives instructed distributors on discounts to be applied when selling Dahua products. – Played a role in disseminating pricing instructions to distributors.

TABLE 10.3 Dahua and distributors (*cont.*)

	Decision No. DOK-5/2023	
Person / Position	**Fine**	**Role and conduct identified by the OCCP**
Chairman of the Board, Alkam Security (Distributor)	PLN 100,000	– Attended Dahua partner meetings where discount policies for distributors were communicated. – Asked Dahua to specify retail prices that Alkam should apply when selling Dahua products, reinforcing price-fixing arrangements.
Sole Proxy, E-commerce Partners (Distributor)	PLN 42,800	– Participated in Dahua partner meetings, during which Dahua representatives communicated discount levels that distributors were expected to apply. – After the meeting, passed on the pricing arrangements to other employees of E-commerce Partners, facilitating implementation of the unlawful agreement.

3.4 Fines for Other Natural Persons

Article 108 provides a legal basis for fining two categories of natural persons: those liable for serious procedural infringements of the Competition Act and those involved in concentration notifications or in providing information as required by the OCCP. A maximum fine of 50 times the average salary may be imposed on managerial or executive figures who, intentionally or not, fail to comply with decisions, notify intentions to concentrate, or provide accurate information.

Second, the same financial sanction may be imposed on persons authorised by the inspected party under Article 105a(6), apartment, premises, building, or transportation holders under Article 91(1), and persons under Article 105a(7) for failure to provide or misleading information, or for not collaborating during inspections under Article 105a; also on witnesses refusing to testify without valid reason.

TABLE 10.4 Veolia PGNiG Termika

Decision No. DOK-5/2020

A concerted practice restricting competition on the market for heat generation within the Warsaw district heating system, as well as on the market for the retail sale of heat in the same system. The infringement consisted of agreeing on heat prices, dividing the heat energy market, and coordinating the terms of bids submitted in tenders for the sale and supply of heat energy.

Person / Position	Fine	Role in the infringement
Chairman of the Board, Veolia Warsaw	PLN 200,000	– Actively participated in negotiations with PGNiG Termika concerning Veolia's abandonment of constructing a new heat source. – Contributed to the development of the Energy Partnership Agreement, which defined the framework of cooperation between the companies. – Negotiated core terms: Veolia to abandon the new heating plant; PGNiG to cease active heat sales to Veolia's end customers. – Signed the Agreement.
Chairman of the Board, PGNiG Termika (leniency applicant)	PLN 0	– Submitted the draft agreement to Veolia. – Agreed additional arrangements concerning PGNiG's withdrawal from the heat sales market. – Accepted termination of the transmission agreement allowing PGNiG to use Veolia's network. – Ordered cessation of sales to end users even before the Agreement was signed. – Signed the Agreement.

The second group of financial sanctions may be imposed for procedural infringements of the Competition Act. In 2024, a fine was levied on a natural person for obstructing a dawn raid. The undertaking was fined 350,000 PLN,[20] and its chairman was fined 50,000 PLN.[21] The CEO was present at the dawn raid and represented the undertaking. Neither during the dawn raid nor for two months afterwards did he grant access to electronic data sets stored on employees' mobile phones. On the one hand, it is positive that the OCCP began fining managers responsible for obstructing dawn raids, which had not happened before. On the other hand, such fines for the undertaking and the CEO are unreasonably lenient and have no deterrent effect, either individually or generally.

3.5 Calculation of Fines

The first Act of 1990 did not provide any rules for calculating fines. It left the authority with almost full discretion when levying fines. Some improvement occurred with the adoption of the 2000 Act. Art. 104 stated that 'when calculating the amount of the fines referred to in Articles 101–103, the duration, gravity and circumstances of the previous infringement of the provisions of the Act should be particularly taken into account'. This regulation was a step forward in establishing limits on the OCCP's discretion, but it remained rudimentary. The introduction of some directives on fine assessment was welcomed and perceived as a great achievement, even though the wording of the statutory provision was imprecise.[22] The Competition Act 2007 repeated the statutory provision with only a slight linguistic change. However, in 2008, the first guidelines on fines were published, introducing a fine calculation algorithm. For the first time, the OCCP's discretion in calculating fines was limited. They were inspired by the European Commission's 1998 guidelines on fines.[23] Until their publication, significant discrepancies were observed in

---

20 OCCP decision RŁO 6/2024.

21 OCCP decision RŁO 7/2024.

22 M. Król–Bogomilska, *Kary pieniężne w prawie antymonopolowym,* Warsaw 2001, 88.

23 Guidelines on the method of setting fines imposed pursuant to Article 15(2) of Regulation No 17 and Article 65(5) of the ECSC Treaty, OJ C 9, of 14.1.1998.

the percentages of fines imposed by the OCCP and in the factors used to determine their amounts.[24]

The most substantial legislative change occurred in 2015, when a significant portion of the guidelines on antimonopoly fines was transferred to the Competition Act, and Article 111 was substantially expanded.[25] This change was important because soft-law rules gained formal significance, and, more importantly, statutory rules provided even more detailed guidance on the assessment of fines.

3.5.1 Statutory Rules on the Determination of Fines and the Circumstances Affecting Their Amount

All the described financial sanctions set a maximum amount or percentage, leaving the OCCP with discretion to determine the fine appropriate in the given case. The minimum amount is not defined, which means that, in each case, the OCCP may impose even a symbolic fine or abstain from fining the undertaking. The OCCP is obliged to assess the grounds for fining undertakings or natural persons for infringements of the Competition Act. The wide margin of administrative discretion does not mean that the OCCP imposes fines arbitrarily. The limitations of administrative discretion are set by the Competition Act itself, case law, and soft law documents issued by the authority. Article 111 sets out three types of circumstances relevant to fine determination. First, there is a general group that must be taken into account in each and every case. The general circumstances include the circumstances of the infringement and any prior infringements of the Act. Second, there is a closed list of aggravating circumstances. Third, there is an open list of mitigating circumstances. This technique is defective because certain general circumstances may lead to a higher fine but are not considered 'aggravating'. This is legal nonsense, but the OCCP sees no reason to change this, even though the solution has been deeply flawed since its introduction in 2015. Mitigating and aggravating circumstances differ between violations of substantive and procedural infringements, as well as between antitrust and merger delicts.

Mitigating circumstances depend on the types of infringements:

i. antitrust: a. voluntarily eliminated adverse effects of his anticompetitive practice, b. desisted from the anticompetitive practice before the initi-

---

24 S. Famirska, *Zmiany w polityce wymierzania kar pieniężnych za praktyki ograniczające konkurencję w świetle wyjaśnień Prezesa UOKiK publikowanych w latach 2008–2024 – zagadnienia wybrane*, iKAR 2024, no.4, 123–135.

25 M. Błachucki, *Judicial control of guidelines on antimonopoly fines in Poland*, Revista de Concorrência e Regulação 2016, no. 25, 47.

ation of the antimonopoly proceedings, c. full cooperation with the authority during the investigation, d. acting under duress when entering into the anticompetitive agreement, e. proved to have been a passive member of the anticompetitive agreement and has been avoiding the implementation of the anticompetitive clauses of the agreement, f. taking action on one's own initiative to stop the infringement or remove its effects;

ii. mergers – a. notifying the OCCP of the completion of the concentration; b. full cooperation with the authority during the investigation;

iii. managers – a. acting under duress, b. contributing to the voluntary removal of the effects of the infringement by the undertaking, c. contributing to the undertaking's voluntary cessation of the unlawful practice before or immediately after the proceedings are initiated, d. taking action on one's own initiative to stop the infringement or remove its effects; d. full cooperation with the authority during the investigation.

A financial penalty imposed on an undertaking on this basis for a procedural infringement occurring in a given antitrust proceeding is independent of the financial penalty for a substantive infringement investigated in that antitrust proceeding.[26]

The aggravating circumstances also depend on the types of infringements:

i. antitrust: a. acting as the leader or initiator of an agreement restricting competition or persuading other undertakings to participate in the agreement – in the case of a breach of the prohibition on agreements restricting competition, b. coercion, pressure or retaliation against other undertakings or persons in order to implement or continue the infringement, c. having previously committed a similar infringement, d. intention;

ii. mergers – a. having previously committed a similar infringement, b. intention;

iii. managers – a. the role of organiser, initiator of an agreement restricting competition or persuading other undertakings or persons to participate in the agreement, b. significant benefits obtained by the manager in connection with the infringement, c. coercion, pressure or retaliation against other undertakings or persons in order to implement or continue the infringement, d. having previously committed a similar infringement,

26 A. Piszcz, *Zasady ustalania przez Prezesa UOKiK wysokości kar pieniężnych za proceduralne naruszenia ustawy o ochronie konkurencji i konsumentów. Glosa do wyroku SN z dnia 27 października 2015 r., III SK 3/15*, Glosa 2016, no.3, 104–110.

When analysing this group, the issue of recidivism warrants explanation. The Competition Act requires the OCCP to record each prior violation of the Act. This does not mean that the occurrence of this condition should affect the amount of the financial penalty imposed in each case. The OCCP and courts adjudicating cases concerning violations of the Competition Act generally do not automatically treat every prior valid violation as grounds for increasing the amount of the financial penalty. Increasing the amount of the fine for a repeat infringement should be based on the similarity of the infringements, not on the mere fact that there has been a previous infringement. The individual prohibitions defined in the Competition Act may not be closely related and may concern different protected goods.[27]

In many cases, the courts set out circumstances the OCCP should consider when calculating the fine amount. Those circumstances are as follows: extent of threat to the public interest; financial profits from the infringement;[28] refraining from the prohibited practice;[29] and irreversible market changes.[30] Not all of those circumstances will be applicable in each case. Sometimes it depends on the specific provisions of the Competition Act, and at other times on the nature of the case. When levying a fine upon the undertaking, the authority should clearly state all established facts and present adequate legal reasoning.[31]

3.5.2 Guidelines on Fines

The historical significance of the guidelines has already been mentioned in the previous section. They continue to play a role in the OCCP's fine policy. This is evidenced by the fact that they are a living document, substantially amended in 2015 and 2021, when the current *Guidelines concerning the determination of fines in cases related to violations of the prohibition of practices restricting competition* (*2024*) were published. New guidelines were necessary after the implementation of Directive ECN+. New provisions gave rise to interpretive problems related to the inclusion of the financial penalty for the turnover generated by the entity exerting decisive influence on the perpetrator of the infringement

27 G. Materna, *Uprzednie naruszenie przepisów ustawy a wymiar kar pieniężnych nakładanych przez Prezesa UOKiK*, PUG 2011, no.11, 10.
28 S. Gronowski, *Polskie prawo antymonopolowe* (*zarys wykładu*), Warsaw 1998, 250.
29 CCCP judgment of 16.11.1994, XVII Amr 31/94.
30 CCCP judgment of 26.04.1995, XVII Amr 74/94.
31 CCCP judgment of 1.03.1995, XVII Amr 63/94.

in the maximum threshold, as well as to the imposition of cumulative penalties.[32]

In addition to the general fining guidelines, the OCCP published guidelines for fining managers. There are no guidelines for calculating fines for procedural infringements or for merger control delicts. Financial sanctions in merger cases are rare, and the OCCP has reserved the option of a case-by-case approach to their calculation.

The guidelines begin with a short preamble explaining the reasons for adopting the document, its scope of application, and its legal character. The guidelines emphasise their interpretative nature and that they do not interfere with statutory provisions. Therefore, they do not constitute binding rules for undertakings. However, undertakings may rely on the OCCP's promise to follow them when levying fines. The latest guidelines limited the scope of this promise. The OCCP stated that the new guidelines are not intended to enable undertakings to precisely determine (calculate) the expected amount of the fine. The amount of fines results from the legal assessment of a specific case considered by the OCCP. The purpose of the guidelines is not to equalise the level of fines across individual categories of cases and enable their comparison, but to standardise the method used to determine their amount. To support its position, the OCCP invoked the Constitutional Tribunal, which stated that Article 101 of the Competition Act or guidelines does not need to make it possible to determine in advance, at the time of concluding the cartel agreement, whether this highly reprehensible anti-market practice is profitable, i.e. whether it will bring its participants profits exceeding the fine. Such an understanding of the sanction referred to in Article 101(1) of the Competition Act would grossly violate the principles of the rule of law.[33]

The 2024 guidelines retained the four-stage process for determining the fine amount but significantly changed both the mechanism for determining the base amount of the financial penalty and the percentage values assigned to individual penalty factors. In the first step, the OCCP determines the initial amount and then the base amount of the fine. The OCCP reserved greater discretion in determining the initial fine amount, indicating it would set the starting amount between 0.01% and 3% of the 'relevant turnover'. The OCCP further noted that a value closer to the upper limit of 3% will be applied in cases of the most serious infringements, such as cartels or practices that exclude the market.

32 S. Famirska, 125.

33 Constitutional Tribunal ruling of 5.04.2017, P 17/16.

The second stage of fine calculation has been approached in a fundamentally different way from before the new guidelines. A closed catalogue of various types of additional factors is taken into account. It includes low revenue from the products concerned by the infringement in their total turnover; a particular threat to the public interest, in particular related to the functioning of secret cartels and the need to ensure general prevention of participation in such infringements; the combined economic potential, including the total turnover of undertakings between which there is a relationship of decisive influence; and a previous infringement of the provisions of the Act (other than a previous similar infringement). At this stage, the starting amount may be adjusted by up to 75% (not, as previously, by up to 50% or reduced to 90%).

The next stage in determining the fine is to multiply the base amount determined in the previous stages by the number of years of participation in the infringement, as set out in the decision finding the infringement. The final step of the analysis is to evaluate mitigating and aggravating circumstances. These may increase or decrease the fine by 25%. As indicated earlier, the list of mitigating and aggravating circumstances is purely descriptive and offers no guidance on the meaning of particular circumstances.

Guidelines have played a significant role in the past and remain an important tool for transparency at the OCCP. The evolution of the guidelines is noticeable. The changes in the methodology for determining the amount of fines presented in the OCCP's official explanations from 2008 to 2024, in my opinion, illustrate a shift in the OCCP's approach to the objectives and functions of fines. In recent years, emphasis has been placed on multiplying the base amount depending on the duration of the practice. The impact of the perpetrator's individual behaviour, in the context of mitigating and aggravating circumstances, has been gradually minimised, and mechanisms have been introduced to give greater account of the objectives of general prevention. It is impossible to miss that the changes are intended to result in increasingly severe penalties, both in percentage and nominal terms. The changes following the implementation of the ECN+ Directive, which take into account the parent company's turnover with a capital interest, will inevitably reinforce this effect.[34] Guidelines are still necessary because the OCCP does not wish to create comprehensive statutory regulations for penalties and prefers to regulate certain matters through soft law. This applies, for example, to the rules for calculating turnover in cases of financial penalties imposed on entities within capital groups, and to issues such as the number of penalties imposed in such cases, even though the subject matter of these regulations

34 S. Famirska, 135.

falls within statutory law.[35] It is not the first time the OCCP has crossed the legal line in adopting guidelines.

3.6 The Leniency Programmes

Cartels are a form of secret agreements, the detection of which can pose significant evidentiary difficulties. In terms of enforcement instruments and persuading participants in illegal agreements to cooperate with state authorities, competition law draws inspiration from criminal law. The leniency programme is a good example of this. The essence of the programme is voluntary disclosure, before or during proceedings, of information about the cartel that meets certain statutory criteria, in exchange for an exemption from, or a reduction in, the fine that would otherwise be imposed on the cartel participant. The leniency programme was a response to the crisis in traditional cartel detection methods and was used by NCAs for many years. This led to cartel enforcement being dominated by the leniency programme, to the detriment of *ex officio* proceedings.[36] The current decline in the enforcement ratio, linked to fewer leniency applications and cartel decisions, may be attributed to this. This seems to be less of an issue in Poland, as the programme has never developed to the same extent here as, for example, at the EU level.

3.6.1 The 'Original' Leniency

To enhance the effectiveness of antitrust enforcement, the leniency programme was introduced into Polish competition law in 2004. It allows the OCCP to grant immunity or reduce fines to the undertaking that cooperates with the authority and provides evidence of an anticompetitive agreement. The programme is open to participants in all types of anticompetitive agreements, whether horizontal or vertical. Before 2014, there were relatively few leniency applications. Hence, fine-tuning the leniency programme has been a core goal of the 2014 amendment. As explained in the narrative memorandum accompanying the amendment, many changes were based on the ECN Model Leniency Programme.[37] The scope for possible fine reductions under the Polish leniency programme has been expanded and rationalised in certain

35 M. Król-Bogomilska, *Zmiany dotyczące*, 32.

36 M. Martyniszyn, *Competition law and policy in crisis and the rise of the expansive state*, JAE 2026, Iss. 2, 324.

37 Available at: https://competition-policy.ec.europa.eu/antitrust-and-cartels/european-competition-network/documents_en.

respects. Since 2015, the leniency programme has also been open to natural persons.

Since its inception, the Polish leniency programme has been broadly consistent with EU programmes, and its subsequent amendments have been strongly influenced by them, as well.[38] An important change occurred in 2023 alongside the implementation of the ECN+ Directive. One of the Directive's aims was to limit differences between national leniency programmes, thereby increasing legal certainty for undertakings about the conditions for applying for leniency, maintaining their incentive to cooperate with the Commission and NCAs, and ensuring that the basic principles of the ECN's model leniency programme are transposed into national legal systems.[39] The Polish leniency programme was shaped on this model in 2014, but some differences remain, including application to non-horizontal agreements, eligibility for natural persons, and an additional leniency-plus reduction. Hence, the 2023 amendment introduced additional procedural harmonising provisions, transferred some provisions from the implementing regulation to the Competition Act, and published the new regulation.[40] Only two new measures show potential to increase the transparency and predictability of the rules for mitigating penalties compared with the previous legal situation. These include a clear definition of the moment when the applicant's obligation to cooperate with the OCCP expires, and the replacement of the requirement that an applicant seeking a waiver of a fine should not induce others to participate in the agreement with a requirement not to take action to compel other undertakings to join or continue to participate.[41] Finally, new guidelines on leniency applications were published in November 2025.[42]

The Polish leniency programme provides for the possibility of a complete exemption from fines for an undertaking that is the first to submit an application for exemption from fines in accordance with the requirements set out in the Act and that has provided evidence or information enabling the OCCP to obtain dawn raid authorisation from the court, which is helpful for initiating administrative proceedings or for issuing a decision concluding such proceed-

---

38 M. Kulesza, *Europejska geneza polskiego programu leniency*, iKAR 2024, no. 4, 61.

39 G. Materna, *Projekt dyrektywy ECN+ (omówienie w aspekcie potrzeby kolejnej nowelizacji polskiego prawa ochrony konkurencji)*, iKAR 2018, no. 2, 44.

40 Regulation of the Council of Ministers of 22.07.2024 on the manner and procedure for handling applications for waiver of fines and applications for reduction of fines, JoL 2024, item 1127,.

41 P. Korycińska-Rządca, *Program łagodzenia kar w Polsce a implementacja dyrektywy Parlamentu Europejskiego i Rady (UE) 2019/1 – wybrane zagadnienia*, PUG 2023, no. 1, 34.

42 Guidelines regarding applications for waiver of assessment and reduction of fines.

ings. In addition, an undertaking seeking complete exemption from fines could not have previously coerced other undertakings into participating in the agreement. A leniency applicant is obliged to terminate their participation in the anticompetitive agreement on the day of filing the application, with the exception of actions which, in the opinion of the OCCP, are necessary to ensure the effectiveness of proceedings conducted by the authority. If the applicant fulfils all of the above conditions, they may be exempt from fines. The Competition Act also provides for cases where the applicant does not meet all conditions for full immunity. In such a case, they may enjoy a reduction of fines.

An undertaking that does not meet any of the above conditions for exemption from a fine may apply for a reduction. To this end, it should submit an appropriate application in accordance with the statutory requirements and present evidence of significant added value to the case, compared with the evidence already in the possession of the OCCP. While, as a rule, only one undertaking can benefit from the waiver of a fine (the one that was first to meet the statutory conditions and submit an appropriate application), there may be more than one undertaking that obtains exemption from the fine after submitting a leniency application. However, each subsequent applicant for a penalty reduction can expect a proportionally smaller reduction. Since 2023, applicants have been able to request written information from the authority regarding the decision on their application. This certainly increases their legal certainty.

The new provision is Article 113j of the Act, which provides that a leniency application covers undertakings that exercise decisive influence over the applicant undertaking, undertakings over which the applicant undertaking exercises decisive influence, and persons managing those undertakings. An entity exercising dominant influence is also an undertaking and, as such, may submit applications for immunity from fines or for a reduction in fines. Therefore, there is no need to include it in the regulation of Article 113h of the Act. OCCP explained in the narrative memorandum that the provision was created to allow applications to be submitted by a category of entities other than undertakings, i.e., by managers. It should also be noted that applications submitted by an undertaking over which decisive influence is exercised and by an undertaking that exercises that influence do not compete with each other in a potential queue of applicants. It should be borne in mind that the proposed Articles 6b and 9b of the Act are intended to give practical effect in the Polish legal system to the EU concept of an undertaking under Article 13(5) of the Directive. For the purposes of imposing fines, undertakings are treated de facto as a single entity, so it is reasonable to treat them in the same way when they submit a request to have the penalty waived or reduced.

3.6.2 The Leniency 'Plus'

The important novelty of the 2014 amendment is the introduction of the so-called 'leniency plus'. This is an extension of the leniency programme originating in the US,[43] but it is also applicable in a few European jurisdictions.[44] The idea behind leniency plus is to reward leniency applicants who secure an additional reduction in the fine by disclosing another anticompetitive activity in which they were involved. The basic assumption is that if undertakings collude once, they tend to collude again. Therefore, by providing adequate incentives, a single leniency application may prompt additional applications that disclose previously unknown cartels. This is described as the 'snowball effect'. These observations were presented as a justification in the narrative memorandum accompanying the amendment introducing leniency plus in Poland. The OCCP ignored reservations about this institution. It poses a moral dilemma, as an additional reward is granted to multimarket firms that participated in more than one prohibited agreement. Moreover, economists have shown that leniency plus can have pro-competitive effects.[45]

Leniency plus is regulated in Art 113d of the Competition Act. According to this provision, if a leniency applicant who does not qualify for full immunity from a fine is the first to disclose another anticompetitive agreement and file a second leniency application, they may obtain an additional 30% reduction in the fine for their first leniency application and full immunity for the second leniency application. The leniency applicant will benefit from leniency plus provided that the second anticompetitive agreement has not been investigated by the OCCP and no previous explanatory or antimonopoly proceedings have been initiated.

From the outset, leniency plus raised doubts about its legitimacy. The poor legislative quality of the provision was emphasised, and, above all, its lack of appeal.[46] The existence of leniency plus was debated during the implementation of the ECN+ Directive.[47] This instrument is not covered by the ECN+ Directive harmonisation, and it was a good opportunity to eliminate or correct it. In the end, the OCCP did not want to discard this instrument of financial policy and proposed no reform.

---

43 It is called 'amnesty plus' in the US.

44 Namely, the UK, Portugal, Bulgaria, and Switzerland.

45 M. Martyniszyn, *Leniency (amnesty) plus: a building block or a Trojan Horse?*, JAE 2015, no. 3, 406.

46 M. Lizurek, *Leniency plus – skuteczny środek walki z kartelami czy martwa instytucja?*, PUG 2015, no. 5, XX.

47 G. Materna, *Projekt*, 44.

3.6.3 Programmed Failure of Leniency Programmes

The number of *leniency* applications is moderate and has changed over the last two decades (Table 10.5).

A notable feature of the Polish leniency programme is that the vast majority of applications concern anticompetitive vertical agreements. This may be perceived as unexpected, since the programme was initially designed to counteract hardcore restrictions at the horizontal level. There is no data on how many natural persons file leniency applications, and the OCCP declined to provide this information in response to PI's request.

More than 20 years after the introduction of leniency plus, there have been no more than three leniency plus applications. However, the OCCP has not provided the public with any further details about this case. Therefore, it is not possible to assess the application's success. Given the highly inefficient general leniency system in public competition enforcement, the small number of leniency plus applications is unsurprising. Therefore, it is very likely that leniency plus will remain an artificial institution until substantial changes are implemented in the general leniency programme.

3.7 Settlement Procedure

Another institution designed to achieve faster and more efficient antitrust enforcement is the settlement procedure (Art 89a of the Competition Act). This is not the first consensual procedure in Polish antitrust practice – the previous Act of 2000 provided for the possibility of concluding an administrative settlement, which, however, due to its ineffectiveness, disappeared from the Competition Act.[48] By introducing this procedure, Polish competition law aligns with EU developments and experience. The settlement procedure was introduced in 2015 to simplify and expedite antimonopoly proceedings.[49] The OCCP immediately published guidelines.[50]

Under the settlement procedure, before the conclusion of antimonopoly proceedings, the OCCP may, *ex officio* or upon a motion, ask all the parties to the proceedings to settle the case, provided that such a settlement will lead to the conclusion of antimonopoly proceedings. Article 89a refers to a party to

48 I. Jackowska, *Dobrowolne poddanie się karze w polskim postępowaniu antymonopolowym*, PPH 2016, no.8, 47–53.

49 A. Piszcz, *Nowe elementy regulacji prawnej kar pieniężnych w ustawie o ochronie konkurencji i konsumentów*, iKAR 2015, no.2, 42–58.

50 Guidelines regarding the settlement procedure (18.11.2015).

TABLE 10.5 Number of leniency applications (Source: OCCP activity reports)

Year	Applications
2004	0
2005	2
2006	3
2007	6
2008	3
2009	6
2010	8
2011	2
2012	16
2013	5
2014	10
2015	2
2016	2 + 1 *leniency plus*
2017	7
2018	6 + 1 *leniency plus*
2019	6 + 1 *leniency plus*
2020	3
2021	4
2022	3
2023	7
2024	8

proceedings, and therefore does not limit the concept to 'undertakings', which allows persons managing an undertaking to make use of this institution.[51] If accepted, the settlement grants the party a 10% reduction in the fine. In essence, the 10% reduction in the financial penalty is equivalent to what the

51 M. Sieradzka, M. Zdyb, *Procedura settlement ugoda w prawie antymonopolowym?*, PUG 2015, no.2, VI–VIII.

party receives in exchange for 'uncomplicating' the proceedings by exercising its right to appeal against the authority's decision.[52]

The party has 14 days to decide whether to participate in the settlement process. If they choose to do so, the OCCP will share its preliminary investigation findings and inform them of the expected fine, which is reduced by 10% due to settlement. The party can respond to this information and submit new evidence. The OCCP then has 14 days to present the final settlement offer. If the party accepts, they must agree to the proposed fine and confirm the facts established during the investigation. At any time, the OCCP may cancel the settlement if it believes it would not resolve the antitrust proceedings. The party can also withdraw their consent to participate at any time. Evidence and facts gathered during the settlement are confidential and cannot be used in other proceedings. The OCCP issues a decision at the end of the settlement process. If the party appeals this decision, the authority must annul it and issue a new one, ignoring the settlement reduction in the new fine.

The described settlement procedure was criticised because it is impossible not to get the impression that, in adapting the European model to Polish realities and in an effort to maintain as strict an approach as possible to the activities of undertakings, the idea of conciliation has been lost. Instead of a consensual way to conclude proceedings more quickly, a procedure has been created in which the undertaking is expected to assume the role of a repentant offender.[53] Moreover, from the outset, the settlement procedure was considered doomed to failure, as a 10% reduction in penalties was a very weak incentive for businesses, even though it was supposed to be the international standard. An undertaking may not be interested in paying a 10% lower fine immediately, since if an appeal is lodged, the decision will likely become final in a few years' time.[54] These forecasts are confirmed by OCCP statistics – in recent years

Table 10.6 shows that the settlement procedure has neither legal nor practical relevance.

52 M. Król-Bogomilska, *Najnowsze zmiany w zakresie sankcji penalnych w polskim prawie antymonopolowym a prawo unijne – kolejne podobieństwa i różnice*, EPS 2015, no. 7, 8.

53 K. Wiese, *Dobrowolne poddanie się karze pieniężnej – uwagi krytyczne do znowelizowanej ustawy o ochronie konkurencji i konsumentów*, ZNUJ 2014, no. 3, 98.

54 A. Piszcz, *Nowe*, 50.

TABLE 10.6 Number of settlements (Source: OCCP activity reports and PI request)

Year	Applications
2015	0
2016	0
2017	0
2018	0
2019	0
2020	3
2021	3
2022	0
2023	0
2024	2

3.8 Whistle-Blowers Programme

The inefficiency of the leniency programme, together with the failure of the settlement procedure, led the OCCP to propose a new tool aimed at encouraging cooperation from anyone aware of antitrust infringements – the Whistle-blowers Programme. The OCCP seeks to follow the European Commission's example, which introduced the Anonymous Whistleblower Tool in 2016.[55] The OCCP calls upon all who become aware of an illegal agreement to report it as a whistleblower (Table 10.7).

The problem is that the OCCP may not guarantee the protection of a whistleblower's identity, nor may the authority offer any reward for cooperation. At the moment, the whole programme relies on the willingness of potential informers to share relevant information voluntarily, on purely altruistic grounds. To remedy this situation, the OCCP was working on legislative proposals to ensure that the concept of a whistleblower was incorporated into antitrust law on a permanent basis. Such regulations are already in force in Germany, Slovakia, and Hungary. The OCCP wanted to introduce a system of financial rewards for whistleblowers' cooperation. Furthermore, the effective protection mechanism should have also been adopted.[56]

55 Refer to http://ec.europa.eu/competition/cartels/whistleblower/index.html.
56 *Introducing the Whistleblower Programme*, https://archiwum.uokik.gov.pl/aktualnosci.php?news_id=13103.

TABLE 10.7 Number of signals (Source: OCCP activity reports and PI request)

Year	Signals
2017	1,862
2018	1,625
2019	1,714
2020	506
2021	547
2022	2,396
2023	15,545
2024	14,038

It is hard to assess the programme's impact because the OCCP does not provide more detailed information. No activity report ever noted that information from signalists has been used as the basis for initiating formal action. I established that signals are rarely relevant from a competition law perspective and are, in fact, consumer complaints. Nonetheless, it is fair to say that the whistleblower programme is as ineffective as the leniency programme. No legislative amendments regarding the programme were adopted despite OCCP's efforts. Under the current rules, the OCCP may not offer any real protection for informant data. Therefore, the whistleblower programme is a toothless tiger and nothing more than a vain propaganda. Should legislative amendments be adopted, the whistleblower programme may have some prospects. However, given the strong cultural restraints against tacit collaboration with state agendas in Poland, we do not expect it to be a great success even after the Competition Act is changed.

3.9 Remedies in Antitrust Investigations

Since 2015, the competition authority has been competent to impose remedies in antitrust cases. Although remedies are not punitive measures, they are considered to be 'a type of legal sanction in real terms'.[57] The institution of remedies is modelled on Article 7 of Regulation No 1/2003.

57 A. Piszcz, *Kilka uwag do projektu założeń ustawy o zmianie ustawy o ochronie konkurencji i konsumenta*, iKAR 2012 No. 2, 11.

When ordering an undertaking to refrain from an anticompetitive practice, the OCCP may determine measures that the undertaking should take to remove the adverse effects of its behaviour. The Competition Act provides examples of such remedies, including granting a licence, granting access to the network, amending a contract, or ensuring supplies on non-discriminatory terms. The list of potential remedies has been left open. Moreover, if behavioural remedies prove unsatisfactory, the OCCP will be entitled to order structural remedies. This is an important change for the Polish competition authority, which will play a much more active role in providing undertakings with positive guidance, not only negative, on how they should execute the administrative decision.

The OCCP should apply remedies only to the most serious restrictions of competition. However, Article 10 does not imply any rule of automatism; remedies are triggered only after undertakings have achieved a dominant position in the market or after conducting market research. When applying a remedy, the OCCP should strive for the broadest possible generalisation of decisions to set the direction for competition policy.[58]

4 Sanctions in Merger Control

Sanctions in merger control share the same legal character, types, and objectives as antitrust sanctions. Financial sanctions play a fundamental role, serving individual and general deterrence, as well as retribution against undertakings that violate regulations. Structural sanctions have never been applied in the history of the OCCP, except for one instance that constituted a clear excess of power by the OCCP (Nord Stream 2[59]), which was quickly corrected by the courts.[60]

To supplement these considerations, it should be noted that although, in relation to merger infringements, natural persons can be punished for the same infringements as undertakings, e.g. failure to notify a merger or respond to an RFI, in the history of the OCCP, this has never been applied, nor have there been any plans to change this aspect of the fining policy. This approach

58 J. Sroczyński, *Tzw. środki zaradcze (remedies) w znowelizowanej ustawie antymonopolowej: istotny wzrost uprawnień Prezesa UOKiK*, PUG 2015, no. 2, XIX.

59 OCCP decision DKK-178/2020.

60 CCCP judgment of 21.11.2021, XVII AmA 11/21.

by the OCCP is incomprehensible and irrational, as the same arguments apply to sanctioning managers for antitrust violations as for merger infringements.

4.1 Financial Sanctions

Sanctions in merger control constitute only a supplementary, albeit marginal, part of competition enforcement. This is because merger control, a legal activity, serves a fundamentally different role from the fight against cartels or abuse of a dominant position, which are essentially illegal activities. The table below shows this quantitatively.

The Table 10.8 shows that fines are the marginal yet visible part of merger enforcement. There is no clear detection or fining policy for merger infringements, as they are treated as incidental occurrences and adjudicated on a case-by-case basis.

4.1.1 Failure to Notify Merger

The most common merger infringement is failure to comply with the notification obligation and carrying out a concentration without first notifying the OCCP of the intention to concentrate. There may be various reasons for this. It may be due to ignorance of the law or a deliberate choice by the undertaking. Ignorance of the law may concern both Polish and EU law.

The type of sanction applied (financial or structural) depends solely on the effects the concentration has had on the market. As indicated earlier, if these effects constitute a significant restriction of competition, the OCCP will be required to apply structural sanctions and, possibly, financial sanctions in parallel. If the concentration did not significantly restrict competition in the market, the OCCP may impose only a financial penalty on the undertaking. Negative effects are not a necessary prerequisite for administrative liability. Therefore, entities that carry out a concentration without the legally required consent of the OCCP will be liable, whether or not the concentration has an adverse effect on competition in the market. Of course, in the latter case, the consequence of such liability will be the initiation of proceedings concerning the concentration and, possibly, the imposition of an administrative fine.[61]

---

61 R. Stankiewicz, *Konsekwencje naruszenia stanu konkurencji na rynku przez przedsiębiorcę dokonującego koncentracji (art. 21 ustawy z 16 lutego 2007 roku o ochronie konkurencji i konsumentów)*, Studia Iuridica 2007, no. 47, 265.

TABLE 10.8 Number of merger infringement decisions (Source: OCCP activity reports)

Year	Failure to notify	Failure to respond	Inaccurate data	Delay in implementation
2025	4	0	0	–
2024	8	0	0	–
2023	1	0	0	0
2022	0	0	0	0
2021	0	0	0	0
2020	3	2	0	0
2019	2	1	0	0
2018	0	0	0	0
2017	3	1	0	0
2016	0	0	0	0
2015	0	0	0	0
2014	1	0	0	0
2013	2	3	0	0
2012	2	1	1	0
2011	0	0	0	0
2010	1	N/A	0	0
2009	2	N/A	0	1
2008	3	N/A	1	0
2007	4	N/A	N/A	0
2006	4	N/A	N/A	0
2005	2	N/A	N/A	0
2004	N/A	N/A	N/A	0
2003	N/A	N/A	N/A	0

A distinctive feature of the Polish system is the absence of sanctions for breaching the standstill obligation, i.e., the obligation to refrain from implementing the concentration until a decision is issued. The OCCP treats such conduct as a breach of the notification obligation. When parties to the transaction partially or fully implement the merger, the OCCP refuses to initiate merger proceedings but commences an infringement procedure. If parties file a merger notification, the OCCP returns it and initiates an infringement procedure.[62] The OCCP treats the same situation when acquiring control of

62 Example OCCP decisions DOK-142/06, DKK-138/2012, DKK-265/2019, DKK-270/2019.

another company: after the competition analysis was terminated and with the intention to re-acquire control, the OCCP requested prior approval.[63] If an undertaking violates the standstill obligation and partially or fully implements the transaction, the only viable strategy is to inform the OCCP of the situation and request the lowest possible fine. Such self-reporting is a statutory mitigating circumstance and affects the amount of the levied fine.[64] It favours undertakings that consciously disregard the notification obligation. Undertakings that wish to self-report and obtain merger clearance are precluded from doing so and will receive an infringement decision, which indirectly serves as the clearance decision (the OCCP acknowledges that the merger is completed and, since financial sanctions are imposed, no negative effect on competition was revealed). This is a flawed solution, and the authority's practice is not entirely convincing. Most of all, it requires legislative intervention.

In cases involving the imposition of this sanction, a situation may arise in which the competences of the Commission and the OCCP are in question. If, under the EUMR provisions, a case concerning a concentration with a Community dimension were referred to the Polish NCA, and after such referral the undertaking carried out the concentration without the OCCP's consent, the competent authority for imposing a possible fine for such an infringement would be the OCCP.[65] This is not merely a theoretical possibility, as undertakings do not always notify the OCCP of cases referred to Poland. For example, the referred-to merger of the television JV was never notified to the OCCP.[66]

The financial penalty for failure to comply with the notification obligation is set out in Article 106(1)(3) of the Competition Act. Pursuant to this provision, the OCCP may impose a financial penalty on an undertaking of up to 10% of the turnover generated in the financial year preceding the year in which the penalty is imposed, if the entrepreneur, even unintentionally, has carried out a concentration without obtaining the consent of the authority. Adverse effects of the merger are not a prerequisite for administrative liability.

Analysis of the list yields several findings. First, the fines are generally unreasonably low (Table 10.9). Second, there is a clear trend towards higher fines, especially after 2016. Third, the Gazprom case was a decisional anomaly with no statistical or substantive relevance. Poland is surprisingly lenient. Such fines do not achieve either individual or general aims. Fourth, infringe-

63 OCCP decision DKK-147/2025.

64 Example OCCP decisions DKK-205/2020, DKK-257/2023.

65 M. Król-Bogomilska, *Zmiany w systemie orzekania kar pieniężnych w polskim prawie antymonopolowym po przystąpieniu Polski do Unii Europejskiej*, Studia Iuridica 2006, no. 46, 164.

66 Case M.9299–DISCOVERY / POLSAT / JV.

TABLE 10.9 The highest fines for failure to notify merger (Source: OCCP activity reports)

Undertaking	Fine amount (thousands PLN)	Outcome of judicial review	Decision number
Gazprom	29,075,726	Fine quashed	DKK-178/2020
AmeriGaz Polska	730	Upheld	DKK-161/2020
Bać Pol	527	Fine quashed	DKK-86/2017
Fermy Drobiu Woźniak	339	Not challenged	DKK-145/2017
Kohler	160	Pending	DKK-147/2025
Dino Polska	100	Not challenged	DKK-270/2019
Podkarpackie Province and PPL	70	Upheld	DKK-37/2009
AGD Market	65	Reduced to 5	DKK-127/2010
Naxicap Partners	60	Not challenged	DKK-257/2023

ment proceedings are initiated ex officio, but around half of cases are initiated through self-reporting by undertakings. This may explain the more lenient approach in many cases.

4.1.2 Failure to Provide Information or Provision of False or Misleading Information

The proper and expeditious conduct of proceedings depends on cooperation among the parties and other participants in the evidentiary process. Failure to provide information or providing false information is sanctioned under Article 106(2)(2). This provision is primarily directed at external undertakings – third parties who are not parties to the proceedings. A party's failure to cooperate, or its unreliable cooperation, is addressed in separate provisions. Other undertakings that violate the obligation to cooperate under Article 50 of the Competition Act may face a fine of up to 3% of the turnover achieved in the financial year preceding the year in which the penalty was imposed. This fine is imposed even if the entrepreneur acted unintentionally.

Failure to cooperate is sanctioned only in response to requests under Article 50(1). This fine is imposed even if the undertaking acted unintentionally. Fault is not a normative prerequisite for imposing sanctions in the form of procedural coercive measures; therefore, OCCP is not obliged to examine it. The mere failure to comply with a procedural obligation may result in a fine, imposed at the authority's discretion.[67] Requests made under Article 49a or Article 50(3) are not subject to sanctions.

Analysis of the list reveals several findings. First, fines for lack of cooperation are often imposed on multiple undertakings during market investigations. This was the case for Engie and Gazprom, as well as for De Longhi, Whirlpool, and Avans. At present, four cases are pending, stemming from the same market investigation. Second, fines for lack of cooperation are, on average, higher than those for substantive infringements. This may reflect a tendency toward fining opportunism – procedural infringements are easier to prove, and undertakings usually offer an unreliable defence. Third, the reasons for the lack of cooperation are varied and usually legally irrelevant. For example, Browary Łódzkie claimed that the requested information was unnecessary for the authority, De Longhi explained that an employee failed to forward four consecutive letters to the management board, and DOM and Linde Gaz pointed out that employees had neglected their duties. Fourth, there is a high success ratio in court proceedings. Even though courts are not willing to quash a decision, significant reductions in fines are often. Only insignificant fines are usually upheld (Table 10.10).

4.1.3 Providing Unreliable and False Information in the Notification Form

Undertakings are required to cooperate honestly with the OCCP during proceedings. The procedural guarantees that ensure an undertaking complies with its obligation to cooperate in good faith are: first, the possibility of resuming merger proceedings under Article 21(1); and second, the possibility of imposing fines under Article 106(2)(1). Unreliability of information should be understood broadly as the presentation of data in the notification application that is inconsistent with the facts. Liability under Article 21(1) is objective and independent of the undertaking's intentions when they present unreliable

67 M. Sachajko, *Istota i charakterystyka prawna antymonopolowych kar pieniężnych*, RPEiS 2002, no. 1, 73.

information. This structure is correct, as only such a regulation can ensure effective and fair cooperation with undertakings. Furthermore, there is no justification for consumers or competitors to bear the potential negative consequences of a party's unprofessional conduct. For this reason, the fears that the provision in question could create scope for abuse have not materialised.[68]

TABLE 10.10 The highest fines for failure to provide information (Source: OCCP activity reports)

Undertaking	Fine amount (thousands PLN)	Outcome of judicial review	Decision number
Gazprom	212,925	Reduced to 174,454	DKK-141/2020
Engie	172,000	Reduced to 430	DKK-217/2019
De Longhi	204	Reduced to 122	DKK-115/2013
Linde Gaz	120	Not challenged	DKK-158/2020
Browary Łódzkie	50	Upheld	DOK-68/2006
Whirlpool	32	Not challenged	DKK-116/2013
DOM Polska	26.5	Upheld	DKK-200/2017
Avans	16	Not challenged	DKK-117/2013

Failure of the undertaking to cooperate in good faith may also result in financial penalties. Pursuant to Article 106(2)(1), the OCCP may impose a financial penalty on an entrepreneur in the amount of up to 3% of the turnover achieved in the financial year preceding the year in which the penalty is imposed, if the undertaking, even unintentionally, provided false information in the notification of the intended concentration.

In the history of the OCCP, two penalties have been imposed for providing unreliable and false information in a notification. The first concerned the largest supermarket chain in Poland, JMD. In the course of proceedings concerning the acquisition of another chain, Plus, the company concealed information in its notification about the expiry of the lease agreement for one of the Plus stores and the conclusion of an agreement with the premises owner by JMD. The fine amounted to PLN 100,000.[69] The courts overturned the penalty on procedural grounds, reaching the bizarre conclusion that a penalty for providing false information can be imposed only if that information is included in the original application. However, if it is provided in a supplement to the

68 R. Stankiewicz, *Konsekwencje*, 268.
69 OCCP decision DKK-101/2008.

application, the penalty applies only if the OCCP reminds the party of this fact.[70] The second penalty concerned UPC Polska, which concealed that it had included numerous market reports in its notification. During the proceedings, the OCCP learned from the author of these reports that he had provided them to the company. UPC was fined PLN 775,000, which the undertaking paid.[71]

4.1.4 Failure to Cooperate during the Inspection

This provision applies to all undertakings, including both parties to the proceedings and third parties, provided that they were inspected by the OCCP. The purpose of this provision is to ensure cooperation from the undertaking during the inspection. Failure to cooperate in such a situation may result in the imposition of a fine of up to 5% of the undertaking's average daily turnover achieved in the financial year preceding the year in which the penalty was imposed, for each day of delay.

In the OCCP's history of merger control cases, inspections of undertakings have been carried out twice. No fine of this type has ever been imposed.

4.1.5 Sanction for Delays

Until the implementation of the ECN+ Directive, Article 107 provided for a financial penalty for delays in the implementation of a decision. The President of the Office could impose a financial penalty of up to EUR 10,000 for each day of delay in implementing a decision or court ruling. The penalty was calculated from the date specified in the decision. In the history of the OCCP, one decision was issued imposing a fine of EUR 130,000 on Carrefour for delay in implementing all remedies.[72] The penalty was calculated at €5,000 per day for the 26-day delay. Remedies included the sale of several outlets, and the delay concerned three locations that Carrefour failed to sell despite having 18 months to do so.

The penalty for delay in implementing concentration decisions, regulated in Article 107 of the Competition Act, has changed its character. The only purpose of levying this fine is clearly stated as being 'to compel' the fulfilment of specific obligations. It applies only to ongoing violations of the Act by an

---

70 PSC judgment of 25.11.2014, III SK 89/13.

71 OCCP decision DKK-6/2012.

72 Decision of the OCCP No. DOK–86/2007.

undertaking.[73] Its sole purpose is to induce the undertaking to comply with the merger decision. Pursuant to this provision, the OCCP may fine an undertaking up to 5% of its average daily turnover achieved in the financial year preceding the year in which the penalty is imposed for each day of delay in implementing the following concentration decisions: (1) conditional – pursuant to Article 19(1); (2) prohibitive – pursuant to Article 20(1); (3) sanctioning – pursuant to Article 21(2) and (4).

It's not clear why the OCCP advocated for this change. There is no rationale for allowing undertakings to disregard their obligations arising from merger decisions, especially when there is no sanction even for months of delay. This was the case of Vectra, which failed to fully implement all remedies in due course. Even though the delay lasted several months, the OCCP discontinued the infringement procedure after the 2023 amendment.[74]

4.2 Structural Sanctions in Merger Cases

In addition to financial sanctions, the OCCP may impose structural sanctions for infringements of competition rules in merger control. The purpose of structural sanctions is to restore the situation prior to the infringement, and they are applied when negative market effects have occurred. Specifically, a structural sanction may be imposed if:

i. a merger decision was based on unreliable information for which the undertakings participating in the concentration were responsible;
ii. the party did not comply with agreed remedies;
iii. the concentration has not been notified to the OCCP;
iv. prohibition decision to proceed with a merger decision has not been respected.

The structural sanction may be applied only if the concentration has already been implemented, and restoring market competition is otherwise impossible. Regarding the mode of implementation and the type of structural sanction to be applied, the OCCP possesses administrative discretion. The application of the structural sanction has one important limit. Structural sanctions may be imposed only within five years from the day the concentration was implemented. This limitation aims at providing legal certainty for undertakings. It should be highlighted that the expiration of the five-year time limit does not preclude the OCCP from imposing financial sanctions.

73 M. Król-Bogomilska, *Zmiany dotyczące*, 19–32.
74 Ruling of the OCCP No. DKK-67/2024.

To date, only one structural sanction has been applied by the OCCP under the present Competition Act. It concerned the establishment of Nord Stream 2 and involved the dissolution of financing agreements between Gazprom and Western oil companies. The courts quashed the decision, so there is no practical experience in enforcing structural sanctions in merger cases.[75]

Although imposing structural sanctions may seem a far-reaching intervention, in reality, it is an extraordinary and extremely limited measure. They apply only to anti-competitive concentrations, whereas financial sanctions apply to other transactions. Structural sanctions can be applied only to concentrations that have already been implemented, whereas the OCCP can fully assess the others and limit itself to financial sanctions.

4.3 Merger Control Fines: Missing Link of the Effective Control Chain

Sanctions in merger control are supplementary and exceptional. Yet sanctioning decisions are important because they clarify formal issues and provide the strongest incentive for undertakings to comply with regulations. A consistent and coherent policy of enforcing the merger regime could contribute to broader prevention and, above all, ensure better cooperation between undertakings and the OCCP. If undertakings know what to expect from the OCCP and how to behave in various contentious situations, such cooperation is much more effective for both parties, even if it ends in a penalty.

Despite the noticeable evolution of sanctions rules in the area of merger infringements, practically nothing has changed; if anything, it has deteriorated. The best example is the ill-considered change to the fine for delay. Thanks to this change, undertakings can delay implementing remedies without any real threat of sanctions. This is not just theoretical speculation but reality. The OCCP has already had to discontinue a case in which, despite several months of delay, no fine could be imposed because of changes made by the OCCP itself. This shows the complete marginalisation of merger control in the enforcement agenda and illustrates the OCCP's poor legislative skills.

Many serious merger infringements remain unsanctioned. The most serious case is the lack of sanctions for gun-jumping. Although the Competition Act contains a standstill obligation, it does not provide sanctions for noncompliance. Although the OCCP treats a breach of the standstill obligation as a form of carrying out a concentration without consent, this policy is flawed and contains significant loopholes. The simplest scenario in which this jurisdictional loophole becomes apparent is when a breach of the standstill obli-

75 Judgment of the CCCP of 21.11.2021, XVII AmA 11/21.

gation is detected after a decision to approve the concentration has already been issued. In such a situation, the OCCP has no legal tools to enforce antimonopoly liability on undertakings. There is also a more practical aspect to this enforcement gap: undertakings have no guidance from the OCCP on what is permitted and what is not in the period before obtaining a decision. There are no clear rules or OCCP guidelines on what is considered acceptable in Poland. Given that the Competition Act, unlike the EUMR, treats even short-term acquisitions of control as concentrations, the requirements for the standstill obligation should be correspondingly higher than at the European level.

A significant problem with merger enforcement is the overly lenient treatment of infringements. Even more problematic are the positions taken by the courts. A striking example of the courts' highly ill-considered and incomprehensible policy on merger infringements is the Supreme Court's judgment, which upheld the lower courts' rulings and reduced the fine for failure to notify to the amount of the notification fee.[76] It is difficult to find a more extreme example of both legal ignorance and alienation from common sense. Recognising that an appropriate fine for disregarding the notification obligation is one that corresponds to the amount of the notification fee is a clear deterrent to such infringements. In this judgment, the Court took an even more revealing position: that the OCCP and courts should adopt a more lenient approach to penalties, with a greater consolidation of market mechanisms and a better understanding of their functioning and the behaviour of undertakings, compared with the rules for assessing the same behaviour in the past. This position is contrary to the basic principles of punishment: lenient penalties may be applied when new regulations and sanctions are introduced, but after a few years, when everyone is familiar with them, penalties should return to a normal level.

5 Civil Law Sanctions

To give the full picture of sanctions, it should be noted that the basic civil-law sanction for infringing the Competition Act is invalidity. Some question whether invalidity can be described as a 'sanction', although 'legal consequence' might be a more appropriate term. They will use this term, similar

76 PSC judgment of 19.11.2014, III SK 15/14.

to civil-law doctrine, because of established custom and the fact that, in a purely linguistic sense, it 'fits' the effects of an antitrust violation.[77]

All agreements whose object or effect is the elimination, restriction, or any other infringement of competition in the relevant market are, in their entirety or in the relevant part, null and void (unless exempted by the de minimis rule or the rule of reason). Similarly, this applies to the consequences of abuse of a dominant position, but the invalidity is absolute in unilateral conduct cases. It means that all the above agreements and legal actions are invalid ex ante. Therefore, an OCCP decision is declaratory. From the outset, the courts emphasised that 'the invalidity sanction is of a civil law nature. This civil-law sanction cannot be enforced by the authorities competent to counteract monopolistic practices, which pursue the objectives of the Act by shaping administrative and legal' relations. Therefore, there are no grounds for including a ruling on the invalidity of the agreement in the operative part of the Antimonopoly Office's decision. Such a ruling may be issued by a civil court'.[78]

Agreements restricting competition have no legal effect between the parties or in relations with third parties – they are legally ineffective. Although such agreements are sometimes implemented in practice, their non-performance or defective performance does not constitute grounds for bringing claims. Therefore, they are not enforceable in court. However, pursuant to Article 6(2), an agreement that meets the conditions for exemption set out in Articles 7 or 8 cannot be declared invalid. This applies to both agreements covered by the de minimis rule (due to the small market share of their participants) and those that meet the conditions set out in block exemption regulations or individually meet the criteria of Article 8. Such agreements are valid from the moment they are concluded and are not subject to the prohibition under Article 6(1).

This sanction applies, inter alia, when a legal act (such as an agreement) has been performed correctly (is a valid legal act) and produces effects – only these effects trigger the sanction of invalidity.[79] The sanction is automatic, without the need for further declarations of intent, and is invalid in relation to legal acts or their relevant parts that constitute practices restricting competition. This effect applies directly to the agreement in question, so a court

---

77 T. Targosz, *Nieważność czynności prawnej jako wynik nadużycia pozycji dominującej*, Transformacje Prawa Prywatnego 2012, no. 2 80.

78 CCCP judgment of 29.12.1993, XVII Amr 44/93.

79 A. Pyrzyńska, *Nieważność czynności prawnej – uwagi na tle art. 6 ustawy o ochronie konkurencji i konsumentów*, PiP 2016, no. 5, 63.

judgment or administrative decision declaring the agreement invalid will be purely declaratory and will not create a new legal situation.[80]

A bilateral legal transaction that constitutes an abuse of a dominant position is one whose content violates the prohibition set out in Article 9(1) in conjunction with Article 9(2) of the Competition Act. This is the case when:

i. the abuse concerns the direct addressee of the act (which excludes the possibility of declaring invalid those acts whose anti-competitive effects concern market participants other than the contractor),
ii. as a rule, it is not necessary to analyse other legal actions of the dominant undertaking in order to establish abuse (i.e. it does not concern actions leading to abuse by differentiating the terms of cooperation with different customers),
iii. it results in a restriction of the economic freedom of the dominant undertaking's counterparty.[81]

The sanction of invalidity does not entail the loss of legal effect of the entire action contrary to the Act – partial invalidity is permissible. A decision of the OCCP (or a judgment of the CCCP) imposing a specific obligation on an undertaking should clearly specify the action to be taken to rule out the possibility of different interpretations. The invalidity of an agreement concluded, for example, between cartel participants does not automatically invalidate contracts they have concluded with third parties. For example, if cartel members have fixed product prices and one of them then concludes a sales contract with a customer using the price resulting from the prohibited agreement, the customer may invoke Article 58 § 2 of the Civil Code, demanding that the contract be declared invalid because it is contrary to the principles of social coexistence.[82] In the case of contracts that have already been fully or partially performed, it is possible to seek damages.

There is a merger control aspect to the invalidity sanction. It concerns the validity of the contract as the basis for the merger. The Competition Act does not contain any sanctions for contract invalidity.[83] Even prohibiting a concentration does not render the contract invalid. Only a decision imposing structural sanctions can require termination of the contract, and in the event of non-compliance with that decision, the OCCP may apply to the court for its

80 M. Lewandowski, *Sankcja nieważności wobec praktyk ograniczających konkurencję–cywilnoprawne aspekty prawa antymonopolowego*, PPH 2010, no. 7, 21.

81 T. Targosz, 96.

82 A. Majer, *Nieważność bezwzględna w ujęciu ustawy o ochronie konkurencji i konsumentów*, Roczniki Administracji i Prawa 2023, no. 3, 329.

83 S. Gronowski, *Glosa do postanowienia Sądu Najwyższego z dnia 27 października 1995 r., III CZP 135/95*, OSP 1996, no. 6, 112.

annulment. This is an extremely ineffective system for ensuring compliance with the notification obligation. Such a regulation contrasts with the conditional invalidity specified in Article 7(4) of the EUMR. In light of this provision, the validity of any transaction depends on a positive final decision. If the parties proceed with the transaction and receive a negative decision from the Commission, the contract is invalid. Interestingly, the system adopted in the Competition Act also stands in clear contrast to the newer regulation contained in the FDI Act. Pursuant to Articles 12(1) and 12k(1) of this Act, the sanction of invalidity of a contract based on which a foreign investment in Polish protected entities is carried out is automatic and occurs *ex lege* in the absence of notification or disregard of a negative decision. This odd and confusing behaviour can only be explained by a widespread failure to uphold the standstill obligation and by the OCCP's negligent enforcement efforts gap.

The Competition Act sets out rules and institutions to protect free competition in the public interest. Although it primarily focuses on administrative law rights and obligations, it also includes an essential supplementary rule on the civil aspects of anticompetitive practices. The invalidity of agreements resulting from anticompetitive practices is a necessary complement to the competition protection system. It is another manifestation of the old Roman principle *nemo potest commodum capere de iniuria sua propria*. The merger control system still awaits similar sanctions.

6 Criminal Sanctions

Neither the Competition Act nor any criminal law provides for criminal liability for infringement of Polish competition law. Interestingly, criminal liability applies to breaches of obligations under public procurement law and regulations on combating unfair competition. However, it should be noted that bid rigging is a separate and independent criminal offence, punishable under Article 305 § 2 of the Criminal Code. This provision provides for a sanction of up to three years' imprisonment for collusive tendering. This crime applies only to natural persons and is independent of the liability of undertakings under the competition law (Table 10.11).

Criminal liability for collusive tendering is modestly imposed. The moderate number of cases brought under Article 305 § 2 of the Criminal Code may reflect the narrowing of the offence's subject matter to public tenders alone. Only three persons were actually imprisoned, whereas fines and some forms of restrictions on liberty were the primary sanctions. It seems that a reasonable proposal to amend this provision would be to extend its scope to cover all

TABLE 10.11 Adult persons adjudicated under Article 305 of the Criminal Code in district courts (courts of first instance) in 2024 (Source: Ministry of Justice)

Persons adjudicated	Persons convicted	Custodial sentence (imprisonment)		Non-custodial sentence – restriction of liberty	Fine as a principal penalty	Conditional discontinuance of proceedings	Acquitted
		Total	of which: suspended custodial sentence				
41	34	14	11	6	14	6	1

tenders, thereby providing criminal-law protection for private tenders and for various tender-type proceedings conducted under specific statutory provisions.[84]

Last but not least, some argue that managers' financial liability should be replaced or supplemented by personal liability, which would consist of the loss of the right to hold a position on the management board or the loss of the right to representation.[85] Such director disqualification is present in some jurisdictions, like the UK.[86]

7 Are Competition Sanctions Severe in Poland?

As provocative as this question may seem, it captures one of the most revealing paradoxes of the OCCP's multitasked jurisdiction. In Polish and, more broadly, European enforcement discourse, competition-law sanctions are routinely portrayed as exceptionally severe. They are often described as quasi-criminal, allegedly justifying heightened procedural safeguards, strict standards of proof, and intensive judicial oversight. For years, this narrative has served as a justificatory framework for cautious enforcement, procedural formalism, and a restrained use of sanctions in antitrust cases.

This perception is difficult to reconcile with the statutory framework. The Competition Act provides for identical maximum fines for infringements of competition law and consumer protection rules (Article 106). The consumer-protection sanctions regime is significantly broader. In addition to fines, it includes measures such as prohibiting unfair contract clauses, requiring mandatory public announcements, and implementing public compensation measures. From the perspective of undertakings, many of these tools are clearly punitive. In normative terms, therefore, the consumer-protection sanctions framework is at least as severe as, and arguably more intrusive than, the competition-law regime.

Empirical data strongly corroborate this conclusion. An examination of fines actually imposed and collected shows that consumer protection is the

---

84 K. Buczkowski, *'Tender collusion' as a form of the offence defined in Art. 305 of the Penal Code*, Prawo w Działaniu. Sprawy karne, 2015, no. 23, 245.

85 Ł. Grzejdziak, *A Barking Dog Seldom Bites: Some Comments on Competition Law Sanctions Policy in Poland* [in:] T. Tóth (ed.), *The Cambridge Handbook of Competition Law Sanctions. Cambridge Law Handbooks*, Cambridge 2022.

86 P. Whelan, *The Emerging Contribution of Director Disqualification in UK Competition Law* [in:] A. MacCulloch, B. Rodger and P. Whelan (eds.), *The UK Competition Regime: A Twenty-Year Retrospective*, Oxford 2021.

truly sanction-intensive field. In 2023 and 2024, competition-law fines totalled PLN 6.2 million and PLN 7.8 million, respectively. In the same period, consumer-protection fines reached PLN 178.2 million in 2023 and PLN 121.8 million in 2024. The disparity is not marginal but extreme: in aggregate, consumer-protection sanctions exceeded competition-law fines by more than 20 times.

This discrepancy exposes a structural paradox at the heart of Polish enforcement practice. While competition-law sanctions are rhetorically framed as draconian and systemically sensitive, consumer protection actually fits this description in practice. Yet consumer sanctions largely remain in the shadow of antitrust in doctrinal debates and public narratives. The paradox is therefore twofold. First, the area presented as the most punitive and normatively demanding – competition law – is, in practice, the least sanction-intensive. Second, the field treated as administratively routine and normatively less sensitive – consumer protection – has become the OCCP's primary source of both reputational capital and fiscal impact. This inversion creates powerful institutional incentives to prioritise consumer enforcement at the expense of antitrust, thereby crowding out competition policy.

Poland stands out not because its statutory maximum fines are unusually high – they are broadly aligned with EU standards – but because of how enforcement discretion is exercised. The OCCP's sanctioning practice reveals not an inherent severity in competition law, but rather its declining importance. The persistent narrative of antitrust exceptionalism masks a reality in which competition enforcement is cautious, selective, and financially modest, while consumer protection has become the de facto flagship of the authority's fining activity.

8 Conclusions

Sanctions play a central role in the Polish competition enforcement system, particularly given the broader institutional and cultural context. On the one hand, limited social condemnation of economic law infringements and historically low cooperation with the OCCP weaken the deterrent effect of enforcement. On the other hand, in jurisdictions where private enforcement functions effectively, public sanctions may play a complementary role, with compensation for damages serving as an additional deterrent. In Poland, however, where private enforcement remains largely ineffective, administrative fines should play a primary deterrent role.[87] This places a particular responsibility on the OCCP and the courts to calibrate sanctions carefully so that they fulfil their preventive role function.

In recent years, the OCCP has faced persistent criticism of its performance in detecting and sanctioning competition-law infringements. Moderate fines and a limited number of high-profile cases have fuelled perceptions of enforcement weakness. Official statistics confirm a decline – outside merger control – in both the number of decisions and the total value of penalties imposed. After a period of very severe sanctions in 2009–2011, the second decade of the twenty-first century saw a marked decrease in both the frequency and magnitude of competition fines.[88] The period since 2019 presents a mixed picture. While there have been notable cases – such as Allegro and the cartels involving Veolia and Benefit Systems – the majority of decisions have concerned resale price maintenance and other vertical restrictions.

Overall, it is difficult to identify clear positive trends. The effects of the 2023 amendment to the Competition Act are not yet evident. Despite expanded powers, no fines have been imposed on associations of undertakings. Leniency, leniency plus, and settlement procedures remain largely ineffective. Although the OCCP highlights its whistleblower programme and the number of signals received, there is no tangible evidence that these signals have led to significant enforcement outcomes. Despite the high volume of notifications, the number of new cases remains low, particularly compared with earlier decades. Similarly, fines imposed on managers are rare and relatively insignificant, while fines for obstruction of dawn raids may even send a counterproductive signal of tolerance.

The 2023 Amendment concerning sanctions brought many changes of various kinds. Some were necessary, while others were manifestly wrong, such as the new version of fines for delay. However, some fundamental issues were not touched. Visible loopholes are the rules governing the liability of the legal or economic successor of an undertaking.[89] Article 13(5) of the ECN+ Directive sets out the rules for imposing penalties on legal and economic successors for infringements of the prohibitions in Articles 101 and 102 TFEU. Unfortunately, the OCCP has decided not to propose any related amendments to the Competition Act. In its case law, the OCCP has consistently recognised the succession

87 M. Modzelewska de Raad, *System*, 93–105.

88 S. Murek, *Wyjaśnienia dotyczące sposobu ustalania kar pieniężnych a proporcjonalność kar pieniężnych nakładanych przez Prezesa UOKiK – próba analizy*, iKAR 2020, no. 5, 106–119.

89 M. Król-Bogomilska, *Najnowsze*, 11.

of antitrust liability and imposed penalties on legal successors in antitrust cases,[90] mergers,[91] and even consumer[92] infringements.

In 2025, the OCCP announced its intention to increase sanctions, most notably through new fining and leniency guidelines. These documents signal higher penalties in both percentage and nominal terms. The OCCP has redefined the role of these guidelines, presenting them less as guarantees and more as reference points. In doing so, it relies on Supreme Court case law rejecting the comparability of fines across cases.[93] This approach marks a fundamental shift, but its acceptance by the courts remains uncertain. Moreover, it stands in tension with a core principle of Polish administrative law – the principle of inspiring trust – which serves as the domestic equivalent of the protection of legitimate expectations. Under Article 7 § 2 of the APC, authorities should not depart from established practice without good reason. The guarantee function of fining guidelines, therefore, lies not in their formal binding force but in stakeholders' legitimate expectation that similar cases will be treated similarly.

Sanctions in merger control remain marginal in enforcement practice. The 2023 amendment has further weakened an already flawed system. Paradoxically, although merger sanctions are rare, they play a crucial role in developing substantive merger law, as regular clearance decisions usually lack reasoning. The neglect of merger sanctions has created an enforcement gap, particularly regarding the standstill obligation and compliance with conditional decisions. Reliance on European Commission guidance is insufficient given the procedural and sanctioning differences between EU and Polish law. The current President of the OCCP has exacerbated this gap by supporting ill-considered amendments, the negative effects of which are already visible.

As a result, no coherent fining policy can currently be identified within the OCCP's competition enforcement practice. Nor have legislative amendments been guided by a clearly articulated and internally consistent conception of the sanctioning system. The implementation of the ECN+ Directive shows that amendments to the Competition Act relied almost exclusively on external sources of inspiration, with limited independent reflection on the appropriate design of sanctions in the Polish context. This deficit in conceptual groundwork led to significant omissions and deficiencies during the transposition process. In particular, substantive harmonisation between the EU and Polish

90 OCCP decision DOK-12/2010.

91 OCCP decision DKK-86/2017.

92 OCCP decision RBG-2/2023.

93 PSC judgement of 3.04.2018, I NSK 7/18.

sanctioning regimes remains incomplete, with important elements left unaddressed, such as liability succession and an effective sanctions system in merger control.

Instruments introduced by the OCCP on its own initiative have largely failed to deliver tangible results. The leniency plus programme is a prominent example of a mechanism that has proven ineffective in practice. Despite the opportunity to revise or recalibrate this instrument during the 2023 legislative amendment, it was left unchanged. More generally, the OCCP's underlying objectives in its fining practice and the intended role of sanctions within the broader enforcement architecture are often difficult to discern. The authority has published very few policy documents clarifying its position on these matters.

The most recent fining guidelines provide guidance and signal two important shifts. First, the OCCP explicitly seeks to limit the guidelines' guarantee function, treating them less as a framework that generates legitimate expectations and more as a flexible reference point. Second, the revised methodology is clearly designed to produce higher fines, both in relative and absolute terms. This tendency will be further reinforced by changes arising from the implementation of the ECN+ Directive, in particular the inclusion of the turnover of parent companies that exercise decisive influence. Taken together, these developments suggest that record-high financial penalties may be imposed in the future in order to strengthen deterrence.[94]

The deficiencies of the sanctioning system and the absence of a coherent fining policy cannot, however, be attributed solely to the OCCP. The role of the judiciary – especially the Supreme Court – has been equally consequential. The Supreme Court has endorsed a fully reformatory model of judicial review of administrative fines imposed by the CCCP. Under this approach, even where the antitrust authority has correctly applied the statutory criteria for imposing a penalty and properly assessed the circumstances of the infringement, the common court remains entitled to reassess the fine in light of its perceived functions.[95]

This judicial stance effectively prevents the OCCP from pursuing a deliberate and consistent policy of fines. While the authority retains formal responsibility for competition enforcement, its capacity to shape sanctioning practice is substantially curtailed. Such extensive judicial intervention has been widely

94 S. Famirska, 134.

95 PSC judgment of 16.04.2015, III SK 24/14.

criticised in the literature, and there have been repeated calls for greater judicial restraint when reviewing the authority's penalty policy.[96]

A further difficulty lies in the unpredictability of judicial reasoning in setting fines. Whereas decisions of the CCCP typically contain detailed calculations grounded in previously issued guidelines, many judgments of common courts display a striking lack of methodological rigour when reducing penalties. Courts frequently fail to provide even an approximate explanation of how revised amounts are derived.[97] The combination of far-reaching judicial activism with insufficient justification for modified fines undermines legal certainty and predictability. Consequently, it makes the development of a stable, transparent, and credible fining policy in Polish competition law extremely difficult, if not altogether infeasible.

96 M. Bernatt, *Między*, 24.

97 See judgments in cases concerning anticompetitive practices, e.g. judgments of the CCCP of 27.01.2011, XVII AmA 73/10, of 11.08.2014, XVII AmA 84/13, of 21.11.2013, XVII AmA, of 13.10.2014, XVII AmA 127/13, of 7.09.2015, XVII AmA 50/14, or judgments of the CA of 17.06.2015, VI ACa 1475/14, of 10.06.2015, VI ACa 1477/14, of 19.12.2012, VI ACa 752/12, of 14.08.2015, VI ACa 1223/14, of 9.11.2010, VI ACa 383/10, of 23.05.2013, VI ACa 1451/12, and merger control, e.g. the judgment of the CCCP of 6.12.2012, XVII AmA 43/11, or the judgment of the CA of 17.05.2016, VI ACa 630/15.

CHAPTER 11

Private Enforcement of Competition Law

1 Introduction

For many years, competition law enforcement was almost exclusively the domain of public authorities. NCAs exist to safeguard the public interest and ensure that markets remain open and competitive. However, administrative decisions do not provide compensation to those harmed by anticompetitive conduct, particularly victims of cartels. To address this gap – and to strengthen the overall effectiveness of competition enforcement – rules on private enforcement gradually emerged within the EU legal framework. The adoption of the Damages Directive provided substantial impetus for reform across Europe, prompting significant changes in national competition law enforcement systems.[1] More than a decade later, it is evident that private enforcement plays very different roles in different Member States.[2] Some continue to rely predominantly on public enforcement for a range of institutional and legal reasons. Poland is a notable example of such a jurisdiction.

Historically, civil damages actions for competition law infringements were exceedingly rare in Poland. This was chiefly due to the difficulties claimants faced in proving the quantum of harm and establishing a causal link between that harm and the infringement. Following the implementation of the Damages Directive in Poland and the adoption of the Private Enforcement Act, this situation has begun to evolve, although the pace of change has been gradual.

This chapter examines the history, current state, and future prospects of private enforcement of competition law in Poland. It begins with a historical overview of the judiciary's evolving approach to private enforcement and concludes that section with a discussion of the very limited – and largely unsuccessful – cases in which claimants sought compensation from undertakings that infringed competition rules. The subsequent section presents and briefly analyses the PEA, situating it within the broader context of the Damages Dir-

1 Directive 2014/104 EU of the European Parliament and of the Council of 26.11.2014 on certain rules governing actions for damages under national law for infringements of the competition law provisions of the Member States and of the European Union Text with EEA relevance, OJ L 349, 5.12.2014, 1–19, hereinafter the 'Damages Directive' or the 'Directive 2014/104'.

2 For an overview, refer to B. Rodger, M. Ferro, F. Marcos (eds.), *Research handbook on private enforcement of competition law in the EU*, Cheltenham 2023.

© 2026 THE AUTHOR(S) | HTTPS://DOI.ORG/10.1163/9789004754638-012
This is an open access publication distributed under the terms of the CC 4.0 license BY-NC-ND.

ective and highlighting the specific features of the Polish regulatory framework. The final section explores the prospects for private enforcement in Poland and assesses the key factors likely to shape its development in the coming years.

2 History of Private Enforcement in Poland

The evolution of private enforcement of competition law in Poland can be divided into three distinct phases. The first phase was characterised by inconsistent Supreme Court case law on whether private enforcement was possible. As a result, civil courts were markedly sceptical about awarding damages for competition law infringements. In the second phase, the judiciary gradually adopted a more favourable view, recognising that civil courts could, in principle, adjudicate antitrust damages claims. However, this doctrinal shift did not immediately translate into a practical increase in litigation: undertakings remained reluctant to initiate compensation proceedings. The third phase began with the first attempts by claimants to seek damages or to request the invalidation of agreements that infringed competition law, marking the initial – though still hesitant – steps towards genuine private enforcement.

The first phase was marked by controversy over whether civil courts were competent to determine whether a given practice was anticompetitive under the Competition Act. Early Supreme Court judgments recognised this competence, allowing civil courts to make their own assessments of whether an infringement had occurred.[3] Subsequently, however, the Supreme Court reversed course, holding that only the OCCP was authorised to determine whether violations of the Competition Act occurred. As a result, civil courts were obliged to stay their proceedings pending a final administrative decision.[4] This approach effectively stalled the development of private enforcement, as civil cases could not proceed until lengthy administrative proceedings had concluded.

Empirical research commissioned by the Ministry of Justice confirmed the consequences of this restrictive stance: only a handful of compensation claims based on competition law infringements were identified, and even fewer resulted in any form of redress.[5] These findings highlight the profound

3 T. Ławicki, 104.

4 PSC order of 27.10.1995, III CZP 135/96.

5 I. Hykawy, *Praktyka sądów cywilnych w sprawach wynikających z zarzutu naruszenia ustawy z 24 lutego 1990 r. o przeciwdziałaniu praktykom monopolistycznym*, Warsaw 2002.

difficulties faced by early claimants and the structural barriers that impeded the emergence of a meaningful private enforcement regime in Poland.

The Supreme Court altered its approach once again roughly a decade later, ruling that civil courts should proceed with private antitrust claims without suspending proceedings pending an OCCP decision.[6] In this new line of case law, the Court held that agreements arising from anticompetitive practices – whether collective or unilateral – were invalid ex lege. Consequently, an OCCP decision had only a declaratory effect: it confirmed an infringement but did not provide the legal basis for the agreement's invalidity. The Court emphasised that public and private enforcement serve different purposes: the former protects the public interest by safeguarding market structure, while the latter protects the private interests of individuals or undertakings harmed by the infringement.

This position was subsequently confirmed and further clarified by a later Supreme Court resolution.[7] The Court explicitly recognised the competence of civil courts to independently determine that a particular undertaking's conduct constituted an abuse of a dominant position, provided the OCCP had not already ruled on the matter. This clarification is particularly significant because it reaffirms that civil courts are bound by OCCP decisions. Once an administrative decision has qualified conduct as anticompetitive, civil courts may not reopen or reinterpret that classification. However, this binding effect does not extend to commitment decisions.[8] Since such decisions do not contain an authoritative finding of infringement, civil courts remain free to determine autonomously whether the conduct at issue was anticompetitive when adjudicating private claims.

The third stage in the development of private enforcement is characterised by claimants' first attempts to rely on competition norms to seek compensation. Before the adoption of the PEA, there were no specific legal provisions governing private enforcement of competition law in Poland. Claimants had to rely exclusively on the general rules of the Civil Code on contractual and tortious liability. As a result, the entire burden of proof – including proof of infringement, harm, and causation – fell on the claimant, making such actions exceptionally challenging.

Although the OCCP President could, in principle, submit an *amicus curiae* opinion in civil proceedings, this mechanism was never invoked. The authority's formal decisions, however, remained significant, as civil courts were

6 PSC judgments of 5.01.2007, I CSK 83/05, or of 2.03.2006, III SK 17/06.
7 PSC resolution of 23.06.2008, III CZP 52/08.
8 PSC resolution of 23.07.2008, I CSK 83/05.

bound by the OCCP's factual and legal findings, which could substantially shape the outcome of private disputes. Claimants were entitled to seek full compensation for harm caused by competition law infringements, though courts retained the power to mitigate damages in accordance with general civil law principles.

No specialised courts existed to hear such claims, and cases were adjudicated under ordinary procedural rules. Depending on the value of the claim, jurisdiction lay with either the district courts or the regional courts.[9] This lack of specialisation, combined with the stringent evidentiary burdens placed on claimants, contributed to the very limited number of antitrust damages actions filed before the enactment of the PEA.

There were several instances in which parties brought antitrust claims before the civil courts. In most of these cases, claimants sought a declaration that the relevant contracts were invalid for breaching the Competition Act, although some also pursued claims for damages. A representative example is a case decided by the Court of Appeals in Szczecin, which reviewed a judgment of the Regional Court.[10] The Regional Court found the parties' agreement invalid for breaching the Competition Act. However, it also held that the claimant had failed to prove the existence and amount of the alleged damage. In the court's view, the evidence was insufficient, and the expert testimony did not conclusively establish harm. On appeal, the Court of Appeals dismissed the claim in its entirety, holding that the agreement did not, in fact, breach competition law and that the claimant had not demonstrated any compensable loss attributable to the agreement.

Another noteworthy case involved an action brought by a radio station against a collective management organisation.[11] The court ruled in favour of the radio station, holding that the organisation's termination of the general licensing agreement was ineffective because it violated the Competition Act. The termination was found to be an abuse of a dominant position. A striking feature of this case was the court's order requiring the organisation to produce licensing agreements with other radio stations. When the organisation refused, the court treated the refusal as indicating unlawful differentiation of licence fees and discrimination against the claimant. This example demonstrates the potential evidentiary value of adverse inferences when a party

9 PSC resolution of 22.02.1994, I CRN 238/93.

10 CA judgment of 26.10.2016, I ACa 693/16.

11 Regional Court judgment of 8.12.2014, I C 932/14.

fails to comply with a disclosure order – although such orders were rare and generally ineffective prior to the PEA.

There are also examples of civil courts relying on OCCP decisions in follow-on damages actions. In one such case, the court dismissed the claim because the claimant failed to prove the fact and the quantum of harm.[12] In another, the court rejected the claim on the basis that the claimant had not established a causal link between the infringement found by the OCCP and the alleged losses.[13] Importantly, the case law makes clear that the absence of an OCCP decision does not preclude civil courts from considering antitrust allegations. On the contrary, the Court of Appeals has held that, in the absence of an administrative decision, civil courts are obliged to assess independently whether the behaviour in question violates competition law.[14]

This brief overview of pre-PEA case law shows that the number of private antitrust actions was very limited, and the success rate was even lower. Nonetheless, these cases demonstrate that civil courts were willing to rule autonomously on the compatibility of contractual arrangements with competition law. Notably, one case resulted in a settlement and the award of damages for a competition law infringement.[15] The principal obstacles were the claimant's heavy burden of proving actual harm and establishing a causal link between the infringement and the loss. One case also highlighted the inefficiency of the general discovery rules in Polish civil procedure, which offered little assistance in obtaining evidence.

The positive development is that many of these systemic difficulties have been addressed by the PEA. By introducing measures such as a presumption of harm for certain infringements and detailed rules on disclosure and the production of evidence, the Act significantly reduces the evidentiary burden on claimants. These reforms create a realistic prospect that antitrust damages claims will become more accessible and more likely to succeed in Polish courts.

3 The Scope of Application of the Private Enforcement Act

To implement Directive 2014/104, Poland adopted a standalone act to regulate claims for damages arising from infringements of competition law. The alter-

12 CA judgment of 10.01.2014, I ACa 1322/13.
13 Regional Court judgment in Lublin of 4.07.2014, I C 759/08.
14 CA judgment of 25.11.2009, VI ACa 1807/14.
15 Refer to fn 39.

native – introducing isolated amendments to several existing statutes – was rightly deemed impractical given the Directive's scope and the specialised nature of the matters it addresses. Likewise, incorporating the implementing provisions into the Competition Act would have been inappropriate, as it would conflict with the public-law character of that legislation.

To begin with, Directive 2014/104 does not apply to infringements of national competition law that are purely domestic – those incapable of affecting trade between Member States and thus outside the scope of Articles 101 and 102 TFEU. Under Article 2(1) of the Directive, an 'infringement of competition law' covers breaches of Articles 101 and 102 TFEU, as well as national rules with essentially the same purpose, as defined in Article 2(3). These provisions apply in parallel with EU law pursuant to Article 3(1) of Regulation 1/2003. However, the Directive explicitly excludes cases that do not affect trade between Member States (recital 10).

In implementing the Directive, national legislators may broaden its scope. Polish law accordingly allows damage claims for infringements of domestic competition rules that lack cross-border effects. Poland chose not to establish separate regimes for purely national and EU-relevant infringements, thereby enhancing the protection of parties harmed by anticompetitive practices, whether these practices affect the EU market or only the domestic market.

The PEA covers all categories of antitrust infringements – horizontal and vertical agreements and abuses of dominance. Extending the PEA to vertical restraints is particularly important, as most decisions of the Polish competition authority concern resale price maintenance and other vertical restrictions; otherwise, opportunities for follow-on actions would be limited. Finally, the Act regulates only actions for damages, leaving other claims, such as injunctions, outside its scope.

The PEA introduces a statutory definition of a cartel as an agreement or concerted practice between at least two actual or potential competitors aimed at coordinating market behaviour or influencing key competitive parameters, particularly through price-fixing, output limitation, market or customer allocation, bid-rigging, import or export restrictions, or other anticompetitive actions. This definition has raised doubts, given that the Polish legal system already defines anticompetitive agreements in Article 6 of the Competition Act. Under Article 30 of the PEA, civil courts may need to determine, as a preliminary issue, whether a practice restricts competition when assessing liability and damages, and these determinations will not always be preceded by an OCCP decision. As the PEA and the Competition Act both address conduct prohibited under Articles 101 and 102 TFEU and Articles 6 and 9 of the Competition Act – prohibitions formally issued by the OCCP – neither statute should be interpreted in isolation. The concept of a cartel should therefore be analysed in light of both Acts rather than exclusively with reference to one or the other. Hence, some commentators argue that the term 'cartel' should be interpreted more broadly than its literal meaning to encompass all forms of anticompetitive agreements.[16]

The PAE also provides that claims for damages arising from competition law infringements fall within the jurisdiction of regional courts. With the written consent of a claimant, actions may also be brought by non-governmental organisations whose statutory mandate includes competition protection (Article 14(1) of the PEA).

The PEA applies only to infringements occurring after its entry into force.[17] Hence, where a situation constituting a violation of competition law began before 27 June 2017 and continued thereafter, only the portion of that conduct occurring after that date should be regarded as an infringement committed following the entry into force of the PEA. The PEA may therefore apply only to claims relating to the segment of the harm attributable to the continuation of the infringement from 27 June 2017 onwards. This approach preserves the principle of non-retroactivity while allowing the PEA to apply to infringements that, although initiated earlier, were completed or manifested in a relevant way only after the Act entered into force.[18]

A notable provision is Article 36(2), which removes the limitation period for access to evidence and for the evidential value of decisions issued by the OCCP. As a result, parties may request disclosure of evidence gathered in antitrust proceedings concluded before the Act's entry into force, and earlier OCCP decisions retain their binding effect. This provision mitigates some of the restrictive consequences of the Act's temporal scope.

4 Grounds of Liability

Article 3(1) of Directive 2014/104 requires Member States to ensure that any natural or legal person who has suffered harm from a competition law infringement can claim and obtain full compensation. PEA extends liability to indirect purchasers harmed by the passing-on of overcharges. It also provides

16 M. Majewski, *Kartel i jego uczestnik w rozumieniu ustawy o roszczeniach o naprawienie szkody wyrządzonej przez naruszenie prawa konkurencji*, iKAR 2019, no. 6, 61.

17 However, procedural provisions, i.e., the discovery process, are applicable to earlier infringements.

18 M. Kłoda, *Przepisy prawa konkurencji z 2017 r. dotyczące przedawnienia a prawo międzyczasowe*, PPH 2020, no. 10, 18.

for joint and several liability among small and medium-sized enterprises (SMEs), subject to the exceptions in Article 5(1). Accordingly, Article 3(1) of the Act – reflecting the Directive – requires compensation for harm caused to any person, thereby aligning Polish law with the Directive's broader personal scope.[19]

The limitation of liability for damages incurred by SMEs arises because such undertakings are liable only to a limited group of persons – namely, their own direct and indirect purchasers. In practice, this means that SMEs participating in a cartel are not jointly and severally liable for harm suffered by the purchasers of other cartel members. The restriction effectively narrows the scope of potential claims against SMEs and reflects the legislator's intention to protect smaller market players from disproportionate financial exposure.

Moreover, this limitation leads to a clear conclusion: SMEs will not be liable to parties with whom they had no commercial relationship, even if those parties suffered harm indirectly, such as through price increases resulting from market-wide adjustments by other cartel participants. Entities affected solely by the broader market impact of the collusive conduct, but not situated within the SME's own supply chain, therefore have no basis for seeking compensation from the SME. This approach is consistent with the Directive's objective of ensuring effective enforcement while preventing excessive burdens on smaller undertakings whose participation in a cartel may be marginal or coerced.[20]

Following the adoption of the ECN+ Directive, it has become clear that a parent company may be held liable, together with its subsidiary, for a competition law infringement committed by that subsidiary. Under the Damages Directive, the 'infringer' may therefore include a parent company that did not directly engage in the anticompetitive conduct but that qualifies as part of the same 'undertaking' for the purposes of EU competition law. The single economic unit doctrine allows the corporate veil to be lifted, imposing liability on the parent company for infringements committed by its subsidiary when the two entities form a single economic unit.[21]

19 A. Jurkowska-Gomułka, *Publiczne i prywatne egzekwowanie zakazów praktyk ograniczających konkurencję*, Warsaw 2013, 131; see also A. Jurkowska-Gomułka, *Private Enforcement of Competition Law in Polish Courts: The Story of an (Almost) Lost Hope for Development*, YARS 2013, no. 6, 107.

20 A. Milewska, *Solidarna odpowiedzialność sprawców naruszenia prawa konkurencji przewidziana w projekcie ustawy o roszczeniach o naprawienie szkody wyrządzonej przez naruszenie prawa konkurencji z 7 lutego 2017 r.–aspekt podmiotowy*, iKAR 2017, no. 1, 78.

21 CJEU Judgment of 6.10.2021, *Sumal SL v Commission*, C-882/19.

However, under the PEA and in light of existing Polish case law, it is difficult – if not impossible – to extend liability in this way. Polish law adopts a formal, entity-based approach: the concept of an 'undertaking' is tied to separate legal personality, and liability is generally grounded in personal responsibility for one's own acts. This domestic framework stands in stark contrast to the functional and purposive interpretation of 'undertaking' under EU law, which focuses on economic reality rather than corporate form. As a result, the Polish approach effectively prevents a parent company from being held liable for damages arising from a competition law infringement committed by its subsidiary, even though such liability would be fully consistent with EU principles.[22] Hence, there are calls for legislative intervention to change this situation.[23]

The right to full compensation under Article 3 of the Directive is consistent with existing principles of Polish civil law. Article 3(2) of the Directive specifies that full compensation includes actual loss, loss of profit, and interest, all of which are already encompassed by Article 361 § 2 of the Civil Code.[24] Thus, no separate implementation was necessary. Polish civil law has long recognised claims for both damnum emergens and lucrum cessans, whether in contractual or tortious contexts. Under prevailing legal doctrine, actual loss is understood as material harm reflected in a concrete reduction in the injured party's assets – i.e., a negative change in their economic position. Lost profits, by contrast, refer to the gains the injured party would reasonably have obtained had the competition law infringement not occurred. Together, these two components constitute the full scope of compensable damage under Polish civil law and the Damages Directive.[25]

The Act rightly confirms that, unless otherwise specified, the general tort provisions of the Civil Code apply. This includes liability for accomplices and beneficiaries of the wrongful act (Article 422 CC), as well as liability for persons entrusted with the performance of tasks (Articles 429 and 430 CC).

A central issue concerns the standard of liability under the new legislation. The Act provides that an undertaking which infringes competition law is liable for the resulting harm unless it proves the absence of fault. This fault-based model reflects the traditional, subjective understanding of culpability in

---

22 M. Mackiewicz, P. Maliszewska, *Rozszerzenie odpowiedzialności za czyn nieuczciwej konkurencji na spółkę dominującą*, PPH 2020, no. 1, 56.

23 M. Dąbroś, *Odpowiedzialność przebijająca w ramach private enforcement*, iKAR 2020, no. 3, 30.

24 A. Majer, *Szkoda antymonopolowa. Zakres pojęciowy oraz przesłanki odpowiedzialności*, Studia Prawnoustrojowe 2023, no. 61, 252.

25 Ibidem.

Polish law. Recital 11 of Directive 2014/104 allows Member States to retain additional conditions of liability – such as fault – provided they comply with EU principles of effectiveness and equivalence. Whether a subjective fault requirement fully satisfies these standards may ultimately require clarification from the Court of Justice, particularly if other Member States adopt objective liability models. A liability regime based solely on unlawfulness – i.e., breach of competition law – might better support the Directive's objectives.

Article 7 of the PEA further introduces a rebuttable presumption that cartel conduct causes harm. This presumption is broader than required by the Directive, as it applies to all infringements within the meaning of Article 2(1). The Directive does not preclude such an extension, thereby enhancing claimants' ability to establish liability in both cartel and non-cartel cases. Given the evidentiary difficulties historically associated with proving anticompetitive conduct, shifting the burden of proof in this way may be essential to ensuring the effectiveness of private enforcement in Poland.

5 Expiry of Claims

Directive 2014/104 introduces harmonised rules on limitation periods to ensure that victims of competition law infringements can effectively pursue damages (recital 4) and to promote consistency across Member States (recital 6). Recital 36 provides that national rules on the commencement, duration, suspension, or interruption of limitation periods must not unduly impede actions for damages, particularly those based on infringement decisions of competition authorities or reviewing courts.

Under Polish law, limitation periods for tort claims not involving personal injury were previously governed by Article 442(1) §§ 1–2 of the Civil Code. This provision did not meet the Directive's requirements for a minimum three-year knowledge-based period combined with a 10-year absolute cap. Article 9(1) of the PEA now provides for a five-year period running from the moment the claimant could become aware of both the harm and the liable party. In cases involving competition law infringements, the conduct at issue is often covert, and its effects may only become apparent after a considerable lapse of time. Importantly, the moment at which an infringement is established does not necessarily coincide with the moment at which concrete financial harm can be identified. For this reason, the concept of 'knowledge' must be interpreted flexibly, taking into account the practical difficulties victims face in detecting and quantifying harm arising from secretive anticompetitive conduct practices.[26] This period does not begin until the infringement has ceased – an event that, in practice, may occur at different times for different entities involved.

The five-year period reflects the Directive's minimum standard, while the 10-year absolute period maintains the traditional approach of Polish civil law. Nonetheless, such a lengthy absolute limit may raise concerns. Extended limitation periods create prolonged uncertainty for undertakings about the scope of potential claimants and overall exposure to liability. As a result, infringing undertakings may delay settlements until the full set of injured parties is known, thereby prolonging dispute resolution.

Judicial practice also highlights the difficulty of identifying the 'end of the infringement' or the 'duration of the practice', particularly in cases involving abuses of dominance.[27] The legislative intent, as reflected in the explanatory memorandum, is that both the five- and ten-year periods commence simultaneously.

Directive 2014/104 further requires the suspension of limitation periods during proceedings before a competition authority (Article 10(4)). Article 9(2) of the PEA implements this rule by suspending the limitation period upon the initiation of such proceedings against the infringer. The period resumes one year after a final infringement decision becomes binding, or, in Member States that do not issue such formal decisions, after the proceedings are otherwise concluded. While the Directive does not specify whether explanatory proceedings should trigger suspension, the PEA explicitly extends this effect to explanatory proceedings as well.[28]

Finally, although the Directive provides that suspension applies only to infringers subject to the authority's proceedings, the PAE does not expressly address this issue. This omission may give rise to interpretative uncertainties where multiple undertakings are jointly and severally liable.

---

26 M. Mackiewicz, *Przedawnienie roszczeń odszkodowawczych z tytułu szkody wyrządzonej naruszeniem krajowego i unijnego prawa konkurencji*, iKAR 2021, no. 4, 65.

27 A. Tworkowska-Baraniuk, *Przedawnienie roszczeń o naprawienie szkody wyrządzonej przez naruszenie prawa konkurencji–polska próba implementacji dyrektywy odszkodowawczej w zakresie terminów przedawnienia*, iKAR 2017, no. 1, 75.

28 M. Mackiewicz, 42.

6 Discovery and Access to Files

A substantial part of the PEA comprises procedural rules governing the disclosure of evidence, reflecting both the central role of disclosure in private enforcement and the significant changes it introduces into Polish civil procedure. The Polish legislator largely followed the framework of the Damages Directive and did not use the possibility under Article 5(8) to broaden disclosure beyond the Directive's minimum requirements. The Act (1) establishes rules and standards for assessing disclosure requests, (2) regulates the procedural course of disclosure proceedings and sanctions for misuse, and (3) sets out absolute and temporal limitations on the disclosure of certain categories of evidence.

Although disclosure orders are not entirely new in Polish law – similar mechanisms are provided for in Article 80 of the Copyright Act and Article 286 of the Industrial Property Act – these earlier instruments have proved ineffective and difficult to apply.[29] PEA is a more detailed and coherent framework that provides parties with clearer procedural rights. Parties may request disclosure, appeal disclosure orders, and seek to modify or revoke them if circumstances change. If the evidence sought contains a trade secret, the party seeking to protect that information may invoke the disproportionate nature of the disclosure as a basis for rejecting the request. The assessment of whether disclosure would be disproportionate must take into account the broadly understood interests of both the parties to the proceedings and the entity holding the evidence. In this context, the court must evaluate the necessity and adequacy of the disclosure, considering, in particular, whether access to the confidential information is genuinely required to establish a specific fact.[30] This balancing exercise reflects the Directive's objective of ensuring effective access to evidence while safeguarding legitimate confidentiality interests. Disclosure orders also constitute enforceable titles, enabling courts to secure compliance through compulsory enforcement mechanisms, thereby enhancing their practical effectiveness. If properly applied, these measures can significantly improve fact-finding in damages actions.

The PEA also introduces sanctions for disclosure. Courts may disregard improperly obtained evidence and impose fines of up to approximately EUR 5,000 where a party (1) requests disclosure in bad faith, (2) breaches condi-

29 M. Błachucki, *Dostęp do informacji przekazywanych Komisji Europejskiej i Prezesowi OCCP w trakcie procedury łagodzenia kar pieniężnych (leniency)*, EPS 2015, no. 5, 21.

30 Z. Ochońska, *Ochrona tajemnicy przedsiębiorstwa w postępowaniu gospodarczym i postępowaniu w sprawach własności intelektualnej*, ZNUJ 2020, no. 3, 112.

tions for accessing or using restricted information, or (3) misuses disclosed evidence in other proceedings. Although these broad grounds for sanctions may deter abuses of the disclosure process, some commentators argue that the fines are too low given the potentially serious consequences of misusing confidential information.[31]

7 The Role of the OCCP

Although the PEA concerns private enforcement, it assigns several important responsibilities to the OCCP.

First, the OCCP must cooperate in disclosure proceedings and comply with production orders issued by civil courts. This marks a fundamental departure from previous practice, under which civil courts were effectively barred from accessing evidence in administrative antitrust files. Historically, the OCCP consistently refused requests for access, and only criminal courts – rarely exercising this option – were permitted to obtain such materials. Under Articles 17–22 of the PEA, civil courts may now order the OCCP to disclose specific documents gathered during administrative proceedings. The OCCP retains the right to object and appeal, providing an appropriate procedural safeguard. Nonetheless, the new framework significantly enhances the evidentiary tools available to civil courts and may improve the accuracy and efficiency of damages adjudication.

Second, civil courts may seek expert assistance from the OCCP or EU NCAs when determining the extent of damages suffered by victims of antitrust infringements. In doing so, courts are encouraged to follow the European Commission's guidelines on quantifying harm, an important measure given that many Polish judges lack the specialised economic expertise needed to assess complex overcharge or market-impact analyses. However, the legislator has imposed a financial cap – approximately EUR 100,000 annually until 2026 – on the resources the OCCP may allocate to such assistance. This limitation is both unusual and difficult to justify. Courts could, in principle, require the parties to cover the costs of expert involvement, making the cap unnecessary. Moreover, the obligation imposed on the OCCP to restrict its support once the cap is nearly exhausted may hinder the consistent application of the Act and the effective quantification of damages.

31 P. Szot, *Ułatwienia dowodowe i rozpoznawania spraw w projekcie ustawy o roszczeniach o naprawienie szkody wyrządzonej przez naruszenie prawa konkurencji*, iKAR 2017, no. 1, 96.

The PEA also governs the evidentiary weight of decisions issued by the OCCP. Under Article 30, civil courts are bound by the operative part of a final OCCP decision confirming a competition law infringement, as well as by final judicial rulings delivered on appeal. However, difficulties may arise in cases involving vertical agreements, as the OCCP rarely identifies all distributors in the operative part of its decisions. In such situations, only those undertakings explicitly named in the operative part 'benefit' from the binding evidentiary effect. Parties not listed remain outside the scope of this rule, and civil courts must independently assess the existence and nature of any infringement with respect to them.[32] Importantly, this binding effect does not extend to discontinued proceedings, which do not prejudge the legality of the conduct.[33] Civil courts may conduct their own fact-finding and admit additional evidence beyond what was established administratively, a mechanism crucial to enabling claimants to meet their burden of proof. However, a civil court may not suspend its proceedings to await an OCCP decision when the same matter is simultaneously the subject of ongoing administrative proceedings.[34] In such circumstances, the civil court is required to adjudicate independently, without deferring to the potential future outcome of the OCCP's investigation.

Decisions of EU NCAs do not have binding force in Poland. Civil courts may treat them as factual presumptions under Article 9(2) of the Damages Directive, but their evidentiary weight remains a matter of judicial discretion. The Polish legislator's decision not to grant such decisions greater probative value may reduce Poland's attractiveness as a jurisdiction for follow-on actions and could hinder the achievement of the Directive's objective of promoting uniform and effective private enforcement throughout the EU.

32 M. Kolasiński, *Wpływ rozstrzygnięć prawomocnych decyzji Prezesa UOKiK dotyczących porozumień ograniczających konkurencję na postępowania w sprawie roszczeń o naprawienie szkody wyrządzonej przez naruszenie prawa konkurencji*, iKAR 2021, no. 4, 55.

33 J. Lenart, T. Kaczyńska, *Związanie sądu ostatecznym rozstrzygnięciem Prezesa UOKiK, SOKiK lub Sądu Apelacyjnego oraz konsekwencje tego rozwiązania dla publicznego i prywatnego egzekwowania prawa konkurencji*, iKAR 2017, no. 1, 69.

34 E. Buczkowska, M. Trepka, *Brak przesłanek do zawieszenia postępowania przez sąd cywilny rozstrzygający sprawę o naprawienie szkody wyrządzonej przez naruszenie prawa konkurencji do czasu rozstrzygnięcia postępowania antymonopolowego lub odwoławczego od decyzji Prezesa UOKiK w przedmiocie tego samego naruszenia–uwagi na tle art. 177 § 1 k.p.c.*, iKAR 2021, no. 4, 31.

8 Prospects for Private Enforcement in Poland

The Damages Directive and the PEA are significant instruments with the potential to reshape the enforcement landscape of competition law in Poland. Whether this potential will be fully realised remains uncertain. The analysis below identifies several factors that may either stimulate or hinder the growth of private enforcement. To provide a comprehensive perspective, I focus on circumstances that, in my view, are most relevant to the future development of private enforcement, regardless of whether their impact is positive or negative.

8.1 Incentives for Development

A historical review of Polish case law shows that the principal obstacles to private enforcement have traditionally centred on evidentiary issues – particularly the difficulty of proving both the anticompetitive nature of the conduct and the resulting harm. Introducing a presumption of harm, together with a detailed and structured framework for the disclosure of evidence, may substantially alleviate these challenges. These mechanisms lower the evidentiary burden on claimants and should make it considerably easier to initiate and substantiate damages actions. Despite the historically low success rate of compensation claims, the PEA tools may encourage undertakings to become more proactive in seeking redress for anticompetitive practices.

The strengthened discovery regime also poses an important – and constructive – challenge for the judiciary. It requires civil courts to engage more actively in evidentiary proceedings, marking a significant departure from the traditionally formalistic approach of Polish civil procedure. This may provide an opportunity for judges to demonstrate greater openness to procedural innovation and to contribute to the evolution of a more modern and responsive civil justice system. Over time, such developments could enable civil courts to play a meaningful role in fostering and disseminating a broader 'competition culture' in Poland, thereby increasing awareness of competition norms and their relevance for market participants.

8.2 Problems

The principal obstacles to the effective functioning of the PEA do not stem from the Act itself but from structural and institutional weaknesses within the Polish legal system.

The most significant concern is the overall efficiency and preparedness of the Polish judiciary. The legislator chose not to establish a specialised court for antitrust damages actions, nor to assign jurisdiction to an existing specialised body, such as the Court for Competition and Consumer Protection. As a result, cases will be adjudicated by ordinary civil courts whose judges generally lack expertise in competition law and economics.[35] The Ministry of Justice has not provided systematic training for judges expected to hear such cases, nor has it allocated additional resources to courts that handle potentially complex and resource-intensive antitrust claims.

This lack of preparation raises doubts about whether civil judges will be willing or able to use expert evidence effectively.[36] Even the CCCP rarely appoints economic experts, despite regularly handling antitrust matters. It is therefore highly uncertain whether general civil courts will be able to evaluate sophisticated economic analyses, cross-examine expert witnesses, or apply advanced quantitative methods to assess damages.

Uncertainty also surrounds the implementation of the new discovery rules. Previous experience with disclosure mechanisms in Polish civil procedure has been largely negative: courts have been reluctant to use them, and the provisions have proved ineffective in practice. Whether judges will now be prepared to issue, enforce, and supervise disclosure orders under the Private Enforcement Act remains an open question. If these mechanisms are applied cautiously or inconsistently, their intended benefits may not materialise.

A second major obstacle is the declining effectiveness of public competition enforcement. Over the past decade, the OCCP's enforcement output has fallen noticeably, with fewer decisions issued each year and, most concerning, fewer decisions addressing vertical restraints. Although vertical restraints fall within the scope of the Private Enforcement Act, they are often less suitable for follow-on actions because damage calculation is difficult and highly fact-specific. Weak public enforcement, therefore, directly limits the pool of infringement decisions on which private damages actions can rely.

This shortfall may be partially offset by decisions of other EU NCAs. Although these decisions lack the binding legal effect of OCCP decisions, they may still carry substantial persuasive weight and guide Polish courts in assessing complex cases. However, their non-binding status and the discretion afforded to courts in evaluating them may limit their practical impact.

---

35 Problem is not typical for Poland–Study on the conditions of claims for damages in case of infringement of EC competition rules, Brussels 2004, 10.

36 Recourse to experts is regarded as an important factor for the development of private enforcement–ibidem, 122.

Third, the OCCP has not been particularly active in promoting the PEA or in cooperating with the courts. Although the OCCP is officially an advocate of private enforcement and supported the Ministry of Justice during the drafting of the PEA, its subsequent engagement has been limited. The authority has shown little initiative in disseminating information about the PEA or in raising awareness among potential claimants of the opportunities it offers for redress. Unfortunately, this modest advocacy effort has been mirrored in its cautious administrative support for the judiciary. By 2025, the OCCP had submitted only seven *amicus curiae* briefs in antitrust damages cases – an extremely small number compared with the several dozen briefs submitted in consumer protection matters. This imbalance clearly reveals the OCCP's enforcement priorities, suggesting that consumer protection continues to dominate its agenda, while private antitrust enforcement remains a significantly lower priority.

Fourth, preparing a compensation claim, including the economic quantification of damages, may pose substantial financial barriers for many Polish undertakings. Drafting a well-founded antitrust damages action often requires sophisticated economic analysis and specialised legal expertise, both of which entail considerable cost. Poland currently lacks a well-developed practice of third-party litigation funding, which in other jurisdictions has played a key role in facilitating access to justice in complex competition cases.[37] As a result, the initial wave of private enforcement actions is likely to come primarily from large market players with sufficient financial and organisational resources to bear the substantial costs of such litigation. Smaller undertakings – despite often being the primary victims of anticompetitive conduct – may remain effectively excluded unless litigation funding mechanisms or collective redress structures evolve to fill this gap.

9 Court Statistics and First Cases

The challenges and structural problems discussed above are evident in the available court statistics. In the first year after the PEA entered into force, there was a modest, but noticeable, increase in interest in filing compensation claims. However, this initial momentum quickly faded. In subsequent years, the number of new cases brought before the regional courts rarely exceeded one or two (Table 11.1).

37 P. Okońska, *Finansowanie sporów sądowych przez podmiot trzeci–perspektywa polska*, iKAR 2024, no. 1, 59.

TABLE 11.1 Record of cases in regional courts concerning claims for infringement of competition law (Source: Ministry of Justice)

Year	New cases	Adjudicated cases
2024	2	1
2023	1	1
2022	1	0
2021	1	3
2020	2	1
2019	1	1
2018	4	3

This trend suggests that the reforms introduced by the PEA – while significant in principle – have not yet led to a substantial increase in private enforcement activity. Persistent barriers, such as limited judicial expertise, high litigation costs, and the scarcity of public enforcement decisions, continue to hinder the development of a robust system of antitrust damages actions in Poland.

From publicly available information, only one clearly successful case is known to date. It involved a dispute between Magna Polonia and Emitel, in which the compensation awarded was PLN 192.5 million.[38] The case is notable for several reasons.

First, the allegations concerned not only an infringement of competition law but also the misuse of confidential information obtained during contractual negotiations. This illustrates the often hybrid nature of complex commercial disputes, where antitrust claims may intersect with other forms of civil liability.

Second, the action was filed in 2013 – well before the adoption of the PEA – demonstrating that, despite significant procedural and evidentiary obstacles, large, well-resourced claimants could occasionally pursue competition-based damages even under the pre-PEA regime.

Third, the case ultimately settled. Although the regional court had upheld Magna Polonia's claim,[39] the parties reached a settlement during the appellate stage. The settlement amount represented over 70% of the damages originally

38 06MAGNA: Ugoda pozasądowa między Magna Polonia S.A. a Emitel S.A., https://www.bankier.pl/wiadomosc/06MAGNA-Ugoda-pozasadowa-miedzy-Magna-Polonia-S-A-a-Emitel-S-A-8562105.html.

39 Regional Court judgment of 2.07.2021, XVI GC 2042/13.

awarded by the Regional Court (PLN 263.44 million), an exceptionally high percentage by the standards of commercial dispute settlements, suggesting that the defendant regarded further litigation as highly risky.

Fourth, and perhaps most significantly for the broader development of private enforcement, the case was made possible by external litigation funding. The financing entity received nearly half of the settlement (PLN 92.9 million). This demonstrates the potential for third-party funding to facilitate large antitrust damages actions – particularly in jurisdictions such as Poland, where the cost and complexity of such litigation may otherwise deter claimants. It highlights the absence of a mature litigation-funding market for smaller claimants, who remain largely unable to pursue similar claims without external support.

10 Conclusions

The enactment of the PEA initially generated considerable interest: it prompted press releases, academic articles, seminars, and conferences – including one organised by the OCCP. Yet this early momentum has largely dissipated. Private enforcement continues to play only a supplementary role alongside public enforcement in Poland. A decade after the adoption of the PEA, the number of damage actions remains modest, and the number of cases in which compensation has actually been paid is even smaller (only one, as described above).

The Act has undeniably equipped undertakings with new legal instruments to pursue damages arising from competition law infringements. The introduction of a presumption of harm – shifting the burden of proof to the infringer – alongside detailed rules on the disclosure of evidence has significantly increased the likelihood that claimants can meet evidentiary requirements in court. These reforms, in principle, should encourage both undertakings and consumers harmed by anticompetitive conduct to seek compensation more frequently.

It remains puzzling that the OCCP provides relatively limited support for using these mechanisms. Given persistent shortcomings in public enforcement, greater engagement from the NCA could substantially strengthen overall enforcement effectiveness. Amicus curiae briefs offer a valuable opportunity for the OCCP to articulate its interpretation of competition law without the constraints of a specific administrative proceeding. Such submissions could exert persuasive influence and help shape the development of competition jurisprudence in Poland. The OCCP's hesitancy to use this tool represents a missed opportunity to enhance the visibility and impact of both private and public enforcement.

Private enforcement also poses a genuine challenge for the judiciary, as courts must adjudicate complex economic issues that fall outside traditional civil jurisdiction. Ultimately, the success of private antitrust enforcement in Poland depends less on legislative reform than on the broader institutional environment – particularly the efficiency of the courts, the availability of expert evidence, and the willingness of undertakings to commit financial resources to lengthy and costly civil litigation.

Despite the weaknesses of public enforcement in recent years, there remains cause for cautious optimism. If effectively utilised, private enforcement could inject new dynamism into Poland's competition culture. It may be private parties – rather than the competition authority – who reinvigorate the enforcement landscape and help develop a more robust, economically informed body of competition case law in the years ahead.

CHAPTER 12

Conclusions: Polish Competition Law and Enforcement – Unfinished Story

As the first President of the Antimonopoly Authority, Anna Fornalczyk recalled that '*a package of ten laws adopted by the Sejm in December 1989, which entered into force on 1 January 1990, initiated systemic reforms in Poland, marking the transition from a centrally planned to a market economy. These reforms were intended to establish conditions conducive to competition, enhance enterprise efficiency, increase market supply, and curb inflationary pressures. The legislative package was soon supplemented by the Antimonopoly Act of 1990, which entered into force on 13 April 1990. On that date, the Antimonopoly Authority – headquartered in Warsaw – began its operations, becoming the first competition authority in a post-communist state.*'[1] This marked the starting point of modern competition law and enforcement in Poland. After the analysis presented in the preceding chapters, this is an appropriate moment to reflect on the trajectory of Polish competition law and assess the lessons it offers.

1 Waiting for (Unlikely) Changes to Come

Historically, competition policy played a central role in Poland's economic transformation. Today, however, competition enforcement constitutes only one – often marginal – component of a broader framework of economic governance. This development is not unique to Poland; it reflects a broader shift from the 'limited state' to the 'expansive state'.[2] Poland now finds itself at another critical juncture, one that calls for reflection on how competition law and enforcement should adapt to this new paradigm. The earlier development model – driven first by external assistance and later by European integration – has reached its limits. The era of readily transferable solutions and broad international consensus in competition law has come to an end.

1 A. Fornalczyk, *Początki*, 419.

2 As rightly presented and analysed by M. Martyniszyn, *Competition law and policy in crisis*.

© 2026 THE AUTHOR(S) | HTTPS://DOI.ORG/10.1163/9789004754638-013
This is an open access publication distributed under the terms of the CC 4.0 license BY-NC-ND.

In this context, the Polish competition authority should not merely follow European regulatory developments, but should actively participate in the international debate on the objectives and instruments of competition law. Such engagement must be selective and context-sensitive: international experiences should be critically assessed and adapted to Poland's specific institutional and enforcement realities. While Poland's participation in international fora – such as the OECD Competition Committee – offers significant analytical and agenda-setting opportunities, these have so far translated only marginally into domestic legal reform or enforcement practice. Strengthening institutional mechanisms that channel comparative experience into national policy remains a key challenge.

At present, no major amendments to Polish competition law are pending. Some changes may arise indirectly from implementing the EMFA. Media regulation remains politically sensitive and conceptually complex. The most likely reform scenario involves mandatory consultation with the media regulator in OCCP-reviewed media merger cases. It remains unclear what legal weight such opinions will carry or whether the substantive merger test will be modified. This arrangement would delegate the assessment of media pluralism to the media regulator, while leaving final decision-making authority with the OCCP. Although the OCCP has some experience with public-interest considerations in merger control, Polish competition law continues to treat non-economic objectives as external to, and competing with, the core aims of the Competition Act.

Further amendments may arise from future European Commission initiatives.[3] Ongoing evaluations of Regulations 1/2003 and 773/2004 have received stakeholder and NCAs' feedback,[4] and reviews of the Technology Transfer[5] and Motor Vehicle Block Exemption Regulations[6] may eventually lead to legislative proposals. By the end of 2025, the Commission is also expected to adopt Guidelines on exclusionary abuses of dominance.[7] However, given the

3 *Timeline for Competition policy reviews 2024–2029*, https://competition-policy.ec.europa.eu/document/download/fb32c5d5-51ec-4344-a9c6-35ebebbb2bc3_en?filename=timeline_competition-policy_review_2024-2029.pdf.

4 *Revision of Regulation 1/2003*, https://competition-policy.ec.europa.eu/antitrust-and-cartels/legislation/regulation-12003_en.

5 *Review of the TTBER and Technology Transfer Guidelines*, https://competition-policy.ec.europa.eu/public-consultations/2023-technology-transfer_en.

6 *Review of the Motor Vehicle Block Exemption Regulation*, https://competition-policy.ec.europa.eu/sectors/manufacturing-basic-industries/review-motor-vehicle-block-exemption-regulation_en.

7 *Application of Article 102 TFEU*, https://competition-policy.ec.europa.eu/antitrust-and-cartels/legislation/application-article-102-tfeu_en.

OCCP's persistently low level of intervention in dominance cases, it is difficult to expect any meaningful shift in Polish enforcement practice.

The Commission's reluctance to reopen the EUMR is even more pronounced. The EC is not eager to open Pandora's Box and discuss possible changes to the EUMR. Instead, there will be an update to the merger guidelines.[8] The Commission is attempting to channel all reform debates into interpretative processes. One may wonder how much 'new content' will emerge from interpreting the EUMR, given the high expectations of many stakeholders. The EC continues to encourage Member States to expand national call-in powers, thereby indirectly resuscitating Article 22 EUMR – despite its recent judicial and practical epic failures in the Illumina/Grail saga.[9]

The Competition Act has formally been aligned with key elements of the EU competition and regulatory framework, in particular the DMA, the FSR, and the FDI screening regime. In the latter area, the OCCP's position has – fortunately – been fundamentally redefined. The OCCP no longer acts as an FDI screening authority; instead, its role has been reduced to a largely consultative one, with the same transaction being assessed in parallel by the OCCP and the competent Polish ministry. However, this parallelism is not supported by any substantive legal framework governing cooperation. In particular, the OCCP is unable to cooperate meaningfully with either the European Commission or national ministries where such cooperation would involve the exchange of legally protected information. As a result, only publicly available information may be shared, rendering FDI screening coordination largely formalistic and practically ineffective.

The application of the DMA in Poland remains opaque, and its practical impact to date appears negligible. In this context, the OCCP's engagement appears largely satisfied by its formal participation in the DMA High-Level Group, while active DMA enforcement does not appear to be a genuine policy priority. The continued relevance of the limited merger control mechanism under Article 14 of the DMA also remains uncertain, particularly in light of the European Commission's revised – and ultimately weakened – approach to Article 22 of the EUMR.[10]

---

8 *Review of the Merger Guidelines,* https://competition-policy.ec.europa.eu/mergers/review-merger-guidelines_en.

9 For an overview of the case: W. Sauter, J. Mulder, *Merger jurisdiction in EU competition law after Illumina/Grail: What's next?,* JAE 2025, no. 1.

10 More on the subject M. Mariniello, *Reinforcing EU merger control against the risks of acquisitions by big tech,* Bruegel Policy Brief 2025, no. 11, https://www.econstor.eu/handle/10419/322592.

Regarding the implementation of the FSR, the OCCP's role is again narrowly circumscribed. It is primarily limited to information gathering, assisting with inspections, and participating in the FSR Advisory Committee. At the national level, FSR implementation suffers from a poorly designed allocation of competencies. The Ministry of Development exercises political leadership and exerts decisive influence over legislative amendments and soft law instruments, yet it has no enforcement role and lacks practical experience in this area. The OCCP, by contrast, is tasked with coordinating cooperation in merger control and public procurement matters and with supporting dawn raids,[11] even though public procurement does not fall within its core jurisdiction. The absence of a clear rationale for this division of responsibilities highlights the opacity and inefficiency of the current institutional design. Ultimately, this arrangement is the product of an incoherent legislative process, compounded by fragmented interagency coordination and, to some extent, selective lobbying by individual authorities.

2 A Multitasked Agency without Strategic Focus

Polish competition law initially developed in line with prevailing international trends, adapted to the needs of a transforming economy, and later shaped by EU accession. However, institutional development followed a predominantly domestic and highly fragmented path, marked by successive ad hoc adjustments rather than a coherent strategy. Over time, successive governments and OCCP presidents transformed the authority into a multitasked agency, without any systematic assessment of whether the cumulative expansion of competences was justified or of the cumulative institutional consequences of these changes. Paradoxically, this evolution also reflected the OCCP's relatively low political salience: new powers were repeatedly assigned to an authority perceived as marginal within the central administration, precisely because these competences were not viewed as politically sensitive or strategically important.

Unlike competition enforcement, consumer protection within the OCCP has continued to expand dynamically. This expansion has been accompanied by the introduction of stronger enforcement instruments, more severe sanc-

11 As in the case of the first-ever dawn raid under FSR: B. Louveaux, C. Jeffs, A. Lyle-Smythe, N. Yeung, *The EU Commission carries out its first dawn raid under the Foreign Subsidies Regulation against a Chinese State-owned company active in the production and sale of security equipment*, e-Competitions 2024, no. 4, Art. N° 118735.

tions, and a progressive centralisation of public enforcement at the expense of judicial competences, most notably in the area of abusive contract clauses. These developments have significantly strengthened the OCCP President's discretionary powers, without corresponding mechanisms of accountability. The resulting enforcement architecture reflects a Caesarist model of administration: highly centralised, hierarchical, and concentrated around the authority's leadership. Although public communication strategies routinely present this evolution as a success in consumer protection, the intensification of consumer enforcement has not been accompanied by a comparable strengthening of advocacy or effectiveness in the OCCP's core mandate of competition enforcement.

The transformation of the OCCP into a multitasked authority has generated structural tensions and jurisdictional conflicts. Competition enforcement presupposes an independent, technocratic regulator insulated from short-term political considerations. FDI screening is inherently political, in the Schmittian sense, involving discretionary judgments about security, sovereignty, and the public interest. For an extended period, the OCCP was required to assess the same transactions simultaneously under competition law and broader public-interest or security considerations. This dual role produced significant institutional strain and a form of jurisdictional schizophrenia. Moreover, a consumer-driven enforcement agenda does not necessarily align with the logic of competition policy. The OCCP's readiness to publicly target foreign banks and advocate measures framed as redistributive or punitive – presented as vindication on behalf of consumers – sits uneasily with the requirement of neutrality and restraint that underpins the legitimacy of an allegedly independent NCA. Such practices risk eroding the OCCP's technocratic credibility in its primary role as a guardian of competitive market structures.

Taken together, these developments have transformed the OCCP into a highly diversified institution with a broad and heterogeneous portfolio of competences – or, less charitably, a repository for assorted regulatory tasks. While there is no universally optimal institutional model, and national arrangements inevitably reflect historical, political, and administrative contingencies, the extent to which political inertia and path dependency have shaped the current configuration is striking. The progressive expansion of the OCCP's mandate has led to a loss of institutional focus and the absence of a coherent, long-term narrative for stakeholders and successive governments. Although the OCCP remains formally part of Poland's economic governance framework, its strategic relevance has diminished. Consumer protection cases attract media attention and resonate with individual consumers, yet they rarely produce systemic or structural effects on market organisation or competitive dynamics. As a result, enforcement activity has become increasingly detached from the broader objectives of economic governance that competition policy is intended to serve. While separating competition enforcement from consumer protection and other ancillary functions – potentially requiring a distinct constitutional and institutional status – would be both theoretically sound and empirically justified, such a reform appears unlikely in the foreseeable future. Budgetary constraints and limited political incentives for institutional restructuring continue to impede more fundamental change.

3 Regime and Organisation of Competition Enforcement

The organisation of a competition authority reflects both its jurisdiction and the ambitions of successive leaderships. While the OCCP operates within Poland's traditional hierarchical model of public administration, the pluralism inherent in competition enforcement would normally justify greater flexibility and shared decision-making. However, the current leadership has transformed this model into a distinctly Caesarist form of administrative governance. Even bodies formally designed to support information exchange and collective deliberation – such as the internal evaluation committee – have been repurposed to reinforce the President's individual authority. A telling example is the nearly two-year delay in appointing a Deputy President; when the post was finally filled, shortly before the change of government, it was assigned a narrowly defined and marginal portfolio.

The OCCP has consistently portrayed the implementation of the ECN+ Directive as a major institutional success. As this analysis demonstrates, such claims are questionable. At a personal level, the reform undoubtedly stabilised the incumbent President's position by introducing guarantees of non-arbitrariness while avoiding any genuinely competitive appointment procedure. Rather than opening the post to meaningful competition, the reform entrenched the existing political appointee. Although the ECN+ Directive introduced most formal guarantees of independence, financial independence was explicitly excluded. The OCCP continues to be financed under general public-administration rules. Given that competition protection accounts for only a limited share of the authority's human and material resources – and competition enforcement in the strict sense an even smaller one – it is difficult to justify granting the OCCP a special budgetary status. Nor does the authority's highly diversified mandate permit the establishment of an autonomous revenue stream comparable to that of sectoral financial regulators.

It remains unclear how these arrangements translate into the OCCP's functioning domestically and within the European administrative space. No significant changes have been observed. The *Sped-Pro* judgment has had no discernible impact on cooperation within the European Competition Network. On the contrary, the OCCP remains active internationally. The current President's advocacy efforts have resulted in membership of the DMA High-Level Group and the vice-chairmanship of the OECD Competition Committee, as well as continued engagement in fora such as the ICN, UNCTAD, and the ECA. While the practical impact of some initiatives – such as regional cooperation memoranda – appears limited and often serves primarily to enhance leadership visibility, they nonetheless demonstrate that domestic rule-of-law concerns and deficiencies in enforcement practices have not constrained international cooperation.

Some of the most serious problems extend beyond the enforcement organisation and are systemic. The OCCP has made no meaningful attempt to address them, particularly in staffing.

The Polish civil service is undergoing gradual erosion, with employment increasingly resembling ordinary labour relations rather than public service. The original vision of an apolitical, professional civil service recruited through open competition has weakened considerably. Although access to the civil service remains formally open, this principle is undermined at senior levels. For presidential posts, recruitment procedures are only nominally competitive, with outcomes determined by political discretion rather than merit. This is the mechanism through which the OCCP President is selected. For director and deputy director positions, neither competitive procedures nor specific qualifications are required. Although competitions have remained legally permissible since 2016, neither of the last two OCCP Presidents has used them. Between May 2016 and September 2025, forty-six directors and sixty-eight deputy directors were appointed without open recruitment. This contrasts sharply with lower-level civil service positions, where competitive examinations remain mandatory. The resulting asymmetry undermines institutional trust, weakens the civil service ethos, and damages organisational performance. Notably, the introduction of formal independence guarantees has not altered this practice, calling into question the OCCP's claims to technocratic legitimacy.

These staffing patterns support the book's broader conclusion that the OCCP has strategically reoriented away from core competition enforcement towards administrative expansion, procedural management, and leadership visibility. Over time, human resources have been redistributed in ways that dilute enforcement capacity, particularly in areas central to competition policy. While competition protection remains part of the formal mandate, its relative weight has declined. This trend is most evident in the marginalisation of merger control, which now operates with limited personnel and diminished institutional influence – despite the irreversible impact of merger decisions on market structure.

Staffing growth has instead concentrated in support, communications, and international cooperation units. This reflects an internal logic prioritising managerial control, throughput, and narrative management over substantive enforcement. Given that personnel costs account for the largest share of the OCCP's budget, staffing allocations serve as a reliable proxy for financial priorities. Resources are increasingly directed towards organisational breadth and leadership exposure rather than analytical depth and enforcement effectiveness.

Taken together, these findings reinforce the book's central thesis: Polish competition enforcement has evolved towards a Caesarist model of governance. Institutional power, resources, and strategic direction are increasingly concentrated around the President rather than embedded in durable enforcement structures. The weakening of merger control, the relative decline of competition protection resources, and the parallel expansion of support and visibility-oriented units are not incidental developments but structural features of a personalised, president-centred regulatory model.

4 From Judicial Conundrum to Judicial Inertia

The jurisdiction and internal organisation of the OCCP are not the only problematic elements of the Polish competition enforcement system. Equally in need of critical reassessment is the allocation of judicial competences in competition cases. The continued jurisdiction of civil courts over appeals against OCCP decisions exemplifies the well-known Polish adage that 'temporary solutions tend to become permanent'. Assigning competition cases – formally administrative in nature – to the civil courts quickly exposed the structural inadequacy of civil procedural rules as a framework for effective judicial review of competition authority decisions. The introduction of a full review on the merits was intended to ensure effective judicial protection and prevent the protracted circulation of cases between administrative authorities and courts. However, these objectives have not been achieved.

High-profile cartel proceedings, such as the cement cartel and the interchange fee (banking cartel) cases, vividly illustrate the gap between these assumptions and procedural reality. Empirical research by other scholars confirms that civil courts adjudicating competition cases operate in a manner closely resembling administrative courts, despite their formally broader powers. They do not exercise comprehensive judicial control over all legally relevant acts of the OCCP. As a result, administrative courts are occasionally required to supplement this fragmented system of review, resulting in jurisdictional overlap and, in some instances, conflicts of competence. Rather than enhancing judicial protection, this dual model has led to procedural complexity, delays, and legal uncertainty.

The retention of civil courts as the primary forum for competition adjudication also raises a systemic question: who, in practice, shapes competition policy in Poland? This issue is particularly acute regarding the fining policy. The CCCP enjoys full discretion to modify OCCP decisions, including the amount of fines imposed. More troubling is that such modifications are often accompanied by little or no substantive reasoning explaining why an effective sanction has been reduced or abandoned altogether. A particularly striking example of this counterproductive approach is the Supreme Court's acceptance of the view that fines for failure to notify a concentration may be set at the level of the applicable notification fees. It is difficult to imagine a clearer illustration of the civil courts' insufficient understanding of the deterrence function of competition enforcement. Such reasoning fundamentally undermines the preventive and dissuasive objectives of merger control sanctions and exposes the deeper deficits of judicial review in Polish competition law.

One possible explanation for this judicial stance and activist approach lies in the courts' attempt to fill the normative and strategic vacuum left by both the OCCP and the government in defining contemporary competition policy, while avoiding responsibility for the systemic consequences of such interventions. Unlike the competition authority or the legislature, courts are insulated from accountability for the long-term coherence, effectiveness, or economic impact of enforcement outcomes, thereby facilitating peculiar reasoning without corresponding responsibility for final market results.

5 Competition Policy: The Great Absentee

In the United States, the need for a more robust antitrust policy has been openly acknowledged.[12] In the Polish context, however, the challenge goes

12 R.W. Crandall, *Towards a More Vigorous Antitrust Policy?*, Review of Industrial Organization (2025) 66: 7–22.

beyond revitalising or strengthening competition enforcement as such. The more fundamental problem lies in the absence of a coherent competition policy and in the lack of any deliberate effort to implement it through clearly defined, measurable objectives. Since at least 2016, Poland has effectively operated without such a policy framework, while regulatory interventions and enforcement activities have increasingly become reactive, fragmented, and ad hoc.

This situation is closely intertwined with persistent deficiencies in accountability and transparency within the OCCP. It is difficult to determine whether these shortcomings are the cause or the consequence of the absence of a clearly articulated competition policy. What is clear, however, is that without defined policy objectives and implementation tasks, any systematic evaluation of the OCCP's performance – particularly at the level of its leadership – is structurally impossible. Assessment is reduced to a piecemeal review of individual cases, divorced from any broader strategic orientation. Although the ECN+ Directive formally empowers national competition authorities to set enforcement priorities, the Polish legal framework lacks an effective mechanism to do so. Following the 2023 amendment to the Competition Act, enforcement priorities remain neither formally articulated nor linked to operational benchmarks, further undermining structured accountability.

The need for a coherent, forward-looking competition policy in Poland is more pressing than ever. At the domestic level, rising concentration across multiple sectors of the economy warrants closer scrutiny and a systematic response. This trend calls for a reassessment of the capacity of competition law and its enforcement to counteract the re-emergence of market power in new and often less visible forms. Both the Polish government and the OCCP face the challenge of adapting competition policy instruments to the dynamics of the digital economy and the renewed prominence of protectionism and economic nationalism. In this broader context, aligning competition policy with other public policies – many of which gain heightened political salience during periods of crisis and systemic transition – becomes indispensable. The mere creation of enforcement networks, as envisaged in the 2015 policy framework, is no longer sufficient. Ultimately, the effectiveness of the institutional architecture depends on the prior articulation of clear policy objectives that guide enforcement choices and enable meaningful accountability.

6 Anticompetitive Practices

From the outset, competition enforcement in Poland focused on the vigorous application of the 1990 Act, particularly on dismantling monopolistic structures at both national and local levels. This enforcement strategy played an important role in Poland's economic transformation, and the OCCP contributed meaningfully to that process. However, these early achievements did not translate into stable, mature antitrust enforcement. Instead, a gradual decline in the intensity of substantive market interventions is evident. While part of this development may be explained by increased awareness of competition law and improved market structures, a significant share of responsibility rests with the OCCP itself.

At present, the OCCP's activity in the field of anticompetitive practices is concentrated primarily on vertical agreements – especially resale price maintenance – and bid rigging, with only sporadic engagement in other categories of cases. There are some positive signals, such as the identification of competition concerns in labour markets and interventions against sports associations. Yet these cases remain rare and, despite their media visibility, are overshadowed by selective and insufficiently transparent enforcement. Cases concerning unilateral conduct, once very common, have become exceptional. This raises serious questions about the OCCP's internal organisation and the marginalisation of regional offices, which historically played a key role in addressing abuses by local dominant undertakings. Moreover, notwithstanding repeated public declarations, enforcement against digital dominant firms remains limited, with only a single truly significant case to date (Allegro).

Even more troubling are the broader directions of enforcement. The selection of cases and interventions warrants critical scrutiny, particularly in the absence of transparent explanations from the OCCP. The growing reliance on procedural instruments and procedural infringements is especially problematic. Treating the number of dawn raids as a proxy for enforcement success reflects both the instrumentalisation of this intrusive tool and a misunderstanding of its exceptional nature and purpose. Similarly, substituting substantive infringement findings with procedural violations is of doubtful value: such an approach contributes little to market correction or societal welfare, while primarily generating higher fines and facilitating relatively easy courtroom outcomes.

Taken together, these trends underscore the pressing need for a coherent competition policy and clearly articulated enforcement priorities. Without such a framework, competition enforcement risks becoming opportunistic, procedurally driven, and detached from its fundamental objective of safeguarding effective competition in the market.

7 Quo Vadis Merger Control?

Merger control in Poland is characterised by stagnation and progressive deprioritisation. Although in the early years of competition enforcement it was a key instrument of market intervention, it has since been marginalised, systematically underdeveloped, and persistently under-resourced within the Polish competition law system. This stagnation is evident at the institutional, substantive, and procedural levels and is clearly reflected in decisional practice. While current enforcement may appear to align with the traditional economic objectives of competition law, this stance is more the result of institutional inertia and resistance to reform than of a deliberate policy choice. Yet the rapidly evolving economic and regulatory environment demands a far more conscious and strategic response. Remaining a time capsule, like a merger control in Poland, is not a valid response.[13]

New challenges require a fundamental reconsideration of which concentrations the OCCP seeks to regulate – and why. At present, it remains unclear why transactions with no meaningful domestic nexus are subject to scrutiny, or why temporary changes in control that do not affect market structure trigger notification obligations. Any recalibration of jurisdiction must be accompanied by a corresponding reallocation of resources. The experience with FDI should serve as a cautionary example against the unreflective incorporation of non-economic objectives into merger control. It is equally implausible that continued reliance on a simplified, narrowly economic approach will remain adequate. Procedural reform should aim to reduce transaction costs for undertakings while enhancing the effectiveness and credibility of enforcement.

Such reforms cannot be pursued without a broader reflection on the increasingly complex 'spider's web' of overlapping merger control regimes. The OCCP should develop a more acute awareness of this institutional architecture and engage more actively in cooperation with other domestic authorities and foreign NCAs. This, however, presupposes a clear articulation of enforcement objectives and a willingness to learn from comparative experience. Persisting in stagnation and marginalising merger control risks rendering an instrument that once played a central role in Poland's demonopolisa-

13 A. Finch, *Merger Law is not–and should not be – in a time capsule*, Columbia Law Review, 2025, no. 1, 76.

tion process obsolete and ineffective – particularly in the face of the structural challenges posed by digital markets and contemporary geoeconomic dynamics.

8 Antimonopoly Proceedings

Antimonopoly proceedings are a special administrative procedure, distinctive in several respects. From a theoretical perspective, they constitute a largely autonomous procedural framework, yet they formally retain their administrative character, with the APC remaining the primary point of reference. Their specificity also stems from the extensive adaptation of procedural solutions traditionally associated with criminal proceedings. At a systemic level, antimonopoly proceedings constitute a distinctive and innovative construct within Polish procedural law, with no close analogues in other branches of administrative adjudication. Finally, their importance within competition law itself is reflected in their sheer normative weight: provisions governing antimonopoly proceedings account for approximately 70% of the Competition Act.

However, 'special' does not necessarily mean 'well designed'. Many procedural solutions persist by institutional inertia, while newer provisions are often imperfectly implemented transplants that fail to establish an optimal procedural framework for resolving competition cases. Rather than forming a coherent and balanced system, the procedural architecture of competition enforcement has developed incrementally and unevenly, without sufficient reflection on its internal consistency or its capacity to safeguard the rights of undertakings subject to enforcement.

Particular concern arises regarding explanatory proceedings. Although formally conceived as a limited and preliminary instrument, explanatory proceedings have become a central pillar of contemporary competition enforcement practice. Their growing intensity and scope are not matched by a corresponding expansion of procedural guarantees. As a result, procedural activity is increasingly treated as an end in itself, rather than a means to substantive enforcement objectives. This trend risks distorting the balance between effective competition enforcement and the protection of procedural rights. Restoring explanatory proceedings to their auxiliary, service-oriented role within competition enforcement – rather than allowing them to dominate it – should therefore be regarded as a priority for any meaningful reform of antimonopoly procedure.

9 Competition Infringements Sanctions

For nearly a decade, successive presidents of the OCCP have sought to portray their approach to sanctions as uncompromising and severe, repeatedly declaring an intention to pursue a strict fining policy unconstrained by formalistic legal limitations. These forceful and often belligerent public statements, however, have not been matched by comparably impressive enforcement outcomes. Courts have largely remained immune to such political rhetoric and have consistently and dispassionately exposed the weaknesses in OCCP decisions. As one commentator aptly observed, *'loud announcements of fines are often followed by silence when they are annulled by the courts'*.[14]

The sanctioning system itself also needs fundamental reconsideration. Successive legislative amendments have tended to replace systemic reflection with piecemeal adjustments, rather than addressing the overall coherence and effectiveness of the enforcement framework. Long-standing jurisdictional gaps remain unresolved, and new deficiencies have emerged from poorly designed reforms. The implementation of the ECN+ Directive provides a particularly telling example: although intended to strengthen enforcement, it has failed to remedy structural weaknesses in the sanctioning regime and, in some respects, has exacerbated them.

Sanctions constitute the final and decisive element of the competition protection system and should therefore be designed only after a comprehensive assessment of the enforcement architecture as a whole. Such an assessment should aim to develop a coherent and predictable fining policy, complemented where appropriate by civil sanctions. Without this broader systemic perspective, sanctioning risks become an isolated and performative exercise, disconnected from the underlying objectives of effective, credible, and legally sustainable competition enforcement.

10 Private Enforcement

Private enforcement of competition law in Poland largely mirrors the state of public enforcement. At the time of the PAE's adoption, there were significant expectations that it would revitalise antitrust enforcement by facilitating follow-on actions. However, several years later, it has become clear that these

14 P. Słowik, *Firmy nie boją się UOKiK. Śmiesznie niskie grzywny budują poczucie bezkarności,* https://biznes.gazetaprawna.pl/artykuly/1412595,firmy-nie-boja-sie-uokik-kary-sa-zbyt-lagodne.html.

expectations have not been realised. Although the OCCP formally supports damages actions and declares its willingness to assist claimants, its actual involvement in private enforcement is more limited and nuanced.[15] To date, the OCCP has submitted only five amicus curiae briefs, and access to these submissions has been restricted in practice. Even now, they are not easily accessible because they are located in sections devoted principally to consumer cases.

The OCCP's advocacy efforts have focused primarily on encouraging reliance on its decisions as a basis for damages claims. Yet the recent volume of infringement decisions does not suggest that they offer many realistic opportunities for private enforcement. Moreover, the nature of these decisions often does not facilitate damages actions. Most importantly, the OCCP's most prominent cases typically take more than a decade to pass through judicial review before becoming final and enforceable. The situation is not substantially better in less complex cases, where proceedings may still take several years.

It would be unwarranted to attribute the weak state of private enforcement solely to the OCCP. Competition damages litigation in Poland remains costly and complex, favouring well-resourced claimants seeking substantial compensation. Structural inefficiencies within the Polish judiciary further exacerbate these difficulties, as proceedings are lengthy and unpredictable. Against this background, it is unsurprising that the first known Polish competition damages cases were resolved through settlement rather than judicial determination. These cases may nonetheless point to a potentially viable model of private enforcement, particularly where claims are supported by external litigation funding.

11 Where Do We Stand? Where Do We Go?

The year 1990 marked the beginning of modern competition law and enforcement in Poland. The analysis shows that this system has evolved continuously and that the process is far from complete. Just as 1990 was a foundational moment, Poland's accession to the European Union on 1 May 2004 was a major turning point. The effects of EU accession on the Polish legal system did not materialise on the day of accession. Although that date undoubtedly served as an important formal threshold, the processes of preparation, app-

---

15 *Odszkodowanie za naruszenie prawa antymonopolowego? Pomogą decyzje Prezesa UOKiK*, https://uokik.gov.pl/odszkodowanie-za-naruszenie-prawa-antymonopolowego-pomoga-decyzje-prezesa-uokik.

roximation, and harmonisation had been underway for many years.[16] The most recent milestone in this evolutionary trajectory was the implementation of the ECN+ Directive. What distinguishes this reform from earlier phases of Europeanisation is that it directly shaped the institutional architecture of competition law enforcement in Poland, whereas previous harmonisation efforts focused primarily on substantive law and, to a more limited extent, procedural rules. While a purely formal assessment of the normative framework might suggest that more than thirty-five years of competition enforcement constitute a success story, the findings presented in this book do not support such an optimistic conclusion.

The early years of the Polish NCA's activity show that even relatively simple and imperfect legal rules need not prevent effective competition enforcement. Experience suggests, however, that within a highly centralised and personalised, i.e. Caesarist, enforcement model, changes to substantive or procedural law alone are not decisive. Today, both the regulatory framework and the institutional design of competition enforcement in Poland are largely shaped by European law. What remains missing are robust mechanisms of accountability and effective, legally permissible oversight that can complement the guarantees of independence introduced at the EU level. The manner in which the ECN+ Directive has been implemented raises serious legal and constitutional concerns, as it risks reducing the OCCP President's independence to a largely formalistic construct. To restore the authority's necessary legitimacy, it is essential to introduce mechanisms that increase the likelihood that OCCP leadership will possess the expertise, experience, and strategic vision required for the authority's effective functioning and the further development of competition policy in Poland.

Periods of crisis and systemic stress tend to expose the underlying foundations of institutional arrangements. The Polish competition enforcement system was, to a significant extent, modelled on foreign examples. As long as international consensus prevailed and the broader economic and geopolitical environment remained favourable, this development path appeared relatively safe, thereby relieving domestic policymakers of the need to make autonomous conceptual choices. Over the past decade, however, both consensus and favourable external conditions have eroded. As a result, Polish competition law – and, in particular, the system responsible for its enforcement – has

16 M. Krasnodębska-Tomkiel, *Wspólnotowe prawo konkurencji. Skutki dla Polski*, Warsaw 2006, 277.

found itself insufficiently prepared to make independent and forward-looking decisions about its own development. Without fundamental reforms and strong, well-prepared leadership, competition enforcement risks further erosion and imitation rather than genuine progress. Persistent inertia and growing distance from international enforcement and conceptual debates increasingly undermine the OCCP's relevance and credibility.

Any attempt to address these challenges must begin with a fundamental reflection on the objectives of competition protection in Poland. The OCCP and other relevant authorities must clarify what they seek to achieve through competition enforcement. All institutions in this governance network need a clear understanding of their respective roles and effective mechanisms for cooperation. The objectives of competition law enforcement itself require reassessment: should Poland adhere strictly to a formalistic, predominantly legal approach, or be open to broader economic and societal considerations? Closely related is the question of institutional design – namely, which bodies should be responsible for pursuing these objectives. Only once these foundational issues have been resolved and a coherent competition policy articulated should the legal framework be adjusted accordingly. Finally, the OCCP's internal organisation and decision-making processes must be adapted to these choices. Notably, no such comprehensive discussion or reform effort has taken place over the past decade, which largely explains the current state of Polish competition enforcement.

Over more than 35 years, the OCCP and its civil servants have demonstrated that competition enforcement in Poland can be effective. Nevertheless, the overall development of the enforcement system cannot be described as an unequivocal success. At a certain point, institutional and organisational transformations deviated from a coherent and sustainable trajectory. Some deficiencies are clearly systemic and external, while others stem from internal governance choices. Yet the OCCP retains significant resources, institutional capacity, and what remains of its credibility and legitimacy. Provided there is sufficient political will, there is a realistic prospect that the authority could return to a more effective and forward-looking path. It is for this reason that this book was written: because I believe the story of Polish Competition Law and Enforcement is not yet complete, and that the best is yet to come.

Index

© 2026 THE AUTHOR(S) | HTTPS://DOI.ORG/10.1163/9789004754638-014
This is an open access publication distributed under the terms of the CC 4.0 license BY-NC-ND.